CHILD SURVIVAL
STRATEGIES FOR RESEARCH

CHILD SURVIVAL
STRATEGIES FOR RESEARCH

W. Henry Mosley
Lincoln C. Chen
Editors

Based on papers for a workshop by the same title
organized by The Rockefeller and Ford Foundations,
Bellagio, Italy, October 1983

POPULATION AND DEVELOPMENT REVIEW
A Supplement to Volume 10   1984

CAMBRIDGE UNIVERSITY PRESS
Cambridge
London   New York   New Rochelle
Melbourne   Sydney

Library of Congress Cataloging in Publication Data
Main entry under title:

Child survival.

"Based on selected papers presented at a
workshop on Strategies for Research on Child
Survival jointly sponsored by The Rockefeller and
Ford Foundations and held at Bellagio, Italy,
October 1983"—Acknowledgments.
"Population and development review, a
supplement to volume 10."
Includes bibliographies and index.
1. Children—Care and hygiene—Congresses.
2. Children—Diseases—Congresses. 3. Children—
Mortality—Congresses. 4. Child health services—
Congresses. 5. Children—Care and hygiene—
Developing countries—Congresses. 6. Children—
Developing countries—Mortality—Congresses.
I. Mosley, W. Henry (Wiley Henry), 1933–   .
II. Chen, Lincoln C. III. Workshop on Strategies for
Research on Child Survival (1983: Bellagio, Italy)
IV. Rockefeller Foundation. V. Ford Foundation.
[DNLM: 1. Child Health Services—congresses.
2. Child Welfare—congresses. 3. Communicable
Diseases Control—congresses. 4. Developing
Countries—congresses. 5. Nutrition Disorders—
prevention & control—congresses.
WA 320 C53498 1983]
RJ101.C527 1984   362.1'9892   84-16970
ISBN 0-521-30193-9

Contents

Analytical Methods

Acknowledgments

This volume is based on selected papers presented at a workshop on Strategies for Research on Child Survival jointly sponsored by The Rockefeller and Ford Foundations and held at Bellagio, Italy, October 1983. The workshop was organized and chaired by W. Parker Mauldin of The Rockefeller Foundation and Oscar Harkavy of The Ford Foundation. Lincoln C. Chen, Jane Menken, W. Henry Mosley, and Samuel H. Preston served on the steering committee for the workshop.

Publication of this volume was made possible by assistance from The Rockefeller and Ford Foundations.

INTRODUCTION AND CONCEPTUAL FRAMEWORK

Child Survival: Research and Policy

W. Henry Mosley

In the developed countries of the world, over 97 percent of all children survive through the preschool years. By contrast, in many poor countries 20 to 25 percent of the children die before reaching their fifth birthday, resulting in an estimated 15 million deaths annually (UNICEF, 1984). Many of these deaths are preventable with available health technology (UN Population Division, 1983). A rising global awareness of the unrealized potential for improving health conditions has led national governments and international agencies to reevaluate health service strategies.[1] Community-based programs have been seized upon by the international health community as the key strategy to make health services accessible, affordable, and socially acceptable.

Yet only two kinds of community-level initiatives are currently undertaken by most health ministries. The first is to extend curative and preventive services to communities through the use of minimally trained paramedical personnel. The second is to concentrate on making a few simple but effective health technologies widely accessible. The latter course of action has particularly captured the attention of the international donor community because of its economy, potential effectiveness in saving lives, and ease of implementation. UNICEF (1984) has been at the forefront in the global promotion of a "child survival revolution" based on what is referred to as the GOBI-FF strategy, an acronym for growth monitoring, oral rehydration therapy for diarrhea, breastfeeding, immunization, food supplements, and family planning.

Recently, this concentration of attention and resources on the delivery of a few technologies to the general population has increasingly come under question (Mosley, 1983; Misra, 1983; UN Population Division, 1983; Chen, 1984). The primary concern is that such a strategy is so strongly supply oriented that it tends to ignore the social constraints to demand for and effective use of health services.[2] This criticism is particularly apposite with respect to efforts to improve child survival. The social factors that constrain families in the use of new technologies may well be the same factors that predispose to higher risks of infant mortality. If so, then limited technology-oriented health intervention programs may be far less cost-effective than their promoters anticipate in the absence of broader development efforts, including investments in education, particularly for women, and in improved economic opportunities for families (Caldwell et al., 1983).

The debate on appropriate program priorities highlights the problems that the international development community faces in trying to determine the best mix of strategies to promote child health. Underpinning this debate are the two dimensions to child survival, the biomedical and the social. Since any health intervention program involves both dimensions, policy-relevant research on child survival should look at both simultaneously (Miró and Potter, 1980: 84). Most health-related field studies in developing countries, however, are carried out by either biomedical or social scientists, each approaching the problems from their own disciplinary perspective with very little recognition accorded the biosocial interrelationships.[3]

The papers in this volume form part of a growing effort to bridge the disciplinary gap between biomedical and social scientists in the study of the determinants of mortality in human populations.[4] The focus is on child survival in the developing world. The purpose is threefold: to propose a simple framework for interdisciplinary communication; to identify key determinants of morbidity and mortality and the methods of analyzing them developed by biomedical and social scientists; and to consider research needs and strategies for multidisciplinary studies on child survival. The comments in this introduction place the volume in the context of current research and highlight programmatic and policy issues that need to be addressed in the future.

Conceptual framework

The barriers to cross-disciplinary communication are almost as great as those across different cultures (Snow, 1971). The difficulties lie in both language and ways of looking at problems. To overcome these hurdles, scientists in the respective disciplines need either to master the jargon and concepts of others, or to define common terms of reference. The paper by W. Henry Mosley and Lincoln C. Chen attempts the latter.

The key concept in the Mosley/Chen framework involves a redefinition of "cause of death." Most biomedical and social scientists identify such conditions as infectious diseases and malnutrition as the main "causes" of high infant and child mortality in poor populations. Biologically that is correct, but the observation is not much more useful than to say that pregnancies are a "cause" of birth rates. It is important to note that both pregnancies and diseases are consequences of biosocial interactions. A fruitful approach to a study of the "causes" of either fertility or mortality in populations is to define and measure these interactions.

In the case of fertility research, Davis and Blake (1956) set the stage for rapid advance by formulating a framework in which live births were viewed as the consequence of a few "proximate determinants," or basic biosocial mechanisms affecting: (1) exposure to intercourse, (2) exposure to the risk of conception, and (3) successful gestation and delivery.

The framework proposed by Mosley and Chen identifies 14 proximate determinants of child mortality. These behaviorally mediated biological mechanisms can be grouped in five categories related to: (1) maternal fertility; (2) environmental contamination; (3) nutrient availability; (4) injuries; and (5) disease control. These proximate determinants provide a conceptual bridge for linking the epidemiologists' concern with identifying biological causes of diseases and deaths in individuals and then seeking control measures by directly manipulating the risk factors (proximate determinants) in the population; and the social scientists' efforts to measure the associations of socioeconomic factors with health behavior (proximate determinants) and their demographic consequences and to propose policies to affect the underlying socioeconomic factors.

As examination of these two major research strategies illustrates, many of the recommendations for health policies and programs coming from the research by scientists in the respective disciplines are not simply a function of empirical results but follow from unspecified assumptions about biosocial interactions. A recognition of this brings us to the roots of the policy debate noted above; it also should provide the impetus for research strategies that incorporate both sociological and biological components.

Biomedical perspectives

Biomedical scientists work in laboratory and clinical settings; their research focuses on disease agents and host–agent interactions. Their applied research is primarily designed to lead to effective therapies and, where possible, vaccines. Such population-based studies as are undertaken in the biomedical field are typically tightly designed to pinpoint the critical risk factors directly associated with specific diseases that might be targeted for intervention programs. The biomedical literature provides the richest source of information about the relationships between the proximate determinants and disease outcomes but has relatively little to say about social interactions.

Infectious and parasitic diseases

Robert E. Black's review of diarrheal diseases documents that any of over two dozen bacterial, viral, or parasitic agents may cause diarrheal disease, though three, *E. coli, Shigella,* and the rotavirus, are most frequent worldwide. These organisms are so prevalent in poor populations that multiple simultaneous infections are not infrequent. Only longitudinal studies can measure the full extent of the disease and elucidate its sources. Because of the intensity of observations and consequent high costs of longitudinal investigations, the search for risk factors for diarrheas has been limited to factors related to food preparation, use of water, and personal hygiene.

Black observes that research to date indicates that the most effective interventions for control of diarrheal disease are programs to interrupt the transmission of infectious agents in the home. This conclusion is based on well-documented findings concerning the overwhelming importance of fecal contamination of food and water in the home, and on controlled studies showing the effectiveness of such simple actions as handwashing in preventing infection. But, a review of the international literature on diarrheal disease research reveals almost no field studies designed to learn how to make household hygiene effective in poor countries (WHO, 1981–1983). By contrast, dozens of studies pour forth from medical centers in the developing world testing minute gradations in the electrolyte content of a rehydration fluid therapy that is already almost 99 percent effective in clinical settings.

Not surprisingly in view of the investment in time and effort, the major medical advances to come from diarrheal disease research in the last two decades have been in rehydration therapy. This development has resulted in a predominantly curative orientation to diarrheal disease control strategy. Beginning in the early 1970s, as health professionals were persuaded to adopt oral rehydration as the treatment of choice, diarrhea case fatality rates fell from 20–30 percent to under 2 percent in treatment facilities around the world (PAHO/WHO, 1983). In light of these extraordinary success rates and the technical simplicity of administering the therapy, the logical next step has been to teach mothers to treat their own children at home. The biomedical literature now includes numerous studies on technical questions relating to how to teach mothers to properly make and mix a wide variety of oral fluids at home, but rarely are there investigations of whether mothers actually use oral rehydration therapy, and how effectively, and whether it has any lasting health benefit (PAHO/WHO, 1983).

Where studies of use and impact of oral rehydration therapy have been done, the results have often been ambiguous because of inadequate consideration of sociocultural factors.[5] The technique's effectiveness in the clinical setting notwithstanding, any community health benefit gained depends upon use of the health facilities by the population. Yet the problem of underutilization of health facilities plagues rural health systems in developing countries (Mosley, 1983). The distance between the community and the health facility is usually not just geographic, but also economic, social, and cultural. At the community level, a mother may be introduced to the technique, but her decision to use it and her ability to use it effectively are powerfully dependent upon the social support system (Mobarak et al., 1980). Curing a child of an episode of life-threatening dehydration, only to return the child to the home situation that led to the attack, may not improve ultimate survival chances. In Bangladesh a one-year follow-up of discharged diarrhea patients aged 3 months to 3 years revealed that these children subsequently experienced much higher mortality than children at comparable ages in the community at large (Roy et al., 1983). In another rural area of Bangladesh, a community-based oral rehydration program reduced the diarrhea case fatality rate by about 80 percent but had a negligible impact on overall mortality experience (Rahaman et al., 1979; ICDDR, B, unpublished data).

For some decades now, biomedical scientists have been aware of the limitations of the curative approach to health care in traditional societies (McDermott, 1966; Rowland and McCollum, 1977; Mata, 1978), and anthropologists have described how belief systems influence choices concerning use of health care (Fabrega, 1972). Policymakers promoting oral rehydration therapy and other technologies are not insensitive to the relevant facts, but in the absence of solid research-based findings about the determinants of success (or failure) of various intervention efforts that could provide better guidelines for program strategies, the trial-and-error approach continues.

Ordinarily, biomedical scientists give little attention to socioeconomic determinants of disease except to note them as "background" variables, which are considered to be beyond the scope of health intervention programs. Not infrequently, social variables are excluded from consideration altogether through "controlled" studies.[6] Yet, as Stanley O. Foster's paper on vaccines implies, there is a need to include consideration of biosocial interactions when new technologies are introduced in mass programs. Three factors that must be considered relate to: (1) acceptance rates; (2) use-effectiveness; and (3) demographic impact—terms familiar to social scientists who have studied the interactions between technology and socioeconomic variables in contraceptive programs. Numerous examples can be cited of the importance of these factors to the success of medical intervention programs. On the point of acceptance, in rural Bangladesh, two-thirds of pregnant women refused to accept tetanus toxoid, even under home delivery (Rahman, 1981). Nor is low vaccine acceptance restricted to underdeveloped countries; measles immunization coverage is less than 20 percent in France and less than 10 percent in Italy (Bart et al., 1983).

Regarding use-effectiveness, medical scientists are acutely aware of biological factors affecting this parameter such as deterioration of vaccines due to poor storage and lack of an adequate immune response in children because of malnutrition. Far less attention has been given to the social constraints to effective vaccine use. For example, for maximum effectiveness, three injections of the "triple" vaccine (diphtheria, tetanus, whooping cough) must be taken, but in many programs around the world, as many as 50 percent of mothers refuse to bring their children for all three injections because of febrile reactions among the children vaccinated. Measles vaccine, to be effective, must be given in a critically short period of time after maternal immunity in the child has declined (age 6–8 months) but before the child is attacked by measles. The means to achieve the requisite compliance in national immunization programs has yet to be found.

In terms of demographic impact, measles vaccine is of the greatest interest because of the high mortality associated with measles among malnourished children in poor countries. Two questions are particularly important. First, is the vaccine program reaching the most disadvantaged segment of the community, those at highest risk of death? Second, among this disadvantaged group, will the elimination of measles lead to improved child survival if poor socioeconomic conditions remain? This latter question was examined in one study in Africa, which found that despite an immediate reduction in measles mortality following immunization, the net gain in child survival over time was very small (Kasongo Project Team, 1981).

These social parameters of vaccine program performance have seldom been the subject of systematic study. In the absence of pertinent data, biomedical scientists make recommendations for mass intervention programs based solely on estimates of the theoretical effectiveness of vaccines. These recommendations consider that the only constraints to program implementation are resources, implicitly assuming that social factors have a negligible influence on program performance.[7]

Parasitic diseases present a special set of problems when it comes to assessing their contributions to child mortality and then determining the priority that should be given to control programs. As David J. Bradley and Anne Keymer report here, although this group of diseases is highly prevalent in poor countries, only a few members of the group, such as malaria, directly cause death; most are characterized by prolonged infestation in the human host that may only indirectly contribute to higher mortality levels in populations.

Most of the research on parasitic diseases has been done by biomedical scientists, but the importance of considering the social dimensions of the problem is being recognized by such agencies as the World Health Organization in their Tropical Diseases Research Program. In this context, it is interesting to note from Bradley and Keymer's paper that many of the biological issues confronting the biomedical scientists have their parallel in the social arena. For example, with the highly prevalent intestinal parasites, an important concern is the biological synergy of malnutrition and infection. The question concerns the degree to which malnutrition predisposes to more severe disease versus the degree to which parasitic infections contribute to growth faltering in children. The answer is important in terms of deciding what role, if any, parasite control may play in nutrition improvement programs. Field studies involving parasite-control activities have not been able to provide a definitive answer to the question because of the effects of "social synergy"; that is, successful programs may not only reduce parasite loads in the populations, but also initiate other behavioral changes in the affected families leading to better child nutrition.

In the area of long-term control of malaria, the biological problem of emerging resistance of the parasite and the vector to insecticides and drugs can render a technical strategy ineffective. Similarly, public health professionals are often faced with the problem of growing social "resistance" in a community after some experience with a new health program intervention— the tendency of the community to revert to former patterns of behavior after the initial enthusiastic reception to the innovation wears off. Both of these problems require research, inasmuch as either can render new initiatives ineffective in the long run.

Studies of malnutrition and health

Papers by Kenneth H. Brown, by Reynaldo Martorell and Teresa J. Ho, and by Sandra L. Huffman and Barbara B. Lamphere deal with dietary intake, malnutrition, and breastfeeding, respectively. Special attention is given to these subjects because of the frequent lack of clarity in the literature when "nutritional problems" are cited as contributing to high mortality. While the expression is used to characterize a population with many malnourished children, it too often also implies that the cause is inadequate food availability. In fact, this may not be the case. Brown stresses that poor dietary intake is only one of several factors influencing the nutritional status of children. (Infection is another factor.) Physical measurements of nutritional status (for example, body weight-for-age) provide an indication of nutrient adequacy in an individual in relation to physiologic needs, but do not reveal how it was produced.

Martorell and Ho describe methods for measuring the nutritional status of children. (While malnutrition can involve deficiencies in any one, or a combination, of many specific nutrients such as vitamins or iodine, or iron, the focus of their discussion is on protein–energy malnutrition). As Martorell and Ho report, among the numerous clinical and biomedical indicators of malnutrition, body measurements of weight and height (anthropometry) have the advantage of being "sensitive over the full range of malnutrition." They are also "highly reliable and are less expensive and easier to obtain than most nutritional data."

Although childhood malnutrition is a serious problem, the only way to confirm food deficiency as a cause would be by direct measurement of dietary intake. This, as Brown's paper reveals, is difficult. Yet, failure to establish which proximate determinants are major contributors to malnutrition in a specific population can jeopardize the success of health intervention efforts. For example, in 1979 Indonesia embarked on a national nutrition program that now involves the monthly weighing of almost 2 million children. Coupled with this, mothers are advised about diets, and some food supplements are provided. The program design is based on the assumption that poor dietary intake is the major problem to overcome. Recent assessments have shown little evidence of a nutritional improvement in children since the program began (Pangestuhadi, 1983). Now the program assumptions are being challenged by Kusin and others (1983), whose research in East Java suggests that the predominant cause of malnutrition may not be poor diet, but frequent recurrent infections. If this is the case, the appropriate intervention strategy to combat malnutrition should emphasize infection control rather than dietary advice.

In India, a debate centers around what factors are the major contributors to malnutrition, and what level of malnutrition should be of concern for nutrition intervention programs (Sukhatme, 1982; Gopalan, 1983). Martorell and Ho summarize data that show a clear association of excess mortality with severe degrees of malnutrition. There is less evidence for the adverse biological consequences of mild to moderate malnutrition even when it produces permanent growth stunting. Indeed, Sukhatme (1982) and others have concluded that the present recommended standards for food (calorie) intake needed to support "adequate" nutrition are unnecessarily high, based on the reasoning that growth faltering is a normal, rather than pathological, physiological adjustment to a reduced diet. Thus, stunted children are simply "small but healthy" (Seckler, 1982). In India, such a redefinition of malnutrition could reduce the estimated number of people who require more food from around 250 million to perhaps 50 million, a difference with major implications for national food and nutrition policies as well as health programs.

Research is needed to assess whether a population of children growing under conditions of limited food intake (such that stunting develops) suffers more adverse consequences (mental and emotional, as well as physical) than a better fed group. This will require a longitudinal (cohort) study; one bias of cross-sectional growth data presented to support the "small but healthy" thesis is that such data pertain to those small children who have survived.

Breastfeeding versus bottlefeeding is another topic of major concern to policymakers. One much debated issue has been the misleading advertising practices of the baby formula industry to promote their products. As Huffman and Lamphere observe in this volume, the advantages of breastfeeding for the health of young infants are manifold and well documented, but breastfeeding makes heavy demands upon the mother's time and energy, and many mothers, by choice or necessity, divert their efforts to other activities. Thus, questions are raised about what health and other social development strategies can provide the best support for both mothers and their children.

Again, we are dealing with a topic that can only be explored through a multidisciplinary approach. Nutritionists are concerned with measurement of breast milk production; anthropologists with the accurate description of beliefs and values associated with breastfeeding practices; sociologists with the determinants of breastfeeding practices; epidemiologists with the environmental conditions predisposing to infection; and demographers with the mortality and fertility consequences of breastfeeding. And, as emphasized by Huffman and Lamphere, all such studies need to be concerned with the fact that proper interpretation of the findings is especially difficult because of the strong association of declines in breastfeeding, which may be expected to have adverse health effects, with other features of modernization that generally enhance child survival.

Social science perspectives

Like research in the biomedical sciences, social science research ranges from the micro to the macro level. At one extreme are the anthropologists who document the beliefs and behavior of individuals and small groups of people; at the next level are those doing household survey research; while at the macro level, social scientists analyze aggregate data from regions or nations. Demographers have developed a variety of sophisticated analytical techniques to estimate trends and differentials in mortality from census and survey records, even where data are quite limited.

Macro-level research strategies and policy implications

Classical macro-level demographic research has relied largely upon existing data sets collected for purposes other than the research objective at hand (Palloni, 1981). This creates great economies in a research program, but limits variables available for study. In spite of these limitations, the macro approach has proven invaluable in defining some of the major determinants of mortality trends and differentials in populations, often yielding findings that have major policy implications.

From the end of World War II until the early 1970s, numerous studies documented unprecedented declines in mortality in the less developed countries. These trends were widely attributed to the introduction of modern medical technology, largely dissociated from socioeconomic development (Davis, 1956; Stolnitz, 1965; Arriaga and Davis, 1969). More recently, a series of studies by Preston (1978, 1980b) demonstrated that both socioeconomic development and technology played important roles, each contributing about 50 percent to the overall mortality decline in the post–World War II period.

As the determinants of mortality in developing countries were being identified, it was expected that the decline would be steady and irreversible until high levels of life expectancy were reached. Thus, the development community was surprised when Gwatkin (1980) presented data suggesting that the pace of improvement in mortality levels had slowed considerably during the late 1960s through the mid-1970s. This prompted a more critical consideration of the connections between development, medical technology, and mortality change, aimed at a fuller understanding of their interrelationships for health policy and programming purposes (Ruzicka and Hansluwka, 1982; UN Population Division, 1983).

Several recent macro-level studies provide important clues in this regard. First, there is the empirical observation that Sri Lanka, Kerala, and Cuba experienced substantial mortality reduction under processes of development structured "in such a way as to increase levels of literacy and spread public health and nutrition programs widely among the population" (Preston, 1978). Preston (1980b) subsequently showed in an analysis of mortality differentials among 52 countries that "the mortality risks facing a family earning $10,000 per year or $100 per year are not strongly influenced by the prevailing level of average income in the nation they reside," the point being that it is the economic capability of the individual family that is important to the survival of their children. This analysis also showed the independent contributions of female education and per capita calorie availability as well as income to mortality differentials.

Palloni (1981), undertaking an analysis of infant and child mortality differentials among Latin American countries, noted the strong influence of the level of literacy, particularly in the high mortality countries where major medical causes of death were diarrheal and respiratory diseases. In these countries Behm (1979) had earlier shown an inverse relationship between child mortality and the level of mother's education. Palloni extended this analysis to show that the relative advantage of mother's education to child survival is contingent on the social circumstances of the community in which she lives. In poor social settings uneducated mothers are at a far greater disadvantage compared with more educated mothers. A graphic illustration of this type of relationship has been presented by Mosley (1983) in an analysis of the mortality differentials in Kenya that revealed far wider child mortality differentials by mother's education in the poorest provinces than in economically more developed areas.

Recent cross-national studies have sought analytically to separate the education and income effects in order to come up with more specific policy recommendations. Flegg (1982) found that the income effect could be explained in part by the number of physicians and nurses per capita. Extending this approach, Jayachandran and Jarvis (1983) found that the number of midwives per capita was a more significant factor than the number of physicians or nurses. Jain (1984) in an analysis of infant and child mortality differentials among states in India was able to demonstrate the independent effects of household poverty and availability and use of medical services, and, consistent with Palloni, found that much of the effect of female literacy operated through these factors.

The implication of these findings is that a rising gross national product does not necessarily translate into improved child survival. Rather, governments must adopt a development strategy that enhances the ability of families to care for themselves. The service components of such a strategy are broadly understood, but macro research cannot provide specific guidelines on how to intervene in a specific country or locality to achieve an effective program. This is exemplified by experience with direct community health intervention programs that have produced mixed results, with failures (relative to the investment) at least equaling successes (Mosley, 1983). For example, in Egypt over 80 percent of women still prefer to use the services of traditional untrained midwives even though enough qualified personnel are available to deliver all babies (Nadim, 1980). In Indonesia a study found that the performance of 94 percent of the village health workers was judged unsatisfactory (Reinks and Iskandar, 1981). In India a community health workers scheme did not achieve its objectives (Bose and Desai, 1983). In Thailand, the Philippines, and Nigeria, major comprehensive health care research projects had negligible or minimal influence on morbidity and mortality (Lampang, 1981; Williamson, 1982; Weiss, 1982).

These experiences do not negate the broad policy conclusions of the research, but they highlight the limitations of macro-level socioeconomic studies. While health services and facilities are factors in reducing the level of disease and death, it is the interaction of these factors with specific political, socioeconomic, and ecological conditions in which families live that determines actual health outcomes.[8]

John Briscoe's paper is interesting in this context. Taking water and sanitation programs as a case study, he shows how in the period before there was a modern scientific understanding of the engineering principles involved, the bases for developing these systems were largely epidemiologic and socioeconomic. Over time, as the science of sanitary engineering advanced, the epidemiologic perspective was essentially lost and economic considerations faded in importance, because the perspective of the engineer was almost entirely on urban systems in advanced countries. As Briscoe illustrates, this narrow technologic perspective can result in sanitary program interventions that fall far short of their planned objectives in developing countries because of severe constraints on effective use of the new systems by families with low incomes and poor hygienic practices.

Micro-level research

Since macro-level research has depended upon existing data sets, little attention has been given to research design and data analysis. The growing interest in going beyond simply describing mortality differentials to explaining why they exist calls for investigations at the household level to measure and interpret the relations between variables. This requires careful consideration of measurement error, detailed specification of the direction of causation, and attention to the presence of disturbing factors (Palloni, 1981). Many of the papers in this volume address these issues.

A key step in the design of household-level research is the development of operational definitions of the variables of interest and the specification of the major structural relationships to incorporate in the analysis. Some of the pioneering work in this area was done by T. Paul Schultz (1979), and in this volume Schultz presents a taxonomy of the variables—health endowments, individual choice variables, and external factors—that influence the health outcome of a given health technology and describes directions empirical study of these relationships may take.

Poor specification of the relationships between variables has frequently led to conclusions that confuse or mislead health policymakers. For example, several studies have specified as independent variables, factors that are better considered as outcomes. Not unexpectedly, if this is done in a multivariate analysis, such factors account for most of the differentials observed, but add little helpful knowledge. Examples are macro studies of child mortality that have taken as independent variables such factors as the level of fertility (Hashmi, 1979) or the prevalence of malaria (Anker and Knowles, 1977; Hogan and Jiwani, 1973). In the two studies of malaria, that variable was meant to serve as a proxy for the ecological setting; however, there were areas in each country being studied—Kenya and Tanzania—that were ecologically highly favorable for malaria transmission, but that were essentially malaria free because of development and health programs. Thus, by using malaria as an explanatory variable, the researchers lost the ability to estimate some of the more significant health program effects. Clearly, the important information for the health planner relates to estimation and explanation of intervention activities and not simply to a finding that malaria can be associated with death.

Problems of interpretation also arise when proximate determinants are handled jointly with independent variables without full consideration of the unobserved factors that are embedded in the determinants. As a rule, because of this bias, the health impact of the proximate variables will be overestimated. Typical examples are survey results in which household environmental facilities, particularly the "presence" of a toilet (which in fact means "use" as well as "access" in most surveys), can be shown to be a strong determinant of health status (Anker and Knowles, 1977; Meegama, 1980; Frenzen and Hogan, 1982). Similar overestimates of impact can relate to health facilities if the effect of actual "use" of services by families is interpreted as the effect of "access to" facilities (Frenzen and Hogan, 1982).

The anthropological approach

One major limitation of survey research is that the variables must be selected a priori. This assumes that the investigator knows in detail the behavioral patterns in the society under investigation, and only wants to make broad generalizations and establish quantitative relationships. In fact, this is not the case for health behavior in much of the developing world, and the lack of knowledge can have important implications for health programs. In Kenya, for example, oral rehydration is being introduced in anticipation that it will save lives by reversing the traditional practice of restricting fluids for children with diarrhea. The impact may be marginal, however, because in one major tribal group infant diarrhea is attributed to poor teething, and the treatment is to cut the child's gums with a sharp object (Maina, 1977). If this practice continues and is ignored by the health system, children with sore gums are likely to refuse to drink the irritating salty oral rehydration solution. In this same tribe, fluids are also withheld in cases of measles. This practice can be catastrophic in the presence of sustained high fever, but the oral rehydration therapy program usually ignores diseases other than diarrheas. Notably, this same study reveals both of these traditional practices to be far less common among educated mothers.

These observations underline the importance of anthropological research to define more precisely what behaviors influence the proximate determinants of child survival and what the motivating factors are. To date, the most extensive research along this line has been done by Caldwell and his colleagues in Africa and Asia in searching for the connections between maternal education and child survival (Caldwell, 1979; Caldwell and MacDonald, 1981; Caldwell et al., 1983). Their investigations address some of the most important questions for health policy around the world: how maternal education operates to influence child survival, and how health and development strategies can influence this process.[9]

In this volume, Helen Ware examines research on women's education, women's roles, and health behavior from an anthropological perspective, revealing the bewildering diversity of hypotheses derived from different cultural settings, and from societies at different stages of development. Ware also highlights the ethnocentric biases that enter into the process of data collection itself. Some questions she raises are: What event is actually reported as a child birth or a child death in a given culture? What is the connection (if any) between "years of schooling" and literacy or functional knowledge about health care? What is the relevance of occupational classifications based on paid employment (usually of men) to the study of women's work and child health? Ware's concluding admonitions, which are relevant for both biomedical and social scientists, are that "the ideal survey [should] be rooted within the local culture . . . [and include] participation by those directly affected," and that it should always "allow room for investigation of unexpected linkages."

Operational strategies in data collection

Two basic approaches to population studies are longitudinal observation and single-round surveys. Biomedical scientists generally conduct longitudinal studies since these are essential for confirming causal hypotheses—for example, in testing the effects of interventions. Furthermore, the longitudinal approach may be the only way to make precise estimates of the incidence and duration of events of interest. The intensity of observation required, however, usually limits longitudinal observations to individual-level (micro) studies in small, selected populations. By contrast, the strength of single-round surveys is that they can cover large, representative populations with considerable economy. This approach is thus favored by social scientists. Most demographic data obtained are retrospective, but precise measurements can be made of the prevalence of conditions in a population, and these data can be used to make indirect estimates of the incidence of events of interest. The large numbers involved permit powerful statistical tests of associations between multiple variables, but causal conclusions must be drawn with great caution. Note, however, that the strength of causal inferences that can be made is not always dependent on longitudinal versus cross-sectional surveys; of equal relevance is the logical conceptualization of the problem being studied and careful identification of the intervening links in a causal chain by either data collection strategy.

Anne R. Pebley describes three longitudinal field studies of health programs—in Guatemala, India, and Bangladesh—that involved controlled trials. The research was hampered by small size of populations studied; selection biases that distorted the comparison of effects of different treatments; and differences in definitions of the variables and in the research methodologies such that a comparison of the results across studies was difficult if not impossible. Most important, because the direct effects of interventions were of primary interest, the controlled studies generally obscured socioeconomic differentials that would naturally occur with large-scale program implementation. This last point reveals a fundamental flaw in using controlled studies as a basis for guiding health strategies: while these studies may measure precisely *what* were the mortality effects of a program intervention, they usually do not give sufficient information on the more important questions regarding *how* and *why* interventions worked or failed to work.[10]

Julie DaVanzo reviews a series of surveys conducted in Malaysia by a multidisciplinary group that paid special attention to research design. The Malaysian study is one of the more comprehensive national studies of mortality undertaken to date, in that the design not only incorporated social determinants and intermediate biological variables, but also combined features of a national sample survey with longitudinal observation.

Analysis of the Malaysian data demonstrates the power of this approach. For example, the association between short birth intervals, low birth weights, and high child mortality is well known. In Malaysia, however, this connection was primarily associated with low family income: high-income families with short birth intervals showed only slight reductions in birth weight. The investigators also found that the connection between reduced breastfeeding and increased infant mortality occurred primarily among families without adequate household sanitation. These findings are perhaps not surprising, but they do indicate that program strategies to promote birth spacing and breastfeeding may not have the health benefits anticipated by their advocates.

Belgin Tekçe and Frederic C. Shorter, reporting on a study in Amman, Jordan, demonstrate how many inferences can be derived from a carefully developed single-round survey. The study was carried out in conjunction with an urban development project, so that physical and economic household data, supplemented with demographic data, were collected from a total household inventory required by the development agency. This was supplemented by interviewing a subsample of households on health-related behavior and health status of children under 3 years of age. In the first stage of the analysis, the traditional estimates of the socioeconomic determinants of mortality revealed sex differentials. At the second stage, which related socioeconomic determinants to health behaviors (intermediate variables), sex differentials in health care and breastfeeding practices were demonstrated. It could then be shown that these differentials in behavior were connected to sex differences in the nutritional status of the surviving children. Finally, nutritional status of the youngest child proved to be associated with previous levels of child mortality in the respective families.

Tekçe and Shorter also provide relevant lessons on program-related research. Since their study was done in connection with an ongoing community development program, it had to be designed to meet the needs of the program implementors. But, because of the scientific input into the study design, it became far more than a passive instrument for evaluation of the project impact. The study provided useful data on such determinants of child mortality as mother's education and hygienic practices that had not been taken into account by the development agency. Since the research was undertaken as a collaborative effort, the agency's participation in the interpretation of the results assured that steps were undertaken to incorporate the findings into program strategies for the community.

Mathematical models and health programs

The paper by James Trussell and Jane Menken provides a brief introduction to life tables that illustrates the power of mathematical models as research tools. With model life tables one can describe the entire age pattern of mortality in a population with just a few index numbers; this not only facilitates the comparison of mortality experiences between populations, but more importantly, permits one to derive estimates of the entire mortality experience of populations from very limited empirical data. Similar models are available to describe the birth patterns in populations, but Bongaarts (1978) has advanced the field of fertility research significantly by developing a simple mathematical model that can be used to assess the contribution of each of the proximate fertility determinants to the levels of births seen in different populations.

A similar achievement in the study of mortality may be possible in the future, but the problem will be much more complex because of the multiple biological processes that can lead to death in infants and children. However, even if this ideal objective can never be reached, there still is a compelling case for researchers to seek common methodologies and frameworks for data collection and analysis so that the experience being accumulated around the world can be tested in mathematical models. This will not only clarify the picture of how various factors operate to produce mortality changes, but also provide better guidance on what health strategies may be effective in improving the situation.

Burton Singer looks at the relevance of mathematical models of infectious diseases to the design, monitoring, and evaluation of public health intervention programs. He observes that the development of mathematical theories of infectious disease transmission has far surpassed the availability of empirical data to test the models; as a result, there are very few models whose predictions may be trusted as a guide to an intervention program strategy. As an illustration of the utility of models, Singer notes that the early work that resulted in the Ross–Macdonald model of malaria transmission was instrumental in supporting strategies for malaria eradication, despite limitations of the model. But now that resistance of the mosquito to insecticides has made eradication an elusive goal, programs aim at a reduction of prevalence and mortality through a mixed strategy of drugs and insecticides. This presents a new challenge to modeling to take into account genetic variability of the vector and of the parasite. Singer makes a strong argument that although the analytical problems have increased in complexity, the need for empirical research and better models is even greater if successful control of malaria and other diseases is to be achieved.

Public health policymakers and program managers unaccustomed to the use of infectious disease models in planning or management may not question their absence. Yet in a number of circumstances in which such models have been used, they have proven important. For example, after the global eradication of smallpox, the logical question was whether the same strategy could be repeated with measles in developing countries. An analysis based on a model of measles transmission dynamics suggests that measles eradication in developing countries will be far more difficult because of the much greater transmission rate of the measles virus in susceptible populations (Bart et al., 1983). Thus current global strategy is aiming primarily for a reduction in measles mortality through mass immunization programs.

Howard N. Barnum and Robin Barlow undertake to construct a model to guide program managers in the allocation of limited health resources. Resource allocation models are intrinsically complex since they must incorporate a range of program intervention strategies as well as biological input–output relationships. In this example, construction of the model requires that relationships and interactions among 51 variables be specified, each with different sets of equations according to the hypothesized functional form of the relationships. Also required is specification of 221 coefficients for the equations that relate to factors ranging from how social determinants will constrain use of medical services, to the effectiveness of health promoters or mass communication in reducing disease incidence, to estimates of the case fatality rates of different diseases complicated with different degrees of malnutrition.

Because quantitative information on most of these coefficients is nonexistent or not readily available, the authors conducted an opinion survey of health professionals with clinical, research, and field experience. In its actual operation, then, the resource allocation model combines the subjective evaluations of health planners with cost data within a framework of predetermined parameters to make the choices about the most cost-effective policies.

The current limitations on input data for planning models should not lead to the conclusion that endeavors in this area have little utility. Rather, work with such models highlights the poor knowledge base that health professionals have about the determinants of child survival and about the effectiveness of intervention efforts. This points up the need for more direct collaboration between researchers and program managers, not just in program design but, more importantly, in the operational phase in which data will be obtained to test and improve models that may guide health policies and programs in the future.

Conclusion

Our central concern is with the survival and health of children in poor developing countries. Advances in the biomedical sciences have given us the potential to assure that over 97 percent of newborns will survive childhood, but reaching this potential is strongly dependent upon the social circumstances in which children are born. To some degree, the technical advances in the medical sciences can transcend the social constraints—particularly when they can be imposed to transform the disease environment, as with the application of insecticides, or when the life-saving effects are easily recognized by the population suffering high mortality, as with antibiotics. But more sustained health improvements require families to be aware of modern scientific concepts of disease causation and to have the means to act on that knowledge.

It is within the family, where the modern (generally Western) health systems interact with the traditional social systems, that most health interventions succeed or fail. And so it is on this crucial interaction that policy-relevant research is needed. Yet it is precisely in this area, where biomedical and social scientists must join together to define and solve the problems, that research has been most neglected. The goal of this volume is to identify some common ground where these two groups can work together to find the answers that will guide health policies and strategies in the future. The task is far from complete, but it is hoped that a few steps in the right direction have been taken in this work.

Notes

1 The recommendations of the 1978 Alma Ata Conference on Primary Health Care, if assiduously implemented, would require a radical reorientation and reorganization of most national health programs in the developing world. Essential elements of the strategy of community-based programs, besides the provision and promotion of the usual health, education, and environmental services, are "involvement of all related sectors and aspects of national and community development"; "maximum community and individual self-reliance and participation in the planning, organization, operation and control of primary care"; "giving priority to those most in need"; and "reliance on health workers (at all levels) including traditional practitioners" (WHO/UNICEF, 1978).

2 The issues currently being raised by those questioning the technology-oriented approach to primary health care have a long history. See, for example, the article by McDermott (1966) discussing "modern medicine and the demographic–disease pattern of overly traditional societies: a technologic misfit." From the perspective of the present author, the problem should be restated as a "sociologic misfit." The technologies do not

fit the diseases. The problem is a failure of top-down, Western-oriented health systems to mesh with traditional cultures and to encourage the socioeconomic changes necessary for improved health in families.

3 An example of the consequences of current disciplinary isolationism is seen in the results of efforts by the World Bank to undertake health policy analysis by examining the relationships between parents' education and childhood diseases. A survey of over 200 health studies from the developing world produced fewer than five that cross-tabulated parents' education with levels of child morbidity, though many more had recorded data on both items (Cochrane, Leslie, and O'Hara, 1980).

4 Notable other efforts in this direction are represented by Preston (1980a) and IUSSP (1983).

5 The latest international annotated bibliography of oral rehydration therapy lists 85 publications where studies "attempted to measure the effect of ORT on diarrheal disease morbidity and on the nutritional status." It concludes: "In these studies both methodological limitations and intervening sociocultural factors often confounded impact mea-

surement. Among the former were poorly chosen or nonexistent comparison groups, variable levels of training and expertise on the part of those administering oral rehydration interventions and often unreliable disease and nutrition surveillance data. Intervening factors included widely varying environmental, cultural and socioeconomic characteristics'' (PAHO/WHO, 1983).

6 For many purposes, the controlled research design is a powerful research tool: it can be used to assess the association of a particular disease with a single behavior factor (e.g., the association of cholera with use of contaminated water) or to measure the biological effect of a technological intervention in a population (e.g., the effect of a vaccine on the incidence of disease) without having to take other variables into account. Typically the former study design is a retrospective case–control study, while the latter is done as a prospective randomized trial. Details of the methodologies are found in most epidemiology textbooks.

7 Examples of such recommendations are found in the articles by Walsh and Warren (1980) and Rohde (1982). A critique of these assumptions may be found in Chen et al. (1981).

8 One example of this interaction comes from the study by Nag (1983), who analyzed life expectancies in West Bengal and Kerala and found that the large differential *use* of medical facilities was a key factor accounting for better health conditions in Kerala. Pursuing these observations further, Caldwell et al. (1982) stress that the behavioral characteristics conducive to good health have their origins in social and cultural factors extending back at least a century.

9 Most micro-level research has assessed the relationship of maternal education to child survival because of the availability of such data in censuses. It should be noted that paternal education is equally important in some settings (Trussell and Preston, 1982).

10 This point comes through most clearly in a comprehensive review of ten health and nutrition intervention projects carried out around the world (including the INCAP and Narangwal studies cited in this volume by Pebley) (Gwatkin et al., 1980). These projects were selected because they represented controlled studies that could give objective data on program impact. But they give little data on the *reasons* for success or failure. This forced the reviewers to make generalizations regarding the key elements of successful projects, such as "the degree to which they depart from the Western tradition of hospital-based, high technology medical services" and "the unusual effectiveness with which the project's service programs were organized, administered, and directed." These are *supply* issues. Information on each community's social constraints to *demand* and on how these were actually overcome would be of more help to administrators seeking to extend the services to larger populations.

References

Anker, Richard, and J. C. Knowles. 1977. "An empirical analysis of mortality differentials in Kenya at the macro and micro level," *Population and Employment Working Paper* No. 60. Geneva: International Labour Office.

Arriaga, E., and K. Davis. 1969. "Patterns of mortality change in Latin America," *Demography* 6: 223–242.

Bart, Kenneth, Walter A. Orenstein, Alan R. Hinman, and Robert W. Amler. 1983. "Measles and models," *International Journal of Epidemiology* 12: 263–266.

Behm, H. 1979. "Socioeconomic determinants of mortality in Latin America," *Proceedings of the Meeting on Socioeconomic Determinants and Consequences of Mortality, Mexico City*. Geneva: WHO, pp. 139–165.

Bongaarts, John. 1978. "A framework for analyzing the proximate determinants of fertility," *Population and Development Review* 4, no. 1 (March): 105–132.

Bose, A., and P. B. Desai. 1983. *Studies in Social Dynamics of Primary Health Care*. New Delhi: Hindustan Publishing Corp.

Caldwell, John C. 1979. "Education as a factor in mortality decline: An examination of Nigerian data," *Population Studies* 23: 395–413.

———, and Peter McDonald. 1981. "Influence of maternal education on infant and child mortality: Levels and causes," *International Population Conference, Manila, 1981*, Vol. 2. Liège; IUSSP, pp. 79–96.

———, P. H. Reddy, and P. Caldwell. 1983. "The social component of mortality decline: An investigation in South India employing alternative methodologies," *Population Studies* 37: 185–205.

Chen, L. C. 1984. "Interaction of health technology and social organization," Takemi Lecture, Harvard School of Public Health, Boston.

———, J. Chakraborty, A. M. Sadar, and Md. Yunus. 1981. "Estimating and partitioning the mortality impact of several modern medical technologies in basic health services," *International Population Conference, Manila, 1981*, Vol. 2. Liège: IUSSP, pp. 113–142.

Cochrane, Susan H., Joan Leslie, and Donald J. O'Hara. 1980. "Parental education and child health: Intracountry evidence," *The Effects of Education on Health*. Washington, D.C.: World Bank Staff Working Paper No. 405, pp. 56–95.

Davis, K. 1956. "The amazing decline of mortality in underdeveloped areas," *American Economic Review* 46: 305–318.

———, and Judith Blake. 1956. "Social structure and fertility: An analytic framework," *Economic Development and Cultural Change* 4: 211–235.

Fabrega, H. 1972. "Medical anthropology," in *Biennial Review of Anthropology*, ed. B. Siegel. Stanford: Stanford University Press, pp. 167–229.

Flegg, A. T. 1982. "Equality of income, illiteracy and medical care as determinants of mortality in underdeveloped countries," *Population Studies* 36: 441–456.

Frenzen, P. D., and D. Hogan. 1982. "The impact of class, education and health care on infant mortality in a developing society: The case of rural Thailand," *Demography* 19: 391–408.

Gopalan, C. 1983. "Small is healthy? For the poor, not for the rich," *Bulletin of the Nutrition Foundation of India*, October, New Delhi.

Gwatkin, D. R. 1980. "Indications of change in developing country mortality trends: The end of an era?" *Population and Development Review* 6, no. 4 (December): 615–644.

———, J. R. Wilcox, and J. D. Wray. 1980. *Can Health and Nutrition Intervention Make a Difference?* Washington, D.C.: Overseas Development Council.

Hashmi, S. S. 1979. "Socioeconomic determinants of mortality levels in Asia and the Pacific," in *Proceedings of the Meeting on Socioeconomic Determinants and Consequences of Mortality, Mexico City*. Geneva: WHO, pp. 119–136.

Hogan, H. R., and S. Jiwani. 1973. "Differential mortality," in *1973 Demographic Survey of Tanzania*, Vol. 6, ed. R. Henin, D. Ewbank, and H. R. Hogan. Dar es Salaam: Bureau of Statistics and University of Dar es Salaam.

IUSSP. 1983. Seminar on Social Policy, Health Policy and Mortality Prospects. Paris: Institut National d'Etudes Démographiques.

Jain, A. 1984. "Determinants of regional variations in infant mortality in rural India," Population Council, New York, mimeo.

Jayachandran, J., and G. K. Jarvis. 1983. "Socioeconomic development, medical care and nutrition as determinants of infant mortality in less developed countries," Discussion Paper No. 34, Department of Sociology, University of Alberta, Edmonton, Canada.

Kasongo Project Team. 1981. "Influence of measles vaccine on survival pattern of 7–35 month old children in Kasongo, Zaire," *Lancet* 1 (4 April): 764–767.

Kusin, J. A., Sri Kardjati, and C. de With. 1983. "Infant feeding and growth in Madura." Paper presented at Workshop on the Interrelationships of Maternal-Infant Nutrition, Airlangga University, Surabaya, Indonesia.

Lampang Health Development Project Documentary Series. 1981. *Summary Final Report of the Lampang Health Development Project*, Vol. 1. Bangkok: Ministry of Public Health.

Maina, B. W. 1977. "A socio-medical enquiry: Modern and indigenous medical care utilization pattern with respect to measles and acute diarrhea among the Akamba," M.A. thesis, University of Nairobi.

Mata, L. 1978. *The Children of Santa Maria Cauque: A Prospective Field Study of Health and Growth.* Cambridge, Mass: The MIT Press.

McDermott, W. 1966. "Modern medicine and the demographic disease pattern of overly traditional societies: A technological misfit," *Journal of Medical Education* 41: 137–162.

Meegama, S. A. 1980. "Socio-economic determinants of infant and child mortality in Sri Lanka: An analysis of post-war experience," *WFS Scientific Report* No. 8. London: World Fertility Survey.

Miró, C., and J. E. Potter. 1980. *Population Policy: Research Priorities in the Developing World.* London: Francis Pinter.

Misra, B. 1983. "A critical analysis of primary health care centers in India." Paper presented in IUSSP Seminar on Social Policy, Health Policy and Mortality Prospects, Paris. Paris: Institut National d'Etudes Demographiques.

Mobarak, A. B. 1980. "Diarrheal disease control study, May through October, 1980." Cairo: Ministry of Health, Rural Health Department.

Mosley, W. H. 1980. "Biological contamination of the environment by man," in *Biological and Social Aspects of Mortality and Length of Life,* ed. S. H. Preston. Liège: Ordina.

————. 1983. "Will primary health care reduce infant and child mortality? A critique of some current strategies with special reference to Africa and Asia." Paper presented in IUSSP Seminar on Social Policy, Health Policy and Mortality Prospects, Paris. Paris: Institut National d'Etudes Demographiques.

Nadim, W. El M. 1980. *Rural Health Care in Egypt.* Ottawa: International Development Research Centre.

Nag, Moni, 1983. "Impact of social and economic development on mortality: Comparative study of Kerala and West Bengal," *Economic and Political Weekly* (Bombay) 18, nos. 19–21, Annual Issue (May): 877–900.

PAHO/WHO. 1983. *Oral Rehydration Therapy: An Annotated Bibliography.* Washington, D.C.: PAHO.

Palloni, A. 1981. "Mortality in Latin America: Emerging patterns," *Population and Development Review* 7, no. 4 (December): 623–649.

Pangestuhadi, M. 1983. "Some notes on the integrated nutrition-family planning program in East Java: A manager's view." Paper presented at Workshop on the Interrelationship of Maternal-Infant Nutrition, Airlangga University, Surabaya, Indonesia.

Preston, S. H. 1976. *Mortality Patterns in National Populations.* New York: Academic Press.

————. 1978. "Mortality, morbidity and development," *Population Bulletin of the UNECWA* 15: 63–78.

————, ed. 1980a. *Biological and Social Aspects of Mortality and Length of Life.* Liège: Ordina.

————. 1980b. "Causes and consequences of mortality declines in less developed countries during the twentieth century," in *Population and Economic Change in Developing Countries,* ed. R. A. Easterlin. Chicago: University of Chicago.

Rahaman, M. M., K. M. S. Aziz, Y. Patwari, et al. 1979. "Diarrheal mortality in two Bangladesh villages with and without community based oral rehydration therapy," *Lancet* 2: 809–812.

Reinks, A., and P. Iskandar. 1981. "Primary and indigenous health care in rural Central Java: A comparison of process and contents," *Hedera Report* No. 4, Faculty of Medicine, Gadjah Mada University, Yogyakarta, Indonesia.

Rohde, J. 1982. "Why the other half dies. The science and politics of child mortality in the third world," Leonard Parsons Lecture, University of Birmingham, England.

Rowland, M. G. M., and J. P. K. McCollum. 1977. "Malnutrition and gastroenteritis in the Gambia," *Transactions of the Royal Society of Tropical Medicine and Hygiene* 71: 199–203.

Roy, S. K., A. K. M. A. Chowdhury, and M. A. Rahaman. 1983. "Excess mortality among children discharged from hospital after treatment for diarrhea in rural Bangladesh," *British Medical Journal* 287: 1097–1099.

Ruzicka, L., and H. Hansluwka. 1982. "Mortality transition in South and East Asia: Technology confronts poverty," *Population and Development Review* 8, no. 3 (September): 567–588.

Schultz, T. P. 1979. "Interpretation of relations among mortality, economics of the household, and the health environment," *Proceedings of the Meeting on Socioeconomic Determinants and Consequences of Mortality, Mexico City.* Geneva: WHO, pp. 382–422.

Seckler, D. 1982. "Small but healthy," in *Newer Concepts in Nutrition and Their Implication for Policy,* ed. P. V. Sukhatme. Pune, India: Maharashtra Association for the Cultivation of Science Research Institute.

Snow, C. P. 1971. "The two cultures and the scientific revolution," in *Public Affairs,* C. P. Snow. New York: Charles Scribner's Sons, pp. 13–46.

Stolnitz, G. 1965. "Recent mortality trends in Latin America, Asia and Africa," *Population Studies* 19: 117–138.

Sukhatme, P. V., ed. 1982. *Newer Concepts in Nutrition and their Implications for Policy.* Pune, India: Maharashtra Association for the Cultivation of Science Research Institute.

Trussell, J., and S. Preston. 1982. "Estimating the covariates of childhood mortality from retrospective reports of mothers," *Health Policy and Education* 3:1–36.

UNICEF. 1984. *The State of the World's Children 1984.* New York: UNICEF.

United Nations. 1982. *Levels and Trends of Mortality Since 1950.* New York: United Nations.

———. Population Division. 1983. "Mortality and health policy. Highlights of the issues in the context of the World Population Plan of Action." Paper prepared for the Expert Group on Mortality and Health Policy, Rome. New York: United Nations.

Walsh, J. A., and Kenneth S. Warren. 1980. "Selective primary health care: An interim strategy for disease control in developing countries," *Social Science and Medicine* 14c: 145–163.

Weiss, E. 1982. "The Calabar Rural Maternal and Child Health/Family Planning Project: The evaluation and research component," International Programs Working Paper No. 16. New York: The Population Council.

Williamson, N. E. 1982. "An attempt to reduce infant and child mortality in Bohol, Philippines," *Studies in Family Planning* 13, no. 4 (April): 106–117.

World Health Organization. 1981–1983. *Bibliography of Acute Diarrheal Diseases,* Vols. 1–3. Geneva: Program for Control of Diarrheal Diseases, WHO.

———, and UNICEF. 1978. *Alma Ata 1978: Primary Health Care.* Geneva: WHO.

An Analytical Framework for the Study of Child Survival in Developing Countries

W. Henry Mosley

Lincoln C. Chen

This essay proposes a new analytical framework for the study of the determinants of child survival in developing countries. The approach incorporates both social and biological variables and integrates research methods employed by social and medical scientists. It also provides for the measurement of morbidity and mortality in a single variable. The framework is based on the premise that all social and economic determinants of child mortality necessarily operate through a common set of biological mechanisms, or proximate determinants, to exert an impact on mortality.[1] The framework is intended to advance research on social policy and medical interventions to improve child survival.

Traditionally, social science research on child mortality has focused on the association between socioeconomic status and levels and patterns of mortality in populations (Figure 1A). Correlations between mortality and socioeconomic characteristics are used to generate causal inferences about the mortality determinants. Income and maternal education, for example, are two commonly measured correlates (and inferred causal determinants) of child mortality in developing country populations. Specific medical causes of death are generally not addressed by social scientists, and the mechanisms by which socioeconomic determinants operate to produce the observed mortality differentials remain largely an unexplained "black box."

Medical research focuses primarily on the biological processes of diseases, less frequently on mortality per se. The differing assumptions and methods are classified in Figure 1B. Studies of cause of death attribute mortality to specific disease processes (such as infections or malnutrition), using information obtained from death reports or clinical case records. Clinical trials assess the therapeutic effect of a particular medical technology. Field intervention studies measure the effectiveness of personal preventive measures on

FIGURE 1   Conceptual models of social science and medical science approaches to research on child survival

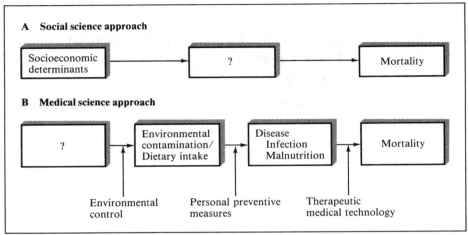

levels of morbidity and mortality in a population. Epidemiological studies may define mechanisms of disease transmission in the environment—for example, the connection between environmental contamination (polluted drinking water) and disease (cholera). Intervention studies alter the environment to reduce disease transmission (as with malaria vector control). Nutrition research focuses on breastfeeding, dietary practices, and food availability as they relate to nutritional status.

The dependent variable most commonly measured in medical research is morbidity, that is, the manifestations of disease processes among survivors—usually calculated as the incidence and prevalence of disease states in a population. The ultimate consequences of disease for mortality in populations at large tend to be neglected, and socioeconomic determinants are generally ignored or dealt with only superficially.

While both the social and medical sciences have made major contributions to our understanding of child mortality in developing countries, the differing concerns and methodologies have compartmentalized such knowledge and constrained the development of potentially more useful approaches to understanding child survival. An even more critical problem is that the selection of a particular research approach usually results in policy and program recommendations biased along disciplinary lines. A new analytical approach incorporating both social and medical science methodologies into a coherent analytical framework of child survival therefore is clearly needed.

The proximate determinants framework

The development of a proximate determinants approach to the study of child survival presented here[2] is based on several premises:

1 In an optimal setting, over 97 percent of newborn infants can be expected to survive through the first five years of life.

2 Reduction in this survival probability in any society is due to the operation of social, economic, biological, and environmental forces.

3 Socioeconomic determinants (independent variables) must operate through more basic proximate determinants that in turn influence the risk of disease and the outcome of disease processes.

4 Specific diseases and nutrient deficiencies observed in a surviving population may be viewed as biological indicators of the operations of the proximate determinants.

5 Growth faltering and ultimately mortality in children (the dependent variable) are the cumulative consequences of multiple disease processes (including their biosocial interactions). Only infrequently is a child's death the result of a single isolated disease episode.

The key to the model is the identification of a set of proximate determinants, or intermediate variables, that directly influence the risk of morbidity and mortality. All social and economic determinants must operate through these variables to affect child survival.[3] The proximate determinants are grouped into five categories:

— Maternal factors: age; parity; birth interval.
— Environmental contamination: air; food/water/fingers; skin/soil/inanimate objects; insect vectors.
— Nutrient deficiency: calories; protein; micronutrients (vitamins and minerals).
— Injury: accidental; intentional.
— Personal illness control: personal preventive measures; medical treatment.

Each of the *maternal factors* has been shown to exert an independent influence on pregnancy outcome and infant survival through its effects on maternal health. Synergism may also exist between maternal variables—for example, short birth spacing combined with young maternal age.

Environmental contamination refers to the transmission of infectious agents to children (and mothers). The four categories representing the main routes whereby infectious agents are transmitted to the human host are air—the route of spread for the respiratory and many "contact"-transmitted diseases; food, water, and fingers—the principal routes of spread for diarrheas and other intestinal diseases; skin, soil, and inanimate objects—the routes for skin infections; and insect vectors, which transmit parasitic and viral diseases.

Nutrient deficiency relates to the intake of the three major classes of nutrients—calories, protein, and the micronutrients. A critical point here is that the survival of children is influenced by nutrients available not only to the child but also to the mother. Maternal diet and nutrition during pregnancy affect birth weight and, during lactation, influence the quantity and nutrient quality of breastmilk.

Injury includes physical injury, burns, and poisoning. Although accidental injuries are often considered random events, their frequency and pattern in a population in fact reflect environmental risks that differ according to socioeconomic and environmental contexts. Injuries may also be intentionally inflicted, the most extreme example being infanticide.

As one component in *personal illness control,* healthy individuals take preventive measures to avoid disease. These include traditional behaviors like observing taboos, as well as modern practices such as immunizations or malaria prophylaxis. An important inclusion is the practices and the quality of care during pregnancy and childbirth. The second component in this category, medical treatment, relates to measures taken to cure diseases after they become manifest.

Figure 2 depicts a framework showing how these five groups of proximate determinants operate on the health dynamics of a population. All proximate determinates in the first four groups influence the rate of shift of healthy individuals toward sickness. The personal illness control factors influence both the rate of illness (through prevention) and the rate of recovery (through treatment). Specific states of sickness (infection or nutrient deficiency) are basically transitory: ultimately there is either complete recovery or irreversible consequences manifested by increasing degrees of permanent growth faltering (or other disability among the survivors) and/or death.[4]

A novel aspect of this conceptual model is its definition of a specific disease state in an individual as an indicator of the operation of the proximate determinants rather than as a "cause" of illness and death. This is not to undervalue the usefulness of etiology-specific classification of disease and death for the development of rational therapeutic and preventive interventions. Rather, the aim is to emphasize the social as well as medical roots of the problem. This in fact is the standard approach of epidemiology, which begins with a biological problem in the host and then searches for its social determinants in order to develop rational control measures. The strategic approach to child survival research implied by this framework parallels methods used in the epidemiology of the chronic diseases rather than of the acute diseases. Chronic diseases such as heart disease are typically multifactorial in causality, have long latency periods between disease exposure and manifestation, and are powerfully influenced by lifestyle and socioeconomic circumstances. There is ample evidence in the medical literature that child mortality, especially in developing countries, also possesses these attributes (Puffer and Serrano, 1975; Mata, 1978).

The proximate determinants (or the intermediate variable) approach to child survival parallels the approach used by Davis and Blake (1956) in developing an analytical framework for the study of fertility. The problems posed

FIGURE 2 Operation of the five groups of proximate determinants
on the health dynamics of a population

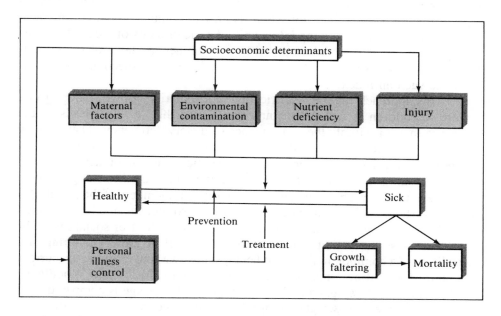

by mortality analysis, however, are far more complex because a child's death
is the ultimate consequence of a cumulative series of biological insults rather
than the outcome of a single biological event. This is quite different from the
fertility model, in which all determinants operate to influence a single biological event (conception to generate a birth). Thus, it appears unlikely that a
proximate determinants framework for mortality is easily amenable to a quantification of component contributions to mortality change, like the elegant
system Bongaarts (1978) has developed for the fertility model.

Development of a conceptual framework for the study of child survival
requires both a definition of the proximate determinants of mortality and a
redefinition of the independent and dependent variables. These definitions are
implied in the premises presented earlier, but greater precision and elaboration
of their measurement and mode of action are indicated.

The dependent variable

Typically, social scientists examine mortality as the dependent variable. This
has strength because deaths are definitive events that may be easily measured
and aggregated. An exclusive focus on mortality, however, handicaps research
because death is a rare event, the measurement of which necessitates the study
of large populations or the cumulation of the morality experience of smaller
populations over long periods. With few exceptions, social scientists pay scant
attention to the health status of survivors. In contrast, medical scientists typ-

ically focus on the diseases or nutritional status of survivors. This approach permits intensive study of smaller populations; it has the shortcoming, however, that past deaths among the birth cohorts being studied are often not taken into account. A logical question, then, is how to combine counts of the dead with observations on the living into a unified scale or index of the health status of a population. The model proposed here combines the level of growth faltering among survivors with the level of mortality of the respective birth cohort to create such an index.

This approach requires clarification. Customarily, growth faltering in a cohort of children is called "malnutrition," and this, in turn, leads to the inference that it is simply the consequence of dietary deficiency. There is now abundant evidence that growth faltering is due to many factors and that it may be more appropriately considered a nonspecific indicator of health status.[5] Thus, combining a measure of growth faltering with mortality can generate a single dependent variable that can be scaled over all members of the population of interest (both survivors and deceased). Doing so reduces one bias common to medical research and strengthens the explanatory power of social research.

To assess the validity of integrating the level of growth faltering and mortality into a common indicator of health status, we first examine the current procedure for scaling "malnutrition" in children (Morley and Woodland, 1979). Children are weighed and their actual weight-for-age is compared with the expected (median) weight-for-age based on standard growth charts (Jelliffe, 1967; American Public Health Association, 1981). Typically, each child's weight is expressed as a percentage of the expected weight-for-age. The degree of growth faltering is a function of the negative deviation from the median.[6] The classification system proposed by Gómez includes three grades of malnutrition: Grade I: 75–89 percent of standard weight-for-age; Grade II: 60–74 percent; Grade III: below 60 percent (Gómez et al.; 1955). Since one standard deviation of the normal weight distribution is usually about 10–11 percent of the median weight-for-age, Gómez Grade I malnutrition overlaps somewhat with the normal range.[7]

The significance of weight-for-age as an indicator of general health status derives from prospective studies in Bangladesh, India, and New Guinea. Measurements of cohorts of children under age 3 years were taken at one point in time, the cohorts were followed prospectively for periods of one to two years, and mortality rates were calculated by weight-for-age groups. The results, summarized in Figure 3, show a consistent increase of death risk with lower weight-for-age. Use of a logarithmic scale illustrates what has long been recognized in newborns, namely, the near exponential increase of mortality risk with greater negative deviations from an expected normal weight (Federici and Terrenato, 1980).[8] The figure also shows a plot of early neonatal deaths by birth weight, which follows much the same pattern.

Based on this pattern of mortality risks among survivors by weight-for-age, our suggested method of incorporating child deaths into a common "health status index" is to assign the child deaths a "score" of Grade IV. A variable

FIGURE 3 Child mortality rates by percentage of expected (median) weight-for-age, based on prospective studies of children in Bangladesh, India, and New Guinea

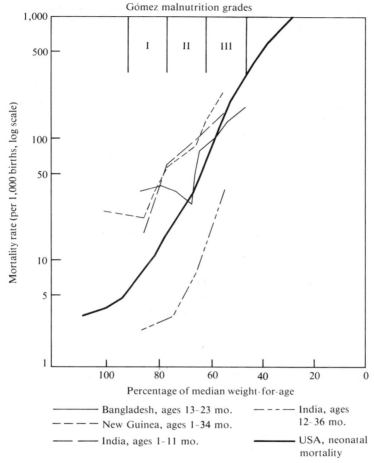

SOURCES: For Bangladesh, 13–23 mo. (Chen et al., 1980); New Guinea, 1–34 mo. (Heywood, 1982); India, 1–11 mo. and 12–36 mo. (Kielman and McCord, 1978); USA (NCHS, 1972).

so constructed can be useful as a relative measure of the current health status of a population cohort, and since this measure reflects cumulative past morbidity experience, it may be suitable for single-round retrospective surveys searching for determinants of child survival.

One caveat needs to be stated regarding the use and interpretation of this combined growth faltering plus mortality variable. Since growth faltering indicates the current health status of a population, it can serve as a measure of the *relative* risk of various subgroups of that population to mortality in the future. However, it will not serve as a valid index to relate specific absolute levels of mortality across populations. This is because the probability of dying at a given level of growth faltering varies greatly between populations according to the prevalence of certain diseases and the availability of medical services. As an example, some Latin American countries as well as New Guinea have documented mortality declines without a significant change in the "nutritional status" of survivors (Solimano and Vine, 1980; Teller et al., 1979; Malcolm, 1974).

Proximate determinants

In order to achieve maximum analytical value, the proximate determinants should not only serve as indicators of the various mechanisms producing growth faltering and death; they also should be measurable in population-based research. In some cases the proximate determinants are measurable directly, in other cases indirectly, as detailed below.

Maternal factors

The maternal factors of age, parity, and birth interval (since last birth and to the next birth where appropriate) are ordinarily measured directly by interview.

Environmental contamination

In field studies, the levels of environmental contamination reflecting the various routes of spread of disease may be measured directly by carrying out microbiological examination of samples of air, water, food, skin washing, or vectors. Usually when this is done for public health surveillance, only a single "indicator organism" is selected for measurement: for example, *E. coli* bacteria from human feces is measured in food or water. A more practical means of assessing the relative intensity of environmental contamination is to measure the number of recent episodes (incidence) of a group of acute infectious diseases in the cohort of children under study. These diseases can be selected to evaluate each of the major routes of environmental contamination (Mosley, 1980a). For example, respiratory diseases (colds, influenza, pneumonia) can be used for airborne infections, diarrheal diseases for food- and water-borne infections, and skin infections/infestations and neonatal tetanus for diseases spread by skin and soil. For chronic diseases, indicators of prevalence in the population are often more useful. Examples are skin tests for tuberculosis, stool examinations for intestinal parasites related to fecal contamination of the environment, physical examinations for scabies and trachoma, and blood smears for malaria.

All of the above are direct means of assessing levels of environmental contamination, either by searching for infective agents in the environment or by measuring those agents' effects in a population. Levels of potential exposure to disease can also be approximated and scaled by using a series of simple physical indexes that are known to be strongly correlated with the levels of biological contamination of the environment. For example, air contamination and risk of contact-acquired respiratory infections can be inferred from the intensity of household crowding (persons per room); water contamination can be scaled by source of supply (ditch, pond, open well, protected well, hand-pump, piped supply); household food contamination, by cleaning, cooking, and storage practices; and potential fecal contamination, by the presence of latrines or toilets, or the use of soap and water.

Where appropriate, more than one measure may be used to obtain a composite index (e.g., incidence of diarrheal disease, prevalence of round-worm parasites, absence of toilet facilities). But when this is done, care should be taken to avoid a common error of treating each measure as an isolated factor, particularly in multivariate models, since the interpretation of the results will be confounded by multicollinearity.

Nutrient deficiency

As with environmental exposure, nutrient availability to the infant (or to the mother during pregnancy and lactation) can be measured directly by weighing of all foods before consumption, accompanied by biochemical analysis of food samples. Less precise measures may be obtained by observing what is eaten, or by a recall history of the diet. These cruder measures may be particularly useful in assessing relative levels of nutrient intake.

Deficiency of specific nutrients in the diet can also be assessed by physical or biochemical measures. Examples are low serum albumin levels for protein deficiency, signs of xerophthalmia for vitamin A deficiency, and anemia for iron deficiency. These physical and biochemical measures of nutritional status, however, should be interpreted with caution, since, as noted earlier, physiological manifestations of nutrient deficiency may also be due to such other factors as recurrent infections.

Injury

The operation of this intermediate variable is measured by the incidence of recent injuries, or the cumulative prevalence of injury-related disabilities (e.g., scarring from burns).

Personal illness control

For preventive measures this variable is commonly assessed by the reported use of such preventive services as immunizations, malaria prophylaxis, or antenatal care. For curative measures, generally the providers of care and types of therapy taken for specific conditions are assessed. Because traditional practices as well as modern scientific medicine should be included in this group, the kinds of therapies or providers must be scaled independently according to probable efficacy.

As these illustrations demonstrate, a variety of procedures can be used to measure and scale the proximate determinants of child survival, ranging from sophisticated biological analysis of environmental and food specimens, to medical examination of individuals, to visual observations of the environment, to simply asking questions. Some methods are more precise than others, but not necessarily better for population-based research. For example, direct microbiological examination of water can give the precise bacterial count of the sample, but since the sample is taken from only one site on one occasion, it is unlikely to be a valid indicator of the risk of infection over an entire year. The observation that the water source is a canal used for bathing, cooking, and fecal waste disposal will be far more appropriate in this case.

Socioeconomic determinants

We next examine a range of socioeconomic determinants (independent variables) and illustrate how they operate through the proximate determinants to influence the level of growth faltering and mortality. The socioeconomic determinants are grouped into three broad categories of variables that are commonly followed in the social science literature.[9]

— Individual-level variables: individual productivity (fathers, mothers); traditions/norms/attitudes.
— Household-level variables: income/wealth.
— Community-level variables: ecological setting; political economy; health system.

Individual-level variables

Individual productivity Three elements that determine the "productivity" of household members are skills (typically measured by educational level), health, and time. If the "product" of interest is a healthy surviving child, the childbearing and childrearing adult (usually the mother) should be considered separately from other adults (usually the father).

For fathers, particularly in the urban sector, educational levels usually correlate strongly with occupation, and therefore with household income. Fathers' education is a strong determinant of the household's assets and the marketable commodities the household consumes. Thus, in many cases correlations between health effects and educational level of fathers (or other nonchildbearing, economically productive adult members in a household) largely occur because of operations on the proximate determinants through the income effects. Father's education may also influence attitudes and thus preferences in choice of consumption goods, including child care services. This effect is likely to be most significant for child survival when more educated fathers are married to less educated mothers.

For mothers, the situation is entirely different. Their skills, time, and health operate directly on the proximate determinants. Because of biological links between the mother and infant during pregnancy and lactation, the mother's health and nutritional status as well as her reproductive pattern influences the health and survival of the child. Because of her responsibility for her own care during pregnancy and the care of her child through the most vulnerable stages of its life, her educational level can affect child survival by influencing her choices and increasing her skills in health care practices related to contraception, nutrition, hygiene, preventive care, and disease treatment. In fact, so many proximate determinants may be directly influenced by a mother's education to radically alter chances for child survival, that one of the authors was prompted to label the process "social synergy" (Mosley, 1983).

Finally, the "production" of a healthy child also requires a mother's time for prenatal visits, attendance at the well-baby clinic, breastfeeding, food preparation, washing clothes, bathing the child, house cleaning, and sickness care. A mother's time may also be required for (or diverted to) other economically productive activities that may or may not be related to child health. In traditional societies, a sharp division of labor by sex tends to maximize the mother's time for child care. On the other hand, in transitional societies characteristic of many developing countries, child care time often competes with time needed for income-generating work (Birdsall and Greevey, 1978; Engle, 1981). The consequences for infant health and mortality depend largely upon the general economic circumstances of the household. For poor families, a mother's outside work may result in child neglect or care by a less skilled sibling, while a wealthy family may hire a skilled and attentive nursemaid (Popkin, 1975; Kumar, 1977). Poor and rich mothers may experience equivalent time-saving and maternal and child health benefits from contraceptive use. By contrast, if both poor and rich mothers find it necessary to use bottlefeeding as a time-saving technology, the consequences to child survival for the two families may be radically different.

Traditions/norms/attitudes Grouped under this category are factors that shape and modify the economic choices and health-related practices of individuals according to the cultural traditions and norms of the society. The following are among the important cultural determinants of child health and survival.

Power relationships within the household—While in most traditional societies the mother has full responsibility for child care, she may have little control over allocation of resources (food) to herself or her child or over critical child care practices (diet, sickness care) (Safilios-Rothschild, 1980). Often decisions in these areas are reserved for the elders, particularly the mother-in-law or the husband, and the latter may rigidly adhere to useless or harmful traditional practices. Caldwell (1979) postulates that one key change in traditional societies produced by mother's education is a shift of intrahousehold power relationships toward the mother to the benefit of her offspring.

Value of children—There is growing evidence that this variable, commonly associated with fertility research, is also important to child survival (Scrimshaw, 1978; Simmons et al., 1982). In economic terms, a family's investments in child care may be conditional on expected returns. Marriage expectations can be a major economic factor in child survival: for example, in Kenya, where girls are valued for the brideprice they bring, child survival rates are slightly higher for females than for males, while in South Asia, where female dowry is the main concern, the reverse is true (Mott, 1979; Poffenberger, 1981). In terms of proximate mechanisms through which this determinant operates, recent studies in rural Bangladesh and Amman, Jordan, have attributed higher female than male child mortality to differential feeding and medical care practices, while Scrimshaw observes that some societies may resort to intentional injury (infanticide) to achieve family size/composition goals (Chen, Huq, and D'Souza, 1981; Urban Development Department, 1982; Scrimshaw, 1978).

Beliefs about disease causation—Anthropological literature is replete with examples of how a society's beliefs about disease causation shape behavior that has an impact on the proximate determinants of child survival. These range from ritualistic disease prevention practices, to choice of therapies and practitioners for sickness care, to sexual taboos and abstinence to prevent illness in the suckling child (Fabrega, 1972; Kleinman et al., 1975). One manifestation of this phenomenon is the commonly reported "underutilization" of modern (Western) health facilities when they are introduced into traditional societies. Probably one of the most powerful influences of formal education is the transmission of concepts of modern scientific medicine. When the mother is exposed to such information, it can transform her preferences for health care practices so as to significantly improve child survival, often without investment of additional economic resources.

Food preferences—Patterns of dietary intake and food choice are probably among the strongest "culturally conditioned" tastes across all societies, as confirmed by the dietary heterogeneity even in developed countries. Because maternal diet during pregnancy and lactation (and even in the mother's own childhood) and patterns of breastfeeding and supplementation are potent determinants of child survival, food preferences can assume importance in many developing countries, particularly where food taboos and restrictions are commonly practiced during pregnancy, lactation, weaning, and illness. A deleterious dietary practice of international concern is the withholding of food and fluids during diarrheal illness, a situation now being addressed through the worldwide promotion of oral rehydration therapy (Grant, 1982).

Household-level variables

Income/wealth/effects A variety of goods, services, and assets at the household level operate on child health and mortality through the proximate determinants. Below are some major ways in which income effects influence child health.

Food—Critical is the stable availability of a basic minimum food supply of sufficient variety to ensure adequate amounts of all nutrients. The sanitary quality of food (clean, fresh, free from spoilage) is also important in preventing disease transmission.

Water—Both quantity and quality of water supply are important determinants of exposure to disease. Adequate quantity is essential to permit bathing, washing, and cleaning, and quality (not only at the source but also in the household) for drinking and food preparation.

Clothing/bedding—Sufficient clothing for protection under local climatic conditions and to allow a change for washing reduces the incidence of skin infections and parasitic infestations.

Housing—Both size and quality are factors. Poor ventilation and crowded sleeping conditions predispose household members to respiratory and skin infections. Adequate sanitation requires vermin-proof screens, construction materials that can be cleaned, and separate rooms for cooking, bathing, toilets, sleeping, storage of food and water, and for livestock. Plumbing and sewer connections greatly simplify hygienic care.

Fuel/energy—An adequate supply of fuel is essential for proper cooking of food, boiling water, and sterilizing stored food and utensils (especially for infant bottles). Energy is needed for refrigeration to prevent diarrheal diseases due to bacterial overgrowth in stored food, as well as for warmth to reduce the likelihood of respiratory infections in cold climates.

Transportation—Access to preventive/curative medical facilities, to markets for consumption goods and food, and to places of income-generating employment is essential.

Hygienic/preventive care—This requires the means to purchase soap, cleansing materials, insecticides, and the like for household use, as well as vitamins, iron supplements, contraceptives, and the means to pay for such preventive services as antenatal care, well-child care, and immunizations.

Sickness care—Included here are costs of services and commodities, such as physicians, hospitalization, and drugs, including maternity care during childbirth.

Information—Through radio, television, newspapers, magazines, books, and informal channels, households can obtain information about proper nutrition, hygiene, contraception, and immunizations.

This brief list of goods and services illustrates why "income" is generally a powerful determinant of child mortality. In poor societies in particular, families may spend 80 percent or more of their disposable income on food; thus variations in income or food prices may be directly translated into rising rates of mortality and malnutrition. This was well documented in the mid-1970s in rural Bangladesh, the tea estates of Sri Lanka, and São Paulo, Brazil (Chowdhury and Chen, 1977; Meegama, 1981; Wood, 1982). In rural subsistence economies, even seasonal variability in income and/or food availability can lead to seasonal swings in mortality (Chambers, 1980; Chen et al., 1979).

Community-level variables

Ecological setting The ecological setting includes climate, soil, rainfall, temperature, altitude, and seasonality. In rural subsistence societies, these variables can have a strong influence on child survival by affecting the quantity and variety of food crops produced, the availability and quality of water, vector-borne disease transmission, the rate of proliferation of bacteria in stored foods, the survival of parasite larvae and eggs in soil, and the drainage of sewage. Ecological variables can also influence the availability of income-generating work, the access to and use of medical facilities, and the time mothers can spend at home in child care.

Political economy The classic study of India's population by Davis (1951) attributed much of the rise in life expectancy (from about 25 years to 50 years) in the first half of this century to the prevention of recurrent famines that had characterized the subcontinent's history; this was achieved by stabilizing food supplies with railroads, road networks, irrigation, markets, and political security. Among the politico-economic factors that can operate to influence child survival are the following.

Organization of production—Whether the mode of production and distribution of benefits is communal or based on individual entrepreneurship can determine the distribution of resources and the availability and stability of food supplies.

Physical infrastructure—Railroad, roads, electricity, water, sewage, and telephone systems can influence health, particularly through their impact on the relative price of staples as well as of health-related goods, services, and information. Many studies have shown, for example, that the poor pay more in money, time, and effort for poor-quality water than do the rich, who have access to an equivalent supply of pure piped water (Briscoe, 1983).

Political institutions—These include organizations at the local level and their ties with centralized authority for policy guidance and/or program implementation, law enforcement and security systems, and popular associations such as labor unions, cooperatives, and political parties. The importance of such political and administrative structures has been emphasized in international comparisons of child mortality, as well as in regional comparisons such as the contrast of Kerala with West Bengal (UN Population Division, 1983; Nag, 1983). Furthermore, the literature on the success or failure of various health action projects, whether national or small-scale, cites the vital roles of local leadership, obstruction by elites, inertia of supporting agencies, and lack of "political will" (Mosley, 1983).

Health system variables How does the formal (Western) health system fit into this conceptual scheme? Interestingly, although there is a general presumption that "modern medicine" must improve the health of populations, there has been little effort to spell out the likely connections or their mechanisms of operation.

Within the proximate determinants model, the formal health system is viewed as operating in the following ways.

Institutionalized (imposed) actions—These are disease-control measures mandated by law (rather than left to individual discretion) to affect the health of populations at large. They potentially can have a powerful impact on mortality. These measures may be financed and directly implemented either by the health system (epidemic control measures such as vector control programs, quarantine, immunizations) or by private enterprise with the health system assuming a supervising/inspection role. Examples of the latter are regulations governing the sanitary quality of commercial foods, milk, water, sewage, air, housing, restaurants, hospitals, and factories.

Implementation of such institutionalized measures is subject to strong economic constraints: the allocation of financial resources to the government health system for preventive activities, its allocation within that system, and the economic resources of private enterprises in the community. Typically in poor countries, in the calculus of many individuals in the community (and of the health system) transfer payments (bribes) to the health system will yield a greater ''benefit'' than the making of investments in the required environmental improvements. While such a stance would seem to have obvious detrimental consequences for the health of populations, there is little research to determine at what economic level mandated health measures might be expected to be effective. Thus, developing countries characteristically are overburdened by ''enforced'' but ineffective health laws.

Cost subsidies—The second major area of health system action consists of cost subsidies to change the relative prices of health-related goods and services. In contrast to institutionalized measures, which are generally designed to reduce disease exposure, these inputs operate primarily through the ''personal illness control'' proximate determinants. They are likely to have a much smaller impact on health status, primarily because most national health budgets are allocated to inputs that operate only after sickness has occurred. This limitation is coupled with the fact that utilization of these services, even if freely available, is voluntary and thus critically dependent upon health beliefs and preferences. In some developing countries, this cultural barrier alone can reduce the health impact of the formal health care system almost to zero (Assaad and Katsha, 1981).

Like institutionalized measures, cost subsidies are subject to economic constraints both within the system and at the individual level. The consequence of cost constraints within the system is rationing of services. This should be carried out equitably; however, few health ministries have planned rationing. The frequent result is concentration of health resources in the urban areas, thereby selectively subsidizing the most advantaged segments of the population. At the individual level, the cost constraint is manifested by such features as the exponential decline of rural health center utilization by residential distance from the facility (Jolly and King, 1966).

Public information/education/motivation—Education/motivation programs can operate at several levels. Politically, they can influence governments to allocate more funds or more effectively use limited resources for health services, or to modify general development strategies to better protect people's health; institutionally, they can upgrade the skills of traditional practitioners or of health workers; individually, they can enhance the skills and change the attitudes and preferences of parents, especially mothers, thereby promoting child survival.

The role of technology—Medical technology improves the effectiveness and efficiency with which the proximate determinants may be manipulated by the health system. Most modern scientific technologies like vaccines and antibiotics are pinpointed to specific disease agents. Often, powerful modern technologies like insecticides have significant adverse side effects as well. Within the health system, technologies can be applied by institutional mandate (DDT, smallpox vaccination, water and sewer systems, proper sanitation and refrigeration in commercial food processing); they can be made available with a cost subsidy (vaccines, drugs, vitamins, oral rehydration salts, contraceptives); or people can be encouraged by education to use them at their own cost (soap, boiling water, toilets).

Since all such technologies are intrinsically "powerful," their health and mortality impact on populations revolves around three issues: (1) what is the potential contribution of the intervention toward improving child survival when analyzed in the proximate determinants model, taking into account biological synergy? (2) to what portion of the population will the technology be available? and (3) will it be used and used effectively? These are analogous to issues in demographic impact analyses to relate contraceptive use to fertility changes in a population. The problem with respect to morbidity and mortality is more complex, as attested by the controversy over the demographic impact of malaria eradication in Sri Lanka (Gray, 1974) and by recent studies of measles mortality after vaccination in Zaire (Kasongo Project Team, 1981; Aaby et al., 1981). The complexity of the problem should not deter research on this issue, however, in view of current proposals to invest vast resources in technology-oriented health strategies with little consideration given to the social and economic constraints that may limit their impact.

As the preceding discussion suggests, the task of delineating and scaling the impact of the socioeconomic variables on the proximate determinants of child health and mortality falls to a wide range of social science disciplines, both those that observe populations and institutions at large and those that quantify economic transactions and the effects of income factors on family goals and outcomes. The need for a multidisciplinary approach to understanding and alleviating child mortality is clear.

Discussion

The purpose of an analytical framework in the study of child survival is to clarify our understanding of the many factors involved in the family's production of healthy children in order to provide a foundation for formulating health policies and strategies. The significance of the proximate determinants model does not lie in simply a listing of the multiplicity of variables of interest or in concerns with scaling and measurement of these factors: many field surveys already address these topics. Rather, the key advantage of the model lies in the organization of seemingly disparate measures of environmental conditions; of dietary, reproductive, and health care practices; and of disease states into a coherent framework in which they are linked to one another and to child survival on the one hand and to socioeconomic factors on the other. The value of the framework is its parsimony. By limiting the proximate determinants to 14 specific factors grouped into five broad categories, we are able to arrive at a scheme that makes feasible the integrated analysis of the biological and social determinants of mortality.

The analytical model implies a major reorientation in research approaches by both health and social scientists looking at child mortality. Specifically, it suggests that child mortality should be studied more as a chronic disease process with multifactorial origins than as an acute, single-cause phenomenon. Use of the model should facilitate specification of the different orders of causality and possible interactions among the socioeconomic determinants. Regarding the dependent variable, the degree of physical deterioration (growth faltering) among surviving children in a population is combined with the mortality experience into a nonspecific measure of the level of adverse conditions facing the population.

There are numerous situations in which a multidisciplinary approach to the study of child survival could provide guidance for health policymakers in the developing world. For example, in many developing countries large differences in infant and child mortality have been observed between various regions, or between mothers with different educational or social characteristics within a given area. In-depth investigation to connect these ecological or socioeconomic factors to specific proximate determinants can give policymakers insights into health-related development strategies that could reduce these differentials.

A rewarding opportunity for multidisciplinary research using this model is provided by "natural experiments," that is, situations in which health or social interventions are being introduced into large populations. For example, rural or urban development projects may change the ecological setting and/or provide additional income-earning opportunities for men and women. Typically these are presumed to lead to improved health in the family, though, in fact, the consequences for child welfare may be mixed. Research in conjunction with such interventions can not only assess the overall health impact of alternative development strategies, but also more sharply define which among a number of specific factors amenable to change by health policymakers are of greatest consequence for child survival.

Notes

1 The terms proximate determinants, intermediate variables, and mechanisms may be used interchangeably.

2 The framework presented here is slightly modified from its original form as developed in Mosley (1983). Specifically,

"nutrient availability" factors have been renamed "nutrient deficiency" factors, and the factors of "vitamins" and "minerals" have been combined to "micronutrients."

3 There are two alternative approaches to solving this problem. One requires a detailed

classification of all known causes of disease and death in every individual in order to make inferences about the social factors contributing to mortality. This approach was used by Puffer and Serrano (1975) in studying mortality among 36,000 children in the Americas. A second approach, proposed here, is to search for and identify several basic mechanisms common to all diseases of interest and through which all socioeconomic determinants must operate.

4 Noteworthy in this framework are biological interactions among the proximate determinants. The effects of the proximate determinant "nutrient deficiency" is modulated by the physiological factors of appetite, absorption, and metabolism. Similarly, the effects generated by "environmental contamination" are influenced by the host's ability to resist infection. In this latter case, host resistance may be compromised by injury, low birth weight, or immaturity at birth. Host defenses may be strengthened by improved nutrition and by vaccines. Also implicit in the framework are the biological mechanisms of synergism between malnutrition and infection. Infections reduce appetite and cause unnecessary metabolic wastage of nutrients, thereby precipitating or aggravating malnutrition; malnutrition, in turn, reduces host resistance, thereby increasing the risk of more severe disease outcomes due to infection.

5 Typically, body wasting and growth retardation are called "malnutrition." While this is the biological situation at the cellular or somatic level, the term "malnutrition" also implies the existence of a specific "cause" of the condition (lack of sufficient food). This assumption commonly leads to a particular public health intervention (feeding programs). There is a growing body of evidence that the level of "malnutrition" among children is as much dependent on maternal health factors and infections as it is on the nutrient deficiency. It is thus more appropriate to consider the levels of physical stunting and wasting in cohorts of children as nonspecific indicators of health status (as is the case with the level of mortality) rather than as a specific indicator of dietary deficiency (Mata, 1978; Cole and Parkin, 1977).

6 For simplicity, the discussion will deal only with weight-for-age measurements, although similar findings have been shown for measures of height-for-age and arm circumference (Chen et al., 1980; Sommer and Loewenstein, 1975; Heywood, 1982).

7 More recent recommendations have proposed that the difference between the observed and expected weight-for-age be expressed in standard deviation units (z score). As noted above, one standard deviation equals roughly 10–11 percent of the expected weight-for-age (Waterlow et al., 1977).

8 The absolute levels and differences between studies shown in Figure 3 are not comparable because of different study designs, treatments available, and so on.

9 Schultz (1979) and Palloni (1981) provide a basis for the organization of socioeconomic determinants in our discussion.

References

Aaby, Peter, Judith Bukh, Ida Marie Lisse, and Arjon J. Smith. 1981. "Measles vaccination and child mortality," *Lancet* 2: 93.

American Public Health Association. 1981. *Growth Monitoring of Preschool Children: Practical Considerations for Primary Health Care Projects*. Primary Health Care Issues, Series I, No. 3. Washington, D.C.: APHA.

Arriaga, Edward, and Kingsley Davis. 1969. "The pattern of mortality change in Latin America," *Demography* 6: 223–242.

Asaad, Marie, and S. Katsha. 1981. "Villagers' participation in the formal and informal health services in an Egyptian delta village," Regional Papers, The Population Council, Cairo.

Behm, Hugo. 1979. "Socioeconomic determinants of mortality in Latin America," *Proceedings of the Meeting on Socioeconomic Determinants and Consequences of Mortality*, Mexico City, 19–25 June. New York and Geneva: UN and WHO.

Belloc, Nedra. 1980. "Personal behavior affecting mortality" in *Biological and Social Aspects of Mortality and Length of Life*, ed. Samuel H. Preston, pp. 449–477. Liège: International Union for the Scientific Study of Population.

Birdsall, N., and W. P. Greevey. 1978. "The second sex in the Third World: Is female poverty a development issue?" Summary of Workshop on Women in Poverty, International Center for Research on Women, Washington, D.C.

Bongaarts, John. 1978. "A framework for analyzing the proximate determinants of fertility," *Population and Development Review* 4, no. 1 (March): 105–132.

Briscoe, John. 1983. "Water supply and health in developing countries: Selective primary health care revisited." Paper presented at the *International Conference on Oral Rehydration Therapy*, USAID, WHO, UNICEF, and International Centre for Diarrheal Disease Research, Washington, D.C., 7–10 June.

Caldwell, John C. 1979. "Education as a factor in mortality decline: An examination of Nigerian data," *Proceedings of the Meeting on Socioeconomic Determinants and Consequences of Mortality*, Mexico City, 19–25 June. New York and Geneva: United Nations and World Health Organization.

Chambers, Robert. 1979. "Health, agriculture and rural poverty: Why seasons matter," Discussion Paper No. 148, Institute of Development Studies, University of Sussex, Brighton, England.

Chen, Lincoln. 1981a. "Child survival: Levels, trends, determinants." Paper presented for chapter on "Supply of Children" in *Determinants of Fertility in Developing Countries: A Summary of Knowledge*. Washington, D.C.: Committee on Population and Demography, National Academy of Sciences.

———. 1981b. "Diarrhea and malnutrition: Interactions, mechanisms, and interventions." Paper presented for *Workshop on Interactions of Diarrhea and Malnutrition*, Bellagio, Italy, 11–15 May. U.N. University World Hunger Programme, Rockefeller Foundation, Ford Foundation and International Center for Diarrheal Disease Research, Bangladesh.

———, A. K. M. Alauddin Chowdhury, and Sandra L. Huffman. 1979. "Seasonal dimensions of energy-protein malnutrition in rural Bangladesh: The role of agriculture, dietary practices and infection," *Ecology of Food and Nutrition* 8: 175–187.

———, A. K. M. Alauddin Chowdhury, and Sandra L. Huffman. 1980. "Anthropometric assessment of energy-protein malnutrition and subsequent risk of mortality among preschool children," *American Journal of Clinical Nutrition* 33: 1836–1845.

———, E. Huq, and S. D'Souza. 1981. "Sex bias in the family allocation of food and health care in rural Bangladesh," *Population and Development Review* 7, no. 1 (March): 55–70.

Chowdhury, A. K. M. Alauddin, and Lincoln Chen. 1977. "The interaction of nutrition, infection, and mortality during recent food crises in Bangladesh," *Food Research Institute Studies* 16: 2.

Cole, T. J., and J. M. Parkin. 1977. "Infection and its effect on growth of young children: A comparison of the Gambia and Uganda," *Transactions of the Royal Society of Tropical Medicine and Hygiene* 71: 196–198.

Davis, Kingsley. 1951. *The Population of India and Pakistan*. Princeton: Princeton University Press.

———, and Judith Blake. 1956. "Social structure and fertility: An analytic framework," *Economic Development and Cultural Change* 4: 211–235.

Engle, P. L. 1981. "Maternal care, maternal substitutes, and children's welfare in developed and developing countries." Paper prepared for Policy Roundtable, International Center for Research on Women, Washington, D.C.

Fabrega, H. 1972. "Medical anthropology," in *Biennial Review of Anthropology*, ed. B. Siegel, pp. 167–229. Stanford: Stanford University Press.

Federici, Nora, and Luciano Terrenato. 1980. "Biological determinants of early life mortality," in *Biological and Social Aspects of Mortality and the Length of Life*, ed. Samuel H. Preston, pp. 331–362. Liège: International Union for the Scientific Study of Population.

Gómez, G., R. Ramos-Galvin, J. Cravioto, and S. Frenk. 1955. "Malnutrition in infancy and childhood with special reference to kwashiorker," in *Advances in Pediatrics*, vol. 7, pp. 131–169. New York: Yearbook Publications.

Grant, James P. 1982. "The state of the world's children 1982–1983." New York: UNICEF.

Gray, R. H. 1974. "The decline of mortality in Ceylon and the demographic effects of malaria control," *Population Studies* 28: 205–229.

Heywood, Peter. 1982. "The functional significance of malnutrition—growth and prospective risk of death in the highlands of Papua New Guinea," *Journal of Food and Nutrition* 39, no. 1: 13–19.

Jellife, Derrick B. 1967. *The Assessment of the Nutrition Status of the Community*, Monograph Series No. 53. Geneva: World Health Organization.

Jolly, Richard, and Maurice King. 1974. "The organization of health services," in *Medical Care in Developing Countries*, ed. Maurice King, pp. 2.1–2.15. Nairobi and Oxford: Oxford University Press.

Kasongo Project Team. 1981. "Influence of measles vaccination on survival pattern of 7–35 month old children in Kasongo, Zaire," *Lancet* 1: 764–763.

Kielmann, A. A., and Colin McCord. 1978. "Weight-for-age as an index of risk for children," *Lancet* 1: 1247–1250.

Kleinman, Arthur, Peter Kunstadter, E. Russell Alexander, and James L. Gale, eds. 1975. *Medicine in Chinese Cultures*. John E. Fogarty International Center, DHEW Publication No. (NIH) 75–653. Washington, D.C.: U.S. Government Printing Office.

Kumar, S. K. 1977. "Composition of economic constraints in child nutrition: Impact of maternal incomes and employment in low income households," Ph.D. Thesis, Cornell University.

Malcolm, L. A. 1974. "Ecological factors relating to child growth and nutritional status," in *Nutrition and Malnutrition Identification and Measurement*, ed. Alexander F. Roche and Frank Falkner, pp. 329–353. New York and London: Plenum Press.

Mata, Leonardo. 1978. *The Children of Santa Maria Cauque: A Prospective Field Study of Health and Growth*. Cambridge, Mass.: M.I.T. Press.

Meegama, Srinivas A. 1981. "The decline in mortality in Sri Lanka in historical perspective," in *International Population Conference, Manila*, vol. 2, pp. 143–164. Liège: International Union for the Scientific Study of Population.

Morley, Davis, and Margaret Woodland. 1979. *See How They Grow—Monitoring Child Growth for Appropriate Health Care in Developing Countries*. London and Basingstoke: The Macmillan Press Ltd.

Mosley, W. Henry. 1980a. "Biological contamination of the environment by man," in *Biological and Social Aspects of Mortality and Length of Life*, ed. Samuel H. Preston, pp. 39–67. Liège: International Union for the Scientific Study of Population.

———. 1980b. "Social determinants of infant and child mortality: Some considerations for an analytical framework," in *Health and Mortality in Infancy and Early Childhood: Report of a Study Group*, pp. 19–43. The Population Council, West Asia and North Africa Region, Cairo.

———. 1983. "Will primary health care reduce infant and child mortality? A critique of some current strategies with special reference to Africa and Asia," *Seminar on Social Policy, Health Policy and Mortality Prospects*, Paris, 28 February–4 March. Paris: Institut National d'Etudes Demographiques (INED).

Mott, Frank L. 1979. "Infant mortality in Kenya: Evidence from the Kenya Fertility Survey," Scientific Report No. 32, World Fertility Survey, London.

Nag, Moni. 1983. "Impact of social and economic development on mortality: Comparative study of Kerala and West Bengal," *Economic and Political Weekly* (Bombay) 18, nos. 19–21, Annual Issue (May): 877–900.

National Center for Health Statistics (NCHS). 1972. *A Study of Infant Mortality from Linked Records: Comparison of Neonatal Mortality from Two Cohort Studies*. US Vital and

Health Statistics, Series 20, No. 13, USDHEW, Public Health Service, Washington, D.C.

Palloni, Alberto. 1981. "Design problems and data collection strategies in studies of mortality differentials in developing countries," *Seminar on Methodology and Data Collection in Mortality Studies*, Dakar, Senegal, 7–10 July. Liège: International Union for the Scientific Study of Population.

Poffenberger, Thomas. 1981. "Child rearing and social structure in rural India: Toward a cross-cultural definition of child abuse and neglect," in *Child Abuse and Neglect, Cross-Cultural Perspectives*, ed. Jill E. Korbin, pp. 71–95. Berkeley: University of California Press.

Popkin, Barry, M. 1975. "Income, time, the working mother and child nutriture," Discussion Paper No. 75-9, Institute of Economic Development and Research, University of the Philippines, Manila.

Puffer, Ruth Rice, and Carlos V. Serrano. 1973. *Patterns of Mortality in Childhood*. Scientific Publication No. 262. Washington, D.C.: Pan American Health Organization.

Safilios-Rothschild, Constantina. 1980. "The role of the family: A neglected aspect of poverty," in *Implementing Programs of Human Development*, ed. Peter T. Knight, pp. 311–373. World Bank Staff Working Paper No. 403. Washington, D.C.: World Bank.

Schultz, T. Paul. 1979. "Interpretations of relations among mortality, economics of the household, and the health environment," *Proceedings of the Meeting on Socioeconomic Determinants and Consequences of Mortality*, Mexico City, 19–25 June. New York and Geneva: United Nations and World Health Organization.

Scrimshaw, Susan C. M. 1978. "Infant mortality and behavior in the regulation of family size," *Population and Development Review* 4 no. 3 (September): 383–404.

Simmons, George B., Celeste Smucker, Stan Bernstein, and Eric Jensen. 1982. "Post-neonatal mortality in rural India: Applications of an economic model," *Demography* 19: 371–389.

Solimano, Georgio R., and Marty Vine. 1980. "Malnutrition, infection and infant mortality," in *Biological and Social Aspects of Mortality and the Length of Life*, ed. Samuel H. Preston, pp. 83–112. Liège: International Union for the Scientific Study of Population.

Sommer, Al, and Matthew S. Loewenstein. 1975. "Nutritional status and mortality: A prospective evaluation of the QUAC stick," *American Journal of Clinical Nutrition* 28: 287–292.

Teller, C., R. Sibrian, C. Talavera, B. Bent, J. del Canto, and L. Saenz. 1979. "Population and nutrition: Implications of sociodemograhic trends and differentials for food and nutrition policy in Central America and Panama," *Ecology of Food and Nutrition* 8: 95–109.

United Nations Population Division. 1983. "Mortality and health policy: Highlights of the issues in the context of the World Population Plan of Action." Paper prepared for Expert Group on Mortality and Health Policy, Rome, 30 May–3 June. New York: United Nations Secretariat.

Urban Development Department. 1982. "A baseline health and population assessment for the upgrading areas of Amman." A Report to the Municipality of Amman by the Population Council.

Waterlow, J. R., R. Buzina, W. Keller, J. Lane, M. Nichaman, and J. Tanner. 1977. "The presentation and use of height and weight data for comparing the nutritional status of groups of children under the age of five years," *Bulletin of the World Health Organization* 55: 489.

Wood, Charles H. 1982. "The political economy of infant mortality in São Paulo, Brazil," *International Journal of Health Services* 12: 215–229.

World Health Organization and UNICEF. 1978. *Primary Health Care*, Alma Ata Conference. Geneva and New York: WHO and UNICEF.

INTERVENING VARIABLES
NUTRITION

Malnutrition, Morbidity, and Mortality

Reynaldo Martorell

Teresa J. Ho

There is no need for further studies to show that severely malnourished children are at greater risk of dying than healthy children. There is a pressing need, on the other hand, for investigations that focus on the survival of children suffering from mild and moderate malnutrition. A strong indication of the need for research in this area is that the number of children with mild and moderate malnutrition is tens of times greater than the number who are severely malnourished.

This paper reviews the literature on the subject of mild and moderate malnutrition and survival. Clinical, epidemiological, and experimental studies are reviewed, and attention is paid to the basic mechanisms underlying key interrelationships. As preface to this discussion, two general issues are discussed. First, how are mild and moderate malnutrition measured and second, what factors are responsible for their existence?

Measurement of nutritional status

Nutritional status can be operationally defined in terms of either "input" or "output" types of indicators. Input indicators are mainly measures of food and nutrient intake: specific examples are home diet consumption and breast-milk ingestion. Intake is difficult to measure reliably, usually requiring highly skilled personnel. Because single measures of intake are poor predictors of the *usual* intake of individuals, many assessments over time are generally required. This is costly and time consuming. Further, individuals differ in terms of the efficiency of nutrient utilization, and such factors as infection also affect utilization. Hence, nutrient intakes, even if perfectly measured, cannot be equated with nutritional status. Nutritional status can alternatively be defined in terms of output measures, including clinical signs of malnutrition, biochemical indicators, physical activity, and anthropometry. Data on output measures can be obtained on a single occasion, an advantage in field research. Output indicators are also more closely related to health and functional capacity.

Inadequacies in nutritional intake eventually result in many adverse effects or outcomes, but not all are manifested at the same level of severity. In situations of inadequate nutritional intake, vital functions like circulation, respiration, and maintenance of body temperature (basal metabolic needs) receive high priority in an organism's adjustment process. Through a variety of mechanisms that include accelerated nutrient absorption and retention and increased mobilization of nutrient stores, the organism attempts to maintain the normal flow of nutrients to the cells and organs. If the cellular nutrient availability becomes affected, functional impairment becomes pronounced and clinical signs become apparent.

The stages in the development of protein–energy malnutrition are shown in Table 1. As dietary intake becomes deficient, children cope by slowing their rate of growth and by reducing physical activity. At this stage one might observe that gains in height, weight, and other measures are less than normal. On the other hand, biochemical indicators (e.g., serum albumin) are normal and clinical signs of malnutrition are absent. At moderate degrees of protein–energy malnutrition, activity and growth rates are affected to a greater degree, and signs of wasting and perhaps some biochemical abnormalities become evident as well. At the final stage of severity, all linear growth ceases, physical activity is severely curtailed, body wasting is marked, and clinical signs (e.g., hair, skin, edema, etc.) are apparent.

TABLE 1   Stages in the development of protein—energy malnutrition

	Physical activity	Growth rates	Biochemical indicators	Body wasting	Clinical signs
Mild	+	+			
Moderate	+ +	+ +	+	+	
Severe	+ + +	+ + +	+ + +	+ + +	+ + +

NOTE: Crosses (+) indicate deviations from normality.

The response to protein–energy malnutrition has two related aspects that can be measured with standard anthropometric techniques: deceleration or cessation of growth, and body wasting. The first can be measured prospectively by means of growth velocities in height or weight; alternatively, the cumulative effect of malnutrition can be estimated by means of indicators of stunting such as height-for-age. Measures of body wasting assess the adequacy of mass relative to length: the most widely used indicator of this type is weight-for-height.

It follows from the scheme presented in Table 1 that where malnutrition is mild to moderate, as in Latin America, children exhibit moderate degrees of stunting (i.e., short stature) but few abnormalities in measures of wasting or body composition. Where malnutrition is moderate to severe, as in India and Nepal, stunting is marked and moderate levels of wasting are observed. Findings from around the world support this view (Martorell, Leslie, and Moock, 1984).

Anthropometry offers many advantages over other indicators of nutritional status. The foremost is that body measurements are sensitive over the full range of malnutrition. Biochemical and clinical indicators, on the other hand, are useful only at the extreme. Data on body measurements are also highly reliable and are less expensive and easier to obtain than most nutritional data. The main disadvantage of anthropometry is its lack of specificity. Body measurements are sensitive to many factors, including all essential nutrients, infection, climate, stress, and genetics. As a result, anthropometric data tell us that there is a problem but reveal very little about its causes.

Determinants of nutritional status

The basic causes of malnutrition in developing countries are socioeconomic. Poverty is pervasive in much of the Third World, and the capacity of families to purchase and/or produce food is limited. Ignorance of the special needs of children and inappropriate cultural beliefs and practices often cause families to give their children diets that are less in quantity and quality than those they could provide. Conditions of environmental sanitation are typically deficient and, combined with limited access to preventive and curative health care, result in high incidences and increased severity of infectious diseases, problems that in turn adversely affect nutrient utilization.

There is general agreement that the small body size of children in developing countries is largely the result of poor diets and frequent infections. Race and climate, two factors once thought to be among the key determinants of variations in body size in children, are not generally given much importance today.

Beaton and Ghassemi (1982) have reviewed the literature detailing the effects of nutrition interventions on the growth of children. Their main conclusion was that food distribution programs were "rather expensive for the measured benefit" (p. 909). They also noted that "close scrutiny of the results of the total experience suggested that anthropometric improvement was surprisingly small" (p. 910). Beaton and Ghassemi argue that the small effect on growth may simply reflect low levels of dietary improvement. In many studies, "leakage" of food to nontarget subjects accounted for a substantial reduction in the amount of food intended for target populations.

The INCAP (Institute of Nutrition of Central America and Panama) supplementation experiment conducted during 1969–77 in four rural villages of Guatemala produced large biological effects relative to other studies (Martorell, Habicht, and Klein, 1982; Martorell, Klein, and Delgado, 1980). Two of the villages received a protein–calorie supplement called "atole," while two others received a low-calorie drink called "fresco." The height and weight of children in the "atole" villages were significantly improved relative to baseline values, while no changes were observed in the "fresco" villages. This differential response was attributed to the low level of supplemental calories ingested in the fresco villages.

While most of the studies from developed nations find no associations between illness and physical growth, those from developing nations report that common childhood ailments—in particular, diarrheal diseases—are clearly associated with physical growth.[1] The findings may reflect contrasting ecological settings. The number of infections experienced by children in developing countries is much greater than in children from industrialized societies. The severity of these infections may also be greater in developing countries, as will be discussed later. Finally, children from well-to-do homes, with plenty of food available and a rebounding appetite, quickly make up the losses caused by infrequent episodes of illness. Catch-up growth in developing countries, on the other hand, may be limited by recurrent infections and a poor convalescent diet.

Most of the studies in developing countries have focused on diarrheal diseases and respiratory infections, the two most important causes of morbidity. Most have found that diarrheal diseases retard growth while respiratory infections usually do not. Some studies have also noted significant negative associations between growth retardation and communicable (e.g., measles) and other (e.g., malaria) diseases.

A number of well-defined mechanisms could account for these findings (Chen and Scrimshaw, 1983). Infections have generalized effects on nutrient metabolism and utilization, and diarrheal diseases interfere with nutrient absorption. Fevers and vomiting frequently accompany episodes of diarrhea and respiratory infections. Dietary intakes are reduced by a poor appetite and by cultural practices that dictate dietary restrictions during infections. During episodes of diarrhea, dietary intakes may be lowered by 20 to 40 percent. Respiratory infections have a smaller effect on appetite (Martorell and Yarbrough, 1983).

Poor dietary intakes and a high incidence of infection are clearly the principal immediate causes of poor nutritional status as measured by physical growth. Some researchers have advanced the notion that infectious diseases, and in particular diarrheal diseases, are more important than the lack of food per se as causes of malnutrition in children (Mata et al., 1977). Most studies of childhood infections in developing countries find relationships with growth that are similar to or stronger than those in studies of nutrition intervention and growth. Hence, a reasonable (even cautious) interpretation of the evidence is that infections are as important a cause of malnutrition as is the limited availability of food.

Mild and moderate malnutrition and survival

The following discussion is organized into four parts. The first deals with immunocompetence and considers whether children with mild and moderate malnutrition are more susceptible to infection. The second part considers whether the frequency and severity of infections are in fact increased in such children. The third part presents epidemiological evidence on the relationship between nutritional status and mortality. Finally, the fourth part summarizes the effects of nutrition interventions on morbidity and mortality.

Nutrition and host resistance to infection

There is sufficient evidence to demonstrate conclusively that malnutrition impairs the body's defense mechanisms (Chandra, 1981; Chandra and New-berne, 1977; Suskind, 1977). However, not all components of the immune system are affected to the same degree. Cell-mediated immunity appears to be most affected. Among the effects found are atrophy of tissues involved in T-cell maturation (thymus gland and the thymic-dependent areas of lymphoid tissue), reduction of the number of T-lymphocytes, interference with lympho-cyte transformation (a process whereby T-cells become mature and sensitized to antigens and able to undergo mitosis), and reduction or absence of the delayed hypersensitivity reaction. Other components of the immune system such as the complement system and phagocytosis are less affected. Least affected are serum antibody titers, but secretory IgA antibody response and antibody affinity are decreased (Chandra, 1981; Suskind, 1977).

We know little about the degree to which the various components of the body's defense mechanism are affected in mild and moderate malnutrition (Chandra, 1981; McMurray et al., 1981; Ziegler and Ziegler, 1975). In one of the few available studies, Kielmann et al. (1976) classified children from rural communities in India according to whether body weight was above the 50th percentile, between the 50th and the 10th percentiles, or below the 10th percentile of the local weight-for-age percentile distribution. The authors found that both the specific antibody response to tetanus immunization and IgG and IgM levels were unrelated to variations in weight-for-age, confirming the findings that the humoral immune system is largely insensitive to malnutrition. However, a gradient in immunocompetence with nutritional status was shown by in vitro and in vivo tests of cell-mediated immunity and for IgA and C_3 levels. Evidence of impaired delayed hypersensitivity reaction has also been reported for Nepalese children with weight-for-height values less than 80 per-cent of normal (Ziegler and Ziegler, 1975).

Reddy et al. (1976) carried out a study on 95 Indian children between 1 and 5 years of age. The 50th percentile values for weight in data from the Indian Council of Medical Research (ICMR) were used as the reference.[2] Children were divided into four groups: I, over 80 percent of median weight (which the authors designate as "normal"); II, 71 to 80 percent; III, 60 to 70 percent; and IV, below 60 percent. The authors' data showed that the phago-cytic activity of leukocytes was impaired in groups II through IV when com-pared with group I. Effects on in vitro tests of cell-mediated immunity were also found. The percentage of lymphocytes that were T-cells (as measured by the rosette formation technique) was 62.5 for group I and 58.5, 50.0, and

39.0 for groups II to IV respectively. Relative to group I, differences were statistically significant for groups III and IV. Similar results were found for in vitro tests of the lymphocyte transformation.[3] The antibody response to typhoid antigen was reduced only in group IV, and all groups showed normal antibody response to diphtheria and tetanus toxoids.

Aspects of cell-mediated immunity were also studied in 71 Colombian children in a prospective study from birth to 2 years of age (McMurray et al., 1981). The children were classified as normal, grade I, or grade II according to the Gómez classification of weight-for-age.[4] There were impaired delayed hypersensitivity reactions (to PPD after BCG vaccination), and the lymphocyte transformation (blastogenic response of lymphocytes to phytohemagglutinin) was reduced in Gómez I and II children. McMurray et al. (1981) also found that tonsil size, an indicator of lymphoid tissue development, was significantly less in children classified as Gómez I and II.

Taken together, these findings in children from Nepal, India, and Colombia suggest that mild and moderately malnourished children have cellular immunity measures consistently lower than those of better nourished children. However, as McMurray et al. (1981) point out, the functional significance of these findings remains unmeasured. They note that no one has "titrated the cellular immune response to determine the minimal activity to prevent disease. While both delayed hypersensitivity and in vitro lymphocyte blastogenesis are related to the antimicrobial function of CMI (cellular-mediated immunity), they do not directly test the ability of the malnourished host to protect himself against infectious disease" (p. 76).

Kielmann et al. (1976), McMurray et al. (1981), and Reddy et al. (1976) relied exclusively on weight-for-age measures, while Ziegler and Ziegler (1975) examined weight-for-height. Weight may be low in children because of low stature and/or because of recent weight loss. Weight, therefore, is an indicator of both stunting (small body size) and wasting (weight loss). As noted earlier, height is a more appropriate indicator of stunting while weight-for-height is more appropriate for measuring wasting. Future studies need to include measures of both wasting and stunting in order to find out which indicator best identifies children with depressed immunocompetence. One would expect immunocompetence to be more closely related to measures of wasting than to those of stunting, inasmuch as severely malnourished children achieve normal levels in all aspects of immunocompetence within four to six weeks of initiating nutritional therapy (McMurray et al., 1981). Finally, previous studies have largely focused on discrete categorizations of nutritional status and have thus been unable to investigate the shape of the relationship between nutritional status and immunocompetence.

The frequency and severity of infections in malnourished infants

Two types of studies provide information on whether children with mild and moderate malnutrition have more severe and frequent infections than found in normal children. The first type is clinical studies of the case fatality for common infections. Although informative, these studies have not generally differentiated between grades of malnutrition. The second type of studies starts with nutritional assessments and relates these findings to the frequency and severity of subsequent infections. Each type is illustrated and discussed below.

Clinical evidence It is widely recognized that relative to the well-to-do, children from the poorer classes in developing countries die from common childhood diseases with inordinate frequency, as they once did in the currently industrialized countries. A good example is measles, a relatively innocuous disease with a reported case fatality ratio (deaths per 100 cases) of around 0.1 percent during the late 1960s in the United States (Morley, 1969). Prospective studies carried out in developing communities around the world show ratios that are dozens of times higher. McGregor (1964) reported a case fatality ratio of 14 to 15 percent in children under age 12 in Gambia, while Morley (1973) reported that in the village of Imesi, Nigeria, the case fatality during an epidemic was 7 percent. In Guatemala, Gordon, Jansen, and Ascoli (1965) found that the case fatality in Indian villages was 4.5 percent; subsequently Mata (1978) found a value of 4 percent. Although a study in West Bengal, India (Sinha, 1977), found that only 2 of 181 children died from measles (1.1 percent), prospective data from Matlab Thana in Bangladesh found a case fatality ratio of 3.7 percent (Koster et al., 1981). Other studies also indicate high case fatality ratios in other areas of the world (Anon., 1968; Morley, 1969; Ifekwunigwe et al., 1980; Koster et al., 1981).

The peak age of incidence of measles is one of the factors that may explain the high case fatality ratio in developing countries. Mortality is higher for infants than for older children; for example, Gordon, Jansen, and Ascoli (1965) found that 11.5 percent of infants who contracted measles died, whereas all children over age 10 who became sick survived. The peak age of incidence is reportedly quite low in Africa (Morley, 1969), and in India and Bangladesh it is about 30 to 36 months (Koster et al., 1981). In industrialized countries, on the other hand, the peak incidence of measles occurs among children attending school for the first time (Gordon, Jansen, and Ascoli, 1965). The quality of health care in and outside the home might also be an important explanatory factor. The hypothesis that the high case fatality ratios are due to more virulent strains of measles in developing countries has never been seriously entertained (Anon., 1968). Another factor may be the coexistence of other infections that aggravate the situation. In developing countries measles is often complicated by many secondary infections, whose presence greatly increases the risk of death (Koster et al., 1981). Among the most serious complications observed are diarrhea and bronchopneumonia (Morley, 1969; Koster et al., 1981). Morley (1969), a pediatrician with vast clinical experience in Africa, believes that nutritional status is the dominant factor in producing the severe form of measles often observed in developing countries. The presence of kwashiorkor greatly increases the case fatality of measles

(Morley, 1969), and complications are more frequent in malnourished children (Ghosh and Dhatt, 1961).

   Nutritional status and risk of infection The focus of this second type of studies is on the relationship between nutritional status and subsequent morbidity. In other words, are malnourished children more often ill and are these infections more severe than in well-nourished children?

   In data from Indian children in Guatemala, Delgado et al. (1983) found that weight-for-height and weight-for-age were stronger predictors of the incidence of simple diarrhea or of diarrhea with mucus and blood than height-for-age. They noted that associations between measures of nutritional status and the incidence of diarrhea were particularly evident during the rainy season.

   James (1972) related the duration and incidence of diarrhea and respiratory infections over a one-year period to weight-for-age at the beginning of the year in 137 children from Costa Rica. The incidence of diarrhea was independent of weight-for-age in children less than 36 months of age, but in children 36 to 60 months the attack rate was twice as large in children with less than 75 percent of the normal weight-for-age than in those who weighed more. No associations were found between weight-for-age and the incidence of respiratory infections. The duration of episodes of diarrhea and respiratory infections was consistently associated with weight-for-age, as shown in Table 2. In low-weight children (less than 75 percent of weight-for-age), the average duration of diarrhea was 9.1 days, compared with 6.9 days in those who weighed more. The duration of respiratory illnesses was 14.5 and 10.9 days for those with low and satisfactory weight respectively. Also, 24 of the 83

TABLE 2   Weight-for-age and the duration of subsequent episodes of diarrhea and respiratory infections: Costa Rican children studied for one year

Group[a]	Sample size	Duration of diarrhea (days)[b]	Duration of respiratory infections[b]
Low weight (N = 83)			
0–12 months	28	9.3	15.0
13–36 months	39	8.3	14.6
37–60 months	16	9.7	13.0
Average		9.1	14.5
Satisfactory weight (N = 54)			
0–12 months	15	8.8	12.9
13–36 months	26	5.6	10.3
37–60 months	13	6.6	9.8
Average		6.9	10.9

[a] Low weight is less than 75 percent of weight-for-age. Satisfactory weight is over 75 percent of weight-for-age.
[b] Differences between low-weight and normal-weight groups were reported to be statistically significant (p < .05). Standard errors were not shown.
SOURCE: James (1972).

children with weight-for-age less than 75 percent of normal were hospitalized, compared with two with satisfactory weights. Twelve low-weight children were hospitalized for severe diarrhea and dehydration and ten for severe respiratory infections. The two hospitalizations in the group with satisfactory weights were for severe respiratory infections. Four children died during the study, all of them from the low-weight groups. Finally, James found no differences between the two groups in environmental and socioeconomic conditions.

Tomkins (1981) investigated the relationship between nutritional status and the incidence of and percent of time ill with diarrhea in 343 children from a village in Nigeria. The period of observation was the three-month rainy season and the children's age ranged from 6 to 32 months. Unlike James (1972), this study also looked at height-for-age and weight-for-height. The incidence of diarrhea was found to be associated only with wasting: as shown in Table 3, the attack rate was 1.90 cases in three months for those with a weight-for-height less than 80 percent of normal, compared with 1.29 for those with greater weight-for-height ($p < .05$). The percent of time children were ill with diarrhea was, however, related to weight-for-age ($p < .01$), height-for-age ($p < .01$), and weight-for-height ($p < .001$). The strongest differences were noted for weight-for-height.

TABLE 3   Attack rate and percent of time ill with diarrhea in relation to nutrition in Nigerian children during the three-month rainy season

Nutritional status	Number of children	Diarrhea attack rate[a]	Percent of time ill with diarrhea
Weight-for-age			
>75%	220	1.25	8.5[c]
<75%	123	1.52	11.3[c]
Height-for-age			
>90%	245	1.37	7.9[c]
<90%	98	1.45	10.8[c]
Weight-for-height			
>80%	302	1.29[b]	7.6[d]
<80%	41	1.90[b]	13.6[d]

[a] Cases per child in three months.
[b] $p < .05$, [c] $p < .01$, [d] $p < .001$.
SOURCE: Tomkins (1981).

In a letter to the editor of *The Lancet* about Tomkins's article, Trowbridge, Newton, and Campbell (1981) reported data from a one-year study of 216 children from El Salvador. The ages of the study subjects ranged from 12 to 36 months. The percent of time during which diarrhea was reported was related to anthropometric status at the beginning and at the end of the period, although relationships with final status were stronger. Weight-for-age at the beginning of the year was not significantly associated with percent of time during which diarrhea was reported, in contrast to height-for-age, weight-for-height, and arm circumference, which were significantly associated. Wasting was a stronger predictor of diarrhea than stunting. Trowbridge, Newton, and Campbell noted that their findings as well as those of Tomkins are confounded by socioeconomic status and that the greater frequency of diarrhea in children with poorer nutritional status may be "related more to increased exposure to enteric pathogens from poor environmental conditions and personal hygiene than to nutritional factors" (p. 1375).

Chen, Huq, and Huffman (1981) have reported on studies carried out in Bangladesh. They found no association between hospitalization for treatment of diarrheal diseases over a two-year period and anthropometric measures (weight-for-age, weight-for-height, and height-for-age) at the beginning of the period. In 207 children ranging in age from birth to 4 years, weight-for-age was not associated with the diarrheal incidence rate as determined by community surveillance. Data on height were not available for study. Also, no relationship was shown between growth rates in weight during the month prior to the period of observation and the subsequent incidence of diarrhea.

Only the studies by Delgado et al. (1983) and Tomkins (1981) support the notion that nutritional status is associated with a greater incidence of infection. On the other hand, a greater number of studies indicate an association with the percent of time ill with diarrhea and with the duration of episodes of diarrhea.[5] Although not all studies agree, weight-for-height, a measure of wasting, tends to be a stronger predictor of future illness than height, a measure of stunting.

Anthropometric indicators and mortality

From the previous sections it follows that children identified as severely malnourished will have greatly increased mortality rates in the months subsequent to the assessment when compared with healthy children. Children with mild and moderate malnutrition might also be expected to show mortality rates greater than those of healthy children but not necessarily intermediate between healthy and severely malnourished children. The evidence suggests that children with mild to moderate malnutrition show some impairment in immunocompetence and that they also tend to have more severe infections than healthy children. Another reason for expecting higher mortality rates in children with mild and moderate malnutrition is that they are more likely to develop severe malnutrition. One would also anticipate that for the short term, measures of wasting would be more predictive of mortality than measures of stunting. However, as the follow-up period is extended, the predictive power would be expected to diminish, particularly for measures of wasting. Measures of stunting, because they are highly correlated with measures of poverty, which are in turn associated with mortality, may, however, continue to be associated with mortality. Finally, one would expect the relationship between malnutrition and mortality to be nonlinear, of the threshold type curves.

Only a few studies on the relationship between anthropometric indicators and mortality have been carried out in large numbers of children. Sommer and Loewenstein (1975) assessed the predictive power of arm circumference-to-height (QUAC stick) over a period of 18 months in 8,292 children from Bangladesh.[6] The basic results of the study are shown in Table 4. Three categories were defined, as specified in the note to the table: I, severe; II, moderate; and III, mild malnutrition.[7] Shown in the table for five age groups are the number of children at risk (C), the percent mortality (M), and the relative risks (R, relative to children in category III). There is clearly a relationship between categories of arm circumference-to-height and mortality. The risk was marked for severe cases (I) and children in the moderate category (II) had only a slightly higher mortality risk than children with mild malnutrition (III). An examination of the relative risks indicates that arm circumference-to-height had better predictive power in children 1–4 years of age than in older children.

TABLE 4   Children at risk (C), percent mortality (M), and relative risks (R) by category of the QUAC stick in children from Bangladesh

| Age at initial assessment (years) | QUAC stick categories[a] | | | | | | | | |
| | I (severe) | | | II (moderate) | | | III (mild) | | |
	C	M	R	C	M	R	C	M	R
1	59	11.9	3.9	408	4.4	1.5	492	3.0	1.0
2	66	13.6	3.6	435	6.0	1.6	507	3.7	1.0
3	62	17.7	7.0	406	4.9	2.0	515	2.5	1.0
4	66	6.1	4.2	321	1.9	1.3	420	1.4	1.0
5–9	389	1.0	2.0	1,791	0.6	1.2	2,032	0.5	1.0

[a] Categories of the QUAC stick (arm circumference-to-height) were made in reference to the local distribution: I, ≤9th percentile; II, 10th–50th percentile; and III, >50th percentile. C is the number of children at risk. M is the percent of children at risk that died in the interval. R is the mortality rate divided by that of category III of the same age group.
SOURCE: Sommer and Loewenstein (1975).

As would be expected, data presented in Table 5 indicate that the relationship with mortality was strongest in the first three months following the assessment. A very interesting fact in Table 5 is that the results for the first three months clearly indicate threshold effects. For example, for the first month, the relative risk for severe cases was 19.8, for moderate cases 1.3, and for mild cases, by definition, 1.0.

Data from the Narangwal project in India (Kielmann and McCord, 1978) are also available. Mortality histories for 2,808 children aged 1–3 years were collected for one year and related to weight-for-age status at the beginning of the year. The results of this study are shown in Table 6. Relative to children with weights of 80 percent or more of weight-for-age, all other groups

TABLE 5   Percent mortality (M) and relative risks (R) since initial assessment in 1—4-year-old children from Bangladesh

	Months since initial assessment							
	<1	1–3	4–6	7–9	10–12	13–15	16–18	Total
	Category I[a]							
M	2.0	3.2	1.6	2.5	2.6	2.6	0.5	12.3
R	19.8	12.2	4.5	3.2	3.0	8.2	2.1	4.5
	Category II							
M	0.1	0.5	0.6	1.3	1.1	0.3	0.7	4.5
R	1.3	2.0	1.8	1.7	1.3	0.8	3.5	1.6
	Category III							
M	0.1	0.3	0.4	0.8	0.8	0.3	0.2	2.7
R	1.0	1.0	1.0	1.0	1.0	1.0	1.0	1.0

[a] For categories of the QUAC stick and descriptions of M and R, see note to Table 4.
SOURCE: Sommer and Loewenstein (1975).

TABLE 6   Percent mortality (M) and relative risks (R) by categories of weight-for-age in children from India

Age at initial assessment (years)	Weight-for-age categories (percent of Harvard weight median)											
	<60			60–69			70–79			80+		
	C	M	R	C	M	R	C	M	R	C	M	R
1–5.9	48	14.6	5.8	109	9.2	3.7	358	9.7	3.9	1,138	2.5	1.0
6–11.9	62	17.7	18.9	212	8.0	8.5	437	3.4	3.6	748	0.9	1.0
12–35.9	218	3.7	13.0	1,025	0.8	2.8	2,126	0.3	1.2	1,776	0.3	1.0

NOTE: For descriptions of C, M, and R, see note to Table 4.
SOURCE: Kielmann and McCord (1978).

of children had higher mortality rates. The relationship implies a gradient in the level of risk and does not support the notion of a threshold effect. Other analyses showed that the predictive power of weight-for-age was greater in the first six months following assessment than in the second six months.

Other data are also available from Bangladesh. Chen et al. (1980) have looked at the relationship between anthropometric indicators and mortality in the subsequent 23 months in 2,019 children. Some of the results of this study are shown in Table 7. Unlike other studies, Chen et al. (1980) investigated the relationship with a number of anthropometric indicators, including weight-for-age, weight-for-height, and height-for-age. The data in the table suggest that all indicators were significant predictors of mortality. On the basis of these and other analyses, the authors concluded that weight-for-height was the weakest predictor of mortality. Inasmuch as the period of follow-up was 1 to 2 years, however, the poor relationship with weight-for-height is not surprising. The data in Table 7 and other data presented by the authors give strong indications of a threshold effect. Cases in the severe category always have higher mortality rates than all other children, while those in the mild and

TABLE 7 Percent mortality (M) and relative risks (R) 0–11 months and 12–23 months after nutritional assessment, classified by percentage weight-for-age, weight-for-height, and height-for-age of the Harvard standard

Nutritional status	Definition (percent of standard)	C	Follow-up period					
			0–11 months		12–23 months		0–23 months	
			M	R	M	R	M	R
Weight-for-age								
Normal/mild	≥75	546	2.38	1.0	1.28	1.0	3.66	1.0
Moderate	60–74	1,046	2.68	1.1	1.53	1.2	4.21	1.2
Severe	<60	427	4.68	2.0	6.56	5.1	11.24	3.1
Weight-for-height								
Normal	≥90	399	3.51	1.0	1.75	1.0	5.26	1.0
Mild	80–89	979	2.66	0.8	2.66	1.5	5.32	1.0
Moderate	70–79	566	2.83	0.8	2.12	1.2	4.95	0.9
Severe	<70	75	6.67	1.9	8.00	4.6	14.67	2.8
Height-for-age								
Normal	≥95	182	1.65	1.0	1.65	1.0	3.33	1.0
Mild	90–94	656	2.29	1.4	1.68	1.0	3.96	1.2
Moderate	85–89	713	2.80	1.7	0.98	0.6	3.79	1.1
Severe	<85	468	5.13	3.1	6.22	3.8	11.32	3.4

NOTE: For descriptions of C, M, and R, see note to Table 4.
SOURCE: Chen et al. (1980).

moderate categories have mortality rates similar to those in the normal category. Trowbridge and Sommer (1981) also suggest that the relationship between mortality and arm circumference is of the threshold type. An odd finding by Chen et al. (1980) is that the discriminating power of the anthropometric indicators does not seem to decline as the period following the initial assessment is increased. In Table 7, the follow-up period is divided into 0–11 months and 12–23 months, and the results indicate that there is actually an increase in the predictive power in the second year. This finding is at odds with previous studies, which suggested a decline in the predictive power over time.

The studies reviewed here all show that severely malnourished children have greatly increased mortality rates relative to normal children. Children with mild and moderate malnutrition also showed increased mortality risks in two of the three studies. Two of the three studies also showed that the discriminating power is greatest immediately following the assessment of nutritional status. Only one study included measures of stunting and wasting; in this instance, mixed indicators such as weight-for-age were better than weight-for-height while height-for-age was intermediate. The period of follow-up was one to two years, however, and the discriminating power of weight-for-height in the short term was not investigated. Arm circumference was found to be an excellent predictor of mortality by all authors who included this measure.[8] To date, no investigation has assessed the relationship between longitudinal data in children (i.e., growth velocities) and mortality risks.

Nutrition interventions and morbidity
and mortality in young children

Another source of information on the relationship between nutritional status and morbidity and mortality comes from studies of the effects of supplementary feeding programs.

The Narangwal study of ten villages in the Punjab, India, is one source of information (Kielmann, Taylor, and Parker, 1978; Taylor et al., 1978; Parker et al., 1978). The villages were divided into four study groups: control, medical care, nutrition, and nutrition and medical care. The villages in the nutrition group had a program of supplementary feeding directed to underweight children less than 3 years of age and to underweight mothers. The supplement provided up to 400 kcal and 11 g of protein per child per day, but attendance by children averaged only 22 percent for those aged 0–12 months and 41 percent for those aged 13–36 months.

Data on morbidity were collected through weekly home visits in all villages, but data collection was more complete in villages receiving services. For this reason, the authors felt that the data were hopelessly biased with regard to incidence. The duration of illness, a variable felt to be less sensitive to bias, was similar in control and nutrition villages for diarrhea (6.3 vs. 5.6 days in nutrition and control villages respectively), fever (3.9 vs. 3.6 days), and infection of the lower respiratory system (3.6 vs 5.0 days). The relationship between nutritional status and mortality, on the other hand, was striking. The infant mortality rate (deaths per 1,000 live births) was 128 in the control villages and 89 in the nutrition villages.[9] The 1–3–year mortality rate was nearly twice as high in the control villages compared with the nutrition villages. There was no evidence of an interaction of services—that is, the combination of nutrition and medical care programs did not result in markedly increased effects on mortality.

The Narangwal project was patterned after an earlier project undertaken by INCAP (Scrimshaw et al., 1966; Ascoli et al., 1967; Gordon et al., 1968; Guzmán et al., 1968).[10] A subsequent INCAP study in four rural Guatemalan villages (1969–77) showed that nutrition supplementation decreased the prevalence of low birth weight; but declines in mortality, on the order of 63 percent for the infant mortality rate and 79 percent for the 1–5 mortality rate, were thought to be more reflective of the medical care program than of the nutrition intervention (Habicht et al., 1975; Lechtig et al., 1978). Because all villages received medical care and some form of nutrition intervention, the separation of these effects proved difficult.

Baertl et al. (1970) have reported on a study carried out in four villages of northern Peru between 1962 and 1967. Villages I and II were controls,[11] while village III received ordinary wheat-flour noodles and village IV received noodles fortified with fish protein concentrate. The weekly distribution of food provided, per person, 250 kcal and 7.5 g of protein in village III and 250 kcal and 12.5 g of protein in village IV. Participation in the nutrition program was high. Medical care was not offered in any of the villages. The nutrition intervention reduced infant and childhood mortality significantly. There appeared to be no differences between villages III and IV and as a result these data were combined. The infant mortality rate was 134.5 per thousand in the control villages and 48 in the nutrition villages. The corresponding figures for the child mortality rate were 40.0 and 21.5 respectively. Relative to mortality data for the 10-year period prior to the study, declines in mortality rates were more marked for the treatment villages than for the control villages.[12]

Martínez and Chávez (1979) studied the incidence and severity of infections in two groups of 17 children each. Mothers of the children in one group received prenatal supplementation and the children received food supplements beginning at the age of 3 months. The second group received no nutritional supplements. All of the children were from the same village, and socioeconomic and environmental conditions were said to be similar in both groups. The incidence of infection was slightly higher in the first six months in the supplemented group, perhaps because patterns of child feeding were changed by the food distribution programs. However, thereafter until 36 months, infections were systematically more frequent in the unsupplemented group. Unsupplemented children had about eight episodes of illness per six-month period, while supplemented children had, on average, about six episodes. Because of the small sample sizes, the findings with regard to incidence were not statistically significant. However, the percent of days per six months that children were sick was significantly greater in the unsupplemented group after six months, roughly twice as high. Thus, effects on duration of illness were more pronounced than on incidence.[13]

Conclusions

The main conclusions derived from the literature review of nutritional status and child survival are as follows:

— Immunocompetence is seriously impaired in severely malnourished children. Effects are more pronounced for cell-mediated immunity and least for the serum immune system. Data are scant on the subject, but it appears that children with less severe forms of malnutrition are also affected, though the functional significance of these effects is unknown.

— Infections are more frequent in malnourished populations but this is best attributed to differences in the quality of the environment between rich and poor. Clinical evidence shows that infections are generally more severe in children from developing countries. Case fatalities for common communicable diseases, such as measles and chicken pox, and for diarrheal diseases are higher than in well-nourished populations.

— The evidence from field studies showing that the frequency of infection is greater in children with mild and moderate malnutrition is weak. On the other hand, there is more support for the notion that poor nutritional status, whether severe or moderate, predisposes children to more severe infections. Wasting appears to be more significantly related to the severity of infections than stunting.

The few large-scale studies that have been carried out all indicate that anthropometric indicators are significant predictors of mortality risks. All studies agree that the risk is many times greater for the severely malnourished and most also show that moderately malnourished children are at greater risk than well-nourished children. A curvilinear relationship best typifies the relationship between anthropometric indicators and mortality. One study suggested a threshold-type curve with enhanced mortality risks only in the severely malnourished.

Nutritional interventions have been shown to improve nutritional status but these same interventions have not been shown to reduce the incidence of infections. Also, there is weak support at best for the hypothesis that nutritional interventions decrease the severity of infections. However, these studies have been plagued by methodological difficulties with the measurement of morbidity and not all intervention studies have been properly analyzed in terms of effects on morbidity. On the other hand, nutrition intervention studies indicate that dietary improvements are associated with lower mortality rates during infancy and early childhood.

It seems to us that the various types of data indicate that the determinants of infections in children with mild and moderate malnutrition are more closely related to the quality of the environment than to the nutritional status of children. However, once a child becomes infected, the severity and duration of the episode will depend on nutritional status.

Moderately malnourished children may be more likely to develop severe infections because of deficiencies in immunocompetence. More severe infections in turn result in a poorer nutritional status and a vicious cycle of effects may eventually bring on severe malnutrition and death. There are many accounts of infections such as measles that can suddenly precipitate kwashiorkor in children. The existence of moderate malnutrition in a child, one should underscore, means that dietary deficiencies and/or frequent infections have been characteristics in the life of the child. While the degree of functional impairment may not be pronounced in moderate malnutrition, the balance is more precarious and such a child is more likely to develop severe malnutrition than one who is well nourished.

Finally, nutrition interventions do not appear to reduce the incidence of infections, although they decrease mortality rates. One explanation for these seemingly contradictory results is that the mortality rates are reduced through improvements in nutritional status. Improving nutritional status has at least two significant effects: better defenses against infection and a lower risk of severe malnutrition. Infection is one of the causes of malnutrition that cannot be ameliorated by nutrition programs.

Notes

1 See literature reviews by Martorell and Yarbrough (1983) and Leslie (1982).

2 Sixty percent of the Boston–Iowa standard corresponds to 80 percent, or the 10th percentile, of the ICMR data.

3 The ^{3}H-thymidine incorporation (cpm, test/control) was 17.3 for group I, 10.0 for II, 3.83 for III, and 4.95 for group IV. Findings for groups III and IV were significantly different from those of group I.

4 Children with more than 90 percent of the expected weight-for-age are classified as normal. Grade I includes those children with weight-for-age values between 75 and 89 percent. Grade II includes children with values between 60 and 74 percent, and grade III encompasses all children with values below 60. Synonyms for grades I, II, and III are mild, moderate, and severe malnutrition respectively.

5 Since this review was written, a related study from Bangladesh has been published (Black et al., 1984). Children were monitored over 60-day periods, and the incidence and duration of diarrheal diseases were examined as a function of anthropometric characteristics recorded at the beginning of the study. No relationship was found between any of the anthropometric indicators and the incidence of diarrheal diseases. On the other hand, children with poorer nutritional status had longer episodes of diarrhea.

6 Arm circumference is a measure highly correlated with weight and weight-for-length (Martorell, Habicht, and Klein, 1982); and while changes from 1 to 4 years of age are not marked, the use of height is a theoretical improvement because it corrects for differences in arm circumference associated with body size and age.

7 The categories in Table 4 differ from those used by Sommer and Loewenstein (1975).

8 Chen, Chowdhury, and Huffman (1981) and Trowbridge and Sommer (1981) argue that the use of height, as in the QUAC stick, does not improve the discriminating power of arm circumference.

9 The rate of 89 in the nutrition villages is the average of villages with nutrition service only (97) and those with nutrition and medical care services (81).

10 The authors of this INCAP study were unable to document effects on the incidence of infections because of the unpredictable nature of epidemics that occurred throughout the study. The authors did find, however, that the case fatality rates for measles and for diarrhea as well as infant mortality rates were reduced in the village receiving a nutrition intervention.

11 Beginning in 1965 village II did receive a feeding program for children 6–30 months of age.

12 Thus infant deaths in the control villages declined from 7.15 to 6.75 per thousand *total* population (a 6 percent decline). In the nutrition villages the decline over the same period was from 6.00 to 2.25 deaths per thousand (a 44 percent decline).

13 A similar study to that of Martínez and Chávez (1979) has been carried out by Barba, Guthrie, and Guthrie (1982) in the Philippines. Twenty-four pairs of infants matched for age, sex, and nutritional status were studied. The children were originally 5–12 months of age. Half were given food supplements for a year while half were not. Although the supplemented children improved significantly in terms of growth, there were no statistically significant differences with regard to the incidence or duration of illnesses other than the finding that children receiving food supplements had more minor colds and coughs.

References

Anon. 1968. "Measles and malnutrition," *Nutrition Reviews* 26: 232–234.

Ascoli, W., M. A. Guzmán, N. S. Scrimshaw, and J. E. Gordon. 1967. "Nutrition and infection field study in Guatemalan villages, 1959–1964: IV. Deaths of infants and preschool children," *Archives of Environmental Health* 15: 439–449.

Baertl, J. M., E. Morales, G. Verastegui, and G. G. Graham. 1970. "Diet supplementation for entire communities: Growth and mortality of infants and children," *American Journal of Clinical Nutrition* 23: 707–715.

Barba, C. V. C., H. A. Guthrie, and G. M. Guthrie. 1982. "Dietary intervention and growth of infants and toddlers in a Philippine rural community," *Ecology of Food and Nutrition* 11: 235–244.

Beaton, G. H., and H. Ghassemi. 1982. "Supplementary feeding programs for young children in developing countries," *American Journal of Clinical Nutrition* 35: 864–916.

Black, R. E., K. H. Brown, and S. Becker. 1984. "Malnutrition is a determining factor in diarrheal duration, but not incidence, among young children in a longitudinal study in rural Bangladesh," *American Journal of Clinical Nutrition* 39: 87–94.

Chandra, R. K. 1979. "Interactions of nutrition, infection and immune response," *Acta Paediatrica Scandinavica* 68: 137–144.

———. 1981. "Immunodeficiency in undernutrition and overnutrition," *Nutrition Reviews* 39: 225–231.

———, and P. M. Newberne. 1977. *Nutrition, Immunity, and Infection: Mechanisms of Interactions*. New York and London: Plenum Press.

Chen, L. C., A. K. M. A. Chowdhury, and S. L. Huffman. 1980. "Anthropometric assessment of energy-protein malnutrition and subsequent risk of mortality among preschool aged children," *American Journal of Clinical Nutrition* 33: 1836–1845.

———, E. Huq, and S. L. Huffman. 1981. "A prospective study of the risk of diarrheal diseases according to the nutritional status of children," *American Journal of Epidemiology* 114: 284–292.

———, and N. S. Scrimshaw, eds. 1983. *Diarrhea and Malnutrition*. New York and London: Plenum Press.

Delgado, H. S., V. Valverde, J. M. Belizan, and R. E. Klein. 1983. "Diarrheal diseases, nutritional status and health care: Analyses of their interrelationships," *Ecology of Food and Nutrition* 12: 229–234.

Ghosh, S., and P. S. Dhatt. 1961. "Complications of measles," *Indian Journal of Child Health* 10: 111–119.

Gordon, J. E., A. A. J. Jansen, and W. Ascoli. 1965. "Measles in rural Guatemala," *Journal of Pediatrics* 66: 779–786.

———, W. Ascoli, L. J. Mata, M. A. Guzmán, and N. S. Scrimshaw. 1968. "Nutrition and infection field study in Guatemalan villages, 1959–1964: VI. Acute diarrheal disease and nutritional disorders in general disease incidence," *Archives of Environmental Health* 16: 424–437.

Guzmán, M. A., N. S. Scrimshaw, H. A. Bruch, and J. E. Gordon. 1968. "Nutrition and infection field study in Guatemalan villages, 1959–1964: VII. Physical growth and development of preschool children," *Archives of Environmental Health* 17: 107–118.

Habicht, J.-P., A. Lechtig, C. Yarbrough, and R. E. Klein. 1975. "Maternal nutrition, birth weight, and infant mortality," in *Size at Birth* (*Ciba Foundation Symposium 27*), ed. K. Elliott and J. Knight. Amsterdam: Associated Scientific Publishers.

Ifekwunigwe, A. E., N. Grasset, R. Glass, and S. Foster. 1980. "Immune response to measles and smallpox vaccinations in malnourished children," *American Journal of Clinical Nutrition* 33: 621–624.

James, J. W. 1972. "Longitudinal study of the morbidity of diarrheal and respiratory infections in malnourished children," *American Journal of Clinical Nutrition* 25: 690–694.

Kielmann, A. A., I. S. Uberoi, R. K. Chandra, and V. L. Mehra. 1976. "The effect of nutritional status on immune capacity and immune responses in preschool children in a rural community in India," *Bulletin of the World Health Organization* 54: 477–483.

———, and C. McCord. 1978. "Weight-for-age as an index of risk of death in children," *The Lancet* (10 June): 1247–1250.

————, C. E. Taylor, and R. L. Parker. 1978. "The Narangwal Nutrition Study: A summary review," *American Journal of Clinical Nutrition* 31: 2040–2052.

Koster, F. T., G. C. Curlin, K. M. A. Aziz, and A. Haque. 1981. "Synergistic impact of measles and diarrhoea on nutrition and mortality in Bangladesh," *Bulletin of the World Health Organization* 59: 901–908.

Lechtig, A., H. Delgado, R. Martorell, D. Richardson, C. Yarbrough, and R. E. Klein. 1978. "Effect of maternal nutrition on infant mortality," in *Nutrition and Human Reproduction,* ed. W. H. Mosley. New York: Plenum Press.

Leslie, Joanne. 1982. "Child malnutrition and diarrhea: A longitudinal study from northeast Brazil," Ph.D. thesis, Johns Hopkins University.

Martínez, C., and A. Chávez. 1979. "Nutrition and development of children from poor rural areas. VII. The effect of the nutritional status on the frequency and severity of infections," *Nutrition Reports International* 19: 307–314.

Martorell, R., J.-P. Habicht, C. Yarbrough, A. Lechtig, and R. E. Klein. 1974. "Morbidity and physical growth in children from rural Guatemala," in *Pediatría XIV,* vol. 5. Buenos Aires: Editorial Médica Panamericana.

————, R. E. Klein, and H. Delgado. 1980. "Improved nutrition and its effects on anthropometric indicators of nutritional status," *Nutritional Reports International* 31: 219–230.

————, J.-P. Habicht, and R. E. Klein. 1982. "Anthropometric indicators of changes in nutritional status in malnourished populations," in *Methodologies for Human Population Studies in Nutrition Related to Health,* ed. B.A. Underwood. NIH Publication No. 82-2462. Washington, D.C.: U.S. Government Printing Office.

————, and C. Yarbrough. 1983. "The energy cost of diarrheal diseases and other common illnesses in children," in *Diarrhea and Malnutrition,* ed. L. C. Chen and N. S. Scrimshaw. New York: Plenum Press.

————, J. Leslie, and P. R. Moock. 1984. "Characteristics and determinants of child nutritional status in Nepal," *American Journal of Clinical Nutrition.* 39: 74–86.

Mata, L. J. 1978. *The Children of Santa María Cauqué: A Prospective Field Study of Health and Growth.* Cambridge, Mass.: MIT Press.

————, R. A. Kromal, J. J. Urrutia, and B. Garcia. 1977. "Effect of infection on food intake and the nutritional state: Perspectives as viewed from the village," *American Journal of Clinical Nutrition* 30: 1215–1227.

McGregor, I. A. 1964. "Measles and child mortality in the Gambia," *West Africa Medical Journal* 13: 251–257.

McMurray, D. N., R. R. Watson, and M. A. Reyes. 1981. "Effect of renutrition on humoral and cell-mediated immunity in severely malnourished children," *American Journal of Clinical Nutrition* 34: 2117–2126.

Morley, D. 1969. "Severe measles in the tropics—I and II," *British Medical Journal* 1: 297–300 and 363–365.

————. 1973. *Paediatric Priorities in the Developing World.* London: Butterworths.

Parker, R. L., C. E. Taylor, A. A. Kielmann, A. K. S. Murthy, and I. S. Uberoi. 1978. "The Narangwal experiment on interactions of nutrition and infections: III. Measurement of services and costs and their relation to outcome," *Indian Journal of Medical Research* 68: 42–54.

Puffer, R. R., and C. V. Serrano. 1973. *Patterns of Mortality in Childhood.* Scientific Publication No. 262. Washington, D.C.: Pan American Health Organization.

Reddy, V., V. Jagadeesan, N. Ragharamulu, C. Bhaskaram, and S. G. Srikantia. 1976. "Functional significance of growth retardation in malnutrition," *American Journal of Clinical Nutrition* 29: 2–7.

Salomon, J. B., L. J. Mata, and J. E. Gordon. 1968. "Malnutrition and the common communicable diseases of childhood in rural Guatemala," *American Journal of Public Health* 3: 505–516.

Scrimshaw, N. S., J. B. Salomon, H. A. Bruch, and J. E. Gordon. 1966. "Studies of diarrheal diseases in Central America: VIII. Measles, diarrhea, and nutritional deficiency in rural Guatemala," *American Journal of Tropical Medicine and Hygiene* 15: 625–631.

Sinha, D. P. 1977. "Measles and malnutrition in a West Bengal village," *Tropical and Geographical Medicine* 29: 125–134.

Snyder, J. D., and M. H. Merson. 1982. "The magnitude of the global problem of acute diarrhoeal disease: A review of active surveillance data," *Bulletin of the World Health Organization* 60: 605–613.

Sommer, A., and M. S. Loewenstein. 1975. "Nutritional status and mortality: A prospective validation of the QUAC stick," *American Journal of Clinical Nutrition* 28: 287–292.

Suskind, R. M., ed. 1977. *Malnutrition and the Immune Response*. New York: Raven Press.

Taylor, C. E., A. A. Kielmann, C. DeSweemer, I. S. Uberoi, H. S. Takulia, C. G. Neumann, W. Blot, H. Shankar, S. Vohra, G. Subbulakshmi, R. S. S. Sarma, R. L. Parker, C. McCord, N. Masih, D. Laliberte, N. S. Kielmann, D. N. Kakar, and A. Forman. 1978. "The Narangwal experiment in interactions of nutrition and infections: Project design and effects upon growth," *Indian Journal of Medical Research* 68: 1–20.

Tomkins, A. 1981. "Nutritional status and severity of diarrhoea among pre-school children in rural Nigeria," *The Lancet* (18 April): 860–862.

Trowbridge, F. L., L. H. Newton, and C. C. Campbell. 1981. Letter to the Editor, *The Lancet* 1: 1375.

——, and A. Sommer. 1981. "Nutritional anthropometry and mortality risk," *American Journal of Clinical Nutrition* 34: 2591–2592.

Wray, J. D. 1978. "Direct nutrition intervention and the control of diarrheal diseases in pre-school children," *American Journal of Clinical Nutrition* 31: 2073–2082.

Ziegler, H. D., and P. B. Ziegler. 1975. "Depression of tuberculin reaction in mild and moderate protein-calorie malnourished children following BCG vaccination," *Johns Hopkins Medical Journal* 137: 59–64.

Measurement
of Dietary Intake

Kenneth H. Brown

The assimilation of exogenous nutrients is a fundamental biological process necessary both to support metabolic functions and to permit physical growth. The study of man's quest to produce or otherwise acquire food has occupied social and biological scientists alike. The quantitative and qualitative description of the food and nutrient intakes of individuals, however, has most commonly been undertaken by nutritionists. This paper reviews the purposes, methods, and interpretation of dietary studies, with emphasis on the measurement and determinants of the dietary intake of children, particularly those in less developed countries.

Before addressing the specifics of dietary studies, it is important to distinguish between the measurement of dietary intake and the assessment of nutritional status. Although it is commonly asserted that dietary studies are undertaken to evaluate the nutritional status of an individual or a population, nutritional status is more appropriately measured by clinical, physiological, or functional parameters. In short, dietary intake is only one of several factors (others being infections, physiological stage of life, and genetic endowment) that may influence the nutritional status of an individual. If an individual's consumption of a certain essential nutrient is habitually lower than the recommended dietary allowance, he may be at risk of nutritional deficiency or he may simply have a lower physiological requirement for that nutrient than the statistically determined recommended allowance. Since the recommended allowance of a nutrient (with the exception of total energy) is usually defined as the level of intake sufficient to satisfy the requirements of 97 percent of the members of the physiological subgroup (defined, for example, by age and sex), it is obvious that many individuals may consume less than these allowances without showing any evidence of nutritional deficiency (Hegsted, 1975). Nutritional status, then, is the physical expression of the relationship between an individual's dietary intake, the bioavailability of these ingested nutrients, and his or her physiological requirements. The bioavailability of nutrients (i.e., their absorption and retention, which may, in turn, be influenced by their dietary source and interactions with specific components of the diet) is measured by metabolic studies and cannot be determined directly by dietary studies.

Research on child survival should consider children's dietary intake, even though the relationship between diet and mortality may not be direct or easy to define. Studies of dietary intake do offer a relatively sensitive, albeit not necessarily specific, tool for predicting nutritional imbalances before they become clinically evident. By contrast, studies of nutritional status, using clinical or biochemical measurements, require that nutritional deficiencies or excesses occur before the problem can be detected. Thus, dietary studies are helpful in evaluating the risk of nutritional problems in an individual or population.

Specific applications of dietary studies as related to child survival might include evaluations of intrasocietal or intrafamilial food distribution throughout the year. Given that food intake can directly affect nutritional status and hence the risk of mortality, information on the availability of food to individual segments of society or to individuals within the family at different seasons of the year could be used to correct inadequacies of food distribution. With such information, targeted educational interventions or food supplementation programs could be planned and subsequently evaluated.

Objectives of dietary studies

Different techniques for measuring dietary intake have been developed to produce either reasonably accurate data from large numbers of individuals or extremely accurate data from limited numbers of individuals. Unfortunately, the more accurate methods are costlier in terms of time, manpower, and money, and hence are generally restricted to studies of relatively small numbers of subjects. Qualitative or quantitative techniques that focus only on food or on both food and nutrients can be used. Clearly, the purpose of the dietary study must first be defined in order to determine the appropriate method of study. Some of the typical objectives of dietary studies and related methodologic issues are shown in Table 1.

Dietary studies have been employed most commonly as part of nutritional surveys or systems of nutritional surveillance (Aranda-Pastor et al., 1978; Beaton, 1976; Jelliffe, 1966; Mason, 1976) to evaluate the availability of foods and nutrients to a group of people, as defined by geographical, physiological (e.g., age, sex), and/or social boundaries. In general, the researcher wants to know the average nutrient intake of individuals within the population, in order to compare different populations or a given population over time, and the distribution of intakes, in order to determine what proportion of individuals are consuming more or less than specific cutoff levels of each nutrient. Studies of populations are often conducted at the household

TABLE 1   Principal applications and objectives of dietary studies

Type of study	Principal application/objective
Nutritional surveys and surveillance	To measure the availability of food and nutrients (expressed in terms of average intake and distribution of intakes) to individuals or groups of individuals
Clinical and epidemiological studies	To determine the relationships between the consumption of specific foods and/or nutrients and the development of disease
Nutritional studies of healthy populations	To estimate nutritional requirements
Studies of dietary practices	To plan food fortification programs To plan and evaluate nutritional education To plan marketing strategy

level—dividing total household intake by the number of individuals in the household—since households are easier to study than individuals, and the true intakes of individuals are not necessarily of interest in this context. Obviously, the per capita consumption data obtained from household studies do not provide information on the consumption of individuals or the intrafamily distribution of food.

Dietary studies are also used to investigate relationships between the current or previous consumption of specific foods or nutrients and the development of disease. For example, a clinician may want to know the relationship between a pediatric patient's energy consumption and either obesity or failure to thrive. Similarly, an epidemiologist may want to study the relationship between vitamin A ingestion and xerophthalmia or between the consumption of smoked fish and gastric carcinoma. Since current dietary intake may not accurately reflect previous consumption patterns, an attempt must be made to elicit earlier dietary patterns when studying diseases that develop over long periods of time.

Ideally, epidemiological studies of diet and disease require accurate data regarding the usual present or past food or nutrient intake of individual subjects; however, the large numbers of subjects necessary for some epidemiological associations to be observed with statistical confidence often make that requirement unachievable. Techniques for the evaluation of groups of individuals in epidemiological studies have also been described (Beaton et al., 1979; Block, 1982; Frank et al., 1978; Liu et al., 1978). Groups of individuals roughly classified by level of intake of a particular substance can be compared for incidence rates of the disease under study. Alternatively, the subjects can be classified by the outcome variable of interest (e.g., body fatness, which has less intraindividual variation than energy intake), and the groups can then be compared with regard to dietary intake.

Studies of dietary intake have also been used to obtain a preliminary approximation of nutrient requirements. For this purpose, the distribution of the usual intake of a nutrient is measured in a population that is free from nutritional deficiency. From these data, one can infer the level of intake above which signs or symptoms of the deficiency would not be expected to occur. The energy requirements of infants during the first 6 months of life have been estimated in this way by observing the intakes of normally growing breastfed babies (FAO/WHO, 1973). For most nutrients (with the possible exception of energy), the observed level of consumption is undoubtedly greater than the minimum sufficient level to maintain normal nutritional status, since most individuals in a well-nourished population consume substantially more than their minimum needs.

In addition to the objectives noted above, there are a variety of miscellaneous applications for dietary studies. When planning a food fortification program, for example, it is critical to know what foods are consumed by the individuals at risk of developing a particular nutritional deficiency. Initially, such information can be obtained from a simple food-frequency questionnaire, but quantitative consumption data will ultimately be required to determine the appropriate level of fortification (Beaton, 1976). Similarly, specific information on dietary practices may be required in order to monitor the effect of an educational campaign. A program to promote breastfeeding, for example, would be well advised to record periodically information on the frequency, duration, and intensity of breastfeeding in the target population. Finally, dietary surveys are often used to determine marketing strategies for commercial enterprises.

Classification of methods to measure dietary intake

Table 2 sets forth the techniques for collecting dietary consumption data and the relative advantages, disadvantages, and costs of these techniques. This review concentrates on quantitative studies of individuals. In general, when quantitative data are required, prospective studies are preferred because they provide more precise information as to what is actually consumed during the period of study. Retrospective techniques are subject to errors of recall, particularly regarding the quantities of food consumed. On the other hand, retrospective studies have been considered advantageous for estimating the individual's usual intake during extended periods of time; prospective studies provide data only for the actual day or days of study. Similarly, the decision to use either self-conducted or observer-administered studies involves possible tradeoffs in the quality of the data. Theoretically, the observer should be able to obtain a more objective assessment of the subject's actual intake. However, it is impossible to determine to what extent the presence of the observer induces the subject to alter his eating pattern. To minimize this problem the observer must be trained to be unintrusive and nonjudgmental. Alternatively, in special circumstances, methods can be devised to observe the subject clandestinely, thus avoiding the observer effect. Despite these concerns, our experience in less developed countries suggests that the occasional attempt by the subject to impress the observer rapidly disappears with repeated visits as

TABLE 2 Advantages and disadvantages of various techniques for measuring dietary intake

Technique	Advantages	Disadvantages	Estimated relative cost[a]
Retrospective studies			
Observer-administered			
Dietary history	Theoretically estimates usual intake	Cannot be validated; requires well-trained dietitian and cooperative subjects	+ +
Recall history	Provides qualitative and (fairly accurate) quantitative data for groups	Requires accurate memory; quantitative information is less accurate than that given by prospective techniques[b]	+ + +
Self-administered			
Dietary questionnaire	Does not require personal interview	Requires literate subject; does not generally provide quantitative data	+
Prospective studies			
Observer-administered			
Food-weighing, home	Provides accurate quantitative data for individuals	Unknown observer effect; logistical difficulties[b]	+ + + +
Food-weighing, clinic	Provides accurate quantitative data for individuals	Requires removal from home setting; unknown effect of technique on dietary intake[b]	+ + + + +
Self-administered			
Food diary (food record)	Provides (fairly accurate) qualitative and quantitative data for individuals	Requires highly motivated, educated subject[b]	+ +
Collaboratively administered			
Duplicate diet	Provides accurate quantitative data for *nutrients* (not foods) *as eaten*	Requires highly motivated, well-trained subject and a laboratory capable of completing analyses[b]	+ + + + +
Preweighed foods	Provides accurate quantitative data for individuals	Can only be completed with a limited range of preprocessed foods[b]	+ + + +

[a] Relative costs were estimated on the basis of number of days of study required, personnel expenses (dietitians, data analysts, laboratory technicians), equipment, and other laboratory, clinical, or transportation expenses.
[b] Technique requires multiple days of study to account for day-to-day, week-to-week, and seasonal variations if accurate information regarding the usual intake of an individual is required.

greater familiarity develops between them. The limited financial resources of families in such settings also preclude major changes in their dietary patterns on days of study.

Description of methods
for dietary studies

Valuable reviews explaining the conventional study methods have been published (Marr, 1971; Pekkarinen, 1970; Reh, 1962). A brief outline of selected methods and some examples of investigations that have applied them are presented here. General issues regarding the planning and organization of studies, the validation and comparison of methods, and the interpretation of dietary data are addressed separately.

The dietary history, also called the "Burke method," was designed "to measure the average intake of an individual during a considerable period of time" (Burke, 1947; Reed and Burke, 1954). The interviewer asks the subject or his caretaker about the usual eating pattern, what meals are taken when, what their composition is (types and amounts of foods), and what other items are eaten as snacks. The quantities of individual foods consumed are calculated from the number of servings of each food per period of time and the estimated size of those servings. These data are cross-checked by asking about additional foods and by reviewing the summarized diet with the subject to ascertain its accuracy. Lubbe (1968) has described slight modifications of this technique for household studies of children in South Africa.

The dietary history intentionally does not ask about actual food consumption on the day or days prior to the survey, but attempts to reconstruct the subject's usual eating habits. This method requires a cooperative, intelligent informant, a skilled dietitian, and a relatively lengthy interview. Its theoretical advantage is that it provides data on the subject's usual intake while not requiring multiple visits to contend with day-to-day variations in intake. Its disadvantage is that many people either do not have a consistent eating pattern or cannot describe their usual diet. The exclusion of these subjects adds a potential source of bias to the data obtained for the group. Furthermore, as explained below, attempts to validate the method have yielded disappointing results.

The dietary recall method requires that the subject report all of the foods consumed during an immediately preceding, fixed period of time. Although some investigators have conducted recall histories covering periods as long as one week, most believe that the data are not reliable beyond 24 to 48 hours. Different dietitians have their preferred interview techniques. Some begin with the previous day's breakfast (often a simple and monotonous meal, which is therefore easily remembered) and then work forward hourly through the activities (and hence snacks and meals) of the day. Others prefer to begin with the last meal of the previous day and work backward. Still others ask only about the main meals initially and then probe regarding additional foods taken during the intervening hours. Some workers have promoted the use of photos or models of foods to aid in the estimation of portion sizes; others request the subject to indicate the amounts consumed using real food, and then weigh the foods directly. It would seem that the more quantitative estimates would be preferable, but such quantification might merely provide an illusion of accuracy in the face of an unreliable memory.

The advantage of the recall history is that it provides semiquantitative information on the real intake during a fixed period of time. The interview is relatively simple and brief. The recently reported successful attempts to complete recall histories by telephone (Krantzler et al., 1982; Posner et al., 1982) are of interest for technologically more advanced societies, but will probably not have much applicability in poorer communities. Assuming the informant is honest and has a reliable memory, the data are probably not unduly influenced by the subject's notion of what he should or would like to eat, since he is asked to report on objective facts rather than estimated patterns of consumption. The major drawback of the technique, and of all others that study a relatively short period of time (i.e., one day), is that an individual's intake varies markedly from day to day. Thus, multiple interviews are required to provide a valid estimate of the individual's "usual" intake.

The dietary questionnaire can be designed to elicit information similar either to the dietary history or to the recall history, or may only request information on the consumption of specific foods. The questionnaire is usually distributed by mail and, thus, is very economical. Nevertheless, its usefulness is restricted by doubts about the validity of responses to any but the simplest types of questions, by the problem of nonresponse, and by the necessity that subjects be literate, a significant constraint in less developed countries.

The food-weighing technique carried out by a trained observer is probably the most reliable method for determining the precise amounts of foods and nutrients consumed during the period of observation and is the standard against which other methods are generally evaluated. The method involves the weighing of all raw food ingredients that are either directly consumed or included in recipes. In the case of recipes ("menu items") composed of several food items, the final weight of the menu item after preparation is determined, and the individual's portion of the menu item minus plate wastes is expressed as a proportion of the entire menu item so that the amounts of individual food items consumed can be calculated. A more detailed description of the method and pertinent calculations has been presented previously (Brown et al., 1982b). The technique has been successfully applied to the study of children in less developed countries (Brown et al., 1982b; Creed et al., 1980).

Food-weighing studies of infants and young children pose special problems, however. Since children's feeding times often do not conform to a strict schedule, continuous observation must be maintained during the day and, ideally, throughout the night. Because 24-hour observation is usually not feasible, though, studies of children often employ a combination of food-weighing during the day and recall history of foods consumed at night. In addition, the consumption of breastmilk and its components must be estimated for breastfed infants. Field techniques for the estimation of the amount and composition of breastmilk consumed have been discussed previously (Brown et al., 1982a; Prentice et al., 1981a). Usually, the amount of milk consumed is estimated by test-weighing before and after feedings, but marker techniques employing stable isotopes have recently been developed (Coward et al., 1979). Additional problems relate to the scheduling and interpretation of studies of children of working mothers. When the children accompany the mother to work, their food consumption (especially breastmilk) cannot be easily quantified. When the children are left with another caretaker, studies may not be convenient because of a change in locale or lack of cooperation. If, on the other hand, the children are evaluated only when their mothers are at home, the intake on those days may not be representative of the customary types and amounts of foods consumed. Finally, there is no convenient way to estimate the milk consumption of a child who breastfeeds only at night. These issues have not been satisfactorily resolved and may preclude the collection of valid data from such subjects.

The obvious advantage of food-weighing studies is their ability to define precisely the dietary intake of cooperative individuals on the day of study. Disadvantages include the need for multiple days of observation, the unknown observer effect, and the cost of equipment (scales) and personnel. In our studies in Bangladesh and Peru, we have successfully trained lay community workers to complete the food-weighing studies, thus reducing personnel expenses for professional dietitians.

Clinic-based food-weighing studies are procedurally similar to the home-based studies described above. They may be used to determine children's food consumption during an illness requiring hospitalization or to observe their eating habits when there is reason to doubt the reliability of information obtained from the caretakers. Although these studies provide accurate and interesting information, their expense and the need to remove the child from the home setting when hospitalization is not otherwise required reduce their practicality.

The food diary is also similar to the food-weighing technique, with the difference that the subject or his caretaker rather than an "outside" observer performs the weighing and recordkeeping. Even among highly educated, well-motivated subjects only 60–80 percent successfully complete their diaries, and compliance tends to diminish rapidly after several days of study. Furthermore, one study has suggested that those who continue recording information beyond the third day of study tend to have a higher level of education (Gersovitz et al., 1978). Individuals capable of completing the technique thus would probably be unrepresentative of populations at large in most of the poorer countries.

Other specialized techniques include the collection of duplicate diets and the preparation of preweighed diets for home delivery. The former technique requires that the subject prepare all food (menu) items in duplicate (Borgstrom et al., 1975). The duplicate diet and any unfinished portions from the subject's diet are saved in separate containers for subsequent laboratory analysis. The difference in the amounts of nutrients in the two specimens equals the amount consumed. The technique is tedious and costly but provides extremely accurate information regarding the nutrients consumed, while avoiding the use of food-composition tables. Furthermore, the analysis is completed on food "as eaten," thus correcting for any changes in nutrient concentrations during cooking. The applicability of the technique in less developed countries depends on the availability of suitable laboratory facilities and cooperative subjects. Poorer subjects would have to be reimbursed for the food lost to the laboratory; whether that payment and other aspects of the study procedures would alter the usual consumption practices is unknown.

The use of preweighed bottles of infant formula and jars of infant foods has been the basis for Fomon's (1971) classic studies of the dietary intake of healthy North American infants. The labeled food containers are delivered to the subject's home daily or weekly, and the emptied, partially emptied, and unused containers and their contents are collected at the time of the following delivery. The mother is asked to place the jars and bottles used during each day of the week in a separate box indicated for that day. Subtracting the weight of the empty or partially emptied containers from the known predelivery weight gives the amount consumed. The technique requires the use of pre-packaged foods, thus restricting its application to societies that customarily use these types of products. The donation of such foods to poorer families could change the subject's consumption patterns; furthermore, other family members might be tempted to share the gift.

A final word about qualitative histories of feeding practices is indicated, since these surveys are frequently useful in less developed countries. To obtain information about children's eating habits, an interviewer systematically asks a series of questions regarding foods that the child is currently receiving and the frequency of consumption. The list of foods may be as general or as detailed as desired, depending on the purpose of the study. Interestingly, in a poor community of the periurban slums of Lima, Peru, we found that retrospective histories of the duration of breastfeeding gave a pattern of age-specific breastfeeding prevalence similar to that observed in a cross-sectional study of the proportion of children actually consuming mother's milk at the time of the survey (see Figure 1). The comparability of the two sets of data for other foods was not as good as for breastfeeding.

FIGURE 1   Comparison of retrospective history of breastfeeding in a periurban slum in Lima, Peru, with age-specific percent of children currently breastfeeding

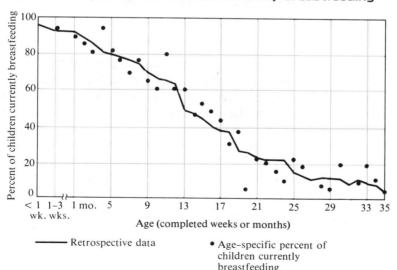

NOTE: Data are for children under age 3 years (N = 779).
SOURCE: Unpublished data from Pueblo Joven Huascar, Canto Grande; Instituto de Investigación Nutricional, Lima, Peru.

Planning and organization
of fieldwork

Careful planning and organization of the fieldwork are critical for the successful outcome of dietary studies. Reh (1962) has written an excellent manual on preparation for such studies, emphasizing the necessity for preliminary conversations with community leaders, statistical sampling from a known population base, adequate training of fieldworkers, and rigorous supervision of field activities. We have found that detailed discussions with health ministry officials as well as local community leaders and individual families—although frustratingly time consuming—are imperative for the success of such a project, particularly in less developed countries, where the subject's level of education and comprehension of the purpose of the study may be limited. While these conversations are taking place, planning of the study sample and training of fieldworkers can also proceed.

The selection and training of fieldworkers require careful attention. We have preferred to teach untrained high school graduates to complete the studies rather than hire previously trained dietitians. The latter are often scarce in less developed countries and may have more difficulty relating to the families being studied. For our studies, congenial individuals selected on the basis of mathematical aptitude tests were enrolled in a one- to two-week intensive training course. The training course for the food-weighing technique included basic nutritional concepts, the use of balances, weighing and taring of food items, recording of data on field forms, and related calculations. Much emphasis was placed on the need for presenting a complete explanation of the studies to the families and for courtesy, confidentiality, and unintrusiveness. Individuals who successfully completed the training course engaged in a series of supervised practice studies before working alone.

Sources of variability in dietary data

Because of the tremendous range in the types and amounts of foods consumed by healthy individuals, attempts to quantify dietary intake must be concerned not only with measurement accuracy, but also with the issues of inter- and intrasubject variability. Since the researcher is most often interested in the subject's usual consumption patterns, the study of a single day's intake—even if perfectly accurate—is not sufficient to define his habitual, or average, intake (Garn et al., 1976). Apart from real differences in dietary intakes among individuals, other potential sources of variation include the day of the week (e.g., weekdays versus weekend days), other day-to-day variability, the season of the year, the physiological status of the subject (age, sex, illnesses, etc.), and the study instrument. Further, the degree of variability differs according to the nutrient studied.

A number of investigators have examined the components of variability in dietary studies (Acheson et al., 1980; Balogh et al., 1971; Beaton et al.,

1979; Beaton et al., 1983; Hankin et al., 1967; Todd et al., 1983; Trulson, 1955; Young and Trulson, 1960; Yudkin, 1951). Intraindividual (day-to-day) variability has been shown to account for approximately 50–60 percent of the total variance of macronutrient intakes of adult Canadians (Beaton et al., 1979), and for 60–100 percent of the variance in their intake of selected vitamins and minerals (Beaton et al., 1983). The within-subject coefficients of variation (SD/mean) reported from four studies of repeated observations of adults are shown in Table 3 for selected nutrients. The day-to-day intake of energy varied from 19 to 26 percent of the mean and the intake of protein, from 25 to 36 percent. Vitamins A and C demonstrated even greater levels of variability, probably because of the irregular consumption of limited numbers of foods with very high concentrations of these vitamins. Because of the magnitude of intraindividual variation, a surprisingly large number of repeated observations are required to estimate confidently ($p < .05$) an individual's usual intake of particular nutrients with reasonable precision (± 20 percent). Beaton et al. (1979) estimated that at least five replicate 24-hour recall histories would be necessary to estimate an individual's energy intake at this level of precision. Balogh et al. (1971) reported that for energy intake nine observations would be required to reach the same level of accuracy for 90 percent of the individuals in her population, and even more observations would be necessary for the estimation of protein and fat consumption.

TABLE 3 Coefficients of variation (percent)[a] of intraindividual daily dietary intakes of selected nutrients: data from 4 studies

Nutrient	Study			
	Hankin (1967) (n = 93 × 7)[b] Adults	Balogh (1971) (n = 161 × 8 to 11)	Beaton (1979) (n = 30 × 6)[c]	Todd (1983) (n = 18 × 30)
Total energy	20	19	26	26
Carbohydrate	22	22	30	
Total protein	25	32,25[d]	36	31
Fat	32	28	31	
Iron			35	
Vitamin A			147	

[a] Coefficient of variation (percent) = SD $\times$ 100/$\bar{x}$.
[b] Number of individuals $\times$ number of studies/individual.
[c] Data for males only presented.
[d] Coefficient of variation for animal protein (32 percent) and vegetable protein (25 percent) presented separately.

In addition to the day-to-day variability noted above, Yudkin (1951) described sizable week-to-week variation among six British graduate students who maintained weekly dietary records for at least four consecutive weeks. Not surprisingly, he found that different subjects varied in the extent of their variability. Comparing one week's day-to-day variation with mean week-to-week variation in the energy intake of 12 adult men, Acheson et al. (1980) found that the coefficient of variation of daily intake (26.2 percent) was substantially greater than for weekly intake (13.2 percent). They found only a minor reduction in the variability with more than one week of study.

The day of the week is often mentioned as an important determinant of dietary intake. Although intuitively it seems reasonable to expect that eating patterns change on weekends, holidays, and during special social events, the few studies that have examined this question critically have not drawn consistent conclusions. Beaton et al. (1979) reported that the day of the week contributed from 3 to 9 percent of the total variance in the intake of different nutrients for women but not for men. The importance of the day of the week disappeared when the nutrients were expressed per 1,000 Kcal rather than as absolute amounts. In other words, although the women consumed approximately 24 percent more food during one of the days of observation (Sunday), they did not alter their patterns of consumption on that day. On the other hand, Todd et al. (1983) found a significant decrease in protein intake (on the order of 11–14 percent), but not energy intake, on Saturday and Sunday among their male graduate student subjects. Despite the poor documentation of dietary changes during socially defined exceptional days, an effort should probably be made to include a representative sampling of these days in dietary studies.

Validation and comparisons of dietary study methods

As with any other scientific measuring device, it is essential to consider the accuracy with which dietary studies quantify dietary intake. Since the objective of dietary intake measurement is to determine the subject's habitual consumption, an evaluation of technique must consider both measurement accuracy and ability to contend with the multiple sources of variation. Variability was discussed above; measurement accuracy is considered here.

Since there is no convenient way to determine with certainty an individual's usual dietary intake during an extended period of time, there is no universally recognized standard against which to compare the data obtained from dietary studies. Block (1982) has recently prepared an excellent review of possible techniques to validate dietary assessment methods and the dilemmas inherent in the performance and interpretation of such validation studies. Three general types of studies have been employed to "validate" dietary methodologies. One type involves the comparison of one dietary methodology with another that is assumed to be more reliable. For example, a 24-hour recall history may be compared with food-weighings obtained on the previous day. This validation method has been criticized, however, on the grounds that the food-weighings may prompt the subject to pay greater than usual attention to his food intake, and thus to recall more accurately than if the recall method alone were used. Thus, it is generally preferable that the food intake be observed without the subject's knowledge—either in an institutional setting or with the help of a collaborative spouse or mother.

A second type of validation study has measured the reproducibility of dietary data obtained from repeated determinations using a single method. Block (1982) has emphasized the conceptual flaw underlying such studies, namely, that the investigator can never be sure whether dietary intake is truly constant during the period of repeated measurements. Thus, poorly reproducible data may indicate a faulty data collection instrument or a real change in dietary intake.

Another way to evaluate dietary study instruments is to compare the intake data, as estimated by the dietary study, with some related physiological parameter. Since the urinary excretion of nitrogen and sodium, for example, is related to the level of intake, dietary data could be compared semiquantitatively with the excreted amounts of such selected nutrients. This type of comparison has been carried out infrequently (Borgstrom et al., 1975; Dahl, 1961; Huse et al., 1974; Isaksson, 1980; Johnstone et al., 1981).

Because of the conceptual problems associated with the second type of validation study and the availability of only limited data from the third, this review concentrates on those studies that have been undertaken to compare dietary methodologies. Comparative studies have usually related the findings from one or more retrospective techniques, such as the 24-hour recall or dietary history, to data obtained from food diaries or food-weighings, assuming that the prospective observations are more accurate. The most interesting comparative studies are those in which an observer monitored the subjects' intake without their knowledge and another dietitian later interviewed the subjects to record their perceived intake. Madden et al. (1976) compared the 24-hour recall data obtained from a group of elderly North Americans participating in a community meal plan with their clandestinely observed, actual intake. With the exception of energy consumption, which was underestimated by 10 percent ($p < 0.05$), there was no significant difference between the group mean ingestion of seven nutrients as determined by either method (paired t-test, $p > 0.05$). When the individual's dietary intake data obtained from both techniques were compared by regression analysis, however, the recall history proved less accurate. The slope of the linear regression of recall data on actual intake data was significantly less than one for energy, protein, and vitamin A. This phenomenon was described as the "flat-slope syndrome," or "talking a good diet." Thus, individuals who consumed less than the mean tended to overestimate their intake and vice-versa. The authors noted that this phenomenon would tend to produce false negative results when differences were sought in the intake of two populations or when evaluating the impact of a feeding intervention program.

In a similar study, Gersovitz (1978) compared the data from both a recall history and a seven-day record with the observed amounts consumed by elderly individuals. The findings were generally similar to the studies of Madden et al. described above. Interestingly, recall data obtained approximately three hours after the meal were no more accurate than the results of 24-hour recalls. As with the recall histories, the seven-day record yielded results similar to the observed intakes for the grouped data except for energy, which was significantly underestimated by the record. The regression analyses of the dietary records indicated that they provided acceptably accurate information about the individuals' intake during the first two days of recordkeeping, but with increased days of study, the concordance of data from the two types of studies began to deteriorate.

An earlier study by Young et al. (1952), which compared 24-hour recall data with results from seven-day records and dietary histories, also indicated that the group means for the recall data and the dietary records were similar, but the data for individual intakes were not reliable. The dietary history, on the other hand, yielded consistently higher values than the other methods, even for grouped data. The actual (observed) intake was not determined in these studies. A more recent study by Morgan et al. (1978) similarly compared a 24-hour recall history, a four-day diary, and a detailed dietary history administered to 100 adult Canadian women. Again, the recall histories and four-day records yielded similar results for average intakes of energy and fat, although the amounts were usually slightly less with the recall data. As with the study by Young et al. (1952), this comparison found that the dietary history produced a substantially higher estimate of average intake.

These results suggest that dietary recall histories may provide reasonably accurate average information for groups of adults, but other studies suggest that children's histories may be less dependable. Emmons and Hayes (1973) surreptitiously observed what children aged 6–12 years ate during school lunches. The observed data for food frequency and nutrient intake were used to evaluate the accuracy of subsequently recorded recall data, obtained either directly from the child or from his mother. The children were able to recall only about 60–80 percent of the primary food items consumed, but showed improved accuracy with increasing age. Certain foods like hot dogs and spaghetti were remembered more consistently than other dishes. The recalls were generally worse with secondary food items such as bread or desserts. The errors in recall occurred in both directions; that is, uneaten foods were reported, and foods consumed were forgotten. Despite these mixed results, the children nevertheless gave a more accurate history than their mothers.

Krantzler et al. (1982) compared the data obtained from recall histories and three-day or seven-day records with the discreetly observed frequency of food selection in a university cafeteria. Seven-day records were the most accurate, producing 87 percent food item agreement. Three-day records and six-hour recalls were intermediate; 24-hour recalls were least accurate (69 percent agreement). Both under- and overreporting were discovered. Foods consumed during breakfast, foods eaten regularly, and those contributing the major part of the meal were better reported; snacks and garnishes were most often underreported.

A final validation study, which measured dietary energy intake by self-administered food-weighings, self-administered written recall histories, or calorimetric analyses of duplicate diets (corrected for nonmetabolizable energy), was reported by Acheson et al. (1980), working in an isolated Antarctic base. Despite the fact that the subjects weighed their own food intakes for the periods covered by the 24-hour recall histories—a fact that theoretically should have aided their memories—they underestimated their energy intake by 21 percent as compared with the food-weighings. The subjects both omitted food items from recall histories and underestimated the portion sizes. The discrepancy between these results and those reported previously may be related to the fact that in the earlier studies dietitians "probed" their informants to help them remember all possible meal items and snacks consumed. The comparison of food-weighings with the calorimetric data produced better agreement during the 96 one-week studies. The results from the food-weighings were 6.7 percent or 4.6 percent greater than from the duplicate diets, depending on which nutrient–energy conversion factors were employed.

Taken as a whole, the results of these and other studies indicate that quantitative, prospective methods for measuring food consumption provide the best estimates of actual intake when the study subjects are sufficiently educated and motivated to comply with the technical demands of the study instrument. Although recall histories provide reliable estimates of the average nutrient intake of groups of adults, such studies can produce misleading results for individuals. The recollected information is probably of better quality when obtained by a dietitian trained to probe for all items consumed during the period of recall.

Since dietary histories are meant to reflect intake during extended periods, they are necessarily more difficult to validate. The comparison method must be completed on a sufficient number of days to account for the variability of intake that occurs over time. The two studies mentioned above that compared dietary histories with one- to two-week dietary records found higher estimated intakes with the dietary history (Morgan et al., 1978; Young et al., 1952). Huenemann and Turner (1942) compared the findings from dietary history interviews with those from ten 14-day, self-administered food-weighings. None of the histories was found to agree with the corresponding dietary record within 20 percent for all nutrients. The authors concluded that "no single dietary history could be considered typical of a subject's food intake over a period of time." Jain et al. (1980) have also compared dietary history results from 16 adult men with food records kept by their spouses for 30-day periods. Mean estimates for all 13 foods and nutrients studied were from 20 percent to 60 percent higher with the dietary history than with the food records. Since positive correlations between methods were found for all nutrients, however, the authors concluded that the recorded intake could be satisfactorily predicted from the dietary history.

These limited studies do not permit a definite conclusion regarding the usefulness of the dietary history method. Nevertheless, since convincing validations are not available and the existing studies suggest that the dietary history overestimates intake, it would seem appropriate to remain skeptical of this technique.

Presentation and interpretation
of results

The nutritionist is usually interested in the subject's consumption of nutrients as well as of foods. To obtain information regarding nutrient intake, either the foods must be analyzed chemically or their nutrient contents must be calculated from food-composition tables. The latter are available for different regions of the world (Gopalan et al., 1977; Krantzler et al., 1982; Watt and Merrill, 1975). Unfortunately, the use of food-composition tables introduces further uncertainty into the dietary data, since the laboratory results presented in these tables are average data from a necessarily limited number of analyses. The nutrient contents of unprocessed agricultural products may vary with the strain of the plant, its position in the field, its size, and whether or not fertilizers were employed during cultivation. The amount of time that food is stored and the time and method of cooking may also affect the concentration of nutrients in the product as consumed. The only way to avoid this uncertainty is to analyze all of the food as consumed, a tedious, expensive, and rarely practical alternative.

Once food intake has been measured or estimated and the nutrient contents of those foods have been calculated, the data must be summarized for communication. Food amounts are usually compiled by food groups, such as cereals, fruits, dairy products, and the like. The Food and Agriculture Organization of the United Nations has suggested the use of 11 groupings (Reh, 1962), but individual investigators may choose to disaggregate the data further for particular interests. Nutrient data should be presented in terms of commonly recognized international units, both as mean or median values of intake and in terms of distribution of intakes. Standard methods of reporting dietary data have been proposed (Durnin and Ferro-Luzzi, 1982), but as yet no international agreement has been reached.

Nutrient intake data are frequently compared with nationally or internationally recommended dietary allowances. Some of the confusion engendered by such comparisons has been mentioned earlier, and has been discussed extensively by Hegsted (1975). Recently there has been increased discussion of the appropriateness of expressing nutrient requirements in terms of energy requirements (i.e., nutrient–energy ratios) rather than formulating separate requirements for different physiological groups. Again, a consensus opinion has not yet been achieved.

A final caution must be observed during the interpretation of dietary data vis-à-vis nutrient requirements. Dietary data reflect only what is consumed; they offer little or no insight into the bioavailability of the nutrients. Different foods may be more or less digestible, and their digestibility can vary according to the age of the consumer, the type of food (e.g., animal versus vegetable), the degree of food processing, and the type and duration of cooking. Furthermore, interactions among foods or nutrients in the diet may inhibit or enhance nutrient absorption. Finally, intestinal parasitosis, diarrhea, and other enteric or systemic illnesses may interfere with intestinal absorption. To resolve these issues of bioavailability of nutrients from particular diets, metabolic studies are required.

Determinants of dietary intake
of infants and children

The determinants of children's dietary intake can be classified as biological, dietary, sociocultural, and other exogenous factors, as follows:

— Biological factors: age, sex, body size, metabolic rate, activity, health status.
— Dietary factors: taste (sweetness, personal preferences, others?), energy density.
— Sociocultural factors: disposable income, parental education, parental occupation, cultural practices.
— Other "exogenous factors": geographic region, climate (season).

Newborns and young children eat primarily in response to hunger and thirst, but the foods made available to them are obviously determined by their caretakers. Biological factors that influence children's metabolic needs and/or sensation of hunger are age, sex, body size, basal metabolic rate, activity, and state of health. Whitehead et al. (1981, 1982) have recently reviewed multiple studies of age- and sex-related changes in the energy intake of infants and children from selected North American and European countries. As expected, the absolute energy intakes increased with age; at each age energy consumption was greater among boys than girls. Although the weanlings included in our studies in rural Bangladesh consumed substantially less than those reported from studies in the technologically more advanced countries, similar age- and sex-related patterns were noted (Brown et al., 1982b).

The metabolic rate of children is directly proportional to their body size, especially when size is expressed in terms of length or surface area. Other factors being equal, bigger children thus tend to eat more. When dietary intake is expressed per kilogram of body weight, however, smaller children generally have larger intakes, possibly because a higher proportion of their body weight is metabolically active tissue and/or because their rates of growth are more accelerated.

Nutrient requirements are often affected by disease, especially by diseases that induce malabsorption or fever (Beisel, 1977; Brown and Black, 1981; Rosenberg et al., 1977). Although increased dietary intake could theoretically compensate for these elevated requirements, the disease may concurrently interfere with dietary intake, either by causing anorexia or through changes in feeding practices. Martorell (1980), for example, has reported an average reduction of nearly 20 percent in the daily intake of Guatemalan village children in association with the common symptoms of diarrhea, "illness-induced apathy," and respiratory infections.

Fomon et al. (1977) have systematically examined the effects of dietary factors on the levels of infants' food consumption. They compared the energy consumption of infants between 4 and 6 months of age who were fed either a commercially available cow's milk formula (67 Kcal/dl) or a vitamin- and linoleic acid–fortified skim milk (36 Kcal/dl). The infants randomized to skim milk feedings consumed significantly more volume but received less energy from their formula. They also tended to eat more solid foods, but those differences were not statistically significant. Interestingly, the infants fed skim milk gained significantly less weight and had a significant decrease in mean triceps and subscapular skinfold thicknesses; there was no difference in length increments between dietary groups.

The same group of investigators also studied the effects of sweetness, saltiness, and the relative proportion of dietary energy as carbohydrate or fat on the volumes and amounts of energy consumed by infants. Infants who received isoenergetic formulas in which the carbohydrate was supplied either as sucrose (sweet) or as a cornstarch hydrolysate (bland) during alternate feeding periods consistently consumed more of the sweeter diet (Fomon et al., 1983). On the other hand, no differences in intake were observed when the salt content of strained infant foods was varied (Fomon et al., 1970). Finally, when the percentages of energy provided by fat (60 percent) and carbohydrates (31 percent) were reversed, no differences in intake or weight gain occurred (Fomon, 1980).

In another fascinating series of long-term studies, Davis observed the self-selection of foods by three weanlings. A large variety of preweighed foods was placed on each child's tray for ad libitum consumption (Davis, 1928). She found that the children were able to select their own foods in quantities sufficient to maintain themselves nutritionally for extended periods of time. Children as young as 8 months of age rapidly indicated preferences for specific foods. They tended to "eat in waves," preferring to eat relatively large amounts of one kind of food for a number of days and then switching to some other food. Several solid foods were usually taken at each meal and liquids were drunk intermittently. No clear preference between raw and cooked food was detectable, although cooked cereals and raw (or rare) meats tended to be selected. The author concluded—despite the limited number of subjects studied—that the self-selection of simple, natural foods by weanlings was a safe means of alimentation.

Sociocultural determinants of children's dietary intake include the family's disposable income, parental education and occupation, and cultural practices. Whereas cropping patterns and the time and quality of the harvest often determine food availability for the family of the subsistence farmer, disposable income and food prices largely determine the amount and types of foods consumed by poorer families in market economies. In urban Peru, for example, total dietary energy intake, as well as the proportion of energy consumed as fat and animal protein, increased with greater per capita expenditure for food (Graham et al., 1981). Calcium, riboflavin, carotene, and vitamin C intakes were also greater in economically advantaged children, largely because of their increased consumption of cow's milk, fruits, and vegetables. Thus, the diets improved qualitatively as well as quantitatively with increased expenditure for food.

The parents' occupations may be an important determinant of dietary intake since this factor will influence the availability of food to the family. The fisherman is more likely to supply his family with fish, and the farmer is more likely to provide the crops harvested from his own fields. This assumption is not always valid, however. Sadly, we have seen children of vegetable gardeners with severe xerophthalmia; the marketable produce was all sold so that rice could be purchased. Parental education may also influence the foods made available to children. Higher rates of breastfeeding have been reported for better educated North American woman, but the opposite may be true in less developed countries (Dodd and Smith, 1982). Similarly, cultural attitudes may encourage the consumption of specific foods and impose taboos on the use of others. These attitudes often have no scientifically evident nutritional or health basis, but can be powerful determinants of consumption patterns.

Other exogenenous factors such as geographic region and climate are major determinants of food availability and, hence, dietary intake. Rice is generally consumed in the humid tropics, while millets are more frequently eaten in arid regions. Mountain people are limited to barley and potatoes at the highest altitudes, but a variety of cereals can be produced in lowland valleys. Unless a relatively sophisticated marketing system has been developed, the inhabitants of a particular ecological zone consume only what can be produced locally. Similarly, there may be dramatic differences in the types and amounts of food available in different seasons. Despite their limited diet, even weanlings are subjected to seasonal fluxes in food availability. In Bangladesh we found that not only did the availability of various staple foods change seasonally, but the consumption of breastmilk varied significantly throughout the year (Brown et al., unpublished). Seasonal changes in breastmilk consumption have also been reported in West Africa (Prentice et al., 1981b). Although the nutritional impact of the seasonal scarcity of some items may be partially mitigated by the availability of other foods, periods of relative nutrient deprivation nevertheless occur.

Conclusions

Studies of dietary intake are necessary to determine the availability of food to individuals and households and its level of consumption by individuals and groups. The methods used to measure dietary intake must be determined in part by the objectives of the study, as well as by the level of financial and human resources at the disposal of the project. Methods include prospective evaluations completed either by the study subject or by an observer, and retrospective assessments using a variety of study instruments. Prospective studies generally provide more reliable quantitative information—especially for individuals—but are costlier and logistically more difficult to complete. In all cases (except for the dubiously reliable dietary history), multiple studies are necessary to estimate the usual intake of an individual with a reasonable degree of confidence, because of the substantial day-to-day variation in intake. Fewer studies are required to determine the usual consumption patterns of groups of individuals.

Practical considerations regarding the implementation of field studies, as well as special problems encountered during the assessment of infants and children, have been described. The interpretation and limitations of dietary information have also been discussed. The principal determinants of the dietary intake of children, including their biological requirements, dietary factors, and social, cultural, geographic, and climatic issues, must all be considered when planning studies and interpreting dietary information.

References

Acheson, K. J., I. T. Campbell, et al. 1980. "The measurement of food and energy intake in man—an evaluation of some techniques," *American Journal of Clinical Nutrition* 33: 1147–1154.

Aranda-Pastor, J., M. T. Mencher, et al. 1978. "Planning a food and nutrition surveillance system: The example of Honduras," *American Journal of Public Health* 68: 748–750.

Balogh, M., H. A. Kahn, and J. H. Medalie. 1971. "Random repeat 24-hour dietary recalls," *American Journal of Clinical Nutrition* 24: 304–310.

Beaton, G. H. 1976. "Food fortification," in *Nutrition in Preventive Medicine*, ed. G. H. Beaton and J. M. S. Bengoa. Geneva: World Health Organization.

———, J. Milner, et al. 1979. "Sources of variance in 24-hour dietary recall data: Implications for nutrition study design and interpretation," *American Journal of Clinical Nutrition* 32: 2546–2559.

———, J. Milner, et al. 1983. "Sources of variance in 24-hour dietary recall data: Implications for nutrition study design and interpretation. Carbohydrate sources, vitamins, and minerals," *American Journal of Clinical Nutrition* 37: 986–995.

Beisel, W. R., ed. 1977. "Symposium on the impact of infections on nutritional status of the host," *American Journal of Clinical Nutrition* 30: 1203ff and 1439ff.

Block, G. 1982. "Review of validations of dietary assessment methods," *American Journal of Epidemiology* 115: 492–505.

Borgstrom, B., A. Norden, et al. 1975. "A study of the food consumption by the duplicate portion technique in a sample of the Dalby, Sweden population," *Scandinavian Journal of Social Medicine* 10: 1–95.

Brown, K. H., and R. E. Black. 1981. "The nutritional cost of infections," Symposia from the XII International Congress of Nutrition. New York: Alan R. Liss, Inc., pp. 467–477.

———, R. E. Black, et al. 1982a. "Clinical and field studies of human lactation: Methodological considerations," *American Journal of Clinical Nutrition* 35: 745–756.

———, R. E. Black, et al. 1982b. "Consumption of foods and nutrients by weanlings in rural Bangladesh," *American Journal of Clinical Nutrition* 36: 878–889.

———, R. E. Black, et al. Unpublished. "Longitudinal studies of infectious diseases and physical growth in rural Bangladesh: Seasonal changes in the consumption of food and nutrients by weanlings."

Burke, B. 1947. "The dietary history as a research tool," *Journal of the American Dietetic Association* 23: 1041–1046.

Coward, W. A., M. B. Sawyer, et al. 1979. "New method for measuring milk intakes in breast-fed babies," *Lancet* ii: 13–14.

Creed, H. M., and G. G. Graham. 1980. "Determinants of growth among poor children: Food and nutrient intakes," *American Journal of Clinical Nutrition* 33: 715–722.

Dahl, L. K. 1961. "Possible role of chronic excess salt consumption in the pathogenesis of essential hypertension," *American Journal of Cardiology* 8: 571–575.

Davis, C. M. 1928. "Self selection of diet by newly weaned infants," *American Journal of Diseases of Children* 36: 651–679.

Dodd, D. A., and N. M. Smith, eds. 1982. *The International Breast Feeding Compendium,* Vol. 2. Columbus: Ross Laboratories.

Durnin, J. V. G. A., and A. Ferro-Luzzi. 1982. "Conducting and reporting studies on human energy intake and output: Suggested standards," *American Journal of Clinical Nutrition* 35: 624–626.

Emmons, L., and M. Hayes. 1973. "Accuracy of 24-hour recalls of young children," *Journal of the American Dietetic Association* 62: 409–415.

FAO/WHO Expert Committee. 1973. *Energy and Protein Requirements.* Geneva: World Health Organization, Technical Report Series No. 522.

Flores, M. 1962. "Dietary studies for assessment of the nutritional status of populations in nonmodernized societies," *American Journal of Clinical Nutrition* 11: 344–355.

Fomon, S. J. 1980. "Factors influencing food consumption in the human infant," *International Journal of Obesity* 4: 348–350.

———, L. N. Thomas, and L. J. Filer. 1970. "Acceptance of unsalted strained foods by normal infants," *Journal of Pediatrics* 76: 242–246.

———, L. N. Thomas, et al. 1971. "Food consumption and growth of normal infants fed milk-based formulas," *Acta Paediatrica Scandinavica,* Supplement 223.

———, L. J. Filer, et al. 1977. "Skim milk in infant feeding," *Acta Paediatrica Scandinavica* 66: 17–30.

———, E. E. Ziegler, et al. 1983. "Sweetness of diet and food consumption by infants," *Proceedings of the Society for Experimental Biology and Medicine* 173: 190–193.

Frank, G. C., G. S. Berenson, and L. S. Webber. 1978. "Dietary studies and the relationship of diet to cardiovascular disease risk factor variables in ten year old children: The Bogalusa Heart Study," *American Journal of Clinical Nutrition* 31: 328–340.

Garn, S. M., F. A. Larken, and P. E. Cole. 1976. "The problem with one-day dietary intakes," *Ecology of Food and Nutrition* 5: 245–247.

Gersovitz, M., J. P. Madden, and H. Smicikclas-Wright. 1978. "Validity of the 24-hour dietary recall and seven-day record for group comparisons," *Journal of the American Dietetic Association* 73: 48–55.

Gopalan, C., B. V. Rama Sastri, and S. C. Balasubramanian. 1977. *Nutritive Value of Indian Foods.* Hyderabad: National Institute of Nutrition.

Graham, G. G., H. M. Creed, et al. 1981. "Determinants of growth among poor children: Relation of nutrient intakes to expenditure for food," *American Journal of Clinical Nutrition* 34: 555–561.

Hankin, J. H., W. E. Reynolds, and S. Margen. 1967. "A short dietary method for epidemiologic studies," *American Journal of Clinical Nutrition* 20: 935–945.

Hegsted, D. M. 1975. "Dietary standards," *Journal of the American Dietetic Association* 66: 13–21.

Hueneman, R. L., and D. Turner. 1942. "Methods of dietary investigation," *Journal of the American Dietetic Association* 18: 562–568.

Huse, D. M., R. A. Nelson, et al. 1974. "Urinary nitrogen excretion as objective measure of dietary intake," *American Journal of Clinical Nutrition* 27: 771–773.

Isaksson, B. 1980. "Urinary nitrogen output as a validity test in dietary surveys," *American Journal of Clinical Nutrition* 33: 4–12.

Jain, M., G. R. Howe, et al. 1980. "Evaluation of a diet history questionnaire for epidemiologic studies," *American Journal of Epidemiology* 111: 212–219.

Jelliffe, D. B. 1966. *The Assessment of the Nutritional Status of the Community*. Geneva: World Health Organization, Monograph Series No. 53.

Johnstone, F. D., M. C. Brown, et al. 1981. "Measurement of variables: Data quality control," *American Journal of Clinical Nutrition* 34: 804–806.

Krantzler, N. J., B. J. Mullen, et al. 1982. "Validity of telephoned diet recalls and records for assessment of individual food intake," *American Journal of Clinical Nutrition* 36: 1234–1242.

Leung, W. T. W., and M. Flores. 1970. *Tabla de composición de alimentos para uso en America Latina*. Guatemala City: INCAP.

Liu, K., J. Stamler, et al. 1978. "Statistical methods to assess and minimize the role of intra-individual variability in obscuring the relationship between dietary lipids and serum cholesterol," *Journal of Chronic Diseases* 31: 399–418.

Lubbe, A. M. 1968. "A survey of the nutritional status of white school children in Pretoria: Description and comparative study of two dietary survey techniques," *South African Medical Journal* 42: 616–622.

Madden, J. P., S. J. Goodman, and H. A. Guthrie. 1976. "Validity of the 24-hour recall," *Journal of the American Dietetic Association* 68: 143–147.

Marr, J. W. 1971. "Individual dietary surveys: Purposes and methods," *World Review of Nutrition and Dietetics* 13: 105–164.

Martorell, R., C. Yarbrough, et al. 1980. "The impact of ordinary illnesses on the dietary intake of malnourished children," *American Journal of Clinical Nutrition* 33: 345–350.

Mason, J. B. 1976. "Surveillance and prediction of food shortages and malnutrition," *Annales de la Société Belge de Medecine Tropicale* 56: 253–261.

Morgan, R. W., M. Jain, et al. 1978. "A comparison of dietary methods in epidemiologic studies," *American Journal of Epidemiology* 107: 488–498.

Pekkarinen, M. 1970. "Methodology in the collection of food consumption data," *World Review of Nutrition and Dietetics* 12: 145–171.

Posner, E. M., C. L. Borman, et al. 1982. "The validity of a telephone-administered 24-hour dietary recall methodology," *American Journal of Clinical Nutrition* 36: 546–553.

Prentice, A., A. M. Prentice, and R. G. Whitehead. 1981a. "Breast-milk fat concentrations of rural African women. 1. Short-term variation within individuals," *British Journal of Nutrition*. 45: 483–494.

———, A. M. Prentice, and R. G. Whitehead. 1981b. "Breast-milk fat concentrations of rural African women. 2. Long-term variations within a community," *British Journal of Nutrition* 45: 495–503.

Reed, R. B., and B. S. Burke. 1954. "Collections and analysis of dietary intake data," *American Journal of Public Health* 44: 1015–1026.

Reh, E. 1962. "Manual on household food consumption surveys," *FAO Food and Nutrition Series* No. 3. Rome: Food and Agricultural Organization.

Rosenberg, I. H., N. W. Solomons, and R. E. Schneider. 1977. "Malabsorption associated with diarrhea and intestinal infections," *American Journal of Clinical Nutrition* 30: 1248–1253.

Todd, K. S., M. Hudes, and D. H. Calloway. 1983. "Food intake measurement: Problems and approaches," *American Journal of Clinical Nutrition* 37: 139–146.

Trulson, M. F. 1955. "Assessment of dietary study methods. II. Variability of eating practices and determinations of sample size and duration of dietary surveys," *Journal of the American Dietetic Association* 31: 797–802.

Watt, B. K., and A. L. Merrill. 1975. "Composition of foods," *Agriculture Handbook* No 8. Washington, D.C.: US Department of Agriculture.

Whitehead, R. G., A. A. Paul, and T. J. Cole. 1981. "A critical analysis of measured food energy intake during infancy and early childhood in comparison with current international recommendations," *Journal of Human Nutrition* 35: 339–348.

————, A. A. Paul, and T. J. Cole. 1982. "Trends in food energy intakes throughout childhood from one to 18 years," *Human Nutrition/Applied Nutrition* 36: 57–62.

Young, C. M., G. C. Hagan, et al. 1952. "A comparison of dietary study methods. II. Dietary history vs seven-day record vs 24-hour recall," *Journal of the American Dietetic Association* 28: 218–221.

————, and M. F. Trulson. 1960. "Methodology for dietary surveys in epidemiological surveys. II. Strengths and weaknesses of existing methods," *American Journal of Public Health* 50: 803–814.

Yudkin, J. 1951. "Dietary surveys: Variation in the weekly intake of nutrients," *British Journal of Nutrition* 5: 177–194.

Breastfeeding Performance and Child Survival

Sandra L. Huffman

Barbara B. Lamphere

Child survival depends upon adequate nutrient intake and the ability of a child to resist or recover from infections. Breastmilk can provide the major nutrient source in a child's diet. It can also be an important contributor to the child's immunologic defense system, increasing resistance to disease. The consumption of breastmilk in place of other food sources that may be contaminated reduces the ingestion of certain infectious agents. Breastfeeding can also contribute to child survival through extending the period of postpartum anovulation, through postpartum abstinence, and by lengthening intervals between births. Enhanced birth intervals have been associated with improvements in child survival (Gray, 1981).

Breastfeeding can therefore affect child survival by its role in nutrient intake, in birth spacing, and its anti-infective properties. Although these factors appear straightforward, the association of breastfeeding and child survival depends upon external conditions facing the child. Breastmilk's role in nutrient intake is important when other products of similar nutrient quality and quantity are unavailable. The anti-infective properties of breastmilk become less important when the load of infection is low, or when health care services are available for early treatment of illness. Its effect on birth spacing is less important as other contraceptive methods become available, or if the mother's nutritional status is not negatively affected by pregnancy.

Figure 1 diagrams the mechanisms by which breastfeeding can influence child survival. (Solid lines depict definite associations; dotted lines suggest possible associations.) Although it is often assumed that breastfeeding affects only infant survival, these pathways may influence the child's health beyond the first year of life. The benefit of enhanced maternal–infant bonding associated with breastfeeding is included in the figure since it may also have an indirect effect on child survival. Mata (1983) observed a decrease in aban-

93

donment of infants in the hospital following delivery associated with increases in the proportion of breastfeeding women. There have also been reports of decreased levels of child abuse and failure to thrive among infants of mothers who breastfeed (Klaus and Kennel, 1976).

FIGURE 1   Effects of breastfeeding on child survival

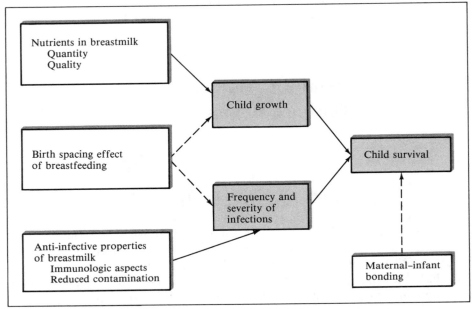

In modern societies, a direct link between breastfeeding and child survival is more difficult to discern than in developing countries. This is not to minimize the role of breastfeeding either as a nutrient source or for its anti-infective properties. Numerous nutrients available in breastmilk whose significance is as yet unknown to researchers may be important for the child's health status. For example, selenium and manganese levels vary substantially between infant formula and breastmilk (Picciano, 1983). The anti-infective properties in breastmilk may also be extremely important in developed countries for reducing morbidity, as demonstrated by a lower rate of otitis media, gastrointestinal illnesses, and allergies among breastfed infants (Cunningham, 1981). This overall impact of breastfeeding on child survival, however, is less dramatic than that seen in developing countries, where noncontaminated foods are not available to replace breastmilk, and where the load of infection is high and health care services are inadequate.

This paper reviews factors influencing the impact of breastfeeding on child survival and details issues in the measurement of the nutrient intake, anti-infective properties, and contraceptive effect of breastfeeding. The final section compares and contrasts differential effects of breastfeeding in a variety of socioeconomic and cultural settings, underlining the need for a clearer understanding of mechanisms of action in general and in specific settings before policy recommendations can be made. It would be simple to say that breastfeeding is beneficial and that all women should breastfeed their infants for at least 6 months. But this simple dictum cannot always be followed. The pressures in societies undergoing modernization mitigating against breastfeeding are often practical as much as psychological or political. Thus, it is argued here, a better understanding of what benefits breastfeeding brings in a specific environment will help policymakers to assess its value and to identify likely problems associated with not breastfeeding in the individual setting.

Factors influencing the impact of breastfeeding

The duration of breastfeeding and timing of introduction of supplements, the pattern of suckling, the type and manner in which supplements are given, and the infection load within the environment all influence breastfeeding performance and its impact on child health and child survival.

Duration of breastfeeding

Although often treated as a dichotomous variable (a woman is either breastfeeding or not, up to a particular point in time), breastfeeding should be thought of as a continuum. Influences on this continuum will be discussed below, but it is helpful first to illustrate some of the definitional problems in assessing duration of breastfeeding.

Full or exclusive breastfeeding has been defined differently depending on the researcher and on the purpose of the study. The most commonly used definition is the consumption of breastmilk as the only nutrient source except for water. Some include juice in full breastfeeding if no other foods are given (Perez et al., 1972). The least rigorous definition of full breastfeeding assumes "exclusive" breastfeeding as long as the child is not receiving a bottle, even if consuming cereals or other supplemental foods (Steckel et al., 1983). Definitions of partial breastfeeding vary accordingly.

The total duration of breastfeeding is the combination of the duration of full and partial breastfeeding. In many populations mixed feeding (both breast and bottle) is the norm, but women are reported to be breastfeeding, not bottlefeeding. As Winikoff (1981) discusses, the mixed-partial-feeding group is the most difficult to define, since it can contain very different breastfeeding patterns. For example, "such a group might include both a predominantly breastfed child given one supplementary bottle during the day when the mother is away and a child who is 'put to breast' just once a day. . . ." It is therefore evident that in discussing the effect of breastfeeding on child survival, it is important to keep in mind which type of breastfeeding is being reported and for what duration.

The determination as to when breastfeeding stops may also differ. In studies of the effect of contraceptives on milk output, Guiloff et al. (1974)

used "complete lack of secretion," while others have used the term when less than two feeds per day are given (Zanartu et al., 1976).

Another important distinction to be made refers to the use of "frequency" and "duration" of breastfeeding, meaning the proportion of women breastfeeding and the number of months breastfed, respectively. This usage of the two terms needs to be differentiated from the frequency (times per day suckled) and duration (number of minutes per feed) of breastfeeding as used to describe suckling patterns (McCann, 1981).

There is a differential effect of breastfeeding on child survival depending on the child's age. Breastfeeding's impact on child survival through its role in nutrient intake and anti-infective properties is strongest in the early months of life, and, although significant in later months, its effect is at a greatly reduced level. Butz et al. (1982) illustrated, using Malaysian data, that an additional week of full breastfeeding in the first month of life was related to a decrease in mortality of 16 deaths per thousand compared with a decrease of 1.8 deaths per thousand for ages 6–12 months.

This effect of breastfeeding on child survival appears in some cases to be primarily dependent on the duration of unsupplemented breastfeeding. For example, it was observed in the Butz study that infants who were fully breastfed during the first month of life had reduced mortality risk both in the first month and in the next 5 months of life regardless of feeding status in the latter period. Infants who survived the first 6 months had lower mortality subsequently if they were fully breastfed in the first 6 months. Plank and Milanesi (1973) found evidence of a similar protective effect of full breastfeeding at age 1 month.

Suckling pattern

The physiologic process of breastmilk production and output is dependent on the suckling process, including its frequency, intensity, and duration. We have a greater understanding of the importance of frequency than of the other two factors, both in terms of milk production and in maintenance of anovulation.

As the infant sucks at the breast, prolactin and oxytocin are released. Prolactin, the hormone necessary for milk production and secretion, is also associated with the maintenance of the anovular state. The mechanism is as yet not well understood (Delvoye and Robyn, 1980; McNeilly et al., 1980). Oxytocin is the hormone necessary for milk ejection from the breast (the let-down reflex). Its release can be inhibited or facilitated by psychological factors (Jelliffe and Jelliffe, 1982). Stress can block the release of oxytocin and prevent the let-down reflex, causing a physiologic but not anatomic inability to breastfeed.

Factors associated with suckling frequency include access of the child to the mother, occurrence of night feeds, the use of pacifiers, the practice of demand versus scheduled feedings, maternal nutritional status, and supplemental feeding practices.

With respect to the child's access to the mother, women who work outside the home have fewer opportunities to breastfeed. Seasonal activity patterns, especially in agricultural societies, can alter frequency of suckling. In Bangladesh, the suckling frequency was reduced during the peak harvest season when women were busy with rice processing activities, even though not working outside their *baris* (Chen et al., 1979). In the Gambia, women reduced breastfeeding frequency with increased demands for work in the fields (Lunn et al., 1981). Similar seasonal patterns have been observed in Zaire and Kenya (Vis et al., 1975; Hennart and Vis, 1980; Van Steenbergen et al., 1978). Sleeping patterns may also affect breastfeeding performance. Infants who sleep with their mothers at night have a greater opportunity for suckling.

Use of pacifiers and practice of scheduled rather than demand feeding also reduce frequency. Breastfeeding fulfills an instinctive need of the child for suckling, both nutritive and non-nutritive. Wolff (1967) has shown that in the early months of life, infants spend a substantial amount of time in non-nutritive suckling. Since the use of pacifiers meets much of the non-nutritive suckling need, it reduces the overall frequency of suckling at the breast. With respect to scheduling of feeds, pediatricians in developed countries often provide instructions on when (time of day) and how long (number of minutes) mothers should breastfeed. In traditional societies, suckling is more likely to be on demand and initiated by the child. For example, in Bangladesh 96 percent of the time suckling was initiated by the child (Huffman et al., 1980).

Some authors have suggested that maternal nutritional status indirectly affects suckling since a well-nourished woman may produce more breastmilk with less suckling than those who are poorly nourished (Whitehead, 1981). This was not supported by data in Bangladesh, which showed that the total amount of time spent suckling by infants aged 18–36 months did not differ by mother's weight-for-height (Huffman et al., 1980). In a Mexican study, however, supplementation of mothers' diets did seem to result in higher milk outputs and was associated with less total suckling time by infants (Chavez et al., 1975), although the major factor affecting suckling time was supplemental feeding of the infant rather than supplements to the mother's diet. In the Gambia, suckling frequency was reportedly reduced when maternal caloric intake increased (Whitehead, 1981), but this may have been related to changes in maternal activity patterns.

Bowen-Jones et al. (1982) report that when milk flow is reduced, suckling rate (sucks per second) increases, even when the baby's hunger is controlled. However, it may be that with frequent suckling as practiced in developing countries, the amount of milk secreted in each bout is less, not because of maternal malnutrition, but because of short intervals since the previous suckling episode. This is supported by data collected by Pao et al. (1980) in a study of US infants in which the volume of milk consumed per feeding was positively correlated with the interval between feeds.

Supplementing the child's diet

The type of supplements (weaning foods) and the manner in which they are given to the child affect the frequency of suckling and the duration of breastfeeding, and therefore the effect breastfeeding has on child survival.

Several studies have indicated that the use of bottles is associated with decreased suckling at the breast. Howie et al. (1981) have shown that as bottles were introduced by Scottish women for feeding infants, the total number of breastfeeds per day declined. The use of bottles was also associated with lower frequencies of suckling in studies in Iran, the United States, and Kenya (Simpson-Hebert, 1977; Kippley and Kippley, 1972; Huntington and Hostetler, 1966; Van Steenbergen et al., 1981). In studies in Chile, Steckel et al. (1983) observed that when women fed their infants milk in bottles, the duration of breastfeeding declined. Studies in the West Indies also support this effect of bottlefeeding (Gueri et al., 1978). Greiner et al. (1981) stated that "the earlier supplementation is introduced, the larger its quantity, and the more it is fed by bottle, the greater its impact on breast milk supply." Van Esterik (1977) reported that mothers in rural Thailand, when considering breastmilk supply to be inadequate, would increase it by more frequent feedings, whereas professional women would supplement infants with infant formula.

Use of bottles has also been suggested to impart greater levels of bacterial contamination to the infant due to a greater difficulty in sterilization in comparison to more easily cleaned cups or spoons (Jelliffe and Jelliffe, 1978).

Aside from how the supplement is given, the type (caloric density), amount, and frequency all influence breastfeeding performance. Frequent feedings with calorically dense foods make the child less dependent on breastmilk for nutrient needs. In developed countries, the most common supplements to breastmilk are cow's milk and formula, both nutrient-dense products easily consumed by infants. In developing countries, when milk is given, it is often diluted (Surjono et al., 1980). Paps or gruels fed to the child are also inadequate in calories to meet the child's nutrient needs. Breastmilk therefore often continues to be the principal source of nutrients for the first few years of life. For example, in Bangladesh, Brown et al. (1982b) have shown that breastmilk provides 50 percent of calories at 2 years of age.

When supplemental foods are inadequate because of low frequency of feeding and caloric density, they are less likely to interfere with suckling. In the Gambia, Zaire, and among the !Kung, where supplementation is begun early but only provides a small part of daily nutrient requirements, suckling frequency is high. In Zaire, the frequency of breastfeeding and the amount of milk consumed did not differ between infants aged less than 6 months receiving supplements and those fully breastfeeding (Hennart and Vis, 1980). The lack of adequate supplementation of breastmilk after 4–6 months postpartum is associated, however, with poor child nutritional status.

The hygienic properties of the supplement contribute to the effect on child survival. Studies of the bacterial content of food and water have illustrated the high level of weaning-food contamination in developing countries. In a study in the Gambia, Barrell and Rowland (1979) found the significant factor was not the type of food prepared, but the conditions under which it was prepared: unboiled water used to prepare foods and to wash bowls and utensils was heavily contaminated with fecal coliforms. Metal bowls and utensils were found to have infective levels of bacteria after being scrubbed with well water and palm leaves and left to dry. They also noted a seasonal variation in the level of contamination. They concluded that a large percentage of foods eaten by infants were contaminated with bacteria to an unacceptable level, even after thorough cooking. Studies in Bangladesh and Indonesia had similar findings (Surjono et al., 1980; Black et al., 1982).

In addition to contamination of water and food, spread of pathogens through contact with the mother is also probable. Studies in Bangladesh have illustrated relatively high levels of rotavirus and *shigella* on the hands of some mothers (Samadi et al., 1983; Khan, 1982). Such contamination may cause infection of food sources or direct infection of the child through bodily contact.

Infection load in the environment

Aside from the direct contamination of supplemental foods, the general level of environmental contamination and prevalence of infectious diseases determine the extent to which breastfeeding performance can influence child survival. When the infection load is high, the immunologic protection provided by breastmilk is more important than when few infectious agents are evident. Availability of water reduces infection load by diluting and washing away the infectious agents. Adequate sanitation facilities help ensure the removal from the environment of infectious agents. Recent studies also have shown the high general level of environmental contamination in poor households and its effect on levels of contaminants on women's hands and breasts (Brunser, 1983). Use of soap in hand washing has been shown to reduce spread of disease in families exposed to shigellae (Khan, 1982).

The interaction between the practice of breastfeeding and water/sanitation availability is shown by Butz et al. (1982) in Malaysia. For children not fully breastfed in the first month of life, the mortality rate in the next 5 months was 94.7 deaths per thousand if no toilet or piped water was available. This rate was reduced to 81.6 deaths per thousand if piped water was present, to 17.3 if there was a toilet, and to 4.2 when both were present in the household. The effects on child survival of the presence of piped water and toilet sanitation are strongest where children are breastfed little or not at all.

Health care services can mediate the effects of high infectious loads. Immunization can protect children from certain infections that antibodies in breastmilk also protect against. Treatment of illnesses can reduce the detrimental impact, both on nutritional status and severity of morbidity (McCord and Kielmann, 1978), and thus may reduce any noticeable effect breastfeeding could have.

Supplementation of the child's diet affects the quantity of breastmilk consumed, the child's total nutrient intake, and the level at which pathogens are introduced to the child's gastrointestinal tract. The general infection load in the environment and availability of health care services affect the frequency and severity of illnesses, and therefore the impact that breastmilk can have on preventing or reducing the severity of such illnesses.

Measuring the impact
of breastfeeding

With this background in mind, the measurement issues involved in assessing breastfeeding performance can be discussed. We will examine the direct and indirect measurements of (1) nutrient intake in relation to quantity of breast-milk, (2) the anti-infective properties of breastmilk, and (3) the contraceptive effect of breastfeeding through postpartum anovulation, abstinence, and birth spacing. Measurement of breastmilk quality will not be considered here. Good reviews of the problems entailed can be found in Allen (1983) and Chandra (1982).

Nutrient intake

The question is whether an infant's nutritional needs are being met by breast-feeding and for how long. Several methods of measuring infant milk intake and lactation performance have been used with varying success. Expression of milk from the breast and the use of the Doppler Ultrasound flowmeter are direct measures of breastmilk output. Test weighing of the infant pre and post feed and measurement of total body water by deuterium oxide breakdown in the saliva are more indirect methods of measuring breastmilk intake. Child growth while on a diet of only breastmilk can in itself be a measure of the adequacy of breastmilk intake, although many other factors come into play. Self-reports of breastmilk production have also been used. The focus here is on methods that are practical for field use in determining lactation perfor-mance.

Mechanical measures The most direct method of determining how much breastmilk can be produced by a woman is the mechanical expression of milk from the breast and its measurement. However, this may not be a true indicator of the quantity of milk received by the child during suckling because the absence of the natural contact between the mother and her child and the resulting lack of stimulus of a baby's suckling may result in inaccurate mea-surements (Gibbs et al., 1977, as discussed by Hibberd et al., 1982).

The Doppler Ultrasound flow transducer is a fairly recent development for the measurement of lactation performance. Developed by the John Rad-cliffe Hospital, Headington, Oxford (How et al., 1979), an electronic trans-ducer is located in the tip of a latex nipple, which is attached to the mother's own nipple before breastfeeding. The intensity and pattern of suckling can be observed as feeding takes place. A small catheter may be placed behind the nipple to allow small amounts of breastmilk to be withdrawn for composition analysis. The composition of breastmilk can then be correlated with the time and intensity of suckling. Further studies are needed to indicate the feasibility of applying this method in the field and in comparing the amount of milk measured by this method to other methods.

Weighing The most commonly known method of estimating breastmilk is to weigh the baby before the breastfeeding session and immediately thereafter, the weight difference representing the amount of milk ingested. The development of electronic scales and the relative ease of training both field-workers and mothers to carry out the weighing have increased the accuracy and practicality of this method (Woolridge et al., 1982). However, the continual observation by a fieldworker, the frequent interruption for weighing, and the mother's level of compliance may all have an effect on the results of the weighings. To get a fairly accurate individual intake measurement, a 24-hour average measurement taken from samples of daily feeding is needed, placing a burden on mother, child, and investigator alike (Brown et al., 1982a).

Deuterium oxide The deuterium dilution technique offers a noninvasive approach to measuring breastmilk intake. After the infant is given a dose of deuterium in sterile water, two saliva samples are taken at intervals up to 14 days to estimate intake of milk through measurement of total body water by deuterium oxide breakdown in the saliva. The method does not interfere with feeding habits or maternal lifestyle nor does it depend on the mother's expertise. However, it may be less accurate when other sources of water are given to the infant, such as in supplemental foods (Butte et al., 1983). In addition, concern has been raised about biological effects on the child's health (Baum and Dobbing, 1979).

Child growth Adequate child growth while on a diet of breastmilk is only an indirect measurement of the quantity and quality of breastmilk intake. Delgado et al. (1982), in a study of four rural villages in Guatemala, suggested effects of maternal nutritional status on milk output since supplementing the diets of lactating women had a positive effect on the growth of infants during the first two trimesters of life. Murray and Murray (1979) stated that breastmilk output was adequate in their study of undernourished Nigerian mothers since they were able to provide breastmilk for normal growth comparable to US standards. In studies of the effect of contraceptive methods on milk output, several researchers have used weight changes as indicators of breastmilk production (Kaern, 1967; Koetsawang et al., 1972; Kora, 1969; Miller and Hughes, 1970, as discussed by Hull, 1981).

Adequate child growth as a measure of breastfeeding performance may be confounded by many factors that influence growth, such as supplemental feeding, infection, health status, and environmental factors. Therefore, measurement by child growth should be used only when these other factors can be controlled.

Subjective impressions have also been used in some studies to assess changes in milk production (Guiloff et al., 1974; Kamal et al., 1969; Koetsawang et al., 1972; Parveen et al., 1977), alone or in conjunction with other measures.

Anti-infective properties of breastmilk

Discussion of the measurement of the anti-infective properties of breastmilk needs to take into account both the direct benefit of the immunologic and other properties in breastmilk, and the indirect effect of the nearly sterile breastmilk contrasted to the possibility of contaminated breastmilk substitutes. The anti-infective properties (including immunoglobulins, lysozyme, the bifidus factor, and lactoferrin) can be measured directly through the assessment of hormonal or cellular components of breastmilk, or indirectly through the study of morbidity of infants with various feeding patterns.

Direct measures Studies that attempt to measure hormonal or cellular components must be able to control for several factors. The quantity of breastmilk produced is likely to affect the amount of anti-infective components the child receives. This can cause problems in interpretation of studies if the quantity of milk collected is not clearly defined. The duration postpartum has a large effect on the concentration of anti-infective properties in the milk. Maternal malnutrition has been observed by some to affect the concentration of antibodies in breastmilk (Miranda, 1983; Cruz et al., 1982), but not by others (Carlsson et al., 1976; Reddy et al., 1977). The child's gestational age may also be associated with immunologic properties (Chandra, 1982).

Indirect measures Numerous studies have observed decreased morbidity rates (both frequency and severity) among breastfed infants compared to those partially breastfed or not breastfed at all. These effects have been seen both in the perinatal and neonatal periods and up to 2 years of age (Cunningham, 1981; Mata, 1978). Several studies have noted a lower rate of mortality or a lower proportion of deaths among breastfed infants (Woodbury, 1922; Janowitz et al., 1981; Lepage et al., 1981; Plank and Milaneski, 1973; Puffer and Serrano, 1973). Most studies find a strong inverse association between breastfeeding and the incidence of gastrointestinal illness (Kumar et al., 1981; Idris et al., 1981; Mata, 1983; Larsen and Homer, 1978; France et al., 1980; Cunningham, 1979; French, 1967). Others have noted a direct association between the practice of breastfeeding and the nutritional status of the child (Kanaaneh, 1972).

Several investigators have noted a decreased prevalence of respiratory illness with the practice of breastfeeding, but when maternal education and family living standards were controlled, this association was no longer significant (Fergusson et al., 1978 and 1981). Frank et al. (1982) noted that when viral infection was documented by culture and serologic tests in US bottlefed and breastfed children, rates of respiratory infection were similar, but breastfeeding may have lessened the severity of illness. The advantage of the Frank study is that in contrast to mothers' reports or hospital admissions data (which may be biased dependent upon maternal care variables), the testing of viral infection was independent.

The problems with using morbidity or mortality as the end point to assess the impact of breastfeeding on health are well discussed by Winikoff (1981). Mortality is affected by social, economic, and medical factors, the historical period, geographic location, and other environmental factors. It is difficult to obtain reliable data on mortality differences if sample sizes are small, since death is a relatively rare event. As for morbidity, such data are difficult to gather accurately due to recall problems, subjective judgments needed to assess severity of illness, and the relationship between recorded illnesses and access to medical care (Winikoff, 1981).

Numerous other methodological issues arise when attempts are made to assess the effect of breastfeeding on morbidity. Sauls (1979) summarizes these issues as:

1 Self-selection bias: women who breastfeed may be different from those who bottlefeed in characteristics (such as socioeconomic status, education) that affect morbidity.

2 Initially breastfed infants can become bottlefed due to factors associated with health, but the opposite is not true.

3 Maternal recognition of disease may be different for breastfeeders than for bottlefeeders (Berksonian bias).

The major factor affecting the relation between breastfeeding performance and child survival is the first listed above: women who breastfeed may have characteristics that differ from those of women not breastfeeding. Important sociocultural, environmental, and economic factors may increase the chance of morbidity among nonbreastfeeders in developing countries. Women who choose not to breastfeed may also have different infant care practices (in terms of treatment of illness, hygiene habits, etc.). However, in research on women of the same socioeconomic class, consistent advantages in the lessened morbidity or mortality associated with breastfeeding have been shown.

Winikoff (1981) suggests that the last two factors listed above could affect the results in the opposite direction, reducing the impact of bottlefeeding rather than enhancing that of breastfeeding on morbidity. For example, mothers who breastfeed may be more aware than bottlefeeders of slight changes in the health of their infants and therefore more likely to report illnesses.

A major methodologic issue relates to the discontinuance of breastfeeding due to child death. Since the cause of not breastfeeding is child death and not the reverse, failure to consider this effect can result in overestimates of the effect of breastfeeding on survival. Based on results from studies in Malaysia, Butz et al. (1982) state that spurious correlations between infant mortality and the duration of breastfeeding can produce large overestimates of the mortality-inhibiting effects of breastfeeding.

Contraceptive effect of breastfeeding

Through associated hormonal changes, breastfeeding causes a delay in the resumption of ovulation in the postpartum period. To a much lesser extent, it may also be associated with delays in conception once ovulation occurs, perhaps due to shortened luteal phases of the menstrual cycle or to problems with implantation of the fertilized ovum (Howie and McNeilly, 1982).

Anovulation The frequency of suckling appears to be the major factor affecting the period of anovulation. Because of the difficulties in measuring ovulation under field conditions, the period of anovulation is usually estimated by the duration of postpartum amenorrhea. Studies are currently being conducted by Gray and colleagues to develop field techniques to determine exactly when postpartum ovulation occurs.

The length of amenorrhea is measured directly by retrospective data on length of amenorrhea during the last closed birth interval, or data on menstrual status in the current open birth interval, or the combination of the two. Measurement of the last closed birth interval requires a sample of women having experienced at least two births, since the interval is defined by the birth occurring prior to the last birth. Open birth interval measurement includes women with at least one birth, since it relates to the status associated with the last birth.

Problems involved with using retrospective data on the last closed birth interval include age heaping and the inclusion of only those women with at least two births. The latter causes a strong downward bias in the estimate, since women with shorter than average intervals are more likely to be included in the sample. The use of the current open interval has the opposite bias, since women with long intervals are more likely to have them currently open (Lesthaeghe, 1982). Figure 2 illustrates these differences for the duration of breastfeeding. Page et al. (1982) suggest the use of data for all births in a fixed period preceding the survey, a period that exceeds the duration studied for most women. The problems involved in using this method include recall errors in reporting the duration of amenorrhea, children that died, and birth dates. It is also important that postpartum bleeding be differentiated from resumption of menses. However, these problems exist in the use of the open and closed interval analyses as well.

Estimates based on suckling patterns—That high frequencies of suckling are related to extended periods of amenorrhea has been observed in field studies in Bangladesh, Zaire, Kenya, the Gambia, and among the !Kung (Huffman et al., 1980; Hennart and Vis, 1980; Van Steenbergen et al., 1981; Konner and Worthman, 1980; Lunn et al., 1981).

The effect of suckling is not clear-cut since the distribution in resumption of menses among women within a population illustrates that some women with frequent suckling patterns resume menses early in the postpartum period, while others with less frequent suckling have more extended amenorrhea.

FIGURE 2 Comparison of measurement of duration of breastfeeding for 28 countries

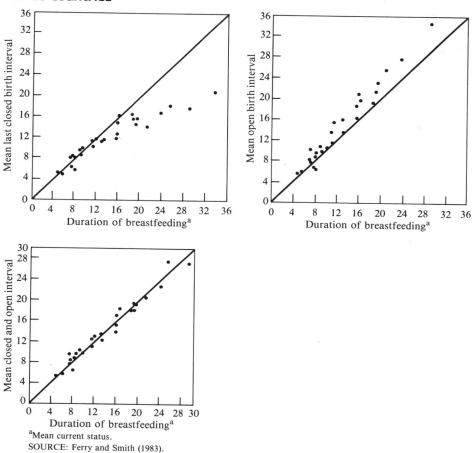

^aMean current status.
SOURCE: Ferry and Smith (1983).

However, the use of suckling frequency to determine when resumption of menses is likely to occur within a population is probably the most accurate indirect means of measurement, though not the most practical. Few studies have been able to directly observe and record suckling. Of those that have, several factors affecting suckling estimates need to be considered. The first is whether the definition of suckling frequency includes total time spent suckling, or the number of suckling bouts. When breastfeeding is on demand, frequent bouts of small duration are common. Whether each bout is defined as a separate event or, alternatively, separate bouts are combined into one event will substantially affect the number of times a woman is considered to breastfeed. Most studies do not explain how a breastfeeding event is defined, thus leaving the area open to misinterpretation.

An equally important factor in measuring frequency of suckling is whether 24-hour or lesser periods of observation are employed (8, 12 hours).

It is often assumed that the frequency of daytime feeds is similar to that of night feeds, but the validity of this assumption is open to question. Even when daytime feeds vary over a period of time, night feeds may remain constant. An important finding from studies in Kenya was that, as a child received supplements (generally through the use of bottles), daytime breastmilk output and daytime suckling decreased, whereas night suckling time and number of feeds remained fairly constant over the first year and a half (Van Steenbergen et al., 1981).

In addition to observations of suckling, self-reports by women on their frequency of suckling (either based on prospective recording or recall of the previous day's pattern or usual pattern) have also been used. These are most appropriate when discrete breastfeeding events are the practice, as is common in developed countries. However, self-reports by women in developing countries can be misleading because of lack of discrete events and because, when night feeds are included, mothers may not be awake when the child feeds.

Estimates based on duration of breastfeeding—The duration of total breastfeeding or of unsupplemented breastfeeding has been used to estimate the duration of the contraceptive effect of breastfeeding, because of their associations with suckling frequency. Populations exhibiting high suckling frequencies have extended periods of breastfeeding. Extended durations of breastfeeding are unlikely unless the child suckles frequently, because with infrequent suckling an older child is not likely to continue breastfeeding since milk supply will be too low. In a US study in which supplementation of infants was delayed until at least 5 months and no bottles were used, the observed duration of amenorrhea was 14 months. This suggests that if infants are fed without the use of bottles and the mother maintains her other "natural" breastfeeding patterns (including night feeds, no use of pacifiers, unscheduled feeds), extended amenorrhea may still result, although it would be of a shorter duration than under circumstances of poor or no supplementation (Kippley and Kippley, 1972). Recent studies in rural Mexico confirm these results: ovulation did not return among women who gave their infants supplemental foods, while continuing to suckle them more than ten times per day (Rivera, 1981).

Through the use of data on breastfeeding patterns, demographers have used mathematical formulas to estimate the duration of amenorrhea. As an example, Bongaarts's (1982) equation converts the mean duration of breastfeeding (BF) into the mean duration of amenorrhea ($Amen$):

$$Amen = 1.753e^{(0.1396BF - 0.001872BF2)}$$

Page and Lesthaeghe (1981) used logit analyses to linearize the pattern of breastfeeding and estimate the median duration of amenorrhea and the curve of its distribution. These equations illustrate on average that the effect of increases in breastfeeding duration is greatest in extending amenorrhea from about 10–24 months postpartum. Before or after this, increases in durations have lesser impacts (Bongaarts, 1982). Table 1 gives data on the proportion of children breastfed in selected developing countries and estimates of the mean duration of breastfeeding and of postpartum amenorrhea.

TABLE 1   Proportion breastfed and mean duration of breastfeeding and of postpartum amenorrhea, from World Fertility Surveys

	Proportion of children breastfed[a]	Mean duration of breast-feeding (mo.)[a]	Mean duration of amenorrhea (mo.)[b]
Bangladesh	.99	31	22
Nepal	1.00	29	21
Indonesia	.98	25	18
Sri Lanka	.98	22	16
Pakistan	.99	21	15
Kenya	.99	17	11
Jordan	.93	11	7
Thailand	.93	20	14
Malaysia	.74	8	5
Peru	.95	14	9
Mexico	.83	12	7
Colombia	.92	10	6
Panama	.80	8	5
Jamaica	.95	8	5
Costa Rica	.75	5	4

[a] Calculated based on current status data for surviving children born in last 36–48 months.
[b] Calculated from mean duration of breastfeeding, using Bongaarts's (1982) equation (see text).
SOURCE: Lesthaeghe (1982).

The measurement problems involved with these estimates are the same as those described above in relation to direct estimation of amenorrhea: age heaping, biases according to which interval (open or closed) is used, inclusion or exclusion of child deaths, and recall errors. An additional problem is that the equations use the same distribution in resumption of menses for each population, with the underlying assumption that suckling patterns are the same. As discussed previously, this in fact is not true, and thus the estimates may be off by a few months. Table 2 compares the calculated estimates of amenorrhea based on Bongaarts's equation with observed durations. As illustrated, the highest difference between the two is 3 months, suggesting a fairly close association of amenorrhea with the duration of breastfeeding on a population basis.

Postpartum abstinence Aside from the direct hormonal effect of breastfeeding on fecundity, it may also have an indirect effect because of its association with postpartum abstinence. In some populations, abstinence exceeds

TABLE 2   Observed and calculated
durations of postpartum amenorrhea

	Observed	Calculated[a]
Brazil		
Bahia	4	5
Rio Grande do Norte	3	3
Paraiba	3	4
Pernambuco	2	3
Dakar	10	13
Guatemala	15	13
Java, Indonesia	21	19
Calabar, Nigeria	9	8
Punjab, India	11	14

[a] Using Bongaarts's (1982) equation (see text).
SOURCE: Lesthaeghe (1982).

the duration of breastfeeding while in others it is shorter (Nag, 1982). Extended postpartum abstinence is seen primarily in parts of Africa, especially sub-Saharan Africa.

Schoenmaeckers et al. (1981) discuss some of the problems involved in measuring postpartum abstinence. Often the duration can be given in terms of events such as "until the child can walk" or "until the child is weaned." This taboo is often related to its effect on "poisoning breastfeed," so that some couples may practice coitus interruptus and be considered to have abstained. Because of the strong cultural proscription against intercourse, reporting errors may also be common. In addition to these problems, recall error, age heaping, and similar problems also arise.

Birth spacing and child survival   The evident association between amenorrhea and duration of breastfeeding has led to the examination of the effect on child survival of increased birth spacing caused by breastfeeding. A major concern with such analyses is that the birth spacing effect of breastfeeding is curtailed by child death, so that there is an automatic direct link between short birth intervals and preceding child death (the child dying before the short birth interval). A problem in studying the effect of birth spacing on the subsequent child (the child born following a short interval) is that a subsequent pregnancy is often the reason for stopping breastfeeding. Winikoff (1983) discusses these problems in detail.

Gray (1981) summarizes the methodological problems involved in assessing the impact of birth spacing on child survival. There is a need to control for other variables affecting birth intervals and child survival—in particular:

1 The association of age and parity with birth intervals: young, high-parity women by definition have short intervals, and they also are at risk to poor outcomes.

2 Short birth intervals may be associated with low socioeconomic which is also associated with high child mortality.

To assess the effect of breastfeeding on child survival through its birth spacing effect, it would be necessary to compare populations who stop breastfeeding early with those who stop later within the same sociocultural group, in order to control for factors other than breastfeeding that will affect death (such as morbidity experience).

Effects of modernization on the impact of breastfeeding

In attempting to make comparisons of populations undergoing changes in the duration of breastfeeding, the impact of societal factors affecting child nutrition and health must be considered.

As modernization occurs, the duration of breastfeeding is often reduced; this could have detrimental effects on child health through the pathways of decreasing nutrient intake, decreased immunologic protection, increased contamination of nutrient sources, and decreased birth spacing. These negative effects can be moderated by changes associated with modernization: increased availability of other food sources for the child; improved environmental and sanitary conditions, which reduce the infection load in the environment; enhanced health services to prevent and treat illnesses among children; and increased use of contraception as an alternative to breastfeeding for child spacing. However, when changes in breastfeeding patterns occur in the absence of such additional improvements, effects on child survival are likely to be substantial. For example, if working patterns of women cause them to abandon breastfeeding, this change is likely to reduce the probability of child survival, especially in the early months of life, unless income increases enough to counter the cost of breastmilk substitutes, and enables preparation and storage of the food in a manner preventing contamination. Among urban slum dwellers, where modernizing influences such as the advertising of infant formula may reduce prevalence of breastfeeding, child health may be negatively affected unless such practices as health care utilization or adoption of birth control are increased.

Examples of the differential effects of modernization on the impact of breastfeeding abound. In a study in rural Chile, where the average age of weaning was about 6 months, rural families with higher incomes, increased availability of running water, and some sewage system had *higher* infant mortality rates than poorer families without these amenities. The high degree of correlation between enhanced socioeconomic status and reductions in the duration of breastfeeding suggests that the improvements in socioeconomic status were unable to counteract the negative effect of early weaning. In this study, partial breastfeeding did not provide a protective effect, while full breastfeeding did (Plank and Milanesi, 1973).

The average length of breastfeeding in Malaysia is greater than in Chile, and the interaction between breastfeeding and socioeconomic status is different. In Malaysia, families with access to toilets and piped water had lower mortality rates in spite of reduced levels of breastfeeding (Butz et al., 1982). These differences suggest that the influence of breastfeeding on survival is dependent on the local ecological context, and on how the latter influences the intervening variables described in this paper, such as differences in availability of health services.

Countries that have illustrated recent declines in breastfeeding—for example, Malaysia and Thailand—have also experienced improvements in the standard of living and associated reductions in infant mortality (Butz and DaVanzo, 1978; Knodel and Debavalya, 1980). This had led some to suggest that breastfeeding is not an important factor in child survival under modernizing conditions. This paper has attempted to illustrate that in order to assess the influence of breastfeeding on survival, it is important to go beyond ecological correlations between declines in breastfeeding and changes in mortality. It is necessary to examine the many conditions affecting breastfeeding's influence on child survival, because subgroups within populations are likely to be influenced differently. Rather than implying an insignificant effect of breastfeeding on child survival, such aggregate results should encourage us to examine which factors are most important in balancing the consequences of declines in breastfeeding, and to understand how to maintain the benefits of breastfeeding in the midst of modernizing influences.

Note

We would like to thank Dr. Beverly Winikoff, Dr. George Graham, and Dr. Tina Sanghvi for their helpful comments on the paper. Support for this paper came from the Determinants of Fertility Award, provided by the Population Council (Contract Nos. CP82.36A and CP83.40A), through a contract with the US Agency for International Development.

References

Allen, L. H., 1983. "Effects of nutritional status on pregnancy and lactation." Paper presented at the Western Hemisphere Nutrition Congress VII, Miami Beach, Florida, 7–11 August.

Anderson, G. H., S. A. Atkinson, and M. H. Bryan, 1981. "Energy and macronutrient content of human milk during early lactation from mothers giving birth prematurely and at term," *American Journal of Clinical Nutrition* 34: 258–265.

Barrell, R. A. E, and M. G. M. Rowland, 1979. "Infant foods as a potential source of diarrhoeal illness in rural West Africa," *Transactions of the Royal Society of Tropical Medicine and Hygiene* 73: 85–90.

Bawn, D., and J. Dobbing, 1979. "Deuterium methods for measuring milk intake in babies," *Lancet* (11 August): 309.

Black, R. E., K. H. Brown, S. Becker, A. R. M. A. Alim, and M. H. Merson, 1982. "Contamination of weaning foods and transmission of enterotoxigenic *Escherichia coli* diarrhoea in children in rural Bangladesh," *Transactions of the Royal Society of Tropical Medicine and Hygiene* 76, no. 2: 259–264.

Blackwood, L. 1981. "Alaska native fertility trends, 1950–1978," *Demography* 18, no. 2: 173–180.

Bongaarts, J., 1983. "The proximate determinants of natural marital fertility," in *Determinants of Fertility in Developing Countries*. Vol. 1: Supply and Demand for Children, ed. R. A. Bulatao and R. D. Lee. New York: Academic Press.

Bowen-Jones, A., C. Thompson, and R. F. Drewett, 1982. "Milk flow and suckling rates during breast-feeding," *Developmental Medicine and Child Neurology* 24: 626–633.

Brown, K. H., R. E. Black, A. D. Robertson, N. A. Akhtar, G. Ahmed, and S. Becker, 1982a. "Clinical and field studies of human lactation: Methodological considerations," *American Journal of Clinical Nutrition* 35: 745–756.

———, R. E. Black, S. Becker, S. Nahar, and J. Sawyer, 1982b. "Longitudinal studies of infectious diseases and physical growth of children in rural Bangladesh: Consumption of food and nutrients by weanlings," *American Journal of Clinical Nutrition* 36: 878–889.

———, R. E. Black, and S. Becker, 1982c. "Seasonal changes in nutritional status and the prevalence of malnutrition in a longitudinal study of young children in rural Bangladesh," *American Journal of Clinical Nutrition* 36: 303–313.

Brunser, O., G. Figueroa, K. Araya, and J. Espinoza, 1983. "Infection and diarrheal disease." Paper presented at the Western Hemisphere Nutrition Congress VII, Miami Beach, Florida, 7–11 August.

Butte, N. F., C. Garza, E. O. Smith, and B. L. Nichols, 1983. "Evaluation of the deuterium dilution technique against the test-weighing procedure for the determination of breast milk intake," *American Journal of Clinical Nutrition* 37: 996–1003.

Butz, W. P., and J. DaVanzo, 1978. "Contracepting, breastfeeding and birthspacing in Malaysia: A model of decision-making subject to economic and biological constraints," *Rand Reports* (unpublished).

———, J. DaVanzo, and J. P. Habicht, 1982. "How biological and behavioral influences on mortality in Malaysia vary during the first year of life," *Population Studies* 37: 381–402.

Carlsson, B., S. Ahlstedt, L. A. Hanson, G. Lindin-Jansson, B. S. Linblad, and B. Sultana, 1976. "*Escherichia coli* O antibody content in milk from healthy Swedish mothers and mothers from a very low socio-economic group of a developing country," *Acta Paediatrica Scandinavica* 65: 417–423.

Chandra, R. K., 1982. "Immunological components of human milk, morbidity and growth," *Journal of the Canadian Dietetic Association* 43, no. 4: 293–299.

———, 1983. "Immune function at the extremes of life: In infancy and in the elderly." Paper presented at the Western Hemisphere Nutrition Congress VII, Miami Beach, Florida, 7–11 August.

Chavez, A., C. Martinez, H. Bourges, M. Coronado, M. Lopez, and S. Basta, 1975. "Child nutrition problems during lactation in poor rural areas," in *Prognosis for the Undernourished Surviving Child*, ed. A. Chavez et al. Basel: S. Karger.

Chen, L. C., S. Ahmed, M. Gesche, and W. H. Mosley, 1974. "A prospective study of birth interval dynamics in rural Bangladesh," *Population Studies* 28: 277–297.

———, A. K. M. A. Chowdhury, and S. L. Huffman, 1979. "Interaction of agriculture, dietary practices, and infection on seasonal dimensions of energy malnutrition," *Ecology of Food and Nutrition* 8: 175–187.

Coward, W. A., M. B. Sawyer, R. G. Whitehead, A. M. Prentice, and J. Evans, 1979. "New method for measuring milk intakes in breast-fed babies," *Lancet* (7 July): 13–14.

Cruz, J. R., B. Carlsson, B. Garcia, M. Gebre-Medhin, Y. Hofuander, J. J. Urrutia, and L. A. Hanson, 1982. "Studies on human milk III. Secretory IgA quantity and antibody levels against *Escherichia coli* in colostrum and milk from underprivileged and privileged mothers," *Pediatric Research* 16, no. 4, Part 1: 272–276.

Cunningham, A. S., 1979. "Morbidity in breast-fed and artificially fed infants. II," *Pediatrics* 95, no. 5: 685–689.

———. 1981. "Breastfeeding and morbidity in industrialized countries: An update," in *Advances in International Maternal and Child Health,* ed. P. B. Jelliffe and E. F. P. Jelliffe. New York: Oxford University Press, pp. 128–168.

Delgado, H. L., R. Martorell, and R. E. Klein, 1982. "Nutrition, lactation, and birth interval components in rural Guatemala," *American Journal of Clinical Nutrition* 35: 1468–1476.

———, V. E. Valverde, R. Martorell, and R. E. Klein, 1982. "Relationship of maternal and infant nutrition in infant growth," *Early Human Development* 6: 273–286.

Delvoye, P., and C. Robyn, 1980. "Breast-feeding and post partum amenorrhoea in Central America. 2: Prolactin and post partum amenorrhoea," *Journal of Tropical Pediatrics* 26: 184–189.

Drewett, R. F., and M. Woolridge, 1979. "Sucking patterns of human babies on the breast," *Early Human Development* 3/4: 315–320.

Fergusson, D. M., L. J. Horwood, F. T. Shannon, and B. Taylor, 1978. "Infant health and breast-feeding during the first 16 weeks of life," *Australia Paediatric Journal* 14: 254–258.

———, L. J. Horwood, F. T. Shannon, and B. Taylor, 1981. "Breast-feeding, gastrointestinal and lower respiratory illness in the first two years," *Australian Paediatric Journal* 17: 191–195.

Ferry, B., and D. Smith, 1983. "Breastfeeding differentials," *Comparative Studies* No. 23 (May). London: World Fertility Survey.

France, G. L., D. J. Marmer, and R. W. Steele, 1980. "Breast-feeding and *Salmonella* infection," *American Journal of Diseases of Children* 134: 147–152.

Frank, A. L., L. H. Taber, W. P. Glezen, G. L. Kasel, C. R. Wells, and A. Paredes, 1982. "Breastfeeding and respiratory virus infection," *Pediatrics* 70: 239–245.

French, J. G., 1967. "Relationship of morbidity to the feeding patterns of Navajo children from birth through twenty-four months," *American Journal of Clinical Nutrition* 20: 375–385.

Gibbs, J. H., C. Fisher, S. Bhattacharya, P. Goddard, and J. F. Bawn, 1977. "Drip breast milk: Its composition, collection, and pasteurization," *Early Human Development* 1: 227–245.

Glass, R. I., A. M. Svennerholm, B. J. Stoll, M. R. Khan, K. N. Hossain, M. I. Huq, and J. Holmgren, 1983. "Protection against cholera in breast-fed children by antibodies in breast milk," *New England Journal of Medicine* 308: 1389–1392.

Goldman, A. S., C. Garza, B. L. Nichols, and R. M. Goldblum, 1982. "Immunologic factors in human milk during the first year of lactation," *Journal of Pediatrics* 100: 563–567.

———, R. M. Goldblum, C. Garza, N. Butte, and B. Nichols, 1983. "Effects of maternal factors upon the immunologic status of the infant." Paper presented at the Western Hemisphere Nutrition Congress VII, Miami Beach, Florida, 7–11 August.

Gray, R. H., 1981. "Birth intervals, postpartum sexual abstinence and child health," in *Child Spacing in Tropical Africa: Traditions and Change,* ed. H. J. Page and R. Lesthaeghe. New York: Academic Press, pp. 93–109.

Greiner, T., P. Van Esterik, and M. Latham, 1981. "The insufficient milk syndrome: An alternative explanation," *Medical Anthropology* 5: 233–247.

Gueri, M., et al., 1978. "Breastfeeding practice in Trinidad," *Bulletin of the Pan American Health Organization* 12: 316–322.

Guiloff, E., et al., 1974. "Effect of contraception on lactation," *American Journal of Obstetrics and Gynecology* 118, no. 1: 42–45.

Hanson, L. A., and J. Winberg, 1972. "Breast milk and defence against infection in the newborn," *Archives of Disease in Childhood* 47: 845–848.

Hennart, P. H., and H. L. Vis, 1980. "Breast-feeding and post partum amenorrhoea in Central Africa. Milk production in rural areas," *Journal of Tropical Pediatrics* 26: 177–183.

Hibberd, C. M., O. G. Brooke, N. D. Carter, M. Haug, and G. Harzer, 1982. "Variation in the composition of breast milk during the first 5 weeks of lactation: Implications for the feeding of preterm infants," *Archives of Disease in Childhood* 57: 658–662.

How, T. V., M. P. Ashmore, et al., 1979. "A doppler ultrasound technique for measuring human milk flow," *Journal of Medical Engineering and Technology* 3, no. 2: 66–71.

Howie, P. W., A. S. McNeilly, M. J. Houston, A. Cook, and H. Boyle, 1981. "Effect of supplementary food on suckling patterns and ovarian activity during lactation," *British Medical Journal* 283: 757–759.

————, and A. S. McNeilly, 1982. "Contraceptive effect of breast feeding," *Journal of Tropical Pediatrics* 28: ii–iv.

Huffman, S. L., A. K. M. A. Chowdhury, J. Chakraborty, and N. Simpson, 1980. "Breast-feeding patterns in rural Bangladesh," *American Journal of Clinical Nutrition* 33: 144–153.

Hull, V. J., 1981. "The effects of hormonal contraceptives on lactation: Current findings, methodological considerations, and future priorities," *Studies in Family Planning* 12, no. 4: (April) 134–155.

Huntington, G. E., and J. A. Hostetler, 1966. "A note on nursing practices in an American isolate with a high birth rate," *Population Studies* 19: 321–324.

Idris, M. Z., S. C. Saxena, G. H. Malik, and B. C. Srivastava, 1981. "Feeding practices and diarrheal episodes among rural and urban infants of Lucknow," *Indian Pediatrics* 18: 311–316.

Janowitz, B., J. H. Lewis, A. Parnell, F. Hefnawi, M. N. Younis, and G. A. Serour, 1981. "Breast-feeding and child survival in Egypt," *Journal of Biosocial Science* 13: 287–297.

Jelliffe, D. B., and E. F. P. Jelliffe, 1978. *Human Milk in the Modern World*. Oxford: Oxford University Press.

————, and E. F. P. Jelliffe, 1982. "Maternal nutrition, breastfeeding and contraception," *British Medical Journal* 285: 806–807.

Kaern, T., 1967. "Effect of an oral contraceptive immediately postpartum on initiation of lactation," *British Medical Journal* 3: 644–646.

Kamal, I., F. Hefnawi, M. Ghoneim, M. Talaat, N. Yainis, A. Tagui, and M. Abdalla, 1969. "Clinical, biochemical, and experimental studies in lactation. I. Lactation pattern in Egyptian women," *American Journal of Obstetrics and Gynecology* 105: 314–323.

Kanaaneh, H., 1972. "The relationship of bottle feeding to malnutrition and gastoenteritis in a pre-industrial setting," *Journal of Tropical Pediatrics* 18: 302–306.

Khan, M. U., 1982. "Interruption of Shigellosis by handwashing," *Transactions of the Royal Society of Tropical Medicine and Hygiene* 76, no. 2: 164–168.

Kippley, S. K., and J. F. Kippley, 1972. "The relation between breastfeeding and amenorrhea: Report of a survey," *Journal of Obstetric, Gynecologic and Neonatal Nursing* 1: 15–21.

Klaus, M. H., and J. H. Kennel, 1976. *Maternal-Infant Bonding: The Impact of Early Separation on Loss of Family Development*. St. Louis: C. V. Mosby Co.

Knodel, J., and N. Debavalya, 1980. "Breastfeeding in Thailand: Trends and differentials, 1969–79," *Studies in Family Planning* 11, no. 12 (December): 355–377.

Koetsawang, S., T. Chiemprajert, and P. Kochananda, 1972. "The effects of injectable contraceptives on lactation." Clinical proceedings of the IPPF Southeast Asia and Oceania Medical and Scientific Congress, Sydney, Australia, 14–18 August, pp. 84–89.

Konner, M., and C. Worthman, 1980. "Nursing frequency, gonadal function, and birth spacing among !Kung hunter-gatherers," *Science* 207: 788–791.

Kora, S. J., 1969. "Effect of oral contraceptives on lactation," *Fertility and Sterility* 20, no. 3: 419–423.

Kumar, V., L. Kumar, and P. Diwedi, 1981. "Morbidity related to feeding pattern in privileged urban and under privileged rural infants," *Indian Journal of Pediatrics* 18: 743–749.

Larsen, S. A., and D. R. Homer, 1978. "Relation of breast versus bottle feeding to hospitalization for gastroenteritis in a middle-class U.S. population," *Journal of Pediatrics* 92, no. 3: 417–419.

Lauber, E., and M. Reinhardt, 1979. "Studies on the quality of breastmilk during 23 months of lactation in a rural community of the Ivory Coast," *American Journal of Clinical Nutrition* 32: 1159–1173.

Lepage, P., C. Munyakazi, and P. Hennart, 1981. "Breastfeeding and hospital mortality in children in Rwanda," *Lancet* (22 August): 409–411.

Lesthaeghe, R., 1982. "Lactation and lactation-related variables, contraception and fertility: An overview of data problems and world trends." Presented at the WHO/NRC Workshop on Breastfeeding and Fertility Regulation: Current Knowledge and Programme Policy Implications, Geneva, Switzerland, February.

Lozoff, B., and G. Brittenham, 1979. "Infant care: Cache or carry," *Pediatrics* 95, no. 3: 478–483.

Lucas, A., P. J. Lucas, and J. D. Baum, 1979. "Pattern of milk flow in breast-fed infants," *Lancet* (14 July): 57–58.

Lunn, P. G., M. Watkinson, A. M. Prentice, P. Morrell, P. Austin, and R. G. Whitehead, 1981. "Maternal nutrition and lactational amenorrhea," *Lancet* (27 June): 1428–1429.

Marin, P., 1982. "The National Breastfeeding Program of Brazil," in Proceedings of a Conference on Actions Needed to Improve Maternal and Infant Nutrition Among Developing Countries, Manila, Philippines.

Mata, L. J., 1978. *The Children of Santa Maria Cauque: A Prospective Field Study of Health and Growth.* Cambridge: MIT Press.

———, et al., 1983. "Effect of hospital and field interventions on breastfeeding, health survival of infants." Paper presented at the Western Hemisphere Nutrition Congress VII, Miami, Florida, 7–12 August.

McCann, M. F., ed., 1981. *Breastfeeding, Fertility and Family Planning. Population Reports* 9, no. 5.

McCord, C., and A. A. Kielmann, 1978. "A successful programme for medical auxiliaries treating childhood diarrhea and pneumonia," *Tropical Doctor* 8: 220–225.

McNeilly, A. S., P. W. Howie, and M. J. Houston, 1980. "Relationship of feeding patterns, prolactin, and resumption of ovulation postpartum," in *Research Frontiers in Fertility Regulation,* ed. Zatuchni, et al. Hagerstown (MD): Harper and Row.

Miller, G. H., and L. R. Hughes, 1970. "Lactation and genital involution effects of a new low-dose oral contraceptive on breastfeeding mothers and their infants," *Obstetrics and Gynecology* 35: 44–50.

Miranda, R., N. G. Saravia, R. Ackerman, N. Murphy, S. Berman, and D. N. McMurray, 1983. "Effect of maternal nutritional status on immunological substances in human colostrum and milk," *American Journal of Clinical Nutrition* 37: 632–640.

Murray, J., and A. B. Murray, 1979. "(Letter) Breast milk and weights of Nigerian mothers and their infants," *American Journal of Clinical Nutrition* 32, no. 4: 737.

Nag, M., 1982. "The impact of sociocultural factors on breastfeeding and sexual behavior," in *Determinants of Fertility in Developing Countries.* Washington, D.C.: National Academy of Sciences, Committee on Population and Demography.

Oo, T. T., and K. M. Naing, 1982. "A comparison of milk output of Burmese mothers by three different methods," *Food and Nutrition Bulletin* 4, no. 4: 66–68.

Page, H. J., and R. Lesthaeghe, eds., 1981. *Child-Spacing in Tropical Africa: Traditions and Change.* New York: Academic Press.

———, R. J. Lesthaeghe, and H. Shah, 1982. "Illustrative analysis: Breastfeeding in Pakistan," *Scientific Reports* No. 37 (December). London: World Fertility Survey.

Pao, E., J. M. Himes, and A. F. Roche, 1980. "Milk intakes and feeding patterns of breast-fed infants," *Journal of the American Dietetic Association* 77: 540–545.

Parveen, L., A. Q. Chowdhury, and Z. Chowdhury, 1977. "Injectable contraception in rural Bangladesh," *Lancet* (November): 946–948.

Perez, A., et al., 1972. "First ovulation after childbirth: The effect of breastfeeding," *American Journal of Obstetrics and Gynecology* 114, no. 6: 1041–1047.

Picciano, M. F., 1983. "The composition of human milk." Paper presented at the Western Hemisphere Nutrition Congress VII, Miami, Florida, August.

Plank, S. L., and M. L. Milanesi, 1973. "Infant feeding and infant mortality in rural Chile," *Bulletin of the World Health Organization* 48: 203–210.

Prema, K., and M. Ravindranath, 1982. "The effect of breastfeeding supplements on the return of fertility," *Studies in Family Planning* 13, no. 10 (October): 293–296.

Puffer, R. R., and C. V. Surrano, 1973. *Patterns of Mortality in Childhood.* Washington, D.C.: Pan American Health Association.

Reddy, V., C. Bhaskaram, N. Raghuramuhi, and V. Jagadeesan, 1977. "Antimicrobial factor in human milk," *Acta Paediatrica Scandinavica* 66: 229–232.

Rivera, R., 1981. Report given at the Annual Meeting of the Association of Planned Parenthood Physicians.

Romaniuk, A., 1980. "Increase in natural fertility during the early stages of modernization: Evidence from an African case study, Zaire," *Population Studies* 34, no. 2: 293–310.

Samadi, A. R., M. I. Huq, and Q. S. Ahmed, 1983. "Detection of rotaviris in handwashings of attendants of children with diarrhea," *British Medical Journal* 286(6360): 188.

Sauls, H. S., 1979. "Potential effect of demographic and other variables in studies comparing morbidity of breast-fed and bottle-fed infants," *Pediatrics* 64, no. 4: 523–527.

Schoenmaeckers, R., I. H. Shah, R. Lesthaeghe, and O. Tambashe, 1981. "The child-spacing tradition and the postpartum taboo in tropical Africa: Anthropological evidence," in *Child-Spacing in Tropical Africa: Traditions and Change,* ed. H. J. Page and R. Lesthaeghe. New York: Academic Press.

Simpson-Hebert, M., 1977. "Breastfeeding in Iran and its relation to fertility," Doctoral thesis, University of North Carolina.

Steckel, A., C. Mardones-Santander, and E. Hertrampf, 1983. "Breastfeeding practices and use of supplemental foods," Institute of Nutrition and Food Technology, University of Chile, Santiago (unpublished).

Surjono, D., S. D. Ismadi, Suwardji, and J. E. Rohde, 1980. "Bacterial contamination and dilution of milk in infant feeding bottles," *Journal of Tropical Pediatrics* 26, no. 2 (April): 58–61.

Vallin, J., 1978. "Fertility in Algeria: Trends and differentials," in *Women's Status and Fertility in the Muslim World.* New York: Praeger Publishers.

Van Esterik, P., 1977. "Lactation, nutrition and changing values: Infant feeding practices in rural and urban Thailand," in *Development and Underdevelopment in S.E. Asia,* ed. G. Means. Canadian Asian Studies Association.

Van Steenbergen, W. M., J. A. Kusin, A. M. Voorhoeve, and A. A. J. Jansen, 1978. "Agents affecting health of mother and child in a rural area of Kenya: Food intake, feeding habits, and nutritional status of the Akamba infant and toddler," *Tropical and Geographical Medicine* 30: 505–522.

———, J. A. Kusin, and M. M. Van Rens, 1981. "Lactation performance of Akamba mothers, Kenya: Breastfeeding behavior, breastmilk yield, and composition," *Journal of Tropical Pediatrics* 27: 155–161.

Vis, H. L., M. Bossuyt, P. Hennart, and M. Caraël, 1975. "The health of mother and child in rural Central Africa," *Studies in Family Planning* 6, no. 12 (December): 437–441.

Whitehead, R. G., ed., 1981. *Maternal Diet, Breast-feeding Capacity, and Lactational Infertility.* Tokyo: The United Nations University.

Winikoff, B., 1981. "Issues in the design of breastfeeding research," *Studies in Family Planning* 12, no. 4 (April): 177–183.

———, 1983. "The effects of birth spacing on child and maternal health," *Studies in Family Planning* 14, no. 10 (October): 231–245.

Wolff, P. H., and A. M. Simmons, 1967. "Non-nutritive suckling and response threshholds in young infants," *Child Development* 38: 631–638.

Woodbury, R. M., 1922. "The relation between breast and artificial feeding and infant mortality," *American Journal of Hygiene* 2, no. 6: 668–687.

Woolridge, M. W., T. V. How, R. F. Drewett, P. Rolfe, and J. D. Baum, 1982. "The continuous measurement of milk intake at a feed in breast-fed babies," *Early Human Development* 6: 365–373.

Yolken, R. H., R. G. Wyatt, L. Mata, J. J. Urutia, B. Garcia, R. M. Chanock, and A. Z. Kapikian, 1978. "Secretory antibody directed against rotavirus in human milk-measurement by means of enzyme-linked immunosorbent assay," *Journal of Pediatrics* 93: 916–921.

Zanartu, J., E. Aguilera, and G. Munoz-Pinto, 1976. "Maintenance of lactation by means of continuous low-dose progestogen given post-partum as a contraceptive," *Contraception* 13, no. 3: 313–318.

INTERVENING VARIABLES

INFECTIOUS AND PARASITIC DISEASES

Immunizable and Respiratory Diseases and Child Mortality

Stanley O. Foster

Four diseases—neonatal tetanus, pertussis, measles, and acute lower respiratory tract infection—cause one-third of deaths under age 5 years in the developing world. In a surveillance area of Matlab Thana, Bangladesh, 2,257 of 7,858 deaths of children under age 5 (35 percent) were attributed to these four diseases (Chen et al., 1980: 27). A recent prospective study of a Javanese village in Indonesia identified pneumonia, tetanus, and measles as responsible for 35 percent of deaths in children under age 2 (Handayani et al., 1983: 91). Although there are other diseases preventable by immunization (e.g., poliomyelitis) and other types of respiratory disease (e.g., croup) that cause mortality in infants and children, these four are the most important.

Neonatal tetanus, pertussis, and measles can be prevented through immunization. Such prevention would eliminate 3–4 million deaths annually. Many respiratory deaths can also be prevented through low-cost drug therapy.

What, then, impedes the application of this technology in the Third World? Discussion of this question requires an understanding of four elements: disease-specific mortality; associated risk factors; availability, feasibility, and acceptability of interventions; and the effectiveness of the interventions.

Neonatal tetanus

Neonatal tetanus, also known as tetanus neonatorum, is caused by infection of the newborn (usually at the umbilical stump) with tetanus organisms. Tetanus typically develops during the first or second week of life and is fatal in 70–90 percent of cases. Expert medical care, rarely available in the developing world where this disease is most common, seldom reduces mortality to less than 50 percent.

Tetanus mortality

Disease-reporting systems in developing countries cannot detect neonatal deaths occurring outside the health care system. Estimates of neonatal tetanus mortality are usually based on single-round retrospective surveys in which household members are questioned about births and infant deaths in the preceding 12 months. The symptom complex of neonatal tetanus—normal breast-feeding at birth, loss of sucking, spasms, and death within the first month of life—is unique and often carries a traditional name, seventh or eighth day disease. Using survey data, the World Health Organization (WHO) has estimated the extent of neonatal tetanus in five countries in the Middle East (155,626 cases and 132,285 deaths) and six countries in Asia (463,429 cases and 393,067 deaths). Less than 5 percent of these cases had been detected through current reporting systems. Country data from these and other surveys are summarized in Table 1.

TABLE 1   Neonatal tetanus incidence rates per 1,000 live births, by country as determined by sample surveys

Country	Live births	Neonatal tetanus deaths	Neonatal tetanus deaths per 1,000 live births	Neonatal tetanus deaths as percent of all neonatal deaths	Source
Bangladesh	2,432	65	27	56	WHO (1982a: 138)
Bhutan	283	5	18	50	WHO (1982a: 138)
Cameroon	2,102	15	7	—	SHDS (1983)
Democratic Yemen	6,224	24	4	20	WHO (1982a: 138)
Egypt	—	228	3	—	WHO (1982a: 138)
India	51,355	415	8	34	Basu (1982: 192)
Indonesia	4,971	53	11	51	WHO (1983a: 56)
Ivory Coast	2,307	41	18	53	WHO (1983b: 72)
Nepal	3,346	49	15	39	WHO (1982a: 138)
Pakistan	13,858	432	31	60	WHO (1982a: 138)
Somalia	5,781	120	21	23	WHO (1982a: 138)
Sudan	9,632	66	9	32	WHO (1982a: 138)
Syrian Arab Republic	6,762	33	5	—	WHO (1982a: 138)
Thailand	13,659	66	5	23	WHO (1982a: 138)
Yemen Arab Republic	5,191	13	3	8	WHO (1982a: 138)

Because deaths, especially infant deaths, are frequently missed in retrospective surveys, these numbers are minimal estimates of neonatal tetanus mortality. Recent data from the Ivory Coast, in which neonatal tetanus mortality was analyzed by length of time since birth ("recall period"), suggest that women forget or are unwilling to report remote fatal events (see Table 2).

TABLE 2 Neonatal tetanus mortality in
Boundiali, Ivory Coast, 1981–83, by
recall period

Recall period (in months)	Births	Neonatal tetanus deaths	Neonatal tetanus deaths per 1,000 live births
1–7	1,052	28	26.6
8–13	731	10	13.7
14–19	524	3	5.7

SOURCE: WHO (1983b: 72).

Prospective longitudinal studies in which all pregnancies are identified and outcomes are followed are a more reliable method for determining the incidence of neonatal tetanus. For example, a national single-round retrospective survey in Bangladesh reported 27 neonatal tetanus deaths per thousand live births as compared with 37 neonatal tetanus deaths per thousand live births in a longitudinal survey in the Matlab surveillance area. The difference probably results from underreporting in the retrospective survey.

Tetanus mortality risk factors

Seven factors are thought to affect the risk of neonatal tetanus infection: environmental exposure to tetanus organisms; sex of the child; place of delivery; type of birth attendant; cord care practice; immunization status of the mother; and socioeconomic status.

Environmental exposure to tetanus organisms Retrospective surveys were carried out in three environmental zones in Punjab Province in Pakistan. Results show significantly higher neonatal tetanus mortality rates in cattle- and horse-raising areas where environmental contamination with tetanus organisms is very high, as compared to farming and urban areas (see Table 3).

TABLE 3 Neonatal tetanus mortality in
Punjab, Pakistan, 1980–81, by area

Area	Live births	Neonatal tetanus deaths	Neonatal tetanus deaths per 1,000 live births
Urban slums	3,000	78	21.0
Rural			
agricultural	6,000	216	33.7
cattle/horse raising	3,000	138	42.5

SOURCE: Suleman (1982: 158–159).

Sex of the child Neonatal tetanus deaths are more frequently reported in males. Reported male-to-female ratios for neonatal tetanus deaths vary from 1.4:1 in Sudan to 2.6:1 in Alexandria, Egypt (WHO, 1982a: 139). In part, the higher mortality of males may result from more complete reporting of male deaths in these traditional Muslim societies; however, tetanus infection resulting from circumcision during the first week of life is the most probable cause of the difference (Suleman, 1982: 161).

Place of delivery Deliveries at home carry a high risk of neonatal tetanus, but hospital delivery does not guarantee protection. In Sri Lanka, 206 of 423 neonatal tetanus deaths (48.7 percent) were among infants delivered in hospitals (DeSilva, 1982: 222). For a country in which 75 percent of deliveries occur in institutions, the relative risk of neonatal tetanus for home delivery is 3:1. It should be noted that hospital stays in Sri Lanka are very short (a few hours), and infection may occur after discharge.

Type of birth attendant Studies in Malaysia have shown that infants delivered by an untrained attendant, family member, or traditional birth attendant (TBA) have a higher rate of neonatal tetanus (34 per thousand live births) than infants delivered by a trained TBA (12 per thousand live births) or by a trained midwife (0 per thousand) (P. Chen, 1976: 96).

Cord care practice Three aspects of umbilical cord care influence the risk of neonatal tetanus: the instrument used to cut the cord, the process of tying or not tying, and materials applied to the unhealed umbilical stump. Data from Bangladesh document these differences (see Table 4).

TABLE 4   Neonatal tetanus mortality in Teknaf, Bangladesh, 1976–77, by cord care practice

	Live births	Neonatal tetanus deaths	Neonatal tetanus deaths per 1,000 live births
Cord cutting			
Razor blade	292	6	20.6
Split bamboo	1,059	31	29.3
Treatment of cord			
Tied, no ash	1,028	25	24.3
Tied, ash	269	6	22.3
Not tied, ash	54	6	111.1

SOURCE: Islam et al. (1982: 301).

Immunization status of the mother Two doses of tetanus toxoid administered at least one month apart and at least one month prior to delivery are nearly 100 percent effective in preventing neonatal tetanus. Thus, lack of tetanus immunization of the mother is a significant risk factor for neonatal tetanus in the infant.

Socioeconomic status Analysis of a series of socioeconomic and exposure variables for neonatal tetanus in Uttar Pradesh, India, by Smucker and colleagues (1980: 329) showed that exposure-related variables (previous neonatal tetanus death in family, presence of large animals in the home, and/or assistance at delivery by an untrained birth attendant) were better predictors of neonatal tetanus than socioeconomic variables (education, income, landholding, and caste).

Availability, feasibility, and acceptability of tetanus prevention

There are two effective strategies for preventing neonatal tetanus: training of birth attendants and immunization of fertile or pregnant women. In Bangladesh, a trial compared the effectiveness of these two strategies (see Table 5). Both strategies reduced the rate of neonatal tetanus, with immunization being the more effective. However, in comparing the two approaches, it is important to recognize that the benefit of TBA training extends beyond neonatal tetanus to other causes of neonatal deaths (see Table 6).

Current coverage of at-risk pregnant women with the desired two doses of tetanus toxoid is low—18 percent in Africa, 10 percent in South America, 16 percent in South Asia, and 4 percent in the Eastern Mediterranean countries.

TABLE 5   Effect of TBA training and tetanus toxoid immunization on neonatal tetanus mortality in Bangladesh

	Live births	Neonatal tetanus deaths	Neonatal tetanus deaths per 1,000 live births
Untrained TBAs	998	24	24.1
Trained TBAs	713	4	5.6
Immunization	771	1	1.3

SOURCE: Rahman (1982: 164).

TABLE 6   Effect of TBA training and tetanus toxoid immunization on neonatal mortality in Bangladesh

	Live births	Neonatal deaths	Neonatal deaths per 1,000 live births
Untrained TBAs	998	85	85.2
Trained TBAs	713	17	23.8
Immunization	771	30	38.9

SOURCE: Rahman (1982: 164).

Recent studies in Bangladesh have shown that acceptance of tetanus toxoid by pregnant women identified by door-to-door household contact was low— 27 percent (WHO, 1981: 209). Investigation of low rates of tetanus toxoid coverage has identified a number of reasons that pregnant women have not made use of available services, including objection by husband or mother-in-law, 35 percent; fear of injection, 33 percent; lack of information, 14 percent; and late detection of pregnancy, 4 percent (WHO, 1981: 210).

Effectiveness of tetanus prevention

The protective effect of tetanus toxoid was best demonstrated in a double-blind controlled field trial carried out in Colombia (see Table 7). Similar results had been reported in 1961 in New Guinea (Schofield, 1961: 787). This protective effect of tetanus toxoid was also shown in the follow-up of children born to women participants in the Matlab Cholera Vaccine trial in which tetanus-diphtheria toxoid was used as a placebo (see Table 8).

TABLE 7   Effectiveness of tetanus toxoid in preventing neonatal tetanus deaths: a double-blind controlled study in Colombia, 1961—66

Group	Live births	Neonatal tetanus deaths	Neonatal tetanus deaths per 1,000 live births
Placebo control—1 injection	270	19	70.4
1 tetanus toxoid injection	224	9	40.2
Placebo control—2/3 injections	347	27	77.8
2/3 tetanus toxoid injections	341	0	0.0

SOURCE: Newell et al. (1966: 869).

TABLE 8   Neonatal mortality of children born to women receiving two doses of cholera vaccine or tetanus-diphtheria toxoid, Matlab, Bangladesh, 1975—77

Interval between vaccination and birth (months)	Cholera vaccine			Tetanus-diphtheria toxoid		
	Live births	Deaths	Neonatal deaths per 1,000 live births	Live births	Deaths	Neonatal deaths per 1,000 live births
9–20	1,652	113	68.4	1,044	46	44.1
21–32	2,734	149	54.5	1,946	73	37.5

SOURCE: Black et al. (1980: 928).

Despite many constraints, neonatal tetanus has been eliminated as a public health problem in many areas. Figure 1 summarizes the experience at the Albert Schweitzer Hospital in Haiti, where four strategies (TBA training, hospital care, immunization of pregnant women, and immunization of all women) were used to eliminate neonatal tetanus. It should be noted that total success was not achieved until nonpregnant fertile women became the target for immunization. Taking into account this experience and the current low tetanus toxoid coverage of at-risk pregnant women, WHO, at its 1983 Global Advisory Group meeting, changed its target for tetanus toxoid to all women of childbearing age (15–44). As the WHO Expanded Programme on Immunization achieves full coverage in infants and young children, single booster doses of tetanus toxoid targeted to young women immunized in childhood will prevent neonatal tetanus.

FIGURE 1   Neonatal tetanus mortality: Deschappels, Haiti, 1940–72

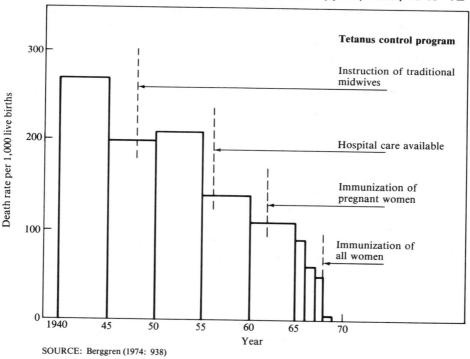

SOURCE: Berggren (1974: 938)

In reviewing the effectiveness of neonatal tetanus prevention, it is important to recognize that tetanus toxoid will, in addition to eliminating neonatal tetanus, also eliminate postpartum and postabortal tetanus (Bennett, 1976: 513).

Pertussis

Among the childhood diseases preventable by immunization, pertussis is the least well understood. In some geographic areas, pertussis is identified as a major cause of childhood mortality directly through damage to the respiratory tract or indirectly as a precipitating cause of severe undernutrition. In other areas, pertussis is not recognizable as a major factor in child health. It is not known whether these geographic differences are real or whether they represent problems in disease recognition and reporting.

Pertussis mortality

Pertussis was first identified as a major cause of mortality in the developing world in reports from Nigeria and Gambia, where case fatalities in community outbreaks were 7.3 and 3.2 percent respectively (Morley et al., 1966: 171; McGregor et al., 1970: 63). The most thorough data come from the Machakos project in Kenya, where a rural highland population of 24,000 was followed prospectively for three years (Voorhoeve et al., 1978: 135). Of the 953 cases of pertussis, 21 died within three months of infection. Twelve of these 21 deaths were attributed to pertussis, a case-fatality rate of 1.26 percent. Although pertussis may have contributed to the other nine deaths, it was not identified as the primary cause. Pertussis accounted for 4.1 percent of all deaths in the 0–15 age group.

Pertussis mortality risk factors

Two factors affect pertussis mortality: age-specific morbidity and complications.

Age-specific morbidity There are two epidemiologic patterns of pertussis: an urban endemic pattern in which most children are infected in the first year of life and a rural pattern in which epidemics occur at infrequent intervals. Inasmuch as age-specific mortality is much higher in children under age 1— 3.2 percent in the Machakos study as compared with 0.9 percent for children over 1 (Voorhoeve et al., 1978: 136)—pertussis mortality is dependent on the underlying pattern of transmission. Factors affecting transmission include population density, mobility, child-rearing practices, and patterns of social interaction. In coastal West Africa where babies are carried by their mothers to market, 88 percent of children are infected with pertussis in the first year of life (McBean, 1978: 292). In contrast, in Dougba, Ivory Coast, a traditional Muslim area in the less densely populated savannah, only 11 percent of the cases occurred in the first year of life (Sokal et al., 1982). In this village, the median age of infection was 3; 46 percent of the cases occurred in children aged 4 and older.

Complications Most reports of pertussis mortality relate to deaths occurring within one month of onset. However, as described by Morley in the prospective follow-up of 203 pertussis cases in a Nigerian village, the cough associated with pertussis is prolonged: five weeks, 43 percent; 10 weeks, 16.5 percent; 15 weeks, 5.8 percent; and 20 weeks, 2.0 percent (Morley et al., 1966: 173). The prolonged cough with its accompanying anorexia and vomiting frequently results in undernutrition. Weight loss of 5 percent or greater was noted in 57 percent of the Nigerian children. Thirty-one percent of children required five or more weeks to regain their weight, and 14 percent took over 12 weeks (1966: 174). Observations in Guatemala have also documented the adverse impact of pertussis on weight (Mata, 1978: 282). The 21 deaths reported within three months of onset of pertussis in the Machakos study may, in fact, represent a better estimate of pertussis-associated mortality, 2.2 percent, than the reported 1.3 percent.

Availability, feasibility, and acceptability of pertussis prevention

DTP vaccine is a standard part of most child health services. The vaccine is available in most countries, primarily through UNICEF, and is usually available at health facilities with cold chain capability (equipment to store vaccine at 0–8°C). Feasibility of vaccine administration is determined by local disease epidemiology and by access to health facilities. In areas of high transmission such as urban West Africa, many children are infected and most deaths occur by five to six months of age—prior to the usual age of complete immunization. To ensure greater protection of young infants, WHO now recommends that DTP immunization be initiated at six weeks (WHO, 1984: 15). In areas where pertussis transmission occurs at older ages, and where vaccine delivery and utilization function effectively, pertussis control is achievable. DTP vaccine is not always readily accepted by mothers. Dropout rates after the first of the required three doses are as high as 50 percent. This resistance to immunization results from several factors: the lack of awareness of pertussis as a disease, lack of belief in the effectiveness of the vaccine, and especially, the sore arms and high fever occurring postimmunization.

Pertussis vaccine effectiveness

Difficulties in clinical diagnosis, especially in children under 1 year of age, in whom the characteristic whoop is often lacking, make estimation of pertussis vaccine efficacy difficult. In addition, bacteriologic and serologic techniques are not always reliable measures of infection. In the United Kingdom, where acceptance of DTP has decreased sharply due to fear of vaccine-associated neurological complications, epidemic pertussis has returned as a health problem. Vaccine efficacy for protected children has been estimated at 85 to 94 percent (Church, 1979: 189). In the developing world, especially in areas of endemic disease, efficacy rates are probably lower due to inability to achieve full protection prior to infection. Studies in Uganda, however, in which DTP immunization was carried out in one of three districts, document the effectiveness of pertussis vaccine (see Table 9). Elimination by immunization of anorexia and vomiting associated with pertussis is also believed to have a key role in preventing undernutrition.

TABLE 9   Pertussis admissions to three district
hospitals, Uganda, 1964–69

Area	Vaccine status	7/1964–6/1966[a]	7/1966–6/1967	7/1967–6/1968	7/1968–6/1969
Ankole	Yes	69	8	11	28
Masaka	No	110	128	211	86
Toro	No	225	171	181	224

[a] Average of two years.
SOURCE: Cook (1978: 286).

Measles

WHO estimates that 1.5 million children die annually of measles and its complications (pneumonia, diarrhea, undernutrition, and systemic infection) (Assaad, 1983: 457). From the perspective of child survival, health planners are challenged by three conflicting hypotheses:

1 Measles immunization will increase child survival in proportion to measles deaths prevented.

2 Measles immunization will, because of its synergistic impact with other major causes of under-5 mortality, increase survival in excess of measles deaths prevented.

3 Measles immunization will not increase child survival because deaths prevented through immunization will be replaced by deaths from other causes.

Is measles immunization a good use of limited health resources? An answer to this question requires a better understanding of the effect of measles immunization on survival as well as on morbidity and mortality related to measles.

Measles mortality

In the early 1960s, measles was recognized as a major cause of child mortality in Africa. Initial studies focused on hospital data, which indicated that inpatient measles case-fatality rates were as high as 25 percent (Morley, 1963: 118). Further studies of measles in communities documented measles as a major killer of African children (Morley et al., 1963: 115; McGregor, 1964: 252; Cantrelle, 1965: 35). Morley's early studies in Imesi identified measles as a chronic as well as an acute disease, with major long-term sequelae in terms of prolonged diarrhea, weight loss, and undernutrition.

For many years, it was thought that high measles-associated mortality was an African phenomenon. However, increased attention to community outbreaks of measles documented high rates of measles-associated mortality in Latin America, the Near East, and Asia. Table 10 provides a range of reported measles case-fatality rates for different geographic areas.

Perhaps the most convincing data on measles mortality are those reported from the Matlab study area in Bangladesh, where 5,775 children in

TABLE 10   Measles case-fatality rates in different geographic areas

Country, year	Location	Cases	Deaths	Case-fatality rate (deaths per 100 cases)	Source
Afghanistan, 1971	Yakaolany	327	90	27.5	Wakeham (1978: 88)
Bangladesh, 1975–76	Matlab	896	33	3.7	Koster (1981: 903)
China					
1950–66	Hebei			1.5	Zhang Yihao (1983: 415)
1967–74	Hebei			0.4	Zhang Yihao (1983: 415)
1975–80	Hebei			0.3	Zhang Yihao (1983: 415)
Guinea Bissau, 1979		98	15	15.3	Aaby (1983: 695)
India					
1971–74	West Bengal	181	2	1.1	Sinha (1977: 125)
1977–78	Tamil Nadu	198	14	7.1	John (1980: 156)
Nigeria, 1950–61	Imesi	222	15	6.8	Morley (1963: 116)
United States, 1960–64				0.009	
Zaire, 1974–77	Kasongo	1,069	65	6.1	Kasongo (1981: 766)

12 villages were followed prospectively for nutritional status and diarrheal incidence (Koster et al., 1981: 903). During the survey period, in which each household was visited on a weekly basis, a measles epidemic developed. Of the 896 children infected, 33 died—a case-fatality rate of 3.7 percent. Extrapolating these findings to the general population, measles mortality is estimated at 160 per 100,000 population.

Almost all recorded studies report measles mortality as deaths within one month of rash. Recently, three measles-infected Gambian villages were followed longitudinally over a nine-month period (Hull et al., 1983: 973). Significant delayed mortality in measles cases as compared with nonmeasles cases was documented (see Table 11). Correcting the two populations for slight differences in age composition, the relative risk of mortality for a child with measles was 13.7:1. In these villages, most of the delayed mortality occurred during the summer rains, the "hungry season"—a period of increased incidence of diarrhea, malaria, and undernutrition. Although these high rates of postmeasles mortality have not been observed in all villages followed longi-

TABLE 11   Acute, 3-month, and 9-month measles mortality in three Gambian villages, 1981

| Time of follow-up | Children with measles | | | Children without measles | | |
	Number	Cumulative deaths	Case-fatality rate (deaths per 100 cases)	Number	Cumulative deaths	Case-fatality rate (deaths per 100 cases)
Acute	146	7	4.8	927	—	—
3 months	145	11	7.6	915	1	0.1
9 months	135	20	14.8	888	9	1.0

SOURCE: Hull et al. (1983: 973).

tudinally, both acute and delayed measles mortality are major factors in determining child survival. In the developing world an estimated 1–5 percent of all children born die of measles or its complications.

Measles mortality risk factors

Four factors determine risk of measles mortality: nutritional status; age at infection; type and severity of complications; and availability of medical care.

Nutritional status Inasmuch as high measles and measles-associated mortality occurs in areas where undernutrition is common, undernutrition is generally accepted as the major cause of measles-associated mortality; however, not all data support this conclusion. In the Matlab prospective study (Koster, 1981: 904) a case–control study of 33 measles deaths showed no significant difference in premeasles nutritional status (weight-for-height) between deaths and controls. Similar conclusions were reached in Zaire, where premeasles nutritional status by four different methods (weight-for-age, weight-for-height, arm circumference-for-age, and arm circumference-for-height) did not correlate with measles mortality (Kasongo Project Team, 1983: 73). Further analyses of these data using international rather than the local anthropometric standards are needed to confirm their findings. Chen reached different conclusions in a study from Matlab, Bangladesh, that showed significantly higher measles mortality for children with low weight-for-age (Chen, 1980b: 1842). Over a two-year period he found a mortality rate of 14.8 per thousand cases of measles among children at less than 65 percent of premeasles weight-for-age as compared with a mortality rate of 6.3 per thousand cases among those over 65 percent premeasles weight-for-age.

In severely undernourished populations, measles-associated mortality rates of 50 percent or higher have been reported. As a current working hypothesis, the association between severe undernutrition and high measles mortality seems clear. For mild and moderate undernutrition, anthropometric measurements are neither sufficiently sensitive to predict mortality nor specific enough to explain it. Specific nutritional deficiencies of micronutrients, low levels of serum albumin as found in Zambia (Savage, 1967: 77), or other as-yet-undemonstrated factors may better explain the relationship of nutrition to measles mortality.

Recent studies have documented an altered immune response in undernourished children. Because this immune response determines severity of initial infection, susceptibility to secondary infection, and ability to handle secondary infection, understanding of the relationship of undernutrition to measles mortality will require better knowledge of the effect of undernutrition on the immune system. A summary of important findings and unanswered questions has been published (*Nutrition Reviews,* 1982: 203). Decreased immune response has been documented in children with severe measles (Whittle et al., 1973: 753). Recent studies have shown that measles virus inoculated into peripheral blood mononuclear (PBM) cells collected from undernourished measles-susceptible children yields significantly more measles virus than inoculations into PBM cells from well-nourished measles-susceptible children (Whittle et al., 1980: 147). In addition, plasma from undernourished measles cases has a suppressive effect on lymphocyte proliferation in vitro (Whittle et al., 1980: 148).

Age at infection Age patterns of measles infection are in part responsible for differences in measles mortality among outbreaks. Several factors determine age-specific incidence: population density, mobility, patterns of human interaction, and child-rearing practices. In Lagos, Nigeria, a high-density urban area where mothers routinely carry their babies on their backs, the median age of measles infection is 14 months. Nearly all children become infected during the first 36 months of life. In comparison, in the less densely populated, more traditional Muslim areas of the African savannah, measles transmits more slowly—the median age in the savannah is 36–48 months (Foster and Pifer, 1971: 153). Using these two age distributions and an average range of age-specific case fatalities for measles (age <1, 8 percent; age 1, 6 percent; age 2, 4 percent; age 3, 2 percent; ages 4 and 5, 1 percent; and ages 6 and over, 0 percent), the mortality for two measles outbreaks—one urban and one rural—would be 6.0 and 1.8 percent, respectively.

Type and severity of complications The fatality rate of uncomplicated measles (rash, fever, conjunctivitis, and cough) is low. During a recent survey of measles in Sri Lanka (Bloch, 1983, II: 12), case-fatality rates were determined by type of complication. Pneumonia, convulsions, and coma were strongly associated with mortality (see Table 12). High case fatality is related not only to the type of complication, but also to the severity of the complication. In the Bangladesh study, diarrhea of seven days or more duration was significantly associated with mortality (see Table 13).

TABLE 12 Measles case-fatality rates by type of complication: Sri Lanka measles survey, March 1983

Complication	Cases	Deaths	Case-fatality rate (deaths per 100 cases)
None	1,047	0	0.0
Diarrhea	879	8	0.9
Pneumonia	263	14	5.3
Convulsions	56	6	10.7
Coma	17	3	17.6

SOURCE: Bloch (1983, II: 12).

Although not a cause of acute mortality, measles is a major precipitating cause of acute vitamin A deficiency, a major cause of blindness in developing countries. In Indonesia, a high correlation was found between a recent history of measles and active corneal and/or stromal disease (Indonesia, 1980: 71).

TABLE 13   Mortality rates due to
measles and diarrhea, and case-fatality
rates: two villages in Matlab,
Bangladesh, 1975–76

Type of episode	Episodes	Deaths	Case-fatality rate (deaths per 100 cases)
Measles, no diarrhea	99	4	4.0
Measles plus diarrhea <7 days	199	2	1.0
Measles plus diarrhea >7 days	67	8	11.9

SOURCE: Koster et al. (1981: 905).

Availability of medical care Most measles deaths are associated with complications, many of which are treatable. The availability of medical care—diagnosis and treatment—is a determinant of survival. In a study from Vellore, India, measles mortality for children with no access to health care (16.1 percent) was significantly higher than that for children with access to medical care (3.7 percent) (John et al., 1980: 156). Deaths occurred primarily among children with treatable complications such as pneumonia, diarrhea, and dysentery. In terms of cost and effectiveness, immunization is less costly and more effective than treatment.

Availability, feasibility, and acceptability of measles prevention

Measles can be prevented by a single dose of vaccine administered at or after 9 months of age. Although some children under 9 months will be infected with measles, 9 months has been determined as the optimum age of immunization (WHO, 1979: 339). Two constraints limit the current use of measles vaccine: the delivery system and public utilization of services. The WHO Expanded Programme on Immunization, through its emphasis on planning, training, and evaluation, has appreciably extended both the quantity and quality of vaccine delivery. In some areas, high levels of measles vaccine coverage have been achieved (WHO, 1983c: 176). However, measles vaccine coverage in at-risk children is still low: in Africa, 27 percent; Latin America, 37 percent; Southeast Asia, 1 percent; Eastern Mediterranean, 22 percent; and Western Pacific, 15 percent. While efforts are being made to expand and extend the delivery system, attention is also being focused on nonacceptors in areas with access to vaccine delivery. Ethnic differences, high migration rates, and lack of knowledge have been identified as major constraints to vaccine acceptance (Brown et al., 1982: 36).

Measles vaccine effectiveness

During the 1960s, there were as many reports of vaccine failure as of success. In a 1972 study in Yaounde, Cameroon, only 17 of every 100 doses of measles vaccine were effective in preventing a case of measles (McBean et al., 1976: 200). Improvements in the cold chain, better identification of the target population, and regular training and supervision have improved the quality of vaccine delivery. In the Gambia study described earlier, vaccine efficacy was 89 percent (Hull et al., 1983: 973). In that country, where measles vaccine coverage increased from 42 percent in 1979 to 71 percent in 1982, an estimated 16,200 cases of measles and 648 measles deaths are being prevented annually (Gambia, 1982: 40). Using cost data on immunization in the Gambia (Robertson, in press) estimates of the average costs to prevent a measles case and a measles death are US$4.66 and $57.89, respectively.

Measles vaccine prevents measles and measles mortality. What of the question presented earlier? Does measles vaccine affect overall child survival? Do children who are saved from measles by vaccine experience "replacement" mortality? To my knowledge, only one study has attempted to answer this question. The Kasongo group used a life table analysis in a controlled measles vaccine study in Zaire. Measles vaccine reduced the risk of dying during the age of maximum measles exposure. The survival probability of the vaccinated cohort at 7–21 months (0.9746) was higher than that of the unvaccinated cohort (0.9461) and of older unvaccinated siblings of the vaccinated cohort (0.9257) (Kasongo Project Team, 1981: 766). The full benefit of vaccination did not appear to be maintained at 35 months. Since further control studies cannot be carried out within existing guidelines for human experimentation, alternative approaches are needed to further review the effect of measles vaccine on child survival.

Acute respiratory infection

Within the World Health Organization, increasing attention is being focused on respiratory disease and the potential of primary health care approaches to reduce attendant mortality. Because acute respiratory infection (ARI) will be increasingly discussed in terms of child mortality and survival, it is important that agreement is reached on a common nomenclature. Table 14, adapted from a recent PAHO publication, provides a system of classification for ARI (PAHO, 1983: 26). Acute lower respiratory tract infections (ALRTI)—primarily pneumonia and bronchiolitis—are the major types of ARI responsible for childhood mortality. This review will be limited to ALRTI.

ALRTI mortality

Prospective surveillance for respiratory disease has been carried out since 1972 among 10,000 people living in Tari in the southern highlands of Papua New Guinea (Riley et al., 1981: 354). In that population, ALRTI mortality was 30 per thousand for infants and 4 per thousand for toddlers. These figures are higher than those reported from Matlab, Bangladesh: 10.4 per thousand for infants and 1.6 per thousand for children 1 to 4 years of age (Chen, 1980a: 28) and for Narangwal, India: 14.8 per thousand in children under age 5 (Taylor et al., unpub. V: 20). For the Papua New Guinea population, 34

TABLE 14   Acute respiratory infections: frequency, nomenclature, etiology, and treatment

Episodes per year per child[a]	Scientific name	Common name	Etiology	Mortality	Preventable	Treatable if other than symptomatic
3.72	Acute nasopharyngitis	Cold	Viral	No	No	—
0.04	Acute otitis media	Ear infection	Bacterial	No	No	Antibiotics
0.08	Acute pharyngotonsilitis	Sore throat	Bacterial and viral	No	No	Antibiotics for beta-haemolytic streptococcus
0.05	Acute laryngitis	Croup	Viral	Rare	No	Surgery for severe obstruction
1.93	Acute bronchitis	Bronchitis	Viral	No	No	—
0.04	Acute bronchiolitis		Viral	Yes	No	Oxygen
0.53	Pneumonia	Broncho-pneumonia	Bacterial and viral	Yes	Yes/No	Antibiotics

[a] Based on cohort study of 45 Guatemalan children followed from birth to age 3 years (Mata, 1978: 260).
SOURCE: PAHO (1983).

percent of deaths of children under age 5 were due to ALRTI as compared to 17.1 percent for Narangwal. Geographic differences in major causes of mortality in children under age 5 (e.g., ALRTI in Papua New Guinea and diarrhea in Asia) appear to be common.

ALRTI risk factors

Four factors influence mortality risk: age of infection; nutritional status; availability of care; and socioeconomic status.

Age of infection ALRTI morbidity is inversely related to age (see Table 15). The case-fatality rate for infants (4.1 percent of severe cases) is higher than that for 1–4-year-olds (2.4 percent of severe cases). High incidence in infants and high infant case-fatality rates explain the observed high ALRTI mortality in infants.

Nutritional status Undernourished children have an increased risk of pneumonia. Data from Costa Rica documented pneumonia rates of 457.8 per thousand undernourished children as compared to 37.0 per thousand children of normal weight (Pio et al., 1982: 20). In Narangwal, mortality, including that due to pneumonia, was observed to double for each decile below 80 percent weight-for-age (Harvard Standard) (Kielmann and McCord, 1978: 1247).

TABLE 15   Acute lower respiratory tract infection (ALRTI), by age: Tari, Papua New Guinea, 1972–73

Age	Moderate ALRTI per 1,000 children	Severe ALRTI per 1,000 children
<1	342	732
1	124	387
2	65	169
3	34	50
4	23	49

SOURCE: Riley (1981: 355).

Availability of care   Because many respiratory infections can be treated with drugs, lack of health care is also a risk factor for mortality from ALRTI.

Socioeconomic status   Studies in the developed world indicate a clear relationship between socioeconomic status as measured by household size, number of rooms, and persons per room and the incidence of respiratory infection. Low economic status and crowding increase the frequency of respiratory infection. No similar data for the developing world have been identified.

Availability, feasibility, and acceptability of ALRTI prevention/treatment

Discussion of prevention and treatment of ALRTI requires an understanding of disease etiology. In Papua New Guinea, 30 to 50 percent of ALRTI was caused by Streptococcus pneumoniae. In other studies where etiology was determined by lung tap, Streptococcus pneumoniae, the most easily treatable cause of ALRTI, was not always the major cause of pneumonia (Abdel-Khalik et al., 1938: 340; Hughes et al., 1969: 480; Mimica et al., 1971: 279; and Pio et al., 1982: 20). Viral infections usually unresponsive to antibiotics, and bacterial infection not responsive to penicillin or other first-line drugs, are frequently responsible for a significant percentage of infections.

Although Streptococcus pneumoniae and Haemophilus influenzae vaccines have been developed and tested, it is doubtful that they will have any application in the developing world in the immediate future. Cost, lack of immune response in young infants, and short duration of protection are major problems to be solved. The observation that infants of mothers immunized with pneumococcal vaccine had a 32 percent lower rate of pneumonia is of interest (Riley and Douglas, 1981: 241). This effect was, however, of short duration.

From a treatment standpoint, use of penicillin in accordance with strict guidelines is proposed as a primary health care approach. Lack of knowledge of cause of individual pneumonias, development of penicillin resistance, and cost factors all need further investigation.

In view of the high public demand for treatment of illness, acceptance of therapy, especially injections, is high. Where organisms are sensitive to the available antibiotics and the antibiotics are available and used appropriately, significant reductions in mortality can be achieved through treatment.

Effectiveness of ALRTI treatment

Appropriate drug therapy will reduce mortality. In a sequential village study in Punjab, the addition of a standing regimen of procaine penicillin led to a decrease in pneumonia case fatality from 10.5 percent to 2.2 percent and a decrease in mean duration of illness from 4.4 to 2.2 days (McCord and Kielmann, 1978: 224).

Discussion

Low-cost, effective techniques exist for prevention of neonatal tetanus, pertussis, and measles through immunization. In many areas, treatment of ALRTI according to a standard treatment algorithm is also feasible. Yet, only 10–25 percent of at-risk developing world populations are currently receiving these services.

No single explanation for this low coverage is applicable on a global basis. Each area, national or subnational, must be evaluated as to current level of services, potential for expansion, and constraints. In some areas, lack of access to any health service is the major constraint, especially in low-density rural areas such as the Sahel in Africa. Without infrastructure and with mobile operations prohibitively expensive, immunization and treatment of respiratory disease in such areas is not possible without significant and prolonged external support. Of immediate concern, however, is the estimated 50 percent of the at-risk population that are within reach of the health system but are not currently receiving basic services.

Although evaluations have identified numerous constraints, administrative, technical, logistic, and/or operational, the single major difference between programs that are obtaining high coverage and those that are not is commitment in three major areas:

— Commitment on the part of governments in allocating priority and resources to prevention, especially among the rural poor.

— Commitment on the part of the health services to work with the public to ensure provision of immunization and basic curative services to all accessible populations.

— Commitment on the part of the public to participate in and be responsible for their own health care.

The technology exists. With the assistance of WHO and UNICEF, basic commodities are available. High levels of coverage can be and are being obtained. Decreased levels of morbidity and mortality are being documented. Expansion of services to the unserved 50 percent of the population with access is the immediate challenge.

References

Aaby, Peter, Jette Bukh, Ida Marie Lisse, and Arjon J. Smits. 1983. "Measles mortality, state of nutrition, and family structure: A community study from Guinea-Bissau," *Journal of Infectious Diseases* 147, no. 4 (April): 693–701.

Abdel-Khalik, A. K., A. M. Askar, and Mohamed Ali. 1938. "The causative organisms of bronchopneumonia in infants in Egypt," *Archives of Disease in Childhood* 13: 333–342.

Assaad, F. 1983. "Measles: Summary of worldwide impact," *Review of Infectious Diseases* 5, no. 3 (May–June): 452–459.

Basu, R. N., and J. Sokkey. 1982. "A baseline study on neonatal tetanus in India," *Pakistan Pediatric Journal* 6, no. 2–3 (June–September): 184–197.

Bennett, M. J. 1976. "Postabortal and postpartum tetanus," *South African Medical Journal* 50 (March): 513–516.

Berggren, Warren L. 1974. "A tetanus control program in Haiti," *American Journal of Tropical Medicine and Hygiene* 23, no. 5: 936–949.

———, Douglas C. Ewbank, and Gretchen C. Berggren. 1981. "Reduction of mortality in rural Haiti through a primary health care program," *New England Journal of Medicine* 304: 1324–1330.

Black, R. E., D. H. Huber, and G. T. Curlin. 1980. "Reduction of neonatal tetanus by mass immunization of non-pregnant women: Duration of protection provided by one or two doses of aluminium-absorbed tetanus toxoid," *Bulletin of the World Health Organization* 58, no. 6: 927–930.

Bloch, Alan B. 1983. "Consultation to determine the public health importance of measles in Sri Lanka," WHO Short-Term Consultant Assignment Report.

Brown, J., P. Djogdom, K. Murphy, G. Kesseng, and D. Heymann. 1982. "Identifying the reasons for low immunization coverage," *Revue d'Épidémiologie et de Santé Publique* (Paris) 30: 35–47.

Cantrelle, P. 1965. "Mortalité et morbidité par rougeole dans les pays francophones de l'Ouest Africain," *Archiv für die Gesamte Virusforschung* 16: 35–45.

Chen, Lincoln C., Mizanur Rahman, and A. M. Sarder. 1980a. "Epidemiology and causes of death among children in a rural area of Bangladesh," *International Journal of Epidemiology* 9, no. 1 (March): 25–33.

———, A. K. M. Alauddin Chowdhury, and Sandra L. Huffman. 1980b. "Anthropometric assessment of energy protein malnutrition and subsequent risk of mortality among preschool aged children," *American Journal of Clinical Nutrition* 33, no. 8 (August): 1836–1845.

Chen, Paul C. Y. 1976. "An assessment of the training of traditional birth attendants of rural Malaysia," *Medical Journal of Malaysia* 31, no. 2 (December): 93–99.

Church, M. A. 1979. "Evidence of whooping-cough vaccine efficacy from the 1978 whooping-cough epidemic in Hertfordshire," *The Lancet* 2 (28 July): 188–190.

Cook, R. 1978. "Pertussis in developing countries: Possibilities and problems of control through immunization," in *International Symposium on Pertussis,* ed. Charles R. Manclark and James C. Hill. Washington, D.C.: DHEW Publication No. (NIH 79-1830), pp. 283–286.

DeSilva, A. V. K. U. 1982. "Neonatal tetanus problem in Sri Lanka," *Pakistan Pediatric Journal* 6, no. 2–3 (June–September): 214–227.

Foster, S. O., and J. M. Pifer. 1971. "Mass measles control in West and Central Africa," *African Journal of Medical Science* 2: 151–158.

Gambia MCH EPI Evaluation. 1982. The Republic of the Gambia.

Handayani, Tri, Mujiani, Valerie Hull, and Jon E. Rohde. 1983. "Child mortality in a rural Javanese village: A prospective study," *International Journal of Epidemiology* 12, no. 1 (March): 88–92.

Hughes, J. R., Dinesh P. Sinha, Mehroo R. Cooper, Keerti V. Shah, and Sisir K. Bose. 1969. "Lung tap in childhood," *Pediatrics* 44, no. 4 (October): 477–485.

Hull, Harry F., Pap John Williams, and Fred Oldfield. 1983. "Measles mortality and vaccine efficacy in rural West Africa," *The Lancet* 1 (April): 972–975.

Indonesia Nutritional Blindness Report. 1980. Government of Indonesia and Helen Keller International.

Islam, M. Shafiqul, M. Mujibur Rahaman, K. M. S. Aziz, M. H. Munshi, Mizanur Rahman, and Yakub Patwari. 1982. "Birth care practice and neonatal tetanus in a rural area of Bangladesh," *Journal of Tropical Pediatrics* 28, no. 6 (December): 299–302.

John, T. Jacob, Abraham Joseph, T. I. George, Janaki Radhakrishnan, Rajdayal P. D. Singh, and Kuryan George. 1980. "Epidemiology and prevention of measles in rural south India," *Indian Journal of Medical Research* 72 (August): 153–158.

Kasongo Project Team. 1981. "Influence of measles vaccination on survival pattern of 7–35 month old children in Kasongo, Zaire," *The Lancet* 1 (4 April): 764–767.

———. 1983. "Anthropometric assessment of young children's nutritional status as an indicator of subsequent risk of dying," *Journal of Tropical Pediatrics* 29 (April): 69–75.

Kielmann, Arnfried A., and Colin McCord. 1978. "Weight-for-age as an index of risk of death in children," *The Lancet* 1 (10 June): 1247–1250.

Koster, F. T., G. C. Curlin, K. M. A. Aziz, and Azizul Haque. 1981. "Synergistic impact of measles and diarrhea on nutrition and mortality in Bangladesh," *Bulletin of the World Health Organization* 59, no. 6: 901–908.

Mahieu, J. M., A. S. Muller, A. M. Voorhoeve, and H. Dikken. 1978. "Pertussis in a rural area of Kenya: Epidemiology and a preliminary report on a vaccine trial," *Bulletin of the World Health Organization* 56, no. 5: 773–780.

Mata, Leonardo J. 1978. *The Children of Santa Maria Cauque: A Prospective Field Study of Health and Growth.* Cambridge, Mass.: MIT Press.

McBean, A. Marshall, Stanley O. Foster, Kenneth L. Herrmann, and Claude Gateff. 1976. "Evaluation of a mass measles immunization campaign in Yaounde, Cameroun," *Transactions of the Royal Society of Tropical Medicine and Hygiene* 70, no. 3: 206–212.

———, Claude Gateff, Charles R. Manclark, and Stanley O. Foster. 1978. "Simultaneous administration of live attenuated measles vaccine with DTP vaccine," *Pediatrics* 62, no. 3 (September): 288–293.

McCord, C., and A. A. Kielmann. 1978. "A successful programme for medical auxiliaries treating childhood diarrhoea and pneumonia," *Tropical Doctor* 8 (October): 220–225.

McGregor, I. A. 1964. "Measles and child mortality in the Gambia," *West African Medical Journal* 13, no. 6 (December): 251–257.

———, A. K. Rahman, A. M. Thompson, W. Z. Billewicz, and Barbara Thompson. 1970. "The health of young children in a West African Gambian village," *Transactions of the Royal Society of Tropical Medicine* 64, no. 1: 48–77.

Mimica, Igor, Eduardo Donoso, Jorge E. Howard, and G. Walter Lederman. 1971. "Lung puncture in the etiological diagnosis of pneumonia," *American Journal of Diseases of Children* 122, no. 4 (October): 278–282.

Morley, D., M. Woodland, and W. J. Martin. 1963. "Measles in Nigerian children," *Journal of Hygiene* 61, no 1 (March): 115–134.

———, Margaret Woodland, and W. J. Martin. 1966. "Whooping cough in Nigerian children," *Tropical and Geographical Medicine* 18: 169–182.

Mosley, W. H., and L. C. Chen. 1984. "An analytic framework for the study of child survival in developing countries," in this issue.

Newell, K. W., A. Duenas Lehmann, D. R. LeBlanc, and N. Garces Osorio. 1966. "The use of toxoid for the prevention of tetanus neonatorum," *Bulletin of the World Health Organization* 35: 863–871.

Nutrition Reviews. 1982. "Severity of measles in malnutrition," 40, no. 7 (July): 203–204.

PAHO. 1983. *Acute Respiratory Infections in Children.* Washington, D.C.: Pan American Health Organization.

Pio, A., J. Leowski, and F. Luelmo. 1982. "Bases for WHO Programme on Acute Respiratory Infections in Children," XXV World Conference on Tuberculosis, Buenos Aires, 15–18 December.

Rahman, Shafiqur. 1982. "The effect of traditional birth attendants and tetanus toxoid in reduction of neo-natal mortality," *Journal of Tropical Pediatrics* 28, no. 4 (August): 163–165.

Ram, E. R. 1978. "Realization of an integrated health services programme in rural India," *Contact* 44: 1–15.

Riley, Ian D., and Robert M. Douglas. 1981. "An epidemiologic approach to pneumococcal disease," *Reviews of Infectious Diseases* 3, no. 2 (March–April): 233–245.

———, Fairlie A. Everingham, David E. Smith, and Robert M. Douglas. 1981. "Immunization with a polyvalent pneumococcal vaccine," *Archives of Disease in Childhood* 56, no. 5 (May): 354–357.

Robertson, R. L., Joe H. Davis, and Kebba Jobe. In press. "Cost study on expanded programme on immunization in the Gambia," *Bulletin of the World Health Organization.*

Savage, F. M. A. 1967. "A year of measles," *Medical Journal of Zambia* 1 (July): 67–77.

Schofield, F. D., V. M. Tucker, and G. R. Westbrook. 1961. "Neonatal tetanus in New Guinea," *British Medical Journal* 2 (23 September): 785–789.

Strengthening Health Delivery Systems (SHDS). Final Report. 1983. Centers for Disease Control, Atlanta, Georgia.

Sinha, D. 1977. "Measles and malnutrition in a West Bengal village," *Tropical and Geographical Medicine* 29 (September): 125–134.

Smucker, C. M., G. B. Simmons, S. Bernstein, and B. D. Misra. 1980. "Neo-natal mortality in South Asia: The special role of tetanus," *Population Studies* 34, no. 2: 321–335.

Sokal, David C., Garba Soga, and Guy Imboua-Bogui. 1982. "Rapport d'une enquête sur la coqueluche-épidémie du village de Dougba," Département de Tingrela, R.C.I. Mai–Aout 1982. OCCGE Technical Report, no. 7: 998/82.

Suleman, Omer. 1982. "Mortality from tetanus neonatorum in Punjab (Pakistan)," *Pakistan Pediatric Journal* 6, no. 2–3 (June–September): 152–166.

Taylor, Carl E., Arnfried A. Kielmann, Cecile DeSweener et al. Unpublished. "Malnutrition, infection growth, and development: The Narangwal experience."

Voorhoeve, A. M., A. S. Muller, T. W. J. Schulpen, W. 't Mannetje, and M. Van Rens. 1978. "Machakos Project Studies IV: Epidemiology of pertussis," *Tropical and Geographical Medicine* 30: 125–139.

Wakeham, P. F. 1978. "Severe measles in Afghanistan," *Tropical Pediatrics and Environmental Child Health* 24, no. 2 (April): 87–88.

Whittle, H. C., Alice Bradley-Moore, A. Fleming, and B. M. Greenwood. 1973. "Effects of measles on the immune response of Nigerian children," *Archives of Disease in Childhood* 48, no. 265 (September): 753–756.

———, J. Mee, H. Werblinska, A. Yakubu, C. Onuora, and N. Gomwalk. 1980. "Immunity to measles in malnourished children," *Clinical and Experimental Immunology* 42: 144–151.

World Health Organization. 1979. "Measles immunization," *WER* (*Weekly Epidemiologic Record*) 54, no. 44 (2 November): 337–339.

———. 1981. "Acceptance of tetanus toxoid immunization among pregnant women," *WER* 56, no. 27 (10 July): 209–210.

————. 1982a. "Prevention of neonatal tetanus," *WER* 57, no. 18 (7 May): 137–142.

————. 1982b. "The use of survey data to supplement disease surveillance," *WER* 57, no. 47 (26 November): 361–362.

————. 1983a. "Neonatal tetanus survey, Indonesia," *WER* 58, no. 8 (25 February): 56–57.

————. 1983b. "Neonatal tetanus mortality survey, Ivory Coast," *WER* 58, no. 10 (11 March): 71–72.

————. 1983c. "Global status report of Expanded Programme on Immunization," *WER* 58, no. 23 (10 June): 173–176.

————. 1984. "Indications and contraindications for vaccine used in EPI," *WER* 59, no. 3 (20 January): 15.

————. EPI Global Medium Term Programme, 1984–1989. EPI/GEN/83/1. 1–12.

Zhang, Yihao, and Su Wannian. 1983. "A review of the current impact of measles in the People's Republic of China," *Reviews of Infectious Diseases* no. 3 (May–June): 411–416.

Diarrheal Diseases and Child Morbidity and Mortality

Robert E. Black

Diarrheal diseases remain one of the most important public health problems in the world. These diseases, commonly defined by an increase in the frequency and fluidity of bowel movements relative to the usual pattern of each individual, have been found to be major contributors to illness and death, particularly in children in developing countries. Recent estimates by the World Health Organization suggest that children of developing countries have three-quarters of a billion episodes of diarrhea each year, causing nearly 5 million deaths (Snyder and Merson, 1982).

For the children of developing countries it is obvious that exposure and response to diseases are conditioned by their social, economic, and environmental milieu. In Addis Adaba, for instance, the prevalence of diarrhea was found to vary according to housing conditions and parental education (Freij and Wall, 1979). In Bangladesh several specific types of diarrhea had higher incidences and longer durations in children from low-income households (Becker, Black, and Brown, unpublished research). These differentials in rates of disease by socioeconomic variables may be due to differences in child care practices, such as preparation of weaning foods, boiling of drinking water, or personal hygiene (Black et al., 1983). On the other hand, they may be due to low-income children's poorer nutritional status, a factor known to be associated with more prolonged diarrhea (Black et al., 1984a). Since the diarrheal diseases are comprised of many specific types of illnesses caused by diverse bacterial, viral, and parasitic enteropathogens with differing modes of transmission, the relationship between the diarrheal diseases and socioeconomic and environmental variables can be determined only if the epidemiology of the diarrheal diseases themselves is better understood.

Until the last several years, studies of children in developing countries had been able to detect a potential causal agent in fewer than 20 percent of stool specimens from children with diarrhea (Feldman, Bhat, and Kamath, 1970). This lack of information about the causes of diarrhea had precluded the complete exposition of the epidemiology of the diarrheal syndromes. Using new techniques to detect enteropathogens, it is now possible to identify an enteropathogen for most of the diarrheal illnesses in young children of developing countries. Furthermore, this knowledge about etiologic agents of diarrhea has permitted a better description of the epidemiology, including the modes of transmission, of specific types of diarrhea.

This paper reviews the major etiologic agents of infant and childhood diarrhea from an epidemiologic perspective. It also discusses the methods for measuring the frequency of diarrheal diseases and for assessing the contribution of these diseases to childhood mortality. Estimates of the importance of specific types or etiologies of diarrhea are given, and the impact of possible interventions, such as vaccines or therapy, is considered.

Etiologic agents of diarrhea

The infectious etiologic agents of diarrhea are numerous. These agents appear to occur worldwide, although some seem to be more frequent in developing countries. Among the bacterial pathogens, diarrheas due to *Escherichia coli* and *Shigella* seem to be particularly common in less developed settings.[1]

The term viral diarrheas has been used to describe a variety of acute, self-limited illnesses, characterized by diarrhea and often vomiting, for which bacterial enteropathogens could not be identified. Although these illnesses were presumed to be due to viral infections, until recently not a single virus could be implicated as an important cause of diarrhea. Since 1972, however, three groups of viruses have been found to be etiologic agents for diarrhea.[2] One group, the rotaviruses, appears to be responsible for a high proportion of the serious sporadic diarrheas of young children.

Of the parasitic causes of diarrhea, *Entamoeba histolytica* and *Giardia lamblia* may be the most common and important.[3] Although the severity of disease with *E. histolytica* varies substantially in different geographic and demographic groups, amoebiasis is the only parasitic diarrheal disease associated with mortality.

The relative importance of these enteropathogens as causes of diarrhea differs somewhat among developing countries. Nevertheless, poor children in most underdeveloped settings share similar environmental hazards, including limited and contaminated water supplies, inadequate feces disposal, and unhygienic home conditions. Thus, most of these enteropathogens tend to occur in developing country populations.

Studies done in Matlab, Bangladesh, during 1978–79 provide the most complete information on the etiology and epidemiology of diarrhea in one area and will be used to demonstrate the frequency and severity of diarrhea associated with different pathogens. In a two-year study of the enteropathogens associated with diarrhea at a rural treatment center, toxigenic *E. coli* was the pathogen most frequently isolated from all patients and from adults (Table 1)

TABLE 1 Percentage of patients with diarrhea associated with enteric pathogens, by age, in the periods February 1977–January 1978 (year 1) and February 1978–January 1979 (year 2), Matlab Thana, Bangladesh

Pathogen identified	Age group and study year							
	<2 years		**2–9 years**		**≥10 years**		**All ages**	
	1(N = 3,500)	2(N = 2,614)	1(N = 1,815)	2(N = 1,391)	1(N = 2,824)	2(N = 2,347)	1(N = 8,139)	2(N = 6,352)
Enterotoxigenic E. coli[a]								
ST	12	17	12	15	16	22	14	18
ST/LT	6	7	6	7	14	19	9	11
LT	5	4	3	1	3	2	4	2
Total	23	28	22	24	33	42	26	32
Rotavirus	—	46	—	12	—	9	—	24
V. cholerae group 0:1	2	2	29	34	14	14	12	14
Non–group 0:1 vibrios	8	5	2	4	8	11	7	7
Shigella	4	5	6	10	4	5	5	6
E. histolytica	1	—	8	—	8	—	4	—
G. lamblia	<1	—	13	—	4	—	2	—
Group F vibriolike organisms	4	<1	4	<1	2	<1	3	<1
Salmonella	<1	<1	2	<1	<1	<1	<1	<1
V. parahaemolyticus	0	<1	<1	0	<1	<1	<1	<1

[a] ST = strain producing heat-stable enterotoxin; LT = strain producing heat-labile enterotoxin.

SOURCE: Black et al. (1980).

(Black et al., 1980). It was second (after rotavirus) in children under age 2 years. Rotavirus was found in the stools of 46 percent of the children under age 2 years and in the stools of 12 percent and 9 percent, respectively, of older children and adults.

Vibrio cholerae group 0:1 was rarely identified in children less than 2 years old but was an important pathogen in older children and adults. Shigella was isolated from 5–6 percent of all patients, but Salmonella and V. parahaemolyticus were rarely found. G. lamblia was identified in 4 percent of the older children, but rarely in children under age 2 years. Vegetative E. histolytica was identified in 13 percent of the older children and in only 1 percent of younger children. An enteropathogen was identified in 70 percent of the children under age 2 years. Infection with more than one pathogen was found in about 20 percent of all patients.

The number of children seen at the treatment center with severe dehydration was determined. Assuming that 50 percent of these children would have died, the number of deaths that would have been expected if treatment had not been available was calculated. An estimated 173 deaths would have occurred in children under 2 years; 60 of these would have been in children with E. coli diarrhea and 73 in those with rotavirus diarrhea. Thus, illnesses associated with these two enteropathogens would have accounted for 77 percent of deaths.

Daily surveillance consisting of household visits and questioning about illness in one Bangladesh village detected 877 episodes of diarrhea in a one-year period (Table 2) (Black et al., 1981a). Enterotoxigenic E. coli were the most common enteropathogens identified in all age groups; shigellae were the second most commonly found enteropathogens, and rotaviruses the third. In

TABLE 2 Number of diarrheal episodes associated with enteric pathogens, by age, in a community-based study, December 1977–November 1978, Matlab Thana, Bangladesh

Pathogen identified	Age group			
	<2 years (N = 377)	2–9 years (N = 380)	≥10 years (N = 120)	All ages (N = 877)
Enterotoxigenic E. coli[a]				
ST	41 (11)	65 (17)	15 (12)	121 (14)
ST/LT	15 (4)	18 (5)	0 (—)	33 (4)
LT	18 (5)	21 (6)	9 (8)	48 (5)
Shigella	57 (15)	32 (8)	5 (4)	94 (11)
Rotavirus	43 (11)	0 (—)	0 (—)	43 (5)
Other and mixed[b]	8 (2)	12 (3)	6 (5)	26 (3)

NOTE: Figures in parentheses are percentages.
[a] For definitions of strains of E. coli, see Table 1.
[b] Includes V. cholerae and Salmonella.
SOURCE: Black et al. (1981a).

the village study, an enteropathogen was identified in 48 percent of children under age 2 years.

Dehydration was significantly more common in children with rotavirus diarrhea and *E. coli* diarrhea than in children with diarrhea of other or unknown etiology. Of 41 children aged less than 2 years with dehydration during a diarrheal episode, 19 (46 percent) had rotavirus detected, and 10 (24 percent) had toxigenic *E. coli*. Of the rotavirus episodes, 44 percent were associated with dehydration, compared with 14 percent for *E. coli* and 5 percent for other diarrheas.

Other studies of the importance of toxigenic *E. coli* and rotaviruses in children with diarrhea have been conducted. Most of these studies have involved few patients and have been carried out during a short period of time, often in either summer or winter months. Taken collectively, however, they suggest that *E. coli* and rotaviruses are important pathogens.

Shigella also appears to be an important pathogen in developing country children. In Bangladesh it has been found to be second in frequency only to enterotoxigenic *E. coli* as a cause of diarrhea. Further, *Shigella* was the pathogen most often associated with prolonged (greater than three weeks) diarrhea; and shigellosis was found to have the strongest negative effect of all types of diarrhea on linear growth of children in Bangladesh (Black, Brown, and Becker, 1984b). Thus, shigellosis may be important not only as a direct cause of death but also because it contributes to malnutrition. Severely malnourished children have been shown to have a higher mortality rate from a variety of infectious diseases (Kielmann and McCord, 1978; Chen, Chowdhury, and Huffman, 1980a).

Subsequent to the studies in Bangladesh, *Campylobacter jejuni* has emerged as an important cause of acute diarrheal disease. Studies in Australia, Canada, the Netherlands, Sweden, the United Kingdom, and the United States have demonstrated *C. jejuni* in the stools of 5–17 percent of persons with diarrhea (Blaser, Taylor, and Feldman, in press). There have been few studies to date in developing countries, but the existing studies indicate that *C. jejuni* may be even more frequently associated with diarrhea there than in developed countries. At the same time, studies of healthy young children in developing countries find a high prevalence of *C. jejuni*. More data are needed on the importance of this pathogen as a cause of diarrhea.

The recent recognition of bacterial and viral agents of diarrhea permits the identification of an enteropathogen in the majority of episodes of diarrhea and in 70–80 percent of the more severe episodes treated at health facilities. Because it is impossible to describe the epidemiology of all the bacterial, viral, and parasitic enteropathogens, this paper concentrates on the agents that appear to contribute most to high diarrheal mortality. Three agents will be included: enterotoxigenic *E. coli*, rotavirus, and *Shigella*. Not only are these the most important causes of severe disease and death, but also their patterns of transmission—direct person-to-person contact (fecal–oral) or ingestion of contaminated food or water—are common to most of the other enteropathogens.

Epidemiology and transmission of important enteropathogens

Escherichia coli

Escherichia coli are gram-negative bacilli that can be found in the normal intestinal flora of man and many animals but can also be an important cause of enteric illness. Some specific *E. coli* serotypes that were implicated in nursery outbreaks of diarrhea, primarily in the 1950s, were referred to as enteropathogenic. This term was used at a time when nothing was known about any *E. coli* pathogenic mechanisms, and it is now used to refer to *E. coli* belonging to serogroups that have been epidemiologically incriminated as pathogens but have not been proven to produce either heat-stable or heat-labile toxins or to have *Shigella*-like invasiveness (Neter, 1983). Investigators from several countries have shown that enteropathogenic *E. coli* are an important cause of epidemic and sporadic cases of infantile diarrhea, which occurs mostly in the summer (Pal et al., 1969; Freiman et al., 1977; Toledo et al., 1983).

In the late 1960s it was first recognized that some *E. coli* produce enterotoxins that cause diarrhea in many animals and in man.[4] Research in the following decade led to the recognition that these toxin-producing organisms are a major cause of diarrhea in developing countries.

Transmission of enterotoxigenic *E. coli* is thought to be primarily by water and food. Water was the vehicle for an outbreak in a national park in the United States (Rosenberg et al., 1977). Foodborne outbreaks have been reported on a cruise ship, and enterotoxigenic organisms have been isolated from foods in Bangladesh and in the United States (Black et al., 1982c; Sack et al., 1977). In Bangladesh, studies suggest that transmission of enterotoxigenic *E. coli* to young children may occur more frequently as a result of consumption of contaminated weaning food (Black et al., 1982c). Person-to-person transmission probably occurs only rarely and then in unusual settings, such as in hospital nurseries (Levine et al., 1980; Ryder et al., 1976).

Because of the association of contaminated water and food with occurrence of this disease, it can be presumed that avoidance of fecally contaminated water and attention to hygienic food handling techniques would help prevent illness. More specific prevention measures, including immunization, may be possible after further epidemiologic and laboratory studies.

Rotavirus

Rotaviruses have been found to be important agents of diarrhea in studies done in scores of countries in every area of the world. In developed countries they are probably the most frequent pathogens causing childhood diarrhea (Brandt et al., 1983). In developing countries, rotaviruses also appear to be frequent pathogens in children hospitalized for acute diarrhea. In 15 hospital-based studies of at least one-year duration done in developing countries, rotaviruses were found in the stool of 14–46 percent of children with diarrhea (average 28 percent).

Rotavirus diarrhea is an endemic problem throughout the world, although clear epidemics have been reported. Community-wide epidemics have primarily involved young children, except among previously isolated populations suddenly exposed to the virus, as on mid-Pacific islands or in remote areas, where epidemics involved substantial proportions of the population of all ages (Foster et al., 1980; Linhares et al., 1981).

Rotavirus infection spreads by fecal–oral transmission. Infectious particles from diarrheal feces have reproduced the disease in volunteers when given orally (Kapikian et al., 1983). The usual mode of transmission is probably by direct person-to-person contact or contact with contaminated objects. Rotaviruses have been demonstrated on the hands of attendants of children with diarrhea (Samadi, Huq, and Ahmed, 1983). The virus is relatively resistant to adverse environmental conditions and can remain on surfaces for prolonged periods. It also maintains structural integrity in water and sewage; and assuming these particles retain infectivity, it is possible that waterborne transmission may occur (Hurst and Gerba, 1980; Steinmann, 1981). The respiratory symptoms associated with rotaviral diarrheal illnesses and the occasional demonstration of rotaviral antigen in nasal wash specimens have led to speculation that transmission could take place via airborne droplets. However, there is currently no evidence to support the possibility of airborne transmission, nor to suggest that rotavirus multiplies with production of infectious particles in any tissue other than small-bowel enterocytes.

Prevention should be possible through the interruption of fecal–oral transmission of the virus. Sanitary waste disposal, avoidance of fecally contaminated water and objects, and particularly such hygienic practices as handwashing would be expected to assist in prevention (Black et al., 1981b).

Immunologic protection from rotavirus diarrhea is not yet well understood. Infants may derive some protection from breastfeeding, since human colostrum and breastmilk have specific rotavirus-neutralizing antibodies, and antirotavirus IgA antibody persists for as long as nine months after delivery (Yolken et al., 1978). Children more than 2 years old and adults have substantial resistance to rotavirus diarrhea. Thus, it seems that natural immunity probably occurs following one or more illnesses in early childhood and repeated asymptomatic exposures to the virus (Black et al., 1982a). It appears that sequential rotavirus illnesses can occur but that such illnesses are usually due to different serotypes (four serotypes are currently recognized based on neutralization assays) (Kapikian, 1981). It is likely that this serotype-specific immunity is due to local intestinal antibody. Because of the importance of the rotavirus as a cause of morbidity and mortality throughout the world, there is great interest in developing a vaccine to prevent rotavirus diarrhea during the first two years of life (Kapikian et al., 1980). Several possible vaccine strains of rotavirus are currently being evaluated in the laboratory and in adult volunteers.

Shigella

Shigella bacteria are classified into four groups: dysenteriae, flexneri, boydii, and sonnei. *S. flexneri* is the most common in developing countries, but *S. dysenteriae* has occurred in several severe epidemics.

Acute diarrhea (usually dysentery) can result from the ingestion of as few as 10 bacteria. This ingested dose is 100–10,000-fold lower than that needed to cause illness with other bacterial organisms, such as *V. cholerae* or *E. coli*. Because of the small infective dose, shigellae are easily spread from person to person. This fecal–oral transmission can occur by direct contact, especially in young children (Black et al., 1977; Pickering et al., 1981). Shigellae can also be transmitted by contaminated food or water (Black et al., 1978). Transmission has also been reported from swimming in contaminated water (Rosenberg et al., 1976). In areas with poor disposal of feces, flies may carry the bacteria and contaminate foods (Watt and Lindsay, 1948).

Shigellae are often endemic in institutions and nurseries (Black et al., 1977; Pickering et al., 1981). These settings are important in the transmission of the bacteria and may also constitute foci from which the community may be infected (Weissman et al., 1974; DuPont et al., 1970). In developing countries, children aged 2–4 years have the highest rate of shigellosis (Black et al., 1982b). Clinical and subclinical infections in childhood probably result in substantial immunity in adults in endemic areas.

Shiga dysentery, due to *S. dysenteriae,* has caused major epidemics in Central America, Africa, Bangladesh, and Sri Lanka (Mendizabal et al., 1971; Rahaman et al., 1975; Frost et al., 1981). The epidemics were caused by multiple antibiotic-resistant bacteria and were associated with a high case-fatality rate in children and adults. In Guatemala alone an estimated 12,000 deaths were due to Shiga dysentery during one year of the epidemic. Why these epidemics occurred and then declined is unknown.

Although shigellosis is usually mild, requiring only supportive therapy including fluid replacement, appropriate antimicrobial therapy can be useful. Such therapy has been shown to shorten the duration of illness and is apparently lifesaving in severe cases (Levine, 1982).

Transmission of shigellae should be preventable by attention to personal hygiene, especially handwashing after a bowel movement or contact with feces. Indeed, proper handwashing has been shown to reduce the spread of the infection in Bangladesh (Khan, 1982). The availability of water for personal hygiene has been found to be inversely correlated with *Shigella* incidence in some areas (Hollister et al., 1955), but it appears that personal hygiene is even more important than the amount of water available (Rajasekaran, Dutt, and Pisharoti, 1977). Various *Shigella* vaccines have been tried but none has been suitable. Additional studies being done with live strains are promising, but, due to the need to confer immunity to multiple serotypes, a vaccine will not be available for some years.

Measuring diarrheal morbidity and mortality

The high rates of disease and death due to diarrhea in developing countries are well recognized but have seldom been accurately measured. Estimates of global morbidity and mortality rates, including those due to diarrhea, have been used to set health care priorities, yet these estimates are based on limited data of questionable quality and unknown generalizability (Snyder and Merson, 1982). Furthermore, although the appropriate tools exist, they have not been frequently applied to determine the variations in diarrheal morbidity and mortality levels between geographic regions or within countries and the reasons for these variations. These epidemiologic tools, which can be used to measure the contributions of the diarrheal diseases to morbidity and mortality of children in developing countries, are described in this section.

Definitions of terms

Population at risk In general, the specific population of interest—classified, for example, by age or area of residence—constitutes the denominator in the calculation of morbidity and mortality rates. In the context of this paper, the population at risk is children under age 5 years living in developing countries. To make more detailed calculations, it would be appropriate to divide this age group into at least two—infants less than 1 year old and children 1–4 years old.

Deaths and cases To calculate the needed rates, the cases that will form the numerator of the analysis must be carefully defined. With crude mortality rates, the definition of death is not usually a problem. However, with specific mortality rates, such as diarrheal mortality or age-specific diarrheal mortality, care must be given to the definition of the numerator. Since it is rarely possible to determine the precise proximate cause of death in developing countries, most calculations use diarrhea-associated deaths: if diarrhea was present at the time of death, it is considered associated with the death. With diarrheal morbidity rates, a definition of diarrhea must be used so that cases can be properly classified. Depending on the measurement methodology and local setting, this definition may be either quantitative (e.g., at least three liquid stools within a 24-hour period) or qualitative (e.g., the mother says that the child has diarrhea).

Incidence rate The number of new cases during a specified time, divided by the population at risk, and multiplied by some unit of population (e.g., 1,000) is the incidence rate. The diarrheal incidence rate would be the number of new cases of diarrhea per 1,000 persons in some period of time (e.g., 1 year).

Prevalence rate The total number of cases present at a point in time, divided by the population at risk, and multiplied by some unit of population (e.g., 1,000) is the point prevalence rate. The numerator includes all persons with diarrhea at that moment, regardless of the time or date of onset of the illness. A similar calculation can be done using all diarrheal cases (old and new) during some specified period; this is called the period prevalence. Period prevalence is the sum of the point prevalence (existing cases) at the beginning of the period and the incidence during the period. Generally, incidence and point prevalence rates are more useful than period prevalence rates.

Death or mortality rate This measure of the frequency of death is calculated using persons dying during a stated period as the numerator and the population at risk during that period as the denominator. The rate of death is expressed per unit of population (e.g., per 1,000 children). Although more detailed calculations are possible, two rates should be sufficient for most purposes; these are the infant (under 1 year) diarrheal mortality rate and the childhood (1–4 years) diarrheal mortality rate.

Death ratio Often it is useful to determine the relative contribution of certain causes of death to the total deaths, or the death ratio. The diarrheal death ratio is the proportion of all deaths that is associated with diarrhea.

Case-fatality rate A disease-specific case-fatality rate can be calculated as the number of persons dying with the disease divided by total persons with the disease. In the present review, it would be the ratio of diarrhea-associated deaths to all cases of diarrhea in the population at risk. This is often calculated in treatment facilities, where it can be useful in evaluating the effectiveness of the current therapeutic approach. However, the case-fatality rate is not very useful as an indication of population-based mortality levels. Only a portion of all diarrheal cases come to treatment facilities, and these are often the more severe cases. The selection biases (nonrandom selection) inherent in the treatment center cases make it difficult to use the case-fatality rate (along with other information such as diarrheal incidence) to estimate diarrheal mortality rates.

Sources of data for calculating diarrheal morbidity and mortality rates

"Routine" surveillance data It is sometimes possible to calculate diarrheal morbidity and mortality rates based on available information from disease reporting, health service statistics, vital records, and censuses. But the information may be severely deficient.

Some countries have a national or regional reporting system that includes diarrheal diseases; more often diarrhea is not a reportable illness. Even if there is a system requiring reporting of the number of cases of diarrhea seen in treatment centers, the completeness and accuracy of the data are influenced by the availability of health facilities, financial and human resources, and the priority given to reporting of diarrhea. For an illness as common (and often as mild) as diarrhea, a major problem is that many cases are treated by local medical practitioners, health workers, and traditional healers who are not part of the reporting system. Furthermore, many cases do not seek medical attention. Thus, calculations based on the reported number of cases of diarrhea are underestimates of the actual number of cases, often by a factor of 100 or even 1,000.

To avoid the problems of incomplete reporting of cases seen at treatment facilities, it is possible to review the records of a sample of facilities and determine the number of diarrheal cases seen there. This may permit a better estimation of the incidence of cases seeking medical attention but would still not provide a true incidence rate. The number of cases treated depends heavily on the extent to which the facilities are used (e.g., service use may be better in urban than in rural areas and better in areas with more available transportation). Thus, diarrheal incidence rates based on health service statistics are not useful indicators of the actual level of diarrheal morbidity.

Vital records or certificates of death and birth are commonly used for calculations of death and birth rates in developed countries. Unfortunately, the usefulness of vital records in developing countries is often restricted because of:

— substantial underregistration of deaths, particularly among newborns, or no death registration at all;
— extensive misreporting of the age at death or excessive numbers of "age not stated" death reports;
— variable availability and quality of information from different areas of the country.

In addition to the problems with the accuracy of death reports in general, there are additional sources of error with cause- (i.e., diarrhea) specific mortality. The most important errors include the following:

— The cause of death is unknown or not provided.
— Standard definitions and classifications for the cause of death are not used.
— Multiple illnesses are present at the time of death, and one of these is arbitrarily selected as the cause of death.

On occasion, the vital records can be used to calculate the infant and childhood mortality rates, but the death registration system does not provide accurate information on cause of death. In this situation it may be possible to estimate the diarrheal mortality rate by multiplying the total mortality rate for children by the diarrheal death ratio. The diarrheal death ratio would need to be calculated based on areas with unusually good death registration or, more likely, based on special surveys to determine the important causes of death.

Sentinel surveillance A sentinel surveillance system can be established to collect information from reporting sites selected for their representativeness and capacity to report accurately. These reporting sites could include selected health facilities and communities. In areas with a reliable routine reporting system, a sentinel system can be used to obtain additional data that would provide a more accurate evaluation of morbidity and mortality. In areas without a reliable routine system, a sentinel system can be used to collect the basic necessary information.

Surveys There are two basic types of surveys: complete surveys and sample surveys. In complete surveys, often censuses, all persons or households in the area are surveyed. In a sample survey only some of the units in the area are selected to be surveyed. Sample surveys are often preferred because they are less difficult, less time-consuming, and less costly than complete surveys.

In addition, surveys can vary in the type of information they collect. The questions can be designed to elicit information on the current situation at the exact time of the survey. For example, the number of children with diarrhea on the day of the survey can be used to calculate the point prevalence of diarrhea. However, the questions are often retrospective, asking about illnesses (or deaths) that occurred some time in the past. Surveys may also use a combination of concurrent and retrospective questions.

A problem in estimating mortality from demographic (census) data is that many developing countries have poor data on mortality, since death reporting is limited or nonexistent. Thus, techniques have been devised to use data from a survey or census to estimate infant and childhood mortality. The survey must obtain retrospective information from women about the woman's age, the number of children ever born, and the number of these children who had died by the time of the survey. William Brass devised methods to convert the calculated proportions of the dead or surviving children into life table measures of mortality (Brass and Coale, 1968). These techniques assume that age-specific fertility and mortality have been relatively stable in the recent past. They also assume that the woman's reported age is accurate and that surviving women are not significantly different from women who died. These techniques can be useful for estimating infant and child mortality rates in some settings, but they may be inaccurate in other situations, such as areas with recent changes in mortality rates. Furthermore, although they permit calculations of age-specific mortality rates, they do not allow determination of cause-specific mortality rates. Thus, to determine the contribution of specific diseases to mortality, they would need to be combined with other calculations, such as the diarrheal death ratio.

Surveys have been used to estimate diarrheal mortality and morbidity rates in a variety of settings. These surveys vary in their methods, depending on specific objectives and necessary precision. The survey methodology can be illustrated using the example of the diarrheal mortality and morbidity surveys that were designed for the Diarrhoeal Diseases Control Programme of the World Health Organization (World Health Organization, 1981). Such surveys have been successfully conducted in more than 20 developing countries to date.

Mortality survey The mortality survey outlined here is designed to determine the total and diarrheal mortality rates in children under age 5 years. It can also be used to calculate age-specific mortality rates of children under age 1 year and aged 1–4 years, if the ages of children in the household and of deceased children are recorded. Workers visiting a sample of households must ask the mother or other child-caretakers in the house a series of questions to determine:

— the number of children under age 5 years in the household (and possibly age of the children) at the time of the survey;
— the number of deaths to children under age 5 years in the previous year;
— the possible causes of these deaths (and possibly age at death).

The number of children (and households) questioned must be sufficient to accurately reflect the true mortality rates. The number of children to be surveyed or the sample size can be determined based on the estimated mortality rates and the desired levels of precision.

This survey uses the cluster sampling method by which villages and interview clusters are selected with a probability proportional to their estimated size. This sample method is more convenient than a random sample, since persons to be interviewed reside in a relatively limited number of villages. Thus, cluster sampling has the advantages of relative speed, low cost, and low personnel requirements. At the same time, it provides accurate information, without undue bias, if carefully designed and conducted.

For convenience the household is the interview unit. To maintain consistency in the survey, the household should be defined based on local customs—for example, all persons eating together and sleeping under the same roof.

In respect to mortality rate calculations, this retrospective survey has several potential sources of error. These are:

— Distortion with respect to the length of the reference period. Since deaths in a population may show a seasonal pattern due to the occurrence of various diseases or environmental conditions, it is highly desirable to consider deaths for a one-year period. It is often difficult for rural people to orient their responses to a calendar year; however, the use of a one-year period oriented toward locally relevant events may permit more accurate placement of deaths in a one-year period.
— Misclassifying the deaths by age. If the deaths of children under age 5 years are the principal target of the survey, this problem will be minimized. Possible misclassifications of children aged 5 years or older as

less than age 5 years may slightly inflate the estimated number of children under age 5; however, it should have relatively little effect on the number of deaths since the mortality rate in 5–9-year-old children is very low in comparison with the rate in younger children. However, if mortality rates are calculated for children under age 1 year and aged 1–4 years, the misclassification by age could be a more serious problem.

— Nonreporting of deaths. This problem must be considered in the design of the survey questionnaire. The deaths that are most likely to be omitted are those of very young children, especially those dying in the first few days of life. Specific questions must be included to attempt to overcome this problem, such as asking the mother her recent pregnancy history and the outcome of each pregnancy.

— Difficulty in attributing cause of death. The mother or other relative of a child cannot be expected to know the cause of death in precise medical terms; however, she will usually remember the events and circumstances of the death. The questions asked in the survey must be designed to determine whether diarrhea was present at the time of death.

The information obtained from such a survey can be used to calculate diarrheal mortality rates as follows:

$$\frac{\text{Deaths due to diarrhea of children under age 5 years in the survey population in the previous year}}{\text{Number of children under age 5 years in the survey population at the time of the survey}} \times 1{,}000$$

Morbidity survey The morbidity survey outlined below is designed to provide an estimate of the diarrheal incidence among children under age 5 years (age-specific morbidity rates could also be obtained). In a sample of households the mother or other child-caretaker in the house must be asked a series of questions to determine:

— the number of children under age 5 years in the household at the present time;
— the number of episodes of diarrhea occurring in a specified time period.

The respondent must remember and report that her child had diarrhea in the time interval in question. The accuracy of her memory is likely to be relatively good for the very recent past but less complete for periods extending two weeks or more before the survey. Thus, to obtain accurate information it is necessary to ask only about a short recent time period such as two weeks. This short period, however, presents a problem in that diarrhea may be seasonal and the particular two-week period chosen for the survey may not be representative of the entire year. There is no easy solution to this problem, but possible answers may be either to repeat the survey at two or more times in the year or to pick a time felt to be most representative of the "usual" diarrhea situation and not a time of extremely high or low diarrheal incidence.

The number of children (and households) questioned must be sufficient to accurately reflect the true diarrheal incidence. The number of children to be surveyed, or the sample size, can be determined based on the estimated diarrheal incidence and desired levels of precision.

The information obtained from the survey questions would be used to calculate the diarrheal incidence for the two-week period as follows:

$$\frac{\text{New episodes of diarrhea in children under age 5 years}}{\substack{\text{Number of children under age 5 years in the survey population} \\ \text{at the time of the survey}}} \times 100$$

The usual practice is to conduct the diarrheal mortality and morbidity surveys at the same time. This survey methodology provides health planners with a rapid, simple, low-cost, yet valid system for obtaining mortality and morbidity information. It can be applied to produce baseline information on the importance of various health problems and to evaluate changes in the levels of these problems as a result of intervention programs.

Prospective studies Prospective or longitudinal studies are extremely useful for describing the natural history of infectious diseases and their transmission. Furthermore, they can be used for identifying risk factors and in assessing causal relationships.

Longitudinal studies of diarrheal morbidity have been performed in several countries. In general, they have been used to determine levels of specific diseases and of malnutrition. Because these studies have extensive logistic requirements, they have been best applied to diseases with a moderately high frequency of occurrence. The prospective methodology has seldom been used to study mortality, especially cause-specific mortality, in developing countries since, even in these areas, mortality is relatively infrequent and the study population would need to be very large. The few sites in developing countries that have prospective demographic (births, deaths, etc.) surveillance of a large population have provided valuable information on age-specific mortality rates; but even with the extensive resources of these projects, the data on cause-specific mortality have not been optimal (Chen, Rahman, and Sarder, 1980b; Becker, 1981). Due to expense and difficulty of operation, high-quality prospective demographic surveillance systems will probably be confined to a few selected areas of the world.

Prospective studies can provide the most accurate information on diarrheal morbidity, and this information can be expressed as incidence rates or prevalence rates. The duration of diarrheal episodes can also be determined. The occurrence of diarrhea is ascertained by means of home visits as frequently as logistically and culturally possible. In most areas of the world, visits must be made at no greater than two-week intervals for the reporting of diarrhea to be reasonably accurate. Visiting more frequently than biweekly is usually advisable: the most intensive studies have conducted household surveillance every other day or three times per week. These intensive prospective studies are usually done in study populations of fewer than 200 persons. After an analysis of 22 prospective studies of diarrheal morbidity, it was suggested that both the frequency of surveillance and the size of the study population affect the incidence of diarrhea calculated by the study (Snyder and Merson, 1982). It is more likely that all episodes will be reported when smaller populations are surveyed more often, resulting in a higher and more accurate incidence.

One requirement for longitudinal studies is continuity of the study population. A high frequency of study subjects dropping out of the study or moving away may compromise the results. It is also an advantage if the investigators and others working on the surveillance continue to be involved for the duration of the study. This may not be a problem for studies of one to two years' duration, but can be for longer studies.

Another issue that must be faced is whether and to what extent the longitudinal study methodology should include providing medical services to the study population. Obviously the provision of such services may alter the state of health or even the transmission of disease. On the other hand, not providing needed services raises serious ethical questions and also may adversely affect the quality of the study data (DeSweemer et al., 1982). Thus, it is usually desirable to provide basic medical services and to try to account for alterations in the disease epidemiology in the study design and analysis.

An advantage of this type of study is that more accurate information can be obtained about individual diarrheal episodes, since they are identified as they occur rather than after. This information may include the association of the illness with specific bacterial, viral, and parasitic enteropathogens. For this to be done specimens of stool must be obtained as early as possible during the illness. Appropriate laboratory tests must then be done to identify the pathogens. Data on the importance of certain pathogens are necessary so that reasonable interventions can be implemented and evaluated.

The limitations of longitudinal studies are their cost and difficulty to conduct. They may be logistically demanding and require constant supervision to ensure accurate data. Another problem is that a small and available study group may not represent the population of the country or region as a whole. Thus, caution must be applied when the data are used to generalize about diarrheal morbidity rates.

Interventions

As discussed earlier, diarrheal pathogens are transmitted by the fecal–oral route. Some, like enterotoxigenic *E. coli,* are commonly transmitted via weaning foods to young children. These foods may become fecally contaminated from impure water, unhygienic utensils, or food-handling. Moreover, the levels of contamination with *E. coli* and other bacterial pathogens may increase due to the multiplication of bacteria that occurs when food is stored at household temperatures. Other pathogens, like *Shigella*, rotavirus, and *G. lamblia*, are infectious in small doses and can be spread via contaminated hands or household objects.

Interventions to interrupt transmission of the enteropathogens could focus at a variety of levels. These may include safe disposal of human feces or protection of water supplies from contamination; however, interventions at these levels have almost invariably been disappointing in their effect on diarrheal morbidity. Perhaps the most promising interventions would focus on the household environment and on the immediate risks to which the child is exposed (Black et al., 1983). Potential areas for intervention would be improvements in the quality of weaning foods from the hygienic point of view and reductions in the degree of household fecal contamination. One such intervention—handwashing—has been found to substantially reduce the incidence of diarrhea (Black et al., 1981b) and the transmission of *Shigella* (Khan, 1982). The other household-level interventions have not been evaluated systematically.

Another approach to prevention is the development of vaccines giving long-lasting protection against the most important enteropathogens. To direct vaccine development, information on the relative importance of the pathogens is needed. Information cited earlier from Bangladesh indicates that three-quarters of the dehydrating and potentially lethal diarrheal episodes were caused by rotavirus or enterotoxigenic *E. coli*. There is also support from other data for the need for a vaccine against *Shigella*, an important cause of dysentery and prolonged diarrhea and a major contributor to malnutrition. New developments have brought vaccines against all three pathogens to the point of studies in volunteers, and a potential rotavirus vaccine is being field tested in infants.

Death from acute diarrhea is most often due to the dehydration that results from loss of water and electrolytes. It is now well accepted that nearly all dehydration-related deaths can be prevented by the prompt administration of rehydration solutions (Hirschhorn, 1980). These solutions can include a glucose– or sucrose–electrolyte mixture or the more recently described rice- or other cereal-based solutions, which may be less expensive and more accessible to children of developing countries. Since acute diarrheal deaths usually constitute 50–60 percent of all diarrheal deaths, an optimal rehydration program should considerably reduce the diarrheal mortality rate. Indeed, reductions in diarrheal deaths of up to 50 percent have been noted in controlled community-based oral rehydration therapy interventions (Rahaman et al., 1979). However, in these studies, reductions in total mortality rates have not always been as great as would be expected from the declines in diarrheal deaths.

Although adequate fluid therapy alone should prevent death from acute dehydrating diarrhea, adjunctive treatment with antibiotics may sometimes be useful to reduce the duration and volume of diarrhea (Wallace et al., 1968; Black, 1982). Of even greater potential importance is the appropriate antibiotic and nutritional therapy of dysentery and prolonged diarrhea that may be associated with *Shigella, Campylobacter, E. histolytica,* or *G. lamblia.* In some areas one-half or more of diarrhea-associated deaths have involved dysenteric or prolonged diarrheal illness, rather than acute diarrhea (Black, unpublished). The possible reduction in diarrheal mortality from prevention of these deaths cannot be qualified at present, but could be substantial.

Notes

1 Until the past decade, a list of bacterial etiologies of diarrhea would have included only a few organisms: "enteropathogenic" *Escherichia coli, Salmonella, Shigella, Staphylococcus aureus, Vibrio cholerae,* and *V. parahaemolyticus.* In the last 10 years additional bacterial agents have been associated with diarrhea. These include *Aeromonas hydrophila, Bacillus cereus, Campylobacter jejuni, Clostridium difficile, C. perfringens,* enterotoxigenic and enteroinvasive *E. coli, V. cholerae,* non-0 group 1, and *Yersinia enterocolitica.* Still other organisms, such as *Plesiomonas shigelloides* and enterotoxin-producing *Klebsiella,* may be enteropathogens, but await more definite proof.

2 Another group, the Norwalk-like viruses, may commonly cause epidemic, as well as endemic, diarrhea. More recently, other groups of viruses have been found in the feces of persons with diarrhea. Sufficient information is available to implicate one such group of adenoviruses as etiologic agents of diarrhea, but the role of the other groups (coronaviruses, astroviruses, minireoviruses, "small round viruses," and calicivirus-like particles) is still uncertain.

3 Other parasites that may be infrequent causes of diarrheal diseases include *Balantidium coli, Capillaria philippinensis, Fasciolopsis buski, Isospora belli, Sarcocystis suihominis, Strongyloides stercoralis,* and *Trichuris trichiura.* A newly recognized cause of diarrhea in man—cryptosporidium—is of uncertain importance. Diarrhea may occur in ascariasis, severe hookworm disease, and trichinosis. Although diarrhea is also sometimes seen with cysticercosis, kala-azar, malaria, and schistosomiasis, these are not usually considered primary diarrheal diseases.

4 Enterotoxigenic *E. coli* are now known to produce two plasmid-mediated enterotoxins: one is heat-labile and the other heat-stable. The heat-labile toxin is structurally similar to cholera toxin and causes loss of fluid and electrolytes in the intestine as a result of adenylate cyclase stimulation. The heat-stable toxin acts in a similar way through stimulation of guanylate cyclase. The relative frequency with which *E. coli* produces the heat-labile toxin, the heat-stable toxin, or both, varies in different regions of the world.

References

Becker, Stan. 1981. "Seasonality of deaths in Matlab, Bangladesh," *International Journal of Epidemiology* 10: 271–280.

Black, Robert E. 1982. "The prophylaxis and therapy of secretory diarrhea," *Medical Clinics of North America* 66: 611–621.

———, Aubert C. Dykes, Susanne P. Sinclair, and Joy G. Wells. 1977. "Giardiasis in daycare centers: Evidence of person to person transmission," *Pediatrics* 60: 486–491.

———, Gunther F. Craun, and Paul A. Blake. 1978. "Epidemiology of common-source outbreaks of shigellosis in the United States, 1961–1975," *American Journal of Epidemiology* 108: 47–52.

———, M. H. Merson, A. S. M. M. Rahman, M. Yunus, A. R. M. A. Alim, I. Huq, R. H.

Yolken, and G. T. Curlin. 1980. "A two-year study of bacterial, viral, and parasitic agents associated with diarrhea in rural Bangladesh," *Journal of Infectious Diseases* 142: 660–664.

———, Michael H. Merson, Imdadul Huq, A. R. M. A. Alim, and Md. Yunus. 1981a. "Incidence and severity of rotavirus and *Escherichia coli* diarrhoea in rural Bangladesh," *Lancet* 1: 141–143.

———, Aubert C. Dykes, Kern E. Anderson, Joy G. Wells, Susanne P. Sinclair, G. William Gary, Jr., Milford H. Hatch, and Eugene J. Gangarosa. 1981b. "Handwashing to prevent diarrhea in day-care centers," *American Journal of Epidemiology* 113: 445–451.

———, Harry B. Greenberg, Albert Z. Kapikian, Kenneth H. Brown, and Stan Becker. 1982a. "Acquisition of serum antibody to Norwalk virus and rotavirus and relation to diarrhea in a longitudinal study of young children in rural Bangladesh," *Journal of Infectious Diseases* 145: 483–489.

———, Kenneth H. Brown, Stan Becker, A. R. M. Abdul Alim, and Imdadul Huq. 1982b. "Longitudinal studies of infectious diseases and physical growth of children in rural Bangladesh. II. Incidence of diarrhea and association with known pathogens," *American Journal of Epidemiology* 115: 315–324.

———, Kenneth H. Brown, Stan Becker, A. R. M. Abdul Alim, and Michael H. Merson. 1982c. "Contamination of weaning foods and transmission of enterotoxigenic *Escherichia coli* diarrhoea in children in rural Bangladesh," *Transactions of the Royal Society of Tropical Medicine and Hygiene* 76: 259–264.

———, Lincoln C. Chen, Oscar Harkavy, M. Mujibur Rahaman, and M. G. M. Rowland. 1983. "Prevention and control of the diarrheal disease," in *Diarrhea and Malnutrition,* ed. Lincoln C. Chen and Nevin S. Scrimshaw. New York: Plenum, pp. 297–303.

———, Kenneth H. Brown, and Stan Becker. 1984a. "Malnutrition is a determining factor for diarrheal duration, but not incidence, among young children in a longitudinal study in rural Bangladesh," *American Journal of Clinical Nutrition* 37: 87–94.

———, Kenneth H. Brown, and Stan Becker. 1984b. "Effects of diarrhea associated with specific enteropathogens on the growth of children in rural Bangladesh," *Pediatrics* 73: 799–805.

Blaser, Martin J., David N. Taylor, and Roger A. Feldman. In press. "Epidemiology of *Campylobacter jejuni* studies," *Reviews of Epidemiology.*

Brandt, Carl D., Hyun Wha Kim, William J. Rodriguez, Julita O. Arrobio, Barbara C. Jeffries, Emma P. Stallings, Caroly Lewis, Audrey J. Miles, Robert M. Chanock, Albert Z. Kapikian, and Robert H. Parrott. 1983. "Pediatric viral gastroenteritis during eight years of study," *Journal of Clinical Microbiology* 18: 71–78.

Brass, William, and Ansley J. Coale. 1968. "Methods of analysis and estimation," in *The Demography of Tropical Africa,* ed. William Brass et al. Princeton: Princeton University Press.

Chen, Lincoln C., A. K. M. A. Chowdhury, and Sandra A. Huffman. 1980a. "Anthropometric assessment of energy-protein malnutrition and subsequent risk of mortality among preschool aged children," *American Journal of Clinical Nutrition* 33: 1836–1845.

———, Mizanur Rahman, and A. M. Sarder. 1980b. "Epidemiology and causes of death among children in a rural area of Bangladesh," *International Journal of Epidemiology* 9: 25–33.

DeSweemer, Cecile, Frederick L. Trowbridge, Robert L. Parker, D. Meriwether, Kenneth H. Brown, Robert E. Black, William A. Reinke, and Carl E. Taylor. 1982. "Critical factors in obtaining data relevant to health programs," in *Methodologies for Human Population Studies in Nutrition Related to Health,* NIH publication no. 82-2462, pp. 59–81.

DuPont, H. L., E. J. Gangarosa, L. B. Reller, W. E. Woodward, R. W. Armstrong, J. Hammond, K. Glaser, and G. K. Morris. 1970. "Shigellosis in custodial institutions," *American Journal of Epidemiology* 92: 172–179.

Feldman, R. A., Prema Bhat, and K. R. Kamath. 1970. "Infection and disease in a group of South Indian families," *American Journal of Epidemiology* 92: 367–375.

Foster, S. O., E. L. Palmer, G. W. Gary, Jr., M. L. Martin, K. L. Herrmann, P. Beasley, and J. Sampson. 1980. "Gastroenteritis due to rotavirus in an isolated Pacific Island group: An epidemic of 3,439 cases," *Journal of Infectious Diseases* 141: 32–39.

Freij, J., and S. Wall. 1979. "Quantity and variation in morbidity: THAID–analysis of the occurrence of gastroenteritis among Ethiopian children." *International Journal of Epidemiology* 8: 313–325.

Freiman, I., E. Hartman, H. Kassel, R. M. Robins-Browne, B. D. Schoub, H. J. Koornhof, G. Lecasas, and O. W. Prozesky. 1977. "A microbiological study of gastro-enteritis in black infants," *South African Medical Journal* 52: 261–265.

Frost, J. A., B. Rowe, J. Vandepitte, and E. J. Threlfall. 1981. "Plasmid characterization in the investigation of an epidemic caused by multiply resistant *Shigella dysenteriae* type 1 in Central Africa," *Lancet* 2: 1074–1076.

Hirschhorn, Norbert. 1980. "The treatment of acute diarrhea in children: An historical and physiological perspective," *American Journal of Clinical Nutrition* 33: 637–663.

Hollister, Arthur C., Jr., M. Dorothy Beck, Alan M. Gittelsohn, and Emmarie C. Hemphill. 1955. "Influence of water availability on shigella prevalence in children of farm labor families," *American Journal of Public Health* 45: 354–362.

Hurst, Christon J., and Charles P. Gerba. 1980. "Stability of simian rotavirus in fresh and estuarine water," *Applied Environmental Microbiology* 39: 1–5.

Kapikian, A. Z., Richard G. Wyatt, Harry B. Greenberg, Anthony R. Kalica, Hyun Wha Kim, Carl D. Brandt, William J. Rodriguez, Robert H. Parrott, and Robert M. Chanock. 1980. "Approaches to immunization of infants and young children against gastroenteritis due to rotaviruses," *Journal of Infectious Diseases* 2: 459–469.

———, W. Lee Cline, Harry B. Greenberg, Richard G. Wyatt, Anthony R. Kalica, Clarence E. Banks, Harvey D. James, Jr., Jorge Flores, and Robert M. Chanock. 1981. "Antigenic characterization of human and animal rotaviruses by immune adherence hemagglutination assay (IAHA): Evidence for distinctness of IAHA and neutralization antigens," *Infection and Immunity* 33: 415–425.

———, R. G. Wyatt, M. M. Levine, R. H. Yolken, D. H. VanKirk, R. Dolin, H. B. Greenberg, and R. M. Chanock. 1983. "Oral administration of human rotavirus to volunteers: Induction of illness and correlates of resistance," *Journal of Infectious Diseases* 147: 95–105.

Khan, Moslem U. 1982. "Interruption of shigellosis by hand washing," *Transactions of the Royal Society of Tropical Medicine and Hygiene* 76: 164–168.

Kielmann, Arnfried A., and Colin McCord. 1978. "Weight-for-age as an index of risk of death in children," *Lancet* 1: 1247–1250.

Levine, Myron M. 1982. "Bacillary dysentery: Mechanisms and treatment," *Medical Clinics of North America* 66: 623–638.

———, Margaret B. Rennels, Luis Cisneros, Timothy P. Hughes, David R. Nalin, and Charles R. Young. 1980. "Lack of person-to-person transmission of enterotoxigenic *Escherichia coli* despite close contact," *American Journal of Epidemiology* 111: 347–355.

Linhares, Alexandre C., Francisco P. Pinheiro, Ronaldo B. Freitas, Yvone B. Gabbay, Jane A. Shirley, and Graham M. Beards. 1981. "An outbreak of rotavirus diarrhea among a nonimmune, isolated South American Indian community," *American Journal of Epidemiology* 113: 703–710.

Mendizabal-Morris, Cesar A., Leonardo J. Mata, Eugene J. Gangarosa, and Guillermo Guzman. 1971. "Epidemic shiga-bacillus dysentery in Central America," *American Journal of Tropical Medicine and Hygiene* 20: 927–933.

Neter, Erwin. 1983. "*Escherichia coli:* An enteric pathogen," *Journal of Pediatric Gastroenterology and Nutrition* 2: 201–203.

Pal, S. C., C. Koteswara Rao, T. Kereselidze, A. K. Krishnaswami, D. K. Murty, C. G. Pandit, and J. B. Shrivastav. 1969. "An extensive community outbreak of enteropathogenic *Escherichia coli* 086:B7 gastroenteritis," *Bulletin of the World Health Organization* 41: 851–858.

Pickering, Larry K., Dolores G. Evans, Herbert L. DuPont, John J. Vollet, II, and Doyle J. Evans, Jr. 1981. "Diarrhea caused by Shigella, rotavirus, and Giardia in day-care centers: Prospective study," *Journal of Pediatrics* 99: 51–56.

Rahaman, M. Mujibur, M. Moslemuddin Khan, K. M. S. Aziz, M. Shafiqual Islam, and A. K. M. Golam Kibriya. 1975. "An outbreak of dysentery caused by *Shigella dysenteriae* type 1 on a coral island in the bay of Bengal," *Journal of Infectious Diseases* 132: 15–19.

———, K. M. S. Aziz, Yakub Patwari, and M. H. Munshi. 1979. "Diarrhoeal mortality in two Bangladeshi villages with and without community-based oral rehydration therapy," *Lancet* 2: 809–812.

Rajasekaran, P., P. R. Dutt, and K. A. Pisharoti. 1977. "Impact of water supply on the incidence of diarrhoea and shigellosis among children in rural communities in Madurai," *Indian Journal of Medical Research* 66: 189–199.

Rosenberg, Mark L., Kenneth K. Hazlet, John Schaefer, Joy G. Wells, and C. Pruneda. 1976. "Shigellosis from swimming," *Journal of the American Medical Association* 236: 1849–1852.

———, Jeffrey P. Koplan, I. Kaye Wachsmuth, Joy G. Wells, Eugene J. Gangarosa, Richard L. Guerrant, and David A. Sack. 1977. "Epidemic diarrhea at Crater Lake from enterotoxigenic *Escherichia coli*," *Annals of Internal Medicine* 86: 714–718.

Ryder, Robert W., I. Kaye Wachsmuth, Alfred E. Buxton, Dolores G. Evans, Herbert L. DuPont, Edward Mason, and Fred F. Barrett. 1976. "Infantile diarrhea produced by heat-stable enterotoxigenic *Escherichia coli*," *New England Journal of Medicine* 295: 849–853.

Sack, Bradley R., David A. Sack, Ira J. Mehlman, Frits Orskov, and Ida Orskov. 1977. "Enterotoxigenic *Escherichia coli* isolated from food," *Journal of Infectious Diseases* 135: 313–317.

Samadi, Aziz R., Mohammad I. Huq, and Quazi S. Ahmed. 1983. "Detection of rotavirus in handwashings of attendants of children with diarrhoea," *British Medical Journal* 286: 188.

Snyder, John D., and Michael H. Merson. 1982. "The magnitude of the global problem of acute diarrhoeal disease: A review of active surveillance data," *Bulletin of the World Health Organization* 60: 605–613.

Steinmann, Jochen. 1981. "Detection of rotavirus in sewage," *Applied and Environmental Microbiology* 41: 1043–1045.

Toledo, Regina, M. F., M. do Carmo B. Alvariza, Jayme Murahovschi, Sonia R. T. S. Ramos, and Luiz R. Trabulsi. 1983. "Enteropathogenic *Escherichia coli* serotypes and endemic diarrhea in infants," *Infection and Immunity* 39: 586–589.

Wallace, C. K., P. N. Anderson, T. C. Brown, S. R. Khanra, G. W. Lewis, N. F. Pierce, S. N. Sanyal, G. V. Segre, and R. H. Waldman. 1968. "Optimal antibiotic therapy in cholera," *Bulletin of the World Health Organization* 39: 239–245.

Watt, James, and Dale R. Lindsay. 1948. "Diarrheal disease control studies. I. Effect of fly control in a high morbidity area," *Public Health Reports* 63: 1319–1334.

Weissman, Jack B., Alan Schmerler, Philip Weiler, Gregory Filice, Norma Godbey, and Inger Hansen. 1974. "The role of preschool children and day-care centers in the spread of shigellosis in urban communities," *Journal of Pediatrics* 84: 797–802.

World Health Organization. 1981. *Manual for the Planning and Evaluation of National Diarrhoeal Diseases Control Programmes.* WHO/CDD/SER/81.5.

Yolken, Robert H., Richard G. Wyatt, Leonardo Mata, Juan J. Urrutia, Berta Garcia, Robert M. Chanock, and Albert Z. Kapikian. 1978. "Secretory antibody directed against rotavirus in human milk—measurement by means of enzyme-linked immunosorbent assay," *Journal of Pediatrics* 93: 916–921.

Parasitic Diseases: Measurement and Mortality Impact

David J. Bradley

Anne Keymer

The animal parasites of man are numerous, and several species infect the average inhabitant of the world at any one time. A few are direct causes of death in children, and among them malaria is of outstanding importance. Many less pathogenic parasites, especially parasitic worms, contribute to malnutrition and to the risk of death.

This paper comprises five parts. The first, after a few words of definition and clearing the background, addresses the major policy issues raised by parasitic disease in relation to child mortality. This is written as far as possible in nontechnical language and also sets out the key areas for future research. The second section summarizes the commoner parasites infecting man and relates their pathology to four phases of child survival and development. Two subsequent sections address the two main areas of parasitic impact in greater detail: the evidence for the scale of malarial mortality in childhood, and the relation between helminthic infection and nutritional damage to children. The last section discusses measurement of parasitic infection. The first major section is specifically intended as a guide to the field for the general reader.

General issues and policy

Infections of man may be due to many types of organism, from the smallest viruses up to tapeworms over a meter in length. Of these infecting organisms, two groups are unequivocally animals (rather than plants, fungi, or not classifiable). These are the protozoa, which are single-celled (or acellular) animals, and the worms or helminths, which are much larger, multicellular, and usually easily visible to the naked eye. The parasitic protozoa and helminths together comprise the animal parasites, and the diseases that result from these infections are usually called the parasitic diseases.

163

The majority of parasitic infections are characterized by having developmental stages of the parasites outside the human host so that their environmental dependence is greater—more stringent and more complex—than for many other infections. Their ultimate determinants in the social, economic, and environmental areas are often capable of precise analysis, and the biological components of their life cycles may be open to very specific interventions.

In discussion of parasites it is helpful to distinguish between infection and disease. When a person harbors living parasites he or she is infected, and some form of dependence of the parasites upon their host, usually for food and shelter, is implied. When the infection actually harms the host, parasitic disease is present. Many people are infected but not apparently harmed by parasites. They have what physicians refer to as subclinical infections, and many of the problems of determining the impact of parasitic infections are related to this phenomenon.

The terminology for measuring parasitic infections needs to be stated. The number of people infected with a particular parasite at a given time comprises the *prevalence* of the infection. We refer to the proportion of the population so infected as the *prevalence rate*. The proportion of people becoming newly infected over a defined period of time comprises the *incidence rate*. If an infection has a very short duration, as in the case of virus infections such as measles, the incidence can be high but the prevalence low. Most children get measles, but few will be ill at any given instant of time. Conversely, because many parasitic infections are very long-lived, the incidence may be quite low but the prevalence very high. In the case of helminth infections, some people may have very few worms while others with much heavier infections may have hundreds. It is therefore necessary to consider the *intensity* of infection or *worm burden* in discussion of parasitic infections.

Infections with parasites are of relatively long duration. We have argued elsewhere (Bradley, 1972) that the comparatively slow replication rate for parasites relative to the time needed for host immune responses to be manifest has had the consequence that most parasites have evolved ways of circumventing these responses in part. So the pattern of parasitic infection is of a chronic or at least a subacute process continuing after an occasionally dramatic initial infection phase, rather than the short acute illness, fatal or cured within the month or even week, that characterizes many viral and bacterial infections.

Moreover, because acquired resistance is incomplete and slowly produced, superinfection, in which an individual acquires more parasites of the same sort before the first infection has died away, is common in parasitic diseases, and often the interval between natural exposures to challenge is much less than the duration of a single infection. The clearest examples of this occur in situations where malaria transmission is very intense (holoendemic malaria) and in some of the soil-transmitted worm (geohelminth) infections. Under such conditions, a child may be infected from a few months after birth through age 6 or 7 years without any intervals free of infection.

The consequences of these two features of parasitic infections, incomplete immunity and superinfection, are to give a very high prevalence, to the point that incidence becomes difficult to measure except in very young children.

The diseases due to animal parasites may affect the survival of children in two ways. A very few, of which malaria is the chief and visceral leishmaniasis or kala-azar the second, can give rise to an initial fatal infection. Malaria in a nonimmune child can be lethal even if the child was in every other respect healthy and well-fed prior to contracting the infection. In pregnant women malaria can cause abortion and maternal death. Disability due to malaria in epidemic form can disrupt family life sufficiently to put some children's lives at risk. Thus malaria is an acute disease contributing both directly and indirectly to child mortality.

By contrast, the vast majority of parasitic diseases (including malaria when the initial infection has not proved fatal) produce their effects on child survival in an indirect and chronic manner. The long duration of these infections and their undramatic effects on survival make it hard to determine and easy to underestimate their consequences. Many effects of parasites result by way of nutritional impairment, and it has proved very difficult to separate out the roles of individual parasites in the multifactorial causation of malnutrition in human populations.

The measurement of parasitic *infections* is a well-studied area. Parasites may be seen with the naked eye or, more usually, with the microscope in samples of blood or other tissues from patients, or in their excreta. Even where the adult parasites are inaccessible, the eggs or larvae of helminths are passed in the excreta or are otherwise accessible to observation. Nevertheless, it is still possible to miss parasites in infected people. Methods have been developed to detect the antibodies to the parasites produced by the infected person, and these techniques have been modified for epidemiological use employing very small samples of tissue. Thus, a single drop of blood, put on a piece of absorbent paper and allowed to dry, may suffice for tests for a half-dozen different parasites.

It has already been pointed out that mere presence or absence data are inadequate for assessment of parasitic infections and that the intensity of infection needs to be determined as well. This is of particular relevance in impact studies, since as a broad generalization the likelihood of serious disease or even of a fatal outcome is positively correlated with the intensity of infection. Among parasitologists the techniques of measuring parasitic infection are a subject of much discussion and of continual scientific progress, with the recent addition of genetic probes to the range of methods available. However, in the present context, measurement of parasitic infection is far advanced relative to the problems of impact measurement. It is relatively easy in community studies to measure the prevalence and to get indications of intensities of parasitic infection. To interpret their contribution to the overall ill health of the children of the community and to the risk of death is altogether a more intractable problem.

In the case of malaria (for which the data are reviewed in a later section) the mortality among children depends on the intensity of transmission of the parasite, which may vary enormously even between malarious regions of the world. The chance or frequency of being bitten by an infective mosquito may vary over a hundredfold between the areas of highly endemic, "stable" malaria in sub-Saharan Africa and those of devastating epidemic, "unstable" malaria in the Punjab and Sri Lanka. Large differences in the biology of the vector mosquitoes are responsible for these differences. The acute malaria attacks of epidemic malaria are undoubtedly associated with both abortions due to the mother's illness and child deaths from mosquito-transmitted, and sometimes congenital, infection. In areas of stable malaria, when babies have maternal antimalarial antibodies, the predominant picture is of infections acquired in infancy and early childhood and associated with heavy mortality in the community. In addition, and because of maternal malaria, which has its greatest effect in those mothers bearing their first child, children are born underweight.

The research implications of what is known about malaria in mothers and children are diverse and lead to operational policy implications. While much has been learned, we are still uncertain of the scale of malarial mortality among infants and young children in most parts of the tropics. Moreover, studies of the "natural" situation are becoming impossible because it is both feasible and necessary to intervene. Nevertheless, the detailed analysis of historical data can add to understanding, as is seen by the results collected over the past 30 years from the Gambia, which continue to provide new information. The value of this for epidemic areas and for those with substantial control measures in operation, such as much of Asia, lies in estimating the risk if malaria were to return and in guiding priorities in the expenditure of health service funds. For the uncontrolled endemic areas of stable malaria, the value is again for setting priorities in planning interventions. The control of malaria is an expensive matter, and, when undertaken by means of vector control, requires staff and activities that are of little use for other types of health care, so that priority-setting is a practical and important task for governments.

In addition to the scale of malarial mortality, the second area needing further study is the mechanisms by which malaria produces its effects, especially on the fetus. It is well known that pregnancy in some way reduces the acquired resistance of women from endemic areas to the disease. McGregor (1983) has demonstrated that this is largely a phenomenon of the first pregnancy. The mechanism is unknown, though he has given good reasons for suggesting it has more to do with hemodynamics than with immunology. A clear understanding of the mechanism would make it feasible to choose between the various patterns of prophylactic or curative use of antimalarials to provide protection to the fetus at the lowest cost.

A third type of priority research in malaria concerns the best way to prevent its effects on children, at low cost. The literature on maternal protection contains several good ideas but little in the way of unequivocal field trials.

The management of infantile and childhood malaria in the community so as to minimize mortality and other less drastic consequences is even less clear. Complete prophylaxis and extremely efficient early treatment of attacks of malaria are both theoretically acceptable alternatives. But which will work better in real health care delivery systems is far from clear, and the practical problems can only be determined by field trials. A final area of anticipated great future relevance will be to explore the relation between vaccination strategies and impact on child health once suitable human vaccines become available for field use. It is likely that protection may improve with delay from the time of birth, and difficulties in deciding the best age for immunization, similar to those found in measles, are likely.

In the case of most other parasites affecting children, the key questions concern the nutritional and growth impact of a heavy burden of helminths and protozoa. The effects of hookworm on the hemoglobin level have been extensively studied, although such studies have characteristically ignored very young children, and more work among the 2–4-year age group would be useful. The effects of hookworm together with *Ascaris, Giardia,* and *Trichuris* upon other aspects of the nutritional state remain unclear at the community level. That they remain so suggests that the impact is not dramatic. It also suggests that the outcome may depend on locally variable details of the nutritional and infective scene, though work in Kenya among a somewhat older age group suggests that growth may be improved by removal of helminths.

The extensive literature on mechanisms of nutritional impairment in infected experimental animals shows that field studies of man can usefully include behavioral observations as well as growth and physiological measurements.

It will be clear to the reader that this discussion has stopped short of definite recommendations for reducing infant mortality by parasite control. This is so only because the scientific evidence is not sufficient to place such action in an accurate priority order with other ways of saving children's lives. There is no doubt that large malaria epidemics should be promptly controlled. The health services will be under great pressure to do this, employing a combination of chemotherapy and vector control, and for many reasons in addition to the effect on child mortality. There also can be no doubt that, wherever malaria transmission is occurring, prompt treatment of symptomatic malaria cases, whether infants, children, or their mothers, is a high priority. Successful and well-maintained control of malaria transmission is always desirable; but in the real world, where it may not be maintained or may not be feasible with the resources available, the correct action is less clear.

Problems surround the use of chemoprophylaxis for mothers or children in the face of continuing intense malaria transmission. There are at least three major difficulties. The first, and perhaps least important in practice, is the question of what happens to the child kept on careful continuous prophylaxis up to 5–6 years of age, with medication then stopping and leaving the school-child without drug protection or acquired immunity. In practice, such children are likely to remain within range of prompt access to chemotherapy. The second problem is the difficulty on a community scale of maintaining pro-phylaxis through early childhood. This involves a mixture of logistics, drug supply, and motivation, and successful long-term programs are rare. Third, even if they succeed, the increasingly rapid emergence and spread of parasitic resistance to the safer chemoprophylactic drugs means that an apparently suc-cessful program probably has a very limited life. Thus although there are obvious areas for field research in all three of these problem areas, a single study is unlikely to solve all the difficulties or lead to universally successful and applicable advice.

Intervention research should focus on how to provide readily available early chemotherapy for symptomatic malaria and on long-term projects to evaluate alternatives such as prolonged chemoprophylaxis. It will be easy to obtain splendid results from the first two years, but very hard to establish a program that is still effective after ten years, for both biological and behavioral reasons.

A similar set of questions surrounds efforts to control chronic parasitism due to protozoa and helminths. Environmental control is slow but very effec-tive in the long run, and parasite control is a byproduct of such programs, which are usually undertaken for other reasons. The pressing questions concern the use of broad-spectrum anthelminthics on a regular basis for large-scale treatment of children. Here, as with malaria, short-term programs tend to demonstrate benefits, but feasible and effective long-term programs are lack-ing, and empirical studies are needed in communities with differing nutritional levels.

In population-based studies of child mortality, it will be useful to include quantitative assessments of parasitic load, and multivariate analyses of risk factors may indicate some role for them. It is, however, highly unlikely that their role can be defined at all precisely except by intervention studies using specific chemotherapy. The exceptions are malaria and kala-azar. The role of each as a cause of death can be defined in autopsy studies and, with some confidence, in clinical studies where good clinical and laboratory records are available.

The diversity of parasites and their contributions to childhood mortality

The parasites of man are numerous and diverse. Often, the illnesses to which they can give rise are known only by local dialect names, and the name of the parasite with "iasis" appended is used for all the conditions in which people are infected. Indeed, a feature of animal parasites even more than of viral and bacterial infections is that many persons are infected, only some are ill, and few die.

There are four ways in which animal parasites may contribute to child mortality. The infection may kill the child even if the child was otherwise in a relatively healthy state. This is here called a *direct* cause of mortality. Parasites may contribute to the complex of malnutrition and infection that increases the risk of death and thus be *indirect* causes of mortality. Third, parasitic infection in the mother may lead to abortion or infection and death of the fetus in the uterus, a *prenatal* effect. Finally, parasitic disease may so disable a mother that she is unable to look after the child properly, so that its chance of survival is reduced. The extreme example of such a *generation delayed* effect occurs when the mother dies of parasitic disease.

Table 1 sets out some of the more important parasites of man and their likely contributions to childhood mortality.

TABLE 1   Contribution of parasites to child mortality: a speculative summary

Parasitic disease	Effect on mortality				World frequency[a] (millions per year)
	Direct	Indirect	Prenatal	Generation delayed	
Malaria	+ + + +	+ + +	+ + +	+ + +	800
Ascariasis	+ +	+ + +			900
Hookworm	+	+ +			800
Schistosomiasis	+	+		+ +	200
Amoebiasis	+ +	+ +		+ +	400
Trichuriasis	+	+			500
Trichinellosis	+				?
Strongyloidiosis	+				?
Trypanosomiasis (African)	+				1
Toxoplasmosis			+		?
Leishmaniasis	+ +				12
Giardiasis	+	+ +			200
Filariasis					250
Onchocerciasis				+ + +	30
Chagas' Disease				+	12

NOTE: Confidence limits are vast, but no better data are available. Appreciable effects on a global scale are shown by increasing numbers of + signs, and are relative not absolute.

[a] From Walsh and Warren (1979). They give a mixture of incidence and prevalence; data are for infection frequency (not disease or death).

While many parasites can and do infect young children, few are commonly fatal. By far the most important is malaria, a protozoan parasite of the red blood cells, transmitted by anopheline mosquitoes and having a broad distribution in the tropics and subtropics, most of all in sub-Saharan Africa and in New Guinea. It is resurgent in much of Asia and in parts of Central and South America. The most lethal form of malaria is due to *Plasmodium falciparum,* which not only gives rise to a high fever and anemia but also can obstruct the blood vessels of the brain, leading to coma and death.

Another parasite that lives inside cells is *Leishmania.* This is transmitted by sandflies. *L. donovani,* which develops in the liver, spleen, and bone marrow, occurs in many tropical areas but chiefly East Africa, India, the Middle East, and the Mediterranean littoral. The Mediterranean form primarily infects young children; for example, over 90 percent of the 3–10,000 cases seen annually in Iraq are under 4 years of age. It is believed that 70 percent of those who contract the disease are likely to die if they are not treated. Other parasitic infections, such as sleeping sickness (African trypanosomiasis), certainly kill children but not selectively nor on a large scale globally. Both *Ascaris* infection and amoebiasis are fatal to a small proportion of those infected, and are recorded in Table 1 because their extremely high global prevalence makes them significant causes of mortality even though the case fatality rate is low.

The indirect contribution of parasites to child mortality is probably large and certainly ill-defined. It is discussed at length in the fourth section. Of the many parasites that play some role, malaria is important, as is a group of parasitic worms that live in the intestine and are spread from the excreta to the mouth by way of a period of development in the soil. They are therefore known as geohelminths. The most important are the two hookworm species that frequently infect man, the large roundworm called *Ascaris,* and possibly the smaller whipworm, *Trichuris.* All these have a wide distribution in developing countries and compete with their human hosts for food in the intestine. In addition, the hookworms suck blood, greatly in excess of their nutritional needs, and give rise to iron deficiency anemia. A minute protozoon, *Giardia,* is also prevalent in the small intestine and is associated with chronic diarrhea. This may also be due to another protozoon, the dysentery amoeba.

Two protozoa have a marked prenatal effect. Malaria in epidemic form may cause the mother to abort, and in endemic areas is associated with a lowered birth weight. Toxoplasmosis, which has a cosmopolitan distribution, can give rise to stillbirths.

Any parasitic infection that is either acute or very heavy or both can impair the mother's health and ability to look after her child. Malaria is again a major problem in this way. Onchocerciasis or river blindness, caused by a worm whose larvae infest the skin and eyes in Africa and Central America, produces disability in several ways, but by far the most serious is blindness. In areas where up to a quarter of adults may be blind from the disease, child rearing is clearly at risk. Hookworm and in some areas schistosomiasis, a group of helminthic infections of the blood vessels, may also cause maternal illness severe enough to make child care difficult.

The two major routes by which child mortality is related to parasitic disease—the direct effects of malaria on infants and children, and the indirect effects of helminthic and some protozoal infections in synergism with malnutrition—are dealt with in greater detail in the next two sections.

Malaria mortality in childhood

The one human parasitic disease that has been unequivocally recognized as a cause of large-scale mortality among children in many parts of the tropics is malaria.

The pattern of infection varies dramatically with the level of transmission, which in turn varies with ambient temperature and the anopheline mosquito density, man-biting habit, and above all, longevity. In areas of low transmission (hypoendemic), few people of any age group may be infected at any time, and parasite burdens may be low. Epidemic malaria in places of variable transmission may give high prevalence at all ages from time to time. But as transmission levels increase in endemic areas, the brunt of infection is moved to a progressively lower age group. In the holoendemic malaria of the *Anopheles gambiae* areas of West and East Africa, prevalences of malaria may reach over 90 percent by the end of the first year of life (Table 2), and the level of malaria in most of the community is determined by acquired immunity rather than by the precise level of transmission. The first form of immunity to develop, that to the gametocyte stages infective to mosquitoes, may already be present before age 2 years, though immunity to other stages in the body may take longer.

TABLE 2   Plasmodium falciparum (P.f.) infection rates: holoendemic malaria in Uganda and Tanzania

Age	P. falciparum: Percent positive	P.f. gametocytes: Percent positive	Percent with P.f. density >100 gametocytes/cu mm	Mean positive P.f. density/cu mm
			Uganda	
2 weeks–2 months	21	8	1	8,000
3–5 months	74	39	6	11,000
6–11 months	87	39	6	11,500
12–23 months	87	39	5	6,000
2–4 years	95	30	3	4,500
5–10 years	84	14	0	1,500
11–14 years	74	10	0	600
15+ years	39	1	0	500
			Tanzania	
2 weeks–3 months	66	41	13	7,000
4–6 months	83	44	3	15,000
7–9 months	90	51	2	13,000
10–12 months	99	44	3	13,000
13–18 months	98	44	2	10,000
19–24 months	98	36	2	11,000
3–5 years	98	35	0	5,000
6–9 years	94	28	1	2,000
10–15 years	88	15	0	1,000
15+ years	31	5	0	100

SOURCES: For Uganda, Davidson and Draper (1953); for Tanzania, Davidson (1955).

Epidemic malaria can have a transient but catastrophic effect on child mortality, as seen in the Punjab epidemic of 1908. The graphic account in Christophers's report (1911) cannot be improved on:

The autumn of 1908 in the Punjab was characterised by an epidemic of extraordinary severity. The effects of this epidemic were first prominently brought before the public by a sudden disorganisation of the train service due to "fever" among the employees at the large railway centre, Lahore. With equal suddenness it made its presence felt throughout the whole Punjab. Where the epidemic was severely felt almost the entire population seems to have been prostrated by sickness; and the mortality almost invariably rose in such places to a rate of several hundreds per mille.

At Amritsar, a city of 160,000 inhabitants, it is stated that almost the entire population was prostrated and the ordinary business of the city interrupted. For many weeks labour for any purpose was unprocurable and even food vendors ceased to carry on their trade. Thus not only was ordinary food difficult to obtain and the prices excessive, but, owing to malaria among the cowkeeper class, milk, a necessity for the very young and the sick, was practically unprocurable even at the exorbitant rate of 8 to 12 annas per seer.

In the two months, October and November, during which the epidemic was at its highest, 307,316 deaths were recorded in the Punjab. In Amritsar the mortality for many weeks was at the rate of over 200 per mille. In Palwal mortality rose to 420 per mille and in Bhera to 493 per mille.

Such data cannot be generalized except as a reminder of what could happen if new insecticides and chemotherapeutic agents do not remain ahead of the development of resistance in mosquitoes and malaria parasites, respectively.

Malaria has been found to be a cause not only of infant death but also of abortion and stillbirth. During the great epidemics in the Punjab in 1908 and Sri Lanka in 1934, dramatic rises in the stillbirth and abortion rates were observed, and Christophers (1911) showed a fivefold rise in stillbirths in Amritsar during the Punjab epidemic and calculated that 30 percent of all pregnancies in that city were interrupted by malaria, accounting for 1,100 abortions and stillbirths and 300 premature births.

The consequences of endemic malaria for the fetus are less generally agreed upon. Blacklock and Gordon (1925) in Sierra Leone found no evidence that malaria predisposed to abortion but found 23 percent mortality in the first week of life in women with malaria-infected placentae as compared with 5 percent in controls, whereas Garnham (1938) in East Africa found little evidence of perinatal mortality from malaria, nor did Bruce-Chwatt (1952).

The most recent study of placental malaria (McGregor et al., 1983) confirms many earlier studies in Africa and showed, on average, a weight deficit at birth of 170 g as compared with controls, but no association of stillbirth with malaria. Malarious placentae were found in 20 percent of singleton births observed.

The consequences of malaria for infant mortality in areas of hyperendemic and holoendemic malaria have been the subject of prolonged (at some stages acrimonious) dispute. Christophers (1949), in summarizing the early literature, emphasized the data of Wilson and of Garnham (1935) showing little malarial mortality among children, and these two authors with Swellengrebel (1950) argued subsequently that a state of natural balance might be present in African holoendemic malaria with rather low mortality. However, Wilson (1936) himself described most children he observed in Tanzania as ill and febrile for about half the first year of life, with hemoglobin levels half of normal. We find it difficult to believe that this would not reduce the child's probability of survival! Moreover, Christophers (1924) showed that children from a hyperendemic area had parasitemia (presence of the parasite in the circulating blood) on 25 percent of their days of life over five times higher than that needed to make adults febrile. All agree that in conditions of heavy endemic transmission there is a phase of acute infestation (Christophers, 1924) in infancy and childhood followed by relative (not absolute) freedom from heavy infection and disease in adults.

The key question here concerns the cost of acquiring immunity, in terms of child mortality. Mortality was rated low by Wilson, Garnham, and Swellengrebel (1950), but they were strongly opposed by Macdonald (1951), particularly on the basis of the 40 percent mortality reduction observed by Farinaud and Choumara (1950) following malaria control on the Indochinese plateau. Moreover, it was found that elimination of the seasonal peak of malaria in Freetown, Sierra Leone, by larval control led to a reduction of 100 per thousand in the infant mortality rate. When transmission of otherwise holoendemic malaria in an area of Tanzania at Pare-Taveta was greatly reduced by residual insecticides, there was a marked fall in infant mortality, and when the program was interrupted it tended to rise again toward the former level. This method of control was specific to malaria and most unlikely to have acted significantly on other contributory causes of death. The most detailed longitudinal studies of malaria in children, which have not been fully published as yet, were by McGregor and his colleagues in the Gambia.

In view of the acknowledged difficulty of malaria control in the African savannah, there has been a series of major field projects attempting to stop transmission. The detailed baseline epidemiological data have also allowed estimates of the effect of control upon infant mortality. None of these projects has completely stopped transmission, but parasite rates have been greatly reduced and the populations substantially protected from malaria. The earliest large project was at Pare-Taveta in East Africa, referred to above. Most subsequent ones were in West Africa, and the most recent was based in Garki district in Northern Nigeria (Molineaux and Grammicia, 1980).

The Garki project came close to stopping malaria transmission in the savannah. The demographic data showed a fall in the infant mortality rate from 245 per thousand live births before intervention to 55 in the first intervention year. However, the rate was 135 in the untreated control villages that year, not significantly different (at the 5 percent level) from the treated. The baseline death rate for the 1–4-year age group was also high at 154 per thousand and fell during intervention to become significantly lower in the treated than untreated villages in the wet season, although the difference was not significant when the first year of intervention is viewed as a whole. The data are compatible with malaria as a common direct cause of death in infants and young children, but with malaria control failing to remove those children who would have died of malaria from the high risk group. The Gambian data of McGregor are similarly compatible with the concept of "competing" causes of death, in that a year with exceptional dry-season mortality due to a measles epidemic was followed by an unusually low wet (malaria) season mortality.

The Garki studies were not sufficiently prolonged to detect delayed falls in mortality due to removing the contribution of chronic malaria to the overall health conditions of children and hence to their risk of dying. The Garki project used two main methods of malaria control: chemotherapy, which was probably specific to malaria, and insecticidal attack with propoxur, which could also affect arboviruses or even flies involved in diarrheal disease transmission, though the effect is very probably focused on malaria largely. The really striking result from the Garki infant mortality data is the very close parallel between the incidence of malaria (infant conversion rate) and the infant mortality rate over the three years of the study, analyzed by ten-week intervals.

It is perhaps of interest that the major texts on malariology, prior to the eradication campaigns of the 1950s, had little to say on the extent of mortality due to malaria when endemic—no more than three or four pages of Boyd's (1949) 1,500-page *Malariology* address the subject. It was clearly assumed in the pre-chloroquine, pre-DDT era that the immensity of the harm done by malaria was so obvious as not to need restatement in most of the world.

Parasitic infection and child survival: indirect effects

With the exception of malaria, parasitic infections do not appear to be significant as direct causes of mortality in children under 5 years of age (Pawlowski, 1983; Walsh and Warren, 1979). The fact remains, however, that their combined prevalence far exceeds the current size of the world population (Peters, 1978), indicating that multiple infection must be the norm throughout much of the developing world. In one study in Guatemala, for example, almost all of the children were found to have been infected at least once with *Giardia* and *Ascaris* by the time they were 3 years old; two-thirds had contracted *Entamoeba histolytica;* and one-half were found to have harbored *Trichuris* (Mata et al., 1977). Infections like these may perhaps contribute indirectly to observed levels of childhood mortality by acting synergistically with other causes of morbidity in the population—for example, malnutrition.

Most children in many developing countries suffer either undernutrition or malnutrition at some time during the first 5 years of life (Latham, 1975). Current figures suggest that 16 percent of the world's children are inadequately fed (US Presidential Commission, 1980), and protein–energy malnutrition is ranked as one of the world's major health problems (Waterlow, 1979). Parasitism and nutrition are inextricably linked for at least two reasons (Crompton and Nesheim, 1982; Scrimshaw et al., 1968). First, many parasites are acquired as a direct result of the feeding behavior of the host; and second, the host by definition provides all the nutrients for the parasites it harbors. The occurrence of synergism in some relationships between host nutrition and the pathology of parasitic infection is now well established (Gordon, 1976; Solomons and Keusch, 1981; WHO, 1965). Such interactions are undoubtedly complex: parasites may respond to inadequate host nutrition by means of alterations in their establishment, survival, and reproductive potential, and may also precipitate continued decline in nutritional status by disturbing the food intake, digestion, and metabolism of their hosts. They may thus become a factor in the etiology of protein–energy malnutrition (FAO/WHO, 1975).

In practice, it seems virtually impossible to decide whether, under naturally occurring conditions, hosts are malnourished because of the presence of parasites or hosts harbor parasites because they are malnourished. Much circumstantial evidence exists, however, to indicate the degree of association between these two factors. For example, malnourished infants often have greater rates of infection with *Entamoeba histolytica* and *Giardia* in the first months of life (Mata, 1975), and intestinal parasites may reach heavier loads in growth-retarded children compared with controls (Jose and Welch, 1970). The results of one study in India indicated that more than three-quarters of the children aged less than 5 years who harbored the intestinal fluke *Fasciolopsis buski* for more than 8 months subsequently died of kwashiorkor (Shah et al., 1974). This is perhaps one specific example of the general and widely made observation that many of the children who suffer both malnutrition and a series of parasitic infections eventually succumb and die (Latham, 1975). Controlled investigations of parasites in laboratory animals have gone some way to untangle the nature of the interrelationships between parasitism and nutrition, but the indirect impact of infection on human morbidity and mortality remains unclear.

The deprivation of nutrients imposed on a host by its parasites may be insignificant if the host is adequately nourished. It has been estimated, for example, that a 5 kg burden of *Ascaris lumbricoides* would probably not take more than 8 percent of ingested food (von Brand, 1979). This proportion may well be greater, however, if the host is a small child and may in addition have serious consequences if the child is already undernourished. Furthermore, the nutrients that a parasite embezzles from its host to meet its own needs are only one facet of the overall disturbance that it may produce in the host's digestive physiology. One of the most striking manifestations of this is malabsorption, associated to some degree with all intestinal parasites but of particular significance in ascariasis, amoebiasis, and giardiasis (Jose and Welch, 1970; Tripathy et al., 1972).

Reductions in host food intake are often observed during the course of parasitic infections in both man (Martorell et al., 1980; Tomkins, 1979; WHO, 1968) and animals (Chapman et al., 1982; Dargie et al., 1979; Sykes et al., 1980; Symons and Jones, 1970), but the physiological processes involved are still poorly understood (see Crompton, 1983). By the end of the first week of an infection with the nematode *Nippostrongylus brasiliensis,* for example, laboratory rats exhibit a reduction of food intake of up to 50 percent (Keymer et al., 1983a). Thereafter, the magnitude of this lesion, which is influenced both by dietary protein and by parasite dose, persists largely unchanged for the remainder of the course of infection and may be associated directly with dose-dependent wasting and mortality in rats that are protein-malnourished.

Some evidence now suggests that a disturbance of host feeding behavior in the form of parasite-induced learned taste aversion may be partly responsible (Keymer et al., 1983b). Anorexia associated with parasitic disease in man may be a vital factor in weight loss or failure to gain weight, particularly in those areas where intake of energy and protein is only just sufficient to maintain health (Tomkins, 1979). Especially in intestinal infections, however, this primary lesion is likely to be compounded by other depredations imposed on nutrient flow to the host tissues. The loss of blood associated with the feeding activity of the hookworms *Ancylostoma duodenale* and *Necator americanus,* for example, can be a contributory factor in the etiology of iron-deficiency anemia (Miller, 1979; Roche and Layrisse, 1966), and must be considered an important association in areas where the prevalence of childhood nutritional anemias may reach 20–25 percent (FAO, 1977).

Some of the ways in which intestinal worms may interfere with the digestion and absorption of food by their hosts have been revealed by studies of *Ascaris suum* in pigs and *Ascaris lumbricoides* in man. One-quarter of the world's population may currently be harboring *Ascaris* infections, and the ubiquity of this parasite is indicated by the daily global contamination of soil by its eggs, which has recently been estimated to reach 9×10^{14} (Pawlowski, 1982). *Ascaris*-infected pigs suffer reductions in food intake and rate of growth, as well as impairment of fat digestion (Forsum et al., 1981; Stephenson et al., 1980b). If this latter finding applies to children infected with *Ascaris lumbricoides,* they will be deprived not only of some energy but also of the fat-soluble vitamin A (Reddy, 1980; Stephenson, 1980; WHO, 1968). Perhaps the overlap between the distributions of vitamin A deficiency and chronic *Ascaris* infection should be investigated with regard to the observation that 50–100,000 children become blind each year as a result of keratomalacia (dryness with ulceration and perforation of the cornea) (FAO, 1977).

Lactase activity has also been found to be significantly reduced in samples of intestinal mucosa taken from *Ascaris*-infected pigs (Forsum et al., 1981); impaired lactase activity has also been demonstrated to be correlated with *Ascaris* infection in Panamanian children (Crompton and Nesheim, personal communication). It seems that one consequence of *Ascaris* infection for some children may be the development of temporary or premature lactose intolerance, which may be of special significance in areas in which the weaning period is highly protracted (Mata et al., 1977).

Further costs must be paid by the parasitized host when nutrients finally make their way into the metabolic pathways. Protein-malnourished rats infected with *Nippostrongylus brasiliensis,* for example, undergo severe hypoalbuminemia as the adult worms become established in the intestine (Crompton et al., 1978). At the same time, abnormally low concentrations of plasma corticosterone and some elevation of insulin levels are detected. These results may be of relevance to the etiology of childhood protein–energy malnutrition, where wasting can be caused by the elevated plasma glucocorticoid concentrations resulting from the stress of frequent infections, and reduced plasma albumin concentration may be of importance in the precipitation of kwashiorkor (Lunn, 1981; Whitehead, 1977).

Studies with domesticated and laboratory animals have established that parasitic infections may often exert considerable effects on the growth of their hosts. The inclusion of pair-fed animals in the experimental design has also indicated that the effect cannot be explained solely in terms of reduced food intake, and that infection must be associated with a reduced capacity to utilize ingested food (Crompton et al., 1981; Platt and Heard, 1965). The impact of parasites on human growth is more difficult to determine, but interpretation of data collected from Kenyan villages has indicated that the removal of *Ascaris* from preschool children by anthelminthic treatment may have led to significant gains in body weight and triceps skin fold thickness during a 14-week period in previously infected as compared with uninfected children (Stephenson et al., 1980a). Similar results have been obtained by Gupta (1980), Rea (1970), and Willett et al. (1979). Although the inference is clear, conclusions concerning the causality of relationships between *Ascaris* infection and retarded growth are unjustified on the basis of studies such as the above (Brown et al., 1981; Freij et al., 1979; Katz, 1980; Schultz, 1981).

A further consequence of protein deprivation is its adverse effect on host immunocompetence (Bell, 1978; Chandra, 1980; Chandra and Newberne, 1977), with the possibility of allowing the course of infection to be extended, the pathology to be increased, and secondary infections to become established. Protein deficiency has been shown experimentally to influence the extent and course of hookworm infection in dogs (Foster and Cort, 1932) and *Ascaris* infection in pigs (Stephenson et al., 1977), and it is tempting to speculate that multiple parasitic infections in children may be facilitated by the effect of protein deprivation on the immune system, especially by the short-term impairment of cell-mediated immune mechanisms (see, for example, Mata, 1975). Circumstantial evidence suggests that certain infections may be synergistically associated—for example, *Trichuris* and invasive amoebiasis (Gilman et al., 1983). Equally, however, antagonistic relationships such as that between *Ascaris* infection and the subsequent contraction of malaria have also been reported (Murray et al., 1977, 1978). An additional feature of helminth infection with regard to susceptibility to secondary infection is that larvae may enhance the passage of microorganisms when they migrate from the intestine to other tissues. There is evidence to suggest, for example, that infection with *Strongyloides stercoralis* may lead to *Escherichia coli* septicemia and meningitis, that *Ascaris suum* infection in pigs may precipitate severe swine influenza, and that *Trichinella spiralis* larvae can act as vehicles of lymphocytic choriomeningitis virus in mice (WHO, 1968).

In conclusion, it is clear that, although circumstantial evidence is available, data do not exist on which to base an assessment of the extent of childhood mortality indirectly mediated by parasitic infection. Synergistic interactions between the pathology of parasitism and malnutrition, however, suggest that parasites must be of far greater significance than is indicated by the numbers of deaths directly attributable to their presence. Whether infection or inadequate nutrition is the initiator, children suffering from the combination enter a positive feedback loop whereby their probability of survival is progressively decreased by the mutual reinforcement of malnutrition and infection. This may result from a single species of parasite or may involve synergism between parasitic agents. For example, although there is as yet little evidence to suggest that malnutrition may enhance the severity or lethality of plasmodial infections (McGregor, 1982), the immunosuppressive effect of malaria is well established, such that the disease may enhance susceptibility to other pathogens, which may in turn cause further nutritional deterioration. Whatever the eventual cause of death, it seems clear that parasitic infection cannot be ruled out as an indirect initiator. The exact magnitude of the influence of each species of parasite on observed levels of childhood mortality may perhaps never be dissected from the existing intricate web of contributory factors, but there is the need and possibility for better understanding than at present.

The measurement of parasitic infection

Although the prevalence of many parasites in endemic areas may be very high by the age of 5 years, children below this age have been neglected in the majority of epidemiological surveys. This is partly because surveys of children at school are much easier to carry out than those of preschool children, which necessitate household visiting. The difficulty of obtaining fecal specimens on demand and the likely fuss over parting with a finger-prick blood sample among young children further discourages study of this age group. In such surveys as are done, the custom of combining data from five-year age groups is often followed. This is reasonable for adult ages but in the 0–5-year age group will usually obscure substantial variation in prevalence rates between years.

If our attention is focused on the first five years of life, there may be great cultural and immunological differences between populations, so that the time course of infection in these early years may differ between endemic communities. The incidence in infancy may be very different from that experienced later in life. The presence of maternal antibodies may complicate the picture (as with viral infections) initially. There are strong environmental and behavioral components to becoming infected that may differentially affect infants—mosquitoes may favor biting the very young or may avoid them, and contact with infective water for schistosomes will depend on patterns of baby bathing. Generalization is difficult, except that in communities highly endemic for a particular parasite substantial numbers of children are likely to be infected and sometimes the peak prevalence and infection load may occur in the first five years of life. Then prevalence may be near zero in one-year-old children and very high (sometimes nearly 100 percent) in those aged 5 years. A great deal changes over a few years, but meaningful analysis of data by single years requires a larger total sample size than is usual in accurate survey work, together with accurate age determinations and an epidemiologically homogenous area. All these may be difficult to obtain in practice; and the geographical heterogeneity of even hamlets and small areas in respect of parasitic infections is increasingly well documented (e.g., Forsyth and Bradley, 1966). If it were part of a general population survey, a total population of over 4,000 would need to be examined to give year-specific age prevalences of useful precision.

Where measurement of parasite burdens is involved, the much smaller size of children raises problems of how to correct or present the results, and sampling issues become more intractable. For example, a fecal egg count of 500 eggs per gram in a 1.5-year-old needs correction for stool volume, which rarely receives much attention at this age, and also needs to be related to the observations of worm-load-dependent pathology made in adults and older children. Alternatively, and perhaps more soundly, the pathological consequences need to be measured in children. In the case of helminths, where intensity of infection is estimated from egg output, the relations of worm burden to egg production may differ from that assumed in adults, as a result of both differing immune responses and density-dependent relations. Five *Ascaris* worms in a baby will be much more crowded than the same number in a large adult.

Detection

Animal parasites are large enough to be seen, and usually identified, under the light microscope while the helminths can be seen by the naked eye. The diagnosis of individual infections, and until recently the techniques of survey, have concentrated on microscopy of the parasites, or more often their reproductive forms in small samples of blood, tissue, or excreta. Such an approach gives tests that are highly specific, lend themselves to quantification, but are of limited sensitivity and subject to sampling error.

The traditional thin fecal smear for helminth eggs and protozoal cysts in feces examines about 3 mg of stool, or one part in 50,000 of an adult's daily excreta, and perhaps 0.01 percent of a young child's. It follows that light infections with helminths laying under 1,000 eggs per female worm daily will often be missed. More appropriate techniques for helminthology examine larger samples, thereby reducing the chance of missing lower egg output levels. Urine volumes of 10 ml are readily examined for schistosome eggs.

Parasites transmitted by biting insects are usually detectable in the blood. In the filarial infections with hematogenous microfilariae, there have been sampling problems as with excreted helminth eggs, but in both cases the use of filtration methods using nucleopore, millipore, filter paper, and other membranes has greatly simplified procedures and increased the samples that can be examined.

For the protozoal parasites, excreta or blood sampling errors are less of a practical difficulty. For malarial parasites the conventional thick smear uses 20 cu mm of blood and thus in theory could detect one parasite in 10^8 red cells.

A more difficult fact to cope with in relation to studies of impact is that the stages of the parasite usually measured may not reflect the intensity of pathogenic activity. Thus *Giardia* may be causing damage to the small intestine and diarrhea, without at that time many cysts being passed in the feces. The nutritional damage done to the host by *Ascaris* may be due primarily to the presence of adult worms and could be significant in infection by male worms alone, in which case no eggs are passed.

As implied above, the helminth infections differ from other microparasites in that the worms cannot increase in number within the human body except by superinfection. By contrast, two weeks after an infection by viruses or protozoa it is impossible to determine the infecting dose because so much replication will have occurred. Therefore helminth infections must be assessed quantitatively—determining not just whether a person has hookworm infection, but by how many hookworms the person is infected. Since as a broad generalization pathology is correlated with the intensity, and sometimes duration, of infection, the need to measure the intensity of infection by parasitic worms is clear. Doing so may also be helpful in protozoal infections in which the parasite burden may give a helpful indication of the extent to which illness or even mortality is due to that infection.

The quantitative nature of helminth infections was well recognized by the Rockefeller Foundation hookworm group (Cort, 1924; Stoll, 1924), and by J. Allen Scott in the case of schistosomes (Scott, 1937). It has been realized and developed with increasing clarity by each successive generation (Scott, 1957; Jordan, 1963; Macdonald, 1965a, b; Bradley, 1963, 1967, 1972) to the present (Warren; Anderson and May, 1982) and can be set out readily. Broad relations between worm burden and pathological consequences have been demonstrated. The absolute severity of illness and its relation to mortality and other diseases are far more speculative.

In population-based studies of the role of parasitic disease in child mortality, two types of problems affect study design greatly. For the acute specific mortality of parasite origin, chiefly relating to malaria, the problem is sampling frequency, because it is the initial infection that is most likely to be lethal. For practical purposes this requires health care facilities so that each child can have a parasitological examination at the time of the terminal illness, for diagnostic purposes. Such information ought to be scientifically self-defeating since appropriate medication should save that child's life. Only in epidemic malaria with gross changes in mortality rates will such data become available.

For the vast majority of parasitic infections, which are contributory factors rather than the sole cause of child mortality, the major design problem in population studies is to sample over a long enough period. While cross-sectional studies may define the general epidemiological picture for a specific parasite in a community, longitudinal observations of children are needed if the role of the parasite as a risk factor is to be analyzed. Grouped observations at regular intervals may overcome some of the sampling problems discussed above. For example, specimens on 5 or 10 consecutive days at intervals of a few months may give useful data. The closely spaced samples help to overcome the difficult task of evaluating whether a single isolated negative sample means loss of infection or is a sampling artifact.

Frequency of sampling over the long term will depend on the precise aims of the study and must consider seasonal regular fluctuations in infection. Logistic considerations and the finite tolerance of children and their parents for sample collection will usually curtail the sampling frequency so that most studies are an uneasy compromise. However, the intractable problems are not in the description of the parasitic infections of child and population in quantitative terms but in determining how far they are risk factors for child mortality.

Techniques

Techniques for the measurement of infection vary both with the habitat and with the reproductive biology of the parasite under consideration. Measurements of the prevalence of infection may be sufficient for studies of microparasites (protozoa), which undergo direct reproduction within the host. For epidemiological purposes, however, knowledge of the prevalence of macroparasitic infection (helminths) is of little value unless combined with some estimate of infection intensity. Most helminth parasites in the definitive host (the one in which sexual stages of the parasite occur) are limited to some form of transmission reproduction, so that both the severity of clinical symptoms and the transmission pattern of infection are critically dependent on the number of parasites harbored per host. Diagnosis of protozoan infection is normally based on direct observation of parasites in samples of tissues, body fluids, or excretory products. In contrast, the presence of helminth parasites may normally only be inferred from the observation of eggs or juvenile stages. For these reasons, methods for the measurement of protozoan infection need only to minimize the number of false negative diagnoses made, whereas methods relating to helminth infections must also attempt to provide an accurate and representative quantitative estimation of the number of transmission stages produced. The inferred relationship between this estimate and actual worm burden creates additional problems for the epidemiological measurement of macroparasitic infection. Examination of blood samples or fecal material is sufficient to identify the majority of parasitic species, but the remainder may require examination of other tissue samples such as skin snips (e.g., *Onchocerca volvulus*) or urine samples (e.g., *Schistosoma haematobium*).

Thin blood films may be used for the specific identification of malaria parasites, trypanosomes, and nematode microfilariae. A correctly prepared thin film consists of a single layer of evenly distributed blood cells in which the structure of the parasite is preserved with a minimum level of distortion. Preparation is made by the even spreading of a single drop of blood along a clean microscope slide. Thick films may be prepared by stirring (to prevent fibrin formation) three drops of blood on a clean slide for 30 seconds to cover an area 2 cm in diameter. Both types of film may be subjected to Giemsa staining after drying in air. A tradeoff exists in these two methods between ease of identification (thin film) and estimation of the numbers of parasites per sample (thick film). Thick films are thus best used when quantitative measurement is required, as is often the case for microfilariae. A further complication occurs in the diagnosis of blood-dwelling filarial nematode infections due to the periodicity of the appearance of microfilariae in the peripheral circulation.

Smears of fresh fecal material may be used for diagnosis of the presence of lumen-dwelling protozoa and helminths. The Kato method, for example, involves a 50 mg sample pressed between a microscope slide and a strip of cellophane soaked in glycerin and malachite green stain. The prepared slide may be stored for relatively short periods of time, but examination is best carried out within a few hours. Although often recommended for use as a quantitative tool, the small amount of material examined limits the usefulness of this method beyond measurements of infection prevalence.

Estimation of the intensity of intestinal helminth infection is normally based on the use of concentration techniques such as the Stoll or formol-ether methods on samples taken from 24-hour stool collections. The former technique involves the examination of a 0.15 ml sample from a suspension made by mixing a known weight of fecal material (approximately 4 g) with a known volume of dilute sodium hydroxide solution. Ether sedimentation is a rather more sophisticated method (therefore requiring the use of rather more sophisticated laboratory facilities) based on the filtration and centrifugation of a known weight of fecal material (approximately 1–3 g) mixed with known volumes of preservative solution and diethyl ether. The advantage of this method is that it can be carried out on material that has been fixed in formalin or Schaudinn's fluid, thereby allowing the collection of specimens at one place and analysis of them elsewhere.

There exist many problems in the use of fecal sample analysis in studies of the epidemiology of intestinal parasites. First are the practical and financial difficulties associated with the collection and analysis of multiple stool specimens: single-specimen analysis has been shown to be unreliable in the detection of low levels of infection and also high levels of infection in which the output of transmission stages is interrupted or periodic (e.g., Sawitz and Faust, 1942). The second related family of problems arises as a result of the highly variable spatial and temporal distribution of parasite transmission stages in the feces, often resulting in a mean estimate of the rate of transmission stage production with an extremely high associated variance (e.g., Croll et al., 1982; Hall, 1981). A third series of possible errors arises as a result of variability in the amount and consistency of stool material produced, especially if this variable is confounded by the presence of the parasites themselves (e.g., Hall, 1982). Lastly, there is much evidence to suggest that the fecundity of intestinal helminth parasites is markedly affected by their density within the intestine (e.g., Anderson and May, 1982), and it seems likely that the degree of density-dependence may be affected by variables such as the size, age, and nutritional status of the host. In view of the foregoing, even if accurate estimates of transmission stage output may be made, they may be of little use in the accurate measurement of intensity.

In conclusion, it seems that measurements of the prevalence and incidence of microparasitic infection are relatively easy to carry out with the required degree of accuracy. Measurements of the intensity of helminth infection are more difficult. This difficulty may turn out to be a major limiting step in the introduction of community control programs based on the diagnosis and selective treatment of the small proportion of individuals who carry heavy worm loads.

References

Anderson, R. M., and R. M. May. 1982. "Population dynamics of human helminth infections: Control by chemotherapy," *Nature* 297: 557–563.

Bell, R. G. 1978. "Undernutrition, infection and immunity: The role of parasites," *Papua New Guinea Medical Journal* 21: 43–45.

Blacklock, D. B., and R. M. Gordon. 1925. "Malaria infection as it occurs in late pregnancy; its relationship to labour and early infancy," *Annals of Tropical Medicine and Parasitology* 19: 327–365.

Boyd, M. F. (ed.). 1949. *Malariology: A Comprehensive Survey of All Aspects of This Group of Diseases from a Global Standpoint.* 2 vols. London: Saunders.

Bradley, D. J. 1963. "A quantitative approach to Bilharzia," *East African Medical Journal* 40: 240–249.

———. 1967. "The measurement of schistosome populations," in *Bilharziasis*, ed. F. K. Mostofi. Berlin: Springer, pp. 301–327.

———. 1972. "Regulation of parasite populations," *Transactions of the Royal Society of Tropical Medicine and Hygiene* 66: 697–708.

Brown, K. H., R. H. Gilman, A. Gafar, S. M. Alamgir, J. L. Strife, A. Z. Kapikian, and R. B. Sack. 1981. "Infections associated with severe protein-calorie malnutrition in hospitalized infants and children," *Nutrition Research* 1: 33–46.

Bruce-Chwatt, L. J. 1952. "Malaria in African infants and children in Southern Nigeria," *Annals of Tropical Medicine and Parasitology* 46: 173–200.

Chandra, R. K. 1980. *Immunology of Nutritional Disorders.* London: Edward Arnold.

———, and P. M. Newberne. 1977. *Nutrition, Immunity and Infection.* New York and London: Plenum Press.

Chapman, H. D., D. L. Fernandes, and T. F. Davison. 1982. "A comparison of the effects of infection with *Eimeria maxima* and dietary restriction on weight gain, plasma metabolites and liver glycogen in the immature fowl, *Gallus domesticus*," *Parasitology* 84: 205–213.

Christophers, S. R. 1911. "Malaria in the Punjab," *Scientific Memoirs by Officers of the Medical and Sanitary Departments of the Government of India,* No. 46.

———. 1924. "The mechanism of immunity against malaria in communities living under hyperendemic conditions," *Indian Journal of Medical Research* 12: 273.

———. 1949. "Endemic and epidemic prevalence," in *Malariology*, ed. M. F. Boyd. London: Saunders, pp. 698–721.

Cort, W. W. 1924. "Investigations on control of hookworm disease. Methods of measuring human infestation," *American Journal of Hygiene* 4: 213–221.

Croll, N. A., R. M. Anderson, T. W. Gyorkos, and E. Ghadinian. 1982. "The population biology and control of *Ascaris lumbricoides* in a rural community in Iran," *Transactions of the Royal Society of Tropical Medicine and Hygiene* 76: 187–197.

Crompton, D. W. T. 1983. "Nutrition and parasitic infection," *Federation Proceedings* (in press).

———, S. Arnold, W. A. Coward, and P. G. Lunn. 1978. "*Nippostrongylus* (Nematoda) infection in protein-malnourished rats," *Transactions of the Royal Society of Tropical Medicine and Hygiene* 72: 195–197.

———, D. E. Walters, and S. Arnold. 1981. "Changes in the food intake and body weight of protein-malnourished rats infected with *Nippostrongylus brasiliensis* (Nematoda)," *Parasitology* 82: 23–38.

———, and M. C. Nesheim. 1982. "Nutritional science and parasitology: A case for collaboration," *Bioscience* 32: 677–680.

Dargie, J. D., C. I. Berry, and J. J. Parkins. 1979. "The pathology of ovine fascioliasis: Studies on the feed intake and digestibility, body weight and nitrogen balance of sheep given rations of hay or hay plus, a polluted supplement," *Research in Veterinary Science* 26: 289–295.

Davidson, G. 1955. "Further studies on the basic factors concerned in the transmission of malaria," *Transactions of the Royal Society of Tropical Medicine and Hygiene* 49: 339–350.

———, and C. C. Draper. 1953. "Field studies of some of the basic factors concerned in the transmission of malaria," *Transactions of the Royal Society of Tropical Medicine and Hygiene* 47: 522–535.

FAO. 1977. *The Fourth World Food Survey*. Rome: FAO.

FAO/WHO. Recommendations. 1975. "Energy and protein requirements," *Food and Nutrition* 1: 11–19.

Farinaud, E., and R. Choumara. 1950. [Malaria infestation and demography of the mountain population of Southern Indo-China.] *Bulletin economique Indochine, supplement* 22: 5–48.

Forsum, E., M. C. Nesheuri, and D. W. T. Crompton. 1981. "Nutritional aspects of *Ascaris* infection in young protein-deficient pigs," *Parasitology* 83: 497–512.

Forsyth, D. M., and D. J. Bradley. 1966. "The consequences of Bilharziasis," *Bulletin of the World Health Organization* 34: 715–735.

Foster, A. O., and W. W. Cort. 1932. "The relation of diet to the susceptibility of dogs of *Ancylostoma caninum*," *American Journal of Hygiene* 16: 582–601.

Freij, L., G. W. Meeuwisse, N. O. Berg, S. Wall, and M. Gebre-Medhin. 1979. "Ascariasis and malnutrition: A study in urban Ethiopian children," *American Journal of Clinical Nutrition* 32: 1545–1553.

Garnham, P. C. C. 1935. "Hyperendemic malaria in a native reserve of Kenya and the influence upon its course of Atebrin and Plasmoquine," *Transactions of the Royal Society of Tropical Medicine and Hygiene* 29: 167.

———. 1938. "The placenta in malaria with special reference to reticulo-enlothelical immunity," *Transactions of the Royal Society of Tropical Medicine and Hygiene* 74: 61–72.

Gilman, R. H., Y. H. Chong, C. Davis, B. Greenberg, H. K. Virik, and H. B. Dixon. 1983. "The adverse consequences of heavy *Trichuris* infection," *Transactions of the Royal Society of Tropical Medicine and Hygiene* 77: 432–438.

Gordon, J. E. 1976. "Synergism of malnutrition and infectious disease," in *Nutrition in Preventive Medicine*, ed. G. H. Beaton and J. M. Bengoa. Geneva: WHO, pp. 193–209.

Gupta, M. C. 1980. "Intestinal parasitic infections and malnutrition," *Indian Journal of Pediatrics* 47: 503–509.

Hall, A. 1981. "Quantitative variability of nematode egg counts in faeces: A study among rural Kenyans," *Transactions of the Royal Society of Tropical Medicine and Hygiene* 75: 682–687.

———. 1982. "Intestinal helminths of man: The interpretation of egg counts," *Parasitology* 85: 605–613.

Jordan, P. 1963. "Some quantitative aspects of Bilharzia with particular reference to suppressive therapy and mollusciciding in control of *S. haematobium* in Sukumaland, Tanganyika," *East African Medical Journal* 40: 250–260.

Jose, D. G., and J. S. Welch. 1970. "Growth retardation, anaemia and infection with malabsorption and infestation of the bowel. The syndrome of protein-calorie malnutrition in Australian aboriginal children," *The Medical Journal of Australia* 1: 349–356.

Katz, M. 1980. "Parasite control in the prevention of malnutrition," in *Proceedings of the Seminar on Parasite Control in the Prevention of Malnutrition*, WHO, UNICEF, JOICFP, JAPC, Tokyo, pp. 79–85.

Keymer, A. E., D. W. T. Crompton, and D. E. Walters. 1983a. "*Nippostrongylus* (Nematoda) in protein-malnourished rats: Host mortality, morbidity and rehabilitation," *Parasitology* 86: 461–475.

———, D. W. T. Crompton, and B. J. Sahakian. 1983b. "Parasite-induced learned taste aversion involving *Nippostrongylus* in rats," *Parasitology* 86: 455–460.

Latham, M. C. 1975. "Nutrition and infection in national development," *Science* 188: 561–565.

Lunn, P. G. 1981. In "Parasitic Infection and Host Nutrition" (Workshop 2, EMOP 3). *Parasitology* 82: 41–42.

Macdonald, G. 1951. "Community aspects of immunity to malaria," *British Medical Bulletin* 8: 33–36.

———. 1965a. "The dynamics of helminth infections, with special reference to Schistosomes," *Transactions of the Royal Society of Tropical Medicine and Hygiene* 59: 489–506.

———. 1965b. "On the scientific basis of tropical hygiene," *Transactions of the Royal Society of Tropical Medicine and Hygiene* 59: 611–620.

McGregor, I. A. 1982. "Malaria: Nutritional implications," *Reviews of Infectious Diseases* 4: 798–804.

———, M. E. Wilson, and W. Z. Billewicz. 1983. "Malaria infection of the placenta in the Gambia, West Africa; its incidence and relationship to stillbirth, birthweight and placental weight," *Transactions of the Royal Society of Tropical Medicine and Hygiene* 77: 232–244.

Martorell, R., C. Yarborough, S. Yarborough, and R. E. Klein. 1980. "The impact of ordinary illnesses on the dietary intakes of malnourished children," *American Journal of Clinical Nutrition* 33: 345–350.

Mata, L. J. 1975. "Malnutrition-infection interactions in the tropics," *The American Journal of Tropical Medicine and Hygiene* 24: 564–574.

———, R. A. Kromal, J. J. Urrutia, and B. Garcia. 1977. "Effect of infection on food intake and the nutritional state: Perspectives as viewed from the village," *American Journal of Clinical Nutrition* 30: 1215–1227.

Miller, T. A. 1979. "Hookworm infection in man," *Advances in Parasitology* 17: 315–384.

Molineaux, L., and G. Gramiccia. 1980. *The Garki Project: Research on the Epidemiology and Control of Malaria in the Sudan Savannah of West Africa*. Geneva: World Health Organization.

Murray, J., A. Murray, M. Murray, and C. Murray. 1977. "Parotid enlargement, forehead edema and suppression of malaria as nutritional consequences of ascariasis," *American Journal of Clinical Nutrition* 30: 2117–2121.

———, A. Murray, M. Murray, and C. Murray. 1978. "The biological suppression of malaria: An ecological and nutritional inter-relationship of a host and two parasites," *American Journal of Clinical Nutrition* 31: 1363–1366.

Pawlowski, Z. S. 1982. "Ascariasis: Host-pathogen biology," *Reviews of Infectious Diseases* 4: 806–814.

———. 1983. "Implications of parasite-nutrition interactions from a world perspective," *Federation Proceedings* (in press).

Peters, W. 1978. "Comments and discussion. In the relevance of parasitology to human welfare today," *Symposium of the British Society for Parasitology* 16: 25–40.

Platt, B. S., and C. R. C. Heard. 1965. "The contribution of infections to protein-calory deficiency," *Transactions of the Royal Society of Tropical Medicine and Hygiene* 59: 571–581.

Rea, J. N. 1970. "Social and nutritional influences on morbidity: A community study of young children in Lagos," *Proceedings of the Nutritional Society* 29: 223–230.

Reddy, V. 1980. "Intestinal helminths and malnutrition," in *Proceedings of the Seminars on Parasite Control in the Prevention of Malnutrition*, WHO, UNICEF, JOICFP, JAPC, Tokyo, pp. 67–78.

Roche, M., and M. Layrisse. 1966. "The nature and causes of hookworm anaemia," *American Journal of Tropical Medicine and Hygiene* 15: 1029–1102.

Sawitz, W. G., and E. C. Faust. 1942. "The probability of detecting intestinal protozoa by successive stool examination," *American Journal of Tropical Medicine and Hygiene* 22: 131–136.

Schultz, M. G. 1981. "The effects of *Ascaris lumbricoides* infection on nutritional status," Workshop on Interactions of Parasitic Diseases and Nutrition, Rockefeller Foundation, Bellagio, Italy.

Scott, J. A. 1937. "Dilution egg counting in comparison with other methods for determining the incidence of *Schistosoma mansoni*," *American Journal of Hygiene* 25: 546–565.

———. 1957. "Egg counts as estimates of intensity of infection with *Schistosoma haematobium*," *Texas Reports on Biology and Medicine* 15: 425–430.

Scrimshaw, N. S., C. E. Taylor, and J. E. Gordon. 1968. *Interactions of Nutrition and Infection*, Monograph Series, 57. Geneva: WHO.

Shah, P. M., P. M. Udani, P. V. Manjarum, and P. A. Naik. 1974. "*Fasciolopsis buski* infestation in children," *Indian Pediatrics* 10: 721.

Solomons, N. W., and G. T. Keusch. 1981. "Nutritional implications of parasitic infections," *Nutritional Reviews* 39: 149–161.

Stephenson, L. S. 1980. "Nutritional and economic implications of soil transmitted helminths with special reference to *Ascariasis*," in *Clinical Disorders in Pediatric Gastroenterology and Nutrition*, ed. F. Lifschitz. New York and Basel: Marcel Dekker Inc.

———, W. G. Pond, L. P. Krook, and M. C. Nesheim. 1977. "The relationship between *Ascaris* infection, dietary protein level, and intestinal pathology in growing pigs," *Federation Proceedings* 36: 1181.

———, D. W. T. Crompton, M. C. Latham, T. W. J. Schulpen, M. C. Nesheim, and A. A. J. Jansen. 1980a. "Relationships between *Ascaris* infection and growth of malnourished preschool children in Kenya," *American Journal of Clinical Nutrition* 33: 1165–1172.

———, W. G. Pond, M. C. Nesheim, L. P. Krook, and D. W. T. Crompton. 1980b. "*Ascaris serum:* Nutrient absorption, growth and intestinal pathology in young pigs experimentally infected with 15-day-old larvae," *Experimental Parasitology* 49: 15–25.

Stoll, N. R. 1924. "The significance of egg count data in *Necator americanus* infestations," *American Journal of Hygiene* 4: 466–500.

Sykes, A. R., R. L. Coop, and B. Rushton. 1980. "Chronic subclinical fascioliasis in sheep: Effects on food intake, food utilization and blood constituents," *Research in Veterinary Science* 28: 63–70.

Symons, L. E. A., and W. O. Jones. 1970. "*Nematospiroides dubius, Nippostrongylus brasiliensis and Trichostrongylus colubriformis:* Protein digestion in infected mammals," *Experimental Parasitology* 27: 496–506.

Tomkins, A. M. 1979. "The role of intestinal parasites in diarrhoea and malnutrition," *Tropical Doctor* 9: 21–24.

Tripathy, K., E. Duque, O. Bolanos, H. Lotero, and L. G. Mayoral. 1972. "Malabsorption syndrome in ascariasis," *American Journal of Clinical Nutrition* 25: 1276–1281.

US Presidential Commission. 1980. *Report of the Presidential Commission on World Hunger*. Washington, D.C.: US Government Printing Office.

von Brand, T. 1979. *Biochemistry and Physiology of Endoparasites*. Amsterdam, New York, and Oxford: Elsevier/North Holland Biomedical Press.

Walsh, J. A., and K. S. Warren. 1979. "Selective primary health care: An interim strategy for disease control in developing countries," *New England Journal of Medicine* 301: 967–974.

Waterlow, J. C. 1979. "Childhood malnutrition—the global problem," *Proceedings of the Nutrition Society* 38: 1–27.

Whitehead, R. G. 1977. "Infection and the development of Kwashiorkor and Marasmus in Africa," *American Journal of Clinical Nutrition* 30: 1281–1284.

WHO. 1968. "Control of Ascariasis," *WHO Chronicle* 22: 155–159.

———. 1981. *Intestinal Protozoan and Helminthic Infections,* Technical Report Series No. 666. Geneva: WHO.

WHO Expert Committee. 1965. *Nutrition and Infection,* Technical Report Series No. 314. Geneva: WHO.

Willett, W. C., W. L. Kilama, and C. M. Kihamia. 1979. "*Ascaris* and growth rates: A randomized trial of treatment," *American Journal of Public Health* 69: 987–991.

Wilson, D. B. 1936. Report of the Malaria Unit, Tanga, 1933–34, together with a report on a study of malaria in India. Dar es Salaam: Government Printer.

———, P. C. C. Garnham, and H. H. Swellengrebel. 1950. "A review of hyperendemic malaria," *Tropical Diseases Bulletin* 47: 677–698.

SOCIOECONOMIC VARIABLES

Effects of Maternal Education, Women's Roles, and Child Care on Child Mortality

Helen Ware

In the developing world there is now clear evidence of differentials in child survival rates associated with the education of mothers. Data from Latin America (Behm, 1976–78; Haines and Avery, 1978), Africa (Caldwell, 1979; Farah and Preston, 1982), and Asia (Cochrane, 1980; Caldwell and McDonald, 1981) all show a negative relationship between the extent of maternal education and the level of child mortality, although the amount of education required to produce a significant reduction in mortality varies from culture to culture.

Evidence of a relationship between women's roles and the mortality of their children is much harder to obtain and to interpret. For a start, while educational levels do not regress and normally remain constant once women have attained maturity, women's roles may vary greatly over time, and data on current status may bear little relationship to the situation at the time when the death occurred or when the child's health first began to decline. For this reason it is not possible, as in the case of education, to make use of data gathered in the vast range of fertility surveys that are now available. To study the relationship between women's roles and the mortality of their children, one should ideally have data for each child extending from birth to age 5, or to death where that came first. Some alternative approaches are discussed below, but is should be recognized that disentangling cause from effect in this area will always require a sophisticated analytical approach and an in-depth knowledge of the culture involved.

Obstacles to measuring child mortality

An eagerness to proceed with the study of differentials in child mortality can result in neglect of the substantial problems involved in collecting the mortality data per se. This neglect is often excused on the grounds that, while there may well be some underreporting of child deaths, more complete reporting would only serve to enhance the differentials discovered since it is the uneducated and poorer women who are most likely to fail to report all deaths that have occurred. This contention merits investigation. In all cultures child death is a threatening subject of conversation, and it does not necessarily follow that women from elite groups in which child mortality is a relatively rare and lonely experience would be more willing to recall such deaths than illiterate village women for whom such events are regrettably commonplace occasions for a small feast and gathering among friends. Indeed, one factor in the study of child mortality should be an awareness of the customs associated with the deaths of young children and of the minimum age at death at which it is deemed appropriate to hold a formal funeral.

Demographers have often suspected older women of forgetting the deaths of children through "recall lapse," without appreciating the cultural factors that make older women reluctant to discuss past tragedies with smart young interviewers. There may also be real problems with cultural variations in the definition of a live birth. Many African groups define any child that dies before it passes through the "outdooring" ceremony as a stillbirth. Although this ceremony usually takes place some seven days after a birth, in the case of a sickly child it is postponed until the infant is more robust. Thus many deaths of infants under the age of one month may be perceived by their mothers as stillbirths (Ware, 1977). There was also a common belief that a woman who suffered a series of child deaths (probably from sickle-cell anemia) was in fact visited by a single child that returned in multiple reincarnations, only to be called back to the spirit world on each occasion (Fadipe, 1970; Onwubalite, 1983). This belief resulted in the brutal mutilation of children's corpses to ensure that, should they return, they would at least be easily recognized (Fadipe, 1970). Such beliefs have clearly been associated with underreporting of child deaths by older, more traditional women whose beliefs have not been altered by conversion to Christianity or Islam. However, from a policy planning viewpoint there is only limited value in studying child mortality differentials among older women whose experiences occurred at a time when conditions were markedly different from those pertaining today. There is no reason to believe that access to primary education will have the same impact today, when it has the potential of affecting the majority of women, as it did under colonial regimes only a generation earlier, when less than one woman in 20 had an opportunity for such an education.

Among younger women, whose children have lived and died in conditions of greater relevance to the current situation, the belief that educated or otherwise more sophisticated women are the most accurate reporters of child deaths needs to be tested. In a wide range of surveys, women whose only child has died are conspicuously absent. It would appear that women in this situation prefer to report themselves as childless rather than admit to what they feel is failure and to discuss the harrowing details. Such reluctance may actually be more rather than less common among educated women. First births are special in all cultures, and one very interesting area of investigation would be the subsequent precautions taken by women whose first children have died prior to the arrival of the second. Are there real constraints of ignorance rather than of income that hinder the adoption of effective preventive measures?

A major source of information on child mortality in the developing countries is the vast range of data from fertility surveys. Such surveys, however, commonly focus on currently married women, with the consequence that the possibly very different mortality experiences of mothers who are widowed, divorced, or deserted are largely neglected.

Much of the discussion that follows concentrates on the relationship between infant and child mortality and maternal education. This is partly because this topic offers both a wealth of data and considerable theoretical debate. Moreover, examination of this specific relationship raises many broader issues, especially those concerning the necessity for identifying the intermediate health variables associated with reduced mortality and the need to distinguish between the effects of greater resources and the impact of greater knowledge in preventing deaths.

Maternal education

Level of education of both sexes is commonly measured in one of four ways: (1) as a dichotomy between the illiterate and the literate (usually defined in terms of being able to read a simple letter in one's mother tongue); (2) by number of years of schooling completed (preferably excluding repeated classes); (3) by highest level of schooling attained (e.g., none, some primary, completed primary, some secondary, etc.); (4) by qualifications or degree obtained (e.g., no schooling, some schooling, school-leaving certificate, etc.). The choice of a measure depends on the purposes for which the data are to be used and local cultural conditions. If it is felt that there is a qualitative in addition to a quantitative difference between primary and secondary schooling, a measure of level rather than of years may be preferred. This choice also avoids problems with changes over time in the years required to pass from one level to the next. In some cultures religious education may take place outside the mainstream and may need to be separately measured. In Nigeria, for example, women who have had Koranic schooling are often more traditional on many measures than those who have never had any formal education (Sembajwe, 1981).

The choice of measure should also be influenced by the working hypothesis as to the ways in which education is thought to influence behavior. If literacy is thought to be the vital element, then questions on literacy or even brief tests of reading ability should be backed up by questions on newspaper reading and other forms of self-instruction and contact with the world at large. If the gaining of specific knowledge is thought to be the vital element, then actual knowledge should be measured in conjunction with questions on the level of education attained. It can be a chastening experience to discover that final-year teacher-trainees know no more about nutrition than primary school leavers and that both groups know little more than the illiterate mothers of malnourished children seen at health clinics (Hoorweg and McDowell, 1979: 91). It is also necessary to be aware of possible distinctions between knowledge and belief. Primary school children and even nurses trained in the methods of Western medicine may absorb information necessary to pass their examinations without incorporating these ''facts'' into the belief systems that determine their behavior.

Theories which hypothesize that education exerts an influence on child care behavior through its effect on the relative power balance between spouses and between younger and older generations need to be tested with data on the education of husbands and wives and of the previous generation (Caldwell, 1979; Farah and Preston, 1982). Data on the education of the previous generation is in any case very useful, for one would expect a considerable difference between the first generation of women to experience formal education and later generations.

Testing the hypothesis that maternal education reduces child mortality

A major theory of the linkage between increased maternal education and reduced child mortality is that education gives women the power and the confidence to take decision-making into their own hands. Caldwell (1979) has argued that three factors are of importance in this regard. In ascending order, these are (1) a reduction in fatalism in the face of children's ill health; (2) a greater capability in manipulating the world (e.g., in knowing where facilities are, and in securing the attention of doctors and nurses); and (3) a change in the traditional balance of family relationships that shifts the focus of power away from the patriarch and the mother-in-law and ensures that a greater share of available resources is devoted to children.

On one level one may test such theories with a range of survey data. An example of the kind of data one would need is information on the differential use of health facilities for sick children by women of various educational levels, incorporating some control for the relative costs in time and money for different groups of women. Actual knowledge of the location of facilities would be easy to test, while measuring the level of attention obtained from medical personnel would require an observational study controlled to see whether, for example, wealthy but illiterate women are reluctant to seek aid or receive inferior service. On the question of the balance of power within the family, it should also be possible to gather data on who actually decides that an ailing infant should be taken to a clinic and, with much greater difficulty, on the allocation of food and other expenditures within the household or within the extended family.

On another level one may question how far it is possible to separate the effects of income and education in matters of child care. (This question is addressed at greater length below.) Decisions about food and sharing may well be different where there is enough to go around from the situation where difficult choices have to be made as to who will have access to a very limited source of protein. It is also possible that food allocation among children depends less on the education of the mother than on the prospective education of the children. Educated parents very rarely plan to have illiterate children, and the food and medical investment in a child who is destined to go to school may well be greater than that in a child who is expected to join its parents in working in the fields. In this context it would be especially interesting to look at investment in the children of educated men with limited incomes who have illiterate wives. If it is indeed the mother's decision-making powers that are vital, then one would expect these children to experience lesser investment and higher mortality than children who have two educated parents.

It is also possible to examine the kinds of mortality effects one would expect to find if the three factors enumerated above are the essential elements in securing the impact of maternal education. One would presumably expect the educational differential in mortality to be much more significant in the latter half of the first year of life and during the second year, when access to solid food gains in importance, rather than in the first six months, when breastmilk is a predominating factor in the diet. This might be counterbalanced to some extent by educated women choosing to deliver in hospital or to use the services of scientifically trained midwives (if these two factors do, in fact, reduce the level of early infant mortality within the community). Here again one faces the problem that these innovative choices are not without financial costs that can usually more readily be met by the educated. Even where educated parents do not have current incomes higher than illiterate ones, their prospects and their credit are usually better, if only because their own parents, who were able to afford to send them to school, may be able to assist.

With respect to perinatal mortality, birth weight is an important intermediate variable. Educated women may achieve higher average birth weights because they receive a larger share of food within the home; because they flout the taboos concerning the consumption of protein sources such as chicken and eggs during pregnancy; because they are more innovative in seeking antenatal care; because they engage in less heavy manual labor during the later months of pregnancy; or because they are a healthier group to start with.

In Bangladesh, where nutrition is an important determinant of health, there is evidence that a link exists between mother's height and the birth weight of the infant and that educated mothers bear heavier infants with a greater chance of survival because of their own greater height and fitness (Chowdhury, 1982). Educated mothers may be taller and fitter not only in cases where their parents were also educated and lived in comfortable circumstances but also in cases where poor parents selected the healthiest and brightest of their children to go to school and then strengthened their investment with preferential treatment in the allocation of food and medical services. (In Nepal height-for-age is the best predictor of school attendance and grades [Moock and Leslie,

1982].) In such cases survey data could show that maternal education was a more important factor in determining the level of child mortality than current household income, while the prior determining factor was the income of the mother's father at the time when her height and her education were being determined (Psacharopoulos, 1983).

Another aspect of the Caldwell hypothesis is the cultural context in which it is set. Caldwell's original data came from the Yoruba areas of Western Nigeria, a culture in which wives keep separate budgets from their husbands. Even in a highly traditional enclave within this culture, Maclean (1974: 122) found that little more than half of the men and fewer of the women thought that a woman should ask the opinion of the household head before taking a sick child to the hospital. With the Nigerian data Caldwell (1979: 400) was able to show that, in comparison with mothers having no formal education, mothers with primary education experienced 42 percent less child mortality, and those with secondary education 36 percent less. Data from ten developing countries, however, showed that a much more common situation is that the fall in child mortality levels associated with the move from primary to secondary education of mothers is twice as important as the original step to primary schooling (Caldwell and McDonald, 1981). Unfortunately the only control for the family's standard of living in this study was a dichotomous division of the father's occupation into white collar and non–white collar. The question arises as to why primary education of the mother should have so much less impact on child mortality in, for example, Bangladesh, Indonesia, Kenya, and Sri Lanka than it does in Western Nigeria. If education works to reduce child mortality through increasing the mother's autonomy and the share of household income allocated to children, why should such a change have to wait upon attainment of secondary education in so many developing countries?

One problem with education as an explanation for changes in family power structures and, through these changes, in mortality levels is that it explains at once too much and too little. Thus in Kerala: "Education appears to be of pivotal importance not only because it enables the woman to become economically independent but because through [independence] she acquires the self-confidence necessary to affirm her dignity and human rights. . . . Education by itself is not enough to liberate women. Only a strong mass-based movement organized by enlightened female leadership will be able to provide women freedom and equality to work in partnership with men for their mutual development" (Murickan, 1975: 95).

Outside observers often underestimate the power of women in traditional societies and overestimate their power in educated households that appear to be somewhat influenced by Western values and cultures. Elmendorf (1975) describes a Mayan woman circumventing her husband so that she could take her child to the clinic despite his opposition; it would be interesting to have other case histories of women whose husbands refused them permission to attend medical facilities with their children. In India, Luschinsky (1980: 146) has described village women adopting a totally new medical practice (viz., bathing young babies) in a context where men played no role in the decision, while the older generation of women adopted a far more empirical approach than they are usually given credit for, declaring that the experiment should be tried on female babies first since they are stronger and less important should the experiment fail.

For sub-Saharan Africa there is a considerable literature on whether educated women do in fact wield more power within the family than their illiterate counterparts (Peil, 1975; Pellow, 1977). The majority view appears to be that educated women who marry men whose status and income are significantly superior to their own actually lose relative power. In any traditional society there is also a life cycle component to women's status within the family. In general the older the woman, the greater her power relative to her husband. Therefore one might expect higher parity children to be in a better position than their older siblings were at the same age; however, mortality data by parity certainly do not corroborate this view (Butz et al., 1982).

For Latin America, Palloni (1981) has shown that literacy has a much greater influence on child mortality than on infant mortality. Instances of excess child mortality are associated with a disproportionate contribution of the complex of water-food-airborne diseases. At one level simply persuading mothers not to cease giving food or drink to children with diarrhea could be extremely beneficial; at another level major improvements in sanitation and water supply are needed. As Palloni has argued, the extent of illiteracy in a society reflects not only the limitations of families but more importantly limitations in the capacity to organize and mobilize to fulfill societal necessities. "From this point of view the proportion illiterate in a population is less an indication of the fraction of mothers with inadequate knowledge to treat and feed a sick child or to challenge the authority of elders than a reflection of the degree of social and political maturity of the system above and beyond the amounts of wealth at its disposal and the degree of equality of its distribution" (Palloni, 1981: 643).

Education has an impact not only through the characteristics of the individual mother but also through the educational level of the society as a whole. At the same level of education a Chilean woman can expect half the proportion of child deaths as her Bolivian counterpart. In a country such as Cuba, which has made enormous efforts to bring health care services within the reach of everyone, differentials in levels of child mortality by the mother's education are quite small. Flegg (1982) has similarly argued that literacy has the greatest impact on child mortality in societies with a relatively egalitarian distribution of income. There has been very little investigation of whether it is possible for education alone to have a significant impact on child mortality (but c.f. Tekçe and Shorter, in this volume). No studies demonstrate that poor but educated women with limited access to effective sanitation or medical facilities nevertheless achieve significant reductions in child mortality. It is true that Khan (1982) has shown that just soap and water and regular washing can reduce the incidence of dysentery by two-thirds. The question then becomes one of having ready access to pure water and the time to secure it, as well as of the cost of soap relative to the family's budget. There are certainly areas of sub-Saharan Africa where women regard access to soap and detergents as one of life's major luxuries.

The interaction between education and income

Few studies have effectively contrasted the relative impacts of maternal education and household income on child mortality levels. This is in part due to the difficulty of obtaining a reasonable measure of income for persons who are not wage earners. In Bangladesh, Chowdhury (1981) failed to find a sufficient number of rural women with formal education to study, but he was able to show that neither the father's education nor the size of the family's landholding was associated with lower mortality. Indeed, the children of the largest landholders experienced relatively high infant mortality levels—possibly, as McCord et al. (1980) found, because of the association between sizable landholdings, ownership of large draught animals, and neonatal tetanus (see also Smucher et al., 1980).

There are also difficulties relating to the type of mortality being studied. If education is associated with significantly reduced neonatal mortality, which in turn results from an association between the mother's education, her height and weight, and the birth weight of the infant, then it can be argued that education in this case acts as a proxy for income. As to the effect of antenatal care on neonatal mortality—one path through which education might operate prior to birth—there does not seem to be a significant impact (Gordon et al., 1965; see also Srivastava and Saksena, 1981, who found no clear relationship despite a conviction that there must be one). On the other hand, the mother's level of nutrition during pregnancy has an important bearing on birth weight (Kielmann et al., 1982). It could be argued that maternal nutrition is determined by mother's education rather than by income because educated mothers eat more sensibly and have a greater share in the food supplies of the household, or because they space their births at greater intervals.

An alternative argument is that education acts as a proxy for command over such resources as clothing, shelter, food, medical care, sanitary facilities, and water supply. This is similar to O'Hara's (1980) view that personal resources can replace environmental resources. It should be noted that educated wives tend to live in wealthier households not only because of any contribution they may make to the household income but also, and possibly more significantly, because educated women can hold out for higher income husbands. Indeed, in areas where educated women are relatively rare, poorer men tend to have a strong bias against marrying such women, who are often perceived as being useless and having ideas above their station.

Identifying the vital intermediate factors

Clearly it would be invaluable for policy planners to be able to isolate a few readily manipulatable factors that act as intermediate variables between a mother's level of education and the mortality of her children. Children do not die because their mothers did not go to school but because they receive insufficient or inappropriate food or are taken to medical services too late when they are ill. If female education is effective because it transmits specific ideas and skills such as a knowledge of germs or sanitary food-handling practices, then one might hope to implement programs to teach these matters specifically, without having to provide eight years of schooling for all potential mothers (Trussell and Hammerlough, 1983; Preston, 1978).

One way of studying this issue is to contrast the knowledge and practices of educated mothers with those of illiterate women. To do so involves comparing behavior related to a large number of practices without having a clear idea of which ones are likely to prove to be relevant. Another approach is to restrict the investigation by trying to isolate the practices that distinguish the illiterate mothers who successfully rear most of their children from those of illiterate mothers who experience repeated child loss. Restricting the study to the illiterate category would exclude many irrelevant factors and make it possible to see whether relatively simple interventions such as the use of trained birth attendants can make a significant impact or whether the real difference is in the level of poverty. Noninterventionist studies in very poor areas may be inappropriate owing to a lack of differentials in infant mortality resulting from the homogeneity of health conditions (Chowdhury, 1981: 4; McCord et al., 1980).

The choice of sites for the study of child mortality differentials among illiterate households should depend on the preexistence of reasonably good demographic data for the area. For example, it would appear that in Sri Lanka child mortality in illiterate households is significantly higher on the estates than in other rural areas (Meegama, 1980). Speculation as to why this should be so dates back to the 1870s, but no one appears to have investigated the relative contributions of the practice of feeding newborns with a compound of powdered nutmeg, castor oil, and sugar for three days prior to initiating breastfeeding; inadequate clothing and warmth in an inclement region; and the lack of trained midwives. Clearly, an in-depth study of several estates with different types of facilities and different levels of mortality could be very rewarding, especially if it covered maternal and child nutrition and sanitary practices.

From another viewpoint, certain interventions could be initiated very rapidly on an experimental basis and monitored as part of a case–control study. Certain estates could be selected to receive combinations of the following inputs: a trained midwife; food supplements for pregnant women and weaned children; baby clothes; improved latrines; and the establishment of mothers' clubs in which women would receive a small bonus for attending demonstrations of effective child care under estate conditions. Part of the research design would involve examining the socioeconomic characteristics of women who accept such innovations. Are those with formal education the first to innovate and, if so, why? Is it because the trained personnel offering the benefits concentrate on those most similar to themselves in their visits and conversations? It is often suggested that food supplements for women and children in very poor families tend to be shared among the entire family (Kielmann et al., 1982). Holding poverty constant, it this less often the case in households where the mother has been to school?

Medical beliefs and practices

One causal link between female education and reduced child mortality might result from a positive association between the educational level of mothers and their use of effective medical services to treat their sick children. It is often implied that such a link does in fact result from educated women abandoning the fatalism and/or belief in traditional remedies of their mothers-in-law and insisting upon taking their children to Western-style medical services. Of more direct concern here is whether to view poverty and deprivation as the cause of the underuse of medical services by the illiterate or alternatively to blame ignorance as the cause.

Since there are few places in the developing world that have a hospital or clinic without also having a school, one of the first controls must be for simple geographic access to a medical facility. Even over the same distance the cost in time and even money may be greater for the illiterate mother than for the educated woman who has access to a car or bicycle. In Uganda in the 1960s, patients spent an average of 35 cents apiece on transport to benefit from 11 cents worth of free treatment (Jolly et al., 1966, Chapter 6, p. 12). In the city of Ibadan in Nigeria, Maclean (1974) undertook a study of differentials in medical beliefs and practices after observing in the hospital context that educated patients and their children received better treatment than their illiterate counterparts although neither group had to pay for the service. This did not simply mean that the educated did not have to join the general queues; it also meant that diagnoses were more specific and more often backed up by tests. In Ibadan more than 90 percent of both traditional illiterate families and elite families had used free hospital services. Additionally, almost two-thirds of both groups had recourse to traditional herbal remedies, while use of proprietary medicines was almost universal outside the faith-healing sects. The most significant difference between the two groups was in private treatment by Western doctors, which had been obtained by 65 percent of elite families compared with only 17 percent of traditional families. The traditional families who could not afford private treatment from a Western-trained practitioner made extensive use of traditional healers. Even in the elite class, belief in and use of traditional medicines declined significantly only among women in professional occupations, almost half of whom were trained nurses. In general, people distinguished between diseases in deciding upon treatment: convulsions in children were generally treated with traditional herbal remedies, as was jaundice, whereas fevers were judged to respond best to Western medicines. Ironically, the belief that certain people are destined to die young and that certain diseases result from divine retribution coincides with an aggressive search for remedies since such judgments are confirmed only after the event.

Asking questions about infant feeding

From a social science viewpoint asking questions about infant feeding is not a simple procedure, especially when the population to be covered is heterogeneous. There are measurement problems associated with definitional issues, with the establishment of durations, and with the possibility of a "politeness response." In examining the nutrition received by the child, it is necessary to distinguish between full and partial breastfeeding and between feeding on demand and feeding according to a schedule (Winikoff and Baer, 1980). Supplementary questions as to where the infant sleeps at night and how often it accompanies its mother during the day will add important information. Artificial feeding may totally supplant breastfeeding, or it may be used as a partial or even incidental supplement. Much of the literature assumes that mothers who bottlefeed cease to breastfeed and that the content of babies' bottles is largely overdiluted infant formula (Chetley, 1979). Both assumptions are matters for investigation rather than speculation. It is necessary to know whether the "milk" used is infant formula or, as is certainly much more common among the poor of sub-Saharan Africa, diluted tinned evaporated or even condensed milk. Equally, from the point of view of potential infection, questions regarding the use of water or other bottlefed drinks of minimal nutritional value are of great importance.

In some cultures weaning is abrupt and dramatic; for example, a mother puts bitter juice on her nipples or the child is sent to stay with its grandmother when the next pregnancy occurs. In other cultures the process involves a gentle tapering off in the proportion of breastmilk to the total dietary intake: some 5-year-old children still suckle at the breast but as a comforter rather than as a source of nourishment (Luschinsky, 1980; Molnos, 1973). In these latter cases it is genuinely difficult for a mother to specify whether or not a child has been weaned. Similarly with the introduction of solids: some mothers give a restless child a stick of sugarcane or an animal bone to gum on before the arrival of the first tooth, without considering this to be a form of feeding. Further, children may be allowed to have tidbits from the communal dish before anyone attempts to start feeding them with pap from a spoon. A response that a child gets some breastmilk, some tinned milk, and some porridge may well not give a very good indication of the nutritional value of its diet. In many areas the basic meal consists of a starchy staple plus a stew of vegetables with perhaps a little meat or fish. The vital question may be how much of the protein content of the sauce is accessible to the child—a matter that is nearly impossible to establish by questioning without on-site measurement under typical conditions (Hoorweg and McDowell, 1979).

The retrospective measurement of the duration of breastfeeding bristles with problems (Lesthaeghe and Page, 1980). First, the cessation of breastfeeding is not an event like a birthday or a death that anyone is likely to recall by exact date. Second, cultural ideals as to how long breastfeeding should last influence responses and result in marked heaping at two-month and six-month durations (with the exception of three months and nine months, it is very rare to find a woman reporting that she breastfed for an odd number of months). Some of this heaping may be perfectly genuine, which means that using procedures to statistically smooth the data may falsify it. There is also the constant problem that differentials in the accuracy of reporting as well as in actual practice may exist between different socioeconomic groups. The ideal solution is to use data on current practice, but this requires a large sample (Lesthaeghe and Page, 1980: 145).

Politeness means that if the interviewers are, or are perceived to be, linked with a health care institution, the extent of breastfeeding may be exaggerated out of a desire to please. Alternatively, a desire to appear ''modern'' or wealthy may result in an overemphasis on bottlefeeding. Responses to questions on how bottles are cleaned and water boiled should also be checked in conjunction with the analysis of data on available water and fuel supplies.

In the case of artificial feeding it is also necessary to ask questions about who feeds the child apart from the mother. In a village setting almost any child that is ambulant may pick up assorted tidbits from house to house. Such snacks are not necessarily an insignificant contribution to the diet. However, access to such goodies may depend on the status of the child's family.

Differentials in breastfeeding practice

It is ironic that the one intermediate variable between education and infant mortality that has been extensively studied is breastfeeding, for the less educated in developing countries generally breastfeed for longer periods and therefore on this ground should have healthier children (Puffer and Serrano, 1973). But studies in both India and Lesotho have shown that bottlefeeding is associated with lower mortality and improved nutrition for children because it is only the relatively wealthy who wean early and switch to bottlefeeding (Srivastava and Saksena, 1981; Lesotho, 1973). One reason shorter periods of breastfeeding by the more highly educated do not result in increased mortality is simply that it is possible to rely exclusively on breastfeeding for too long (Plank and Milanesi, 1973; Rowland et al., 1981). Indeed, mothers who are compelled to rely exclusively on breastfeeding for prolonged periods are poorer and less well educated (Butz et al., 1982).

In examining the relationship between breastfeeding and mortality it is important to have data on the age at death of infants because of the different impact of breastfeeding in the first six months as compared with later months (Butz et al., 1982). Indeed, a fully breastfed infant will not be malnourished during the first six months of life unless it is exposed to infection (Scrimshaw et al., 1968). Although great emphasis has been placed on the promotional efforts of infant formula companies, little research has been done on why mothers adopt bottlefeeding (Chetley, 1979). In Yemen women prefer not to take their children with them when they work in the fields because it is inconvenient and the child is exposed to the evil eye. Bottlefeeding enables women to leave infants at home with older siblings; it also obviates problems associated with local beliefs that a mother's moods and characteristics are passed on to her child through her milk (Melrose, 1981). Another common reason for abandoning breastfeeding is the belief that a breastfeeding mother should abstain from sexual relations since the semen will sour her milk (Bracher and Santow, 1982). In areas where breastfeeding is declining, the trend has been attributed to the deleterious impact of formal labor force participation, but scant attention has been paid to the factors encouraging some women to continue breastfeeding (although it has been hypothesized that women's groups and traditional birth attendants play some role [Van Esterik, 1983]).

Women's roles

It is in part a measure of the male bias of the social sciences that one rarely finds a generic discussion of men's roles. Discussions of men's experiences generally take their roles for granted, focusing instead on such specific groups as the elite, migrants, or the rural poor. Discussions of women's experiences, whether by men or by women, tend to assume that, despite barriers of class, caste, religion, or experience, women have more in common with one another than with male members of their own group. There has also been a less than rewarding obsession with dividing women into two categories: "workers" and "nonworkers." Indeed, a growing body of literature is devoted to demonstrating the falsity of this dichotomy in the Third World context (Boserup, 1970; Reiter, 1975; Dixon, 1978, 1982; Rogers, 1980). Work has too often been defined as tasks performed by men. By this criterion, housework is not work even where it entails head-carrying heavy loads of water over a dozen kilometers or de-husking rice with a 12-kilo weight for 14 hours a day.

Because so much attention has been devoted to the influence of women's economic activities on the fulfillment of child care practices, it is worthwhile to concentrate here on examining data needs in this area.

Economic activity and child care practices

Women may perform economic activities within the home, in the informal sector outside the home, in such occupations as farm laborer, petty trader, or domestic worker in other households (in which cases it may be possible to take young children along), or in the formal sector in factories and offices (where children are clearly not allowed). From this point of view it is not the occupation that is of importance, but the circumstances in which it is carried out. Women's economic activities will have a negative impact on child care only where the activity is incompatible with simultaneous childrearing or where the mother lacks access to another person able to care for the child.

A great deal of confusion has been generated by the tendency to equate work for women with paid employment outside the home and therefore to label all other women as nonworkers despite their indispensable contributions to the household (Rogers, 1980; Ware, 1981). In reality, in developing countries almost the only women who do not have to perform hard labor are those who live in households wealthy enough to support domestic servants or to provide mechanical and electrical alternatives (Lindenbaum et al., 1983). However, in the demographic literature the discussion of the relationship between women's work and child mortality has almost always focused on paid employment outside the home, which is believed to be a possible cause of child neglect and child malnutrition due to the abandonment of breastfeeding.

Put another way, both level of nutrition and standards of care may be significantly affected by the nature of the mother's employment, but the problem lies in separating the effects of poverty or ignorance from those of the mother's work per se. Ideally, one would wish to divide mothers who work outside the home into two groups: those who work because of the driving pressure of poverty and those whose work is more a source of interest and a higher standard of living.

Very little is known about the fate of children in very poor families who are left at home when their mothers go out to work. In the slums of San Salvador, Nieves (1979) has described how women move in to live with their sisters or mothers so that domestic and income-earning tasks can be shared. In the Bataan Export Processing Zone of the Philippines, Zosa-Feranil (1982) found that 20 percent of working mothers believed it was impossible to provide adequate care and discipline for their children. Some chose to send their children to stay with their grandparents in the rural areas, while a larger number brought in relatives to live with them and care for the children (Zosa-Feranil, 1982). Construction workers in Chiang Mai City in northern Thailand have an arrangement whereby mothers pay for one of their number to mind all the children rather than doing construction work. Day care centers for children of working mothers are appearing in the villages of northern Thailand because grandmothers themselves are economically active and older siblings are at school (Singhanetra-Renard, 1982).

One apparent cost associated with formal work force participation by the mothers of infants is the necessary abandonment of breastfeeding. However, the pattern is not quite so simple. In San Salvador, Nieves (1979) found poor women preferring two part-time jobs to one full-time one so that they could return home to breastfeed at lunch time. Elsewhere, another pattern is for the mothers of young children to avoid work that is incompatible with breastfeeding. In northern Thailand female construction workers time their births to avoid a period of peak job availability and do not return to work until the child is at least one year old (Singhanetra-Renard, 1982).

To read some of the breastfeeding literature, one might be pardoned for thinking that Asia has an abundance of mothers working in factories while their children die due to early initiation of bottlefeeding (Chetley, 1979). In reality, outside of Singapore and Hong Kong, few married women and even fewer mothers are employed in factories. In Java women give up working when they become pregnant or at least after the birth of the child. Of mothers who do work in the factories, 84 percent live in a household containing at least one other able-bodied female who is responsible for child care. Young girls may be kept home to care for their younger siblings if their mothers cannot be profitably employed in farming or trading activities to which they can take their unweaned children (Wolf, 1982). In South Korea nearly all rural women work on the farm, but very few married urban women work outside the home (Koo, 1982). Mothers in the Philippines frequently choose petty trading as an occupation since it interferes relatively little with child care. In Malaysia the employment of married women in factories is still extremely uncommon.

If the abandonment of breastfeeding is one possible cost of formal employment for poor mothers, problems that arise when the child is ill may well be another. Factory workers who disappear for the morning to the clinic with a sick child may well face the sack in a labor buyer's market. When factory workers' children are ill, is the time-consuming search for treatment simply delayed for as long as possible, or do the siblings or grandmothers who care for the children take them to the clinic? Apart from this problem it would appear that the poorer the household the smaller the difference in the quality of care between the mother and the substitute care giver. The elite working mothers stand to lose the most by entrusting the care of their children to poorly educated servants. In Java educated women realize this and generally avoid paid employment while their children are young (Rahardjo and Hull, 1982). Alternatively, in West Africa, elite women consider it wasteful to postpone entering a professional career and are beginning to send their children to Western-style day care centers (Lewis, 1977; Oppong, 1975). In Sudan, Farah and Preston (1982) found that the mother's participation in the labor force raised infant mortality by 27 percent in the capital, as compared with 10 percent for the country as a whole, possibly because educated women employed in the capital are more seriously disadvantaged by entrusting child care to illiterate maids or relatives.

Childrearing is often thought of as being incompatible with women's economic activities only where women work in the modern formal sector. However, three factors are relevant here: the compatibility of the task itself with child care, the availability of relatives to provide substitute child care, and the distance between the workplace and the home. Neither transplanting paddy nor craftwork is a task compatible with the care of a young child; however, in the villages older siblings or grandmothers are usually available to care for young infants while a mother is employed at such a job. With movement to the town the grandmother has often been left behind and the older daughter is not available because she is in school or even working in the factory alongside her mother. Similarly in the town the woman's workplace is likely to be at such a distance from the home that she is not even available for periodic breastfeeding (Manderson, 1982).

Village infants may retain the advantages of being breastfed even when their mothers work over 12 hours a day in the fields, but other aspects of child care may well be neglected and supplementary feeding may be absent or totally unsuitable. Even in the 1950s Luschinsky (1980: 123) reported Indian village mothers discussing the decline in the custom of giving tastes of opium to quiet babies whose mothers had no time to be with them.

Sex preference and differentials in care

Another way in which the status of women contributes to child mortality levels is through the effect of sex preferences on child care. Where there is a strong preference and need for sons, boys will receive preferential treatment in feeding and medical treatment (Rosenberg, 1973; Williamson, 1976). While infanticide may be on the decline, the "mania for sons" has now resulted in requests to Indian hospitals to determine the sex of fetuses so that sex-selective abortions may be carried out (Ramanamma and Bambawale, 1980). In Bangladesh advantages given to male infants by way of parental care, feeding patterns, food distribution within the family, and the treatment of illness (especially where financial expenditure is involved) result in a female postneonatal mortality rate that is 21 percent higher than the male rate (D'Souza and Chen, 1980). In a later study the authors note that in 1974–77, "excess female to male mortality in the 1–4-year group was noted even among wealthy landowning families" (Chen et al., 1981: 67). It should be recognized that the daughters of educated women may have better life chances not simply because their mothers place a greater value on daughters but also because such women are less likely to have to make these vital decisions regarding allocation of resources.

The actual measurement of sex differentials in resource allocation for child care is very complex. This is so because the degree of discrimination against girls depends on the sex composition of the family as a whole and the total number of surviving children. A first child evokes a special reaction in almost all cultures irrespective of sex, and an only daughter may experience positive discrimination from her mother (Luschinsky, 1980). Field surveys have generally suggested that cultural prescriptions that boys should be breastfed longer than girls or should receive supplementary feeding earlier are not reflected in statistical data, which reflect instead the impact of individual considerations. However, it is worth pursuing questions about actual expenditures on infants, and especially on medical treatment, in order to examine possible sex differentials. One Korean study showed that the chief effect of introducing a minimal fee for immunizations was to reduce the proportion of girls receiving injections (Ware, 1981).

Children are not only unwelcome when they are of the "wrong" sex, they may simply be the latest addition to a family that the parents feel is already large enough. In Thailand, Frenzen and Hogan (1982) showed that health information, social class, district development level, and whether births were wanted all continued to have significant independent effects on infant mortality even when the effects of other social variables were taken into account. Neither maternal education nor parental beliefs about intergenerational wealth transfers had any significant impact on infant survival, net of the other social variables in the model.

The design of household surveys

If women's education has an independent effect on the mortality of their children, it should be possible to show that this impact operates even after controlling for income of the household and birth weight of the child. A real educational impact should be independent of household income in that, with the same resources, educated women should be able to provide healthier lives for their children than their illiterate counterparts.

Ideally a survey designed to address this question would be located in an area where strong educational differentials in mortality are already known to exist. The aim would be to follow up two samples of births to currently married women aged 20–29 from a maternity center with recorded birth weight data: one, a random sample of births to women with no education; the other, a random sample of births to women with the minimum level of education necessary to produce an apparent education effect. Infants would be followed up at one month, six months, and one year after birth. The first interview would establish the basic data base for each household; later interviews would monitor changes in feeding, child care, and sanitation once survival had been established. The first interview would attempt to measure income in two ways. One would be the standard measure of all sources of income from wages, sale of produce, household consumption, and so on. The other would be a measure of the household's standard of living, that is, of the resources demonstrably available to the household in the way of the quality of housing, access to clean water, mosquito nets, cooking equipment, and so on. Clearly these items need to be selected with a view to their impact on health, and they would need to be counterbalanced with some local luxuries to enable researchers to examine whether families who do not spend money on items related to health may be spending it elsewhere. For agricultural and other self-employed households, one option is to put profits back into the family enterprise, and it would be very interesting to look at the expenditure patterns of farmers and small businessmen at different levels of education. Of course one of the findings may well be that educated women are much less likely to be found in households where the man of the house is a farmer and especially a landless farm laborer. However, even when they have equivalent incomes, village school teachers and petty officials are likely to have very different priorities from the farmer. Having no land to leave to their children, parents in the former professions have little choice but to invest in the education and hence in the overall quality of their children.

Another aspect of such a prospective study should be to examine the time budgets of women with children of different ages. One benefit that educated mothers may have is simply enough disposable time to enable them to prepare special food for an infant, to take an ailing child to the clinic at the first sign of distress, and so forth. Educated women simply do not have to spend hours in water porterage nor, in many developing countries, in working in the fields. The time budgets would thus fit questions about food preparation and hygienic precautions into their proper framework. In one adult education project in Upper Volta, it was found that wells had to be dug, grain grinding mills had to be provided, and donkey carts had to be introduced to transport firewood before illiterate women could find time to attend literacy classes (Lavrencic, 1979). The same is often true of classes to teach improved child care or basic nutrition: captive audiences may be found in the queues waiting for medical treatment for sick children, but under ordinary circumstances poor women simply do not have time to attend classes.

One remarkable feature of the available time budget studies around the world is just how little time adult women spend in child care (Ware, 1981: Table 7.2). In reports that include a specific category of child care, this activity rarely occupies much more than 10 percent of women's time. This is so for several reasons: daughters often spend more time on child care than their mothers (White, 1976; Weisner and Gallimore, 1977); average figures disguise the greater expenditure of time by mothers who have only very young children; and, in any case, child care is often combined with a productive activity that is given preference in recording. Time budget studies do not normally examine educational differentials in women's expenditure of time, but a prospective study like the one suggested here could clearly fill this gap and incorporate data on who cares for the child when the mother is absent and how and by whom it is actually fed, washed, toileted, and kept from accidents.

The study should also incorporate basic questions on nutrition and health to establish whether educated women do, in fact, have useful knowledge in this area that the illiterate do not share. It would also be important to measure the use of health facilities over the year and to examine differentials in the circumstances defined as being appropriate occasions for seeking outside aid.

Other elements of such a study should be adapted to fit in with local conditions. Albert Schweitzer (1941) believed that infant mortality was significantly lower in polygynous marriages because the various wives were able to share domestic and agricultural tasks and therefore had time to provide a better standard of child care. Schwartz (1978) investigated this hypothesis in the Ivory Coast in a polygynous community where 31 percent of children died before the age of 3. He found that the overall standard of living was so low that there were no significant differentials. Infants were weaned onto a diet almost exclusively composed of rice-water gruel, and women were so busy working in the fields and gathering shellfish while their husbands were away at sea that none of them had the benefit of a respite from hard labor.

No single survey design is ideal for all circumstances and cultures. Indeed, many of the apparently contradictory results of studies in this area stem from the fact that different elements are significant at different levels of development and in different regions. However, some general comments can be made about the features of a study of infant and child mortality differentials that will prove valid for most contexts. Table 1 lists features that should be incorporated into all surveys unless there is a good reason for omitting specific items. Much of the discussion in the first two sections of this paper has

TABLE 1   Elements of a good survey

Coverage of conditions prior to birth
Education and occupation of grandparents
Education and occupation of parents (*Fernando, 1981*)
Female circumcision
Timing of previous pregnancies (*Locoh, 1979*)
Special behavior/nutrition during pregnancy (*Gordon et al., 1965*)
Height of mother
Whether the child was wanted (*Frenzen and Hogan, 1982*)

Coverage of conditions surrounding the birth (*Hart, 1965; Mead and Newton, 1967*)
Place of birth
Attendance at birth (*Smucker et al., 1980*)
Birth customs/circumcision/treatment of umbilical cord (*Bhatia, 1981*)
Birth weight
Diet of infant for days 1–3 (*Winikoff and Baer, 1980*)

Coverage of conditions during infancy
Breastfeeding (*Van Esterik, 1983*)
Supplementary feeding (*Bairagi, 1980*)
Who cares for the infant (*Kinzer, 1975; Weisner and Gallimore, 1977*)
Whether the mother is separated from the infant (*Shah, 1982*)
Mother's work of all kinds (*DaVanzo and Lee, 1977; Chaudhury, 1979*)
Action taken in case of illness/how decision is arrived at (*Dennis, 1974–75; Conco, 1979*)
Knowledge of possible health care services for infants (*Population Reports, 1982*)
Hygiene directly affecting the infant (*Kamien, 1978*)

Coverage of ambient conditions (*Hobart, 1975; Anker and Knowles, 1977*)
Building materials of house
Access to water supply/sanitation (*Butz et al., 1982*)
Access to medical facilities (*Mosley, 1983*)
Cooking method/kitchen inventory
Mosquito nets and other preventive measures
Medicines kept within the household
General possessions index
Income data (*Flegg, 1982; Simmons et al., 1982*)

Mortality data
Previous experience of child mortality in the family (*Ben-Porath, 1976*)
Age of death: under 1 month, 1–6 months, 7–11 months, 12–23 months (*Meegama, 1980*)
Where the infant died
Medical remedies tried prior to death/specialists seen
Sex of infant and of siblings (*Williamson, 1976; Schultz, 1982*)

envisaged a retrospective survey, not because this is the ideal but because the costs of prospective surveys of mortality differentials are likely to be great. Where mortality levels are very high, there is also the problem of providing a moral justification for funding and fielding a trained staff to observe the conditions under which children die without intervening. An ideal survey, then, would collect retrospective data, current data, and prospective data. It would seek to measure the impact of a proposed intervention but would avoid the assumption that social change can be achieved at the push of a button. Whatever the impact of education may be, it is usually the end product of several years of attending school for at least five hours a day, five days a week.

The ideal survey is also rooted within the local culture and includes participation by those directly affected. How else is it possible to know that measles vaccinations can be highly popular in a population that does not believe that the disease is contagious yet perceives the vaccination to be a powerful amulet (Imperato and Traore, 1979)? The ideal survey also allows room for investigation of unexpected linkages. In the United States declines in infant mortality appear to be associated with increased reliance on induced abortion as a backup to contraceptive failure (Grossman and Jacobowitz, 1981). In the developing countries infant mortality is rarely seen as resulting from choices in which that child's welfare takes second place to some other goal. However, studies of sex differentials in areas with a strong preference for sons show that it may be important to think of the avoidance of mortality as but one of a number of competing objectives. The educated may pursue child survival with greater single-mindedness, or their access to greater resources may spare them some of life's more difficult decisions.

Conclusion

We know that women who have been to school lose fewer of their children in childhood and infancy than their unschooled peers. We do not know why this should be so either in terms of the impact of education on women's behavior in general or in terms of their specific contribution to their children's health. The relationship between women's economic and other roles and the survival of their children remains even more uncertain.

What is needed is much more pragmatic investigation of the intermediate factors involved, for it is these factors that are most amenable to policy intervention in the short and medium term. Clearly, for example, if the relationship between mother's education and her child's survival is largely established by controlling for the birth weight of the child, then the policy implications are very different from those that would result from a proven link between maternal education, hygienic practices, and child survival. It is also necessary to be aware of the importance of cultural variations. While education in one culture may have a strong effect because it acts as a form of assertiveness training, in another culture the significant element may be the prestige associated with education, which results in educated young women being spared the burdens of heavy manual labor. Finally, while there is an urgent need for information on the exact nature of the maternal behaviors associated with increased child survival, we should be wary of attributing the blame for high mortality levels directly to mothers.

References

Anderson, P. 1983. "The reproductive role of the human breast," *Current Anthropology* 24, no. 1: 25–45.

Anker, R., and J. Knowles. 1977. "An empirical analysis of mortality differentials in Kenya at the macro and micro level," *Population and Employment Working Paper* 60. Geneva: ILO.

Bairagi, R. 1980. "Is income the only constraint on child nutrition in rural Bangladesh," *Bulletin of the World Health Organization* 58: 767–772.

Behm, H. 1976–78. *La Mortalidid en los Primeros Años de Vida en Países de la America Latina*. Santiago: CELADE.

Ben-Porath, Y. 1976. *Child Mortality and Fertility*. Santa Monica: Rand Corporation Paper, P. 5772.

Bhatia, S. 1981. "Traditional childbirth practices: Implications for a rural MCH program," *Studies in Family Planning* 12, no. 2 (February): 66–75.

Boserup, E. 1970. *Women's Role in Economic Development*. New York: St. Martin's Press.

Bracher, M., and G. Santow. 1982. "Breastfeeding in Central Java," *Population Studies* 36, no. 3: 413–429.

Butz, W., et al. 1982. *Biological and Behavioral Influences on the Mortality of Malaysian Infants*. Santa Monica: Rand Corporation.

Caldwell, J. 1979. "Education as a factor in mortality decline," *Population Studies* 33, no. 3: 395–413.

———, and P. McDonald. 1981. "Influence of maternal education on infant and child mortality," *International Population Conference Manila,* Vol. 2. Liège: International Union for the Scientific Study of Population.

Chaudhury, R. 1979. "Marriage, urban women and the labor force: The Bangladesh case," *Signs* 5, no. 1: 154–163.

Chen, L. C., et al. 1981. "Sex bias in the family allocation of food and health care in rural Bangladesh," *Population and Development Review* 7, no. 1 (March): 55–76.

Chetley, A. 1979. *The Baby Killer Scandal*. London: War on Want.

Chowdhury, A. 1981. *Infant Deaths, Determinants and Dilemmas*. Dacca: ICDDR, Scientific Report 46.

———. 1982. "Factors influencing infant survival in rural Bangladesh," *Glimpse* 4 (9–10).

Cochrane, S. 1980. *The Effects of Education on Health*. Washington, D.C.: World Bank, Staff Working Paper 405.

Conco, W. 1979. "The African Bantu traditional practice of medicine," in *African Therapeutic Systems,* ed. Z. Ademuwagun. Waltham, Mass.: Crossroads Press.

DaVanzo, J., and D. Lee. 1978. *The Compatibility of Child Care with Labor Force Participation and Non-market Activities*. Santa Monica: Rand Corporation.

Dennis, R. 1974–75. "The traditional healer in Liberia," *Rural Africana* 26: 17–23.

Dixon, R. 1978. *Rural Women at Work*. Baltimore: Johns Hopkins University Press.

———. 1982. "Women in agriculture: Counting the labor force in developing countries," *Population and Development Review* 8, no. 3 (September): 539–566.

D'Souza, S., and L. Chen. 1980. "Sex differentials in mortality in rural Bangladesh," *Population and Development Review* 6, no. 2 (June): 257–270.

Elmendorf, M. 1975. "The Mayan woman and change," in *Women Cross-Culturally*, ed. R. Rohrlich-Leavitt. The Hague: Mouton.

Fadipe, N. 1970. *The Sociology of the Yoruba*. Ibadan: Ibadan University Press.

Farah, A., and S. Preston. 1982. "Child mortality differentials in Sudan," in *Demographic Transition in Metropolitan Sudan*. Canberra: Australian National University Press.

Fernando, D. 1981. "Factors influencing the infant mortality rate in Sri Lanka," *Journal of Biosocial Science* 13, no. 2: 287–297.

Flegg, A. 1982. "Inequality of income, illiteracy and medical care as determinants of infant mortality," *Population Studies* 36, no. 3: 441–458.

Frenzen, P., and D. Hogan. 1982. "The impact of class, education and health care on infant mortality in a developing society: The case of rural Thailand," *Demography* 19, no. 3: 391–408.

Gael, B., et al. 1980. "Lack of time as an obstacle to women's education: The case of Upper Volta," *Comparative Education Review* 24, no. 2: S.124–139.

Gordon, J., et al. 1965. "A field study of illnesses during pregnancy, their management and pre-natal care in Punjab villages," *Indian Pediatrics* 2, no. 9: 330–335.

Grossman, M., and S. Jacobowitz. 1981. "Variations in infant mortality rates among counties of the United States," *Demography* 18, no. 4: 695–713.

Haines, M., and R. Avery. 1978. "Patterns of differential mortality during infancy and early childhood in developing nations." Paper prepared for the American Population Association Meeting, Atlanta, Georgia.

Hart, D., et al. 1965. *South Asian Birth Customs*. New Haven: HRAF Press.

Hobart, C. 1975. *Socio-Economic Correlates of Mortality and Morbidity among Inuit Infants*. Edmonton: University of Alberta, Population Research Laboratory.

Hoorweg, J., and I. McDowell. 1979. *Evaluation of Nutritional Education in Africa*. The Hague: Mouton.

Imperato, P., and D. Traore. 1979. "Traditional beliefs about measles," in *African Therapeutic Systems*, ed. Z. Ademuwagun, Waltham, Mass.: Crossroads Press.

Jolly, R., et al. 1966. "The economy of a district hospital," in *Medical Care in Developing Countries*, ed. R. King. Nairobi; Oxford University Press.

Kamien, M. 1978. *The Dark People of Bourke*. Canberra: Australian Institute of Aboriginal Studies.

Khan, M. 1982. "Interruption of shigellosis by hand washing," *Transactions of the Royal Society of Tropical Hygiene* 76: 164–168.

Kielmann, A., et al. 1982. "Nutrition intervention: An evaluation of six studies," *Studies in Family Planning* 13, no. 8/9 (August/September): 246–257.

Kinzer, N. 1975. "Socio-cultural factors mitigating role conflict of Buenos Aires professional women," in *Women Cross-Culturally*, ed. R. Rohrlich-Leavitt. The Hague: Mouton.

Koo, S-Y. 1982. "Trends in female labor force participation and occupational shifts in urban Korea," Conference on Women in the Labour Force in Asia, Development Studies Centre, Australian National University, Canberra.

Lavrencic, K. 1979. "Reading and writing is not enough," *African Woman* 19: 42–43.

Lesotho. 1973. *Report of the Lesotho Pilot Survey on Population and Food Consumption*. Maseru: Bureau of Statistics.

Lesthaeghe, R., and H. Page. 1980. "The post-partum non-susceptible period," *Population Studies* 34, no. 1: 143–170.

Levine, R. 1980. "Influences of women's schooling on maternal behavior in the Third World," *Comparative Education Review* 24, no. 2 (2): S78–105.

Lewis, B. 1977. "Economic activity and marriage among Ivorian urban women," in *Sexual Stratification*, ed. A. Schlegel. New York: Columbia University Press.

Lindenbaum, S., et al. 1983. *The Influence of Education on Infant and Child Mortality in Bangladesh*. Dhaka: International Centre for Diarrhoeal Disease Research.

Locoh, T. 1979. "Child spacing in Africa," African Traditional Birth Spacing Workshop, Brussels.

Luschinsky, M. 1980. *The Life of Women in a Village of North India.* Ann Arbor: University Microfilms.

McCord, C., et al. 1980. *Deaths Rates, Land the Price of Rice,* Dacca: Noakhali, Campanigonj Health Project, Evaluation Unit Report 4.

Maclean, U. 1974. *Magical Medicine: A Nigerian Case Study.* London: Penguin.

Manderson, L. 1982. "Infant feeding practice, market expansion and the patterning of choice in South East Asia," *New Doctor* 26: 27–32.

Martin, L., et al. 1983. "Covariates of child mortality in the Philippines, Indonesia and Pakistan," *Population Studies* 37, no. 3: 417–432.

Mead, M., and N. Newton. 1967. "Cultural patterning of perinatal behaviour," in *Childbearing,* ed. S. Richardson and A. Guttmacher. Baltimore: Williams and Wilkins.

Meegama, S. 1980. "Socio-economic determinants of infant and child mortality in Sri Lanka," *World Fertility Survey Scientific Report* 8.

Melrose, D. 1981. *The Great Health Robbery: Baby Milk and Medicine in Yemen.* Oxford: Oxfam.

Molnos, A. 1973. *Cultural Source Materials for Populations Planning in East Africa.* Nairobi: East African Publishing House.

Moock, M., and Leslie, J. 1982. *Child Malnutrition and Schooling in the Terai Region of Nepal.* Washington, D.C.: World Bank.

Mosley, W. 1983. "Will primary health care reduce infant and child mortality?" Paris: IUSSP Seminar.

Murickan, J. 1975. "Women in Kerala," in *Women in Contemporary India,* ed. A. de Souza. Delhi: Manohar.

Nieves, I. 1979. "Household arrangements and multiple jobs in San Salvador," *Signs* 5, no. 1: 134–142.

O'Hara, D. 1980. "Towards a model of the effects of education on health," in *The Effects of Education on Health.* Washington, D.C.: World Bank Staff Working Paper 405.

Onwubalite, J. 1983. "Sickle-cell anaemia: An inflammation for the ancient myth of reincarnation in Nigeria," *The Lancet* 2, no. 8348 (27 August): 503–505.

Oppong, C. 1975. "Nursing mothers: Aspects of the conjugal and maternal roles of nurses in Accra," Canadian African Studies Meeting, Toronto.

Palloni, A. 1981. "Mortality in Latin America: Emerging patterns," *Population and Development Review* 7, no. 4 (December): 623–649.

Peil, M. 1975. "Female roles in West African towns," in *Changing Social Structure in Ghana,* ed. J. Goody. London: International African Institute.

Pellow, D. 1978. *Women in Accra: Options for Autonomy.* Algonac, Mich.: Reference Publications.

Piho, V. 1975. "Life and labour of the women textile workers in Mexico City," in *Women Cross Culturally,* ed. R. Rohrlich-Leavitt. The Hague; Mouton.

Plank, S., and M. Milanesi. 1973. "Infant feeding and infant mortality in rural Chile," *Bulletin of the World Health Organization* 48: 203–210.

Population Reports. 1982. *Community Based Health and Family Planning.* Baltimore: Johns Hopkins University.

Preston, S. 1978. "Mortality, morbidity and development," *Population Bulletin of the United Nations Economic Commission for Western Asia* 15: 63–75.

Psacharopoulos, C. 1983. "Educational research at the World Bank," *World Bank Research News* 4 no. 1: 3–17.

Puffer, R., and C. Serrano. 1973. *Patterns of Mortality in Childhood.* Washington, D.C.: Pan American Health Organization.

Rahardjo, Y., and V. Hull. 1982. "Employment patterns of educated women in Indonesian cities," Conference on Women in the Labour Force in Asia, Development Studies Centre, Australian National University, Canberra.

Ramanamma, A., and U. Bambawale. 1980. "The mania for sons," *Social Science and Medicine* 14, no. 8: 107–110.

Reiter, R., ed. 1975. *Towards an Anthropology of Women.* New York: Monthly Review Press.

Rogers, B. 1980. *The Domestication of Women: Discrimination in Developing Societies.* New York: St. Martin's Press.

Rosenberg, E. 1973. "Ecological effects of sex differential nutrition." Paper prepared for the American Anthropological Association.

Rowland, D., et al. 1981. "Lactation and infant nutrition," *Medical Bulletin* 37, no. 1: 77–82.

Schultz, T. 1982. "Women's work and their status: Rural Indian evidence of labour market and environmental effects on sex differentials in childhood mortality," in *Women's Roles and Population Trends in the Third World*, ed. R. Anker. London: Croom Helm.

Schwartz, A. 1978. "Fécondité et mortalité avant l'âge de trois ans chez les Krou de Côte d'Ivoire," in *Marriage, Fertility and Parenthood in West Africa*, ed. C. Oppong. Canberra: Australian National University Press.

Schweitzer, A. 1941. *Histoires de la Forêt Vierge.* Paris: Payot.

Scrimshaw, N., et al. 1968. *Interactions of Nutrition and Infection.* Geneva: World Health Organization.

Sembajwe, I. 1981. *Fertility and Infant Mortality amongst the Yoruba in Western Nigeria.* Canberra: Australian National University Press.

Shah, N., ed. 1982. *Pakistani Women.* Honolulu: East West Population Institute.

Simmons, G., et al. 1982. "Post-neonatal mortality in rural India: Implications of an economic model," *Demography* 19, no. 3: 371–389.

Singhanetra-Renard, A. 1982. "Effect of female labor force participation on fertility: The case of construction workers in Chiang Mai City," Conference on Women in the Labour Force in Asia, Development Studies Centre, Australian National University, Canberra.

Smucker, G., et al. 1980. "Neonatal mortality in South Asia: The special role of tetanus," *Population Studies* 34, no. 2: 321–335.

Srivastava, J., and D. Saksena. 1981. "Infant mortality differentials in an Indian city," *Journal of Biosocial Science* 13, no. 4: 467–478.

Trussell, J., and C. Hammerlough. 1983. "A hazards model analysis of the covariates of infant and child mortality in Sri Lanka," *Demography* 20, no. 1: 1–26.

Van Esterik, P. 1983. "Integrating ethnographic and survey research: A review of the ethnographic component of a study of infant feeding practices in developing countries," *Population Council International Programs Working Paper* 17.

Ware, H. 1977. "Language problems in demographic field work in Africa," *World Fertility Survey Scientific Reports* 2.

———. 1981. *Women, Demography and Development.* Canberra: Australian National University Press.

Weisner, T., and R. Gallimore, 1977. "My brother's keeper: Child and sibling caretaking," *Current Anthropology* 18, no. 2: 169–190.

White, B. 1976. "Population, involution and employment in rural Java," *Development and Change* 7: 267–290.

Williamson, N. 1976. *Sons or Daughters: A Cross Cultural Survey of Parental Preferences.* Beverly Hills: Sage.

Winikoff, B., and E. Baer. 1980. "The obstetrician's opportunity: Translating 'Breast is Best' from theory to practice," *Population Council International Programs Working Paper* 11.

Wolf, D. 1982. "Making the bread and bringing it home: Female factory workers and the family economy in rural Java," Conference on Women in the Labour Force in Asia, Development Studies Centre, Australian National University, Canberra.

Zosa-Feranil, I. 1982. "Female employment and the family: A case study of the Bataan Export Processing Zone," Conference on Women in the Labour Force in Asia, Development Studies Centre, Australian National University, Canberra.

Studying the Impact of Household Economic and Community Variables on Child Mortality

T. Paul Schultz

Empirical studies of child survival make use of many types of information and are guided by many research paradigms. Statistical analyses of the determinants of child survival may deal with observations on regional conditions and population aggregates, characteristics of systematically selected populations, such as those encountered in a clinical practice, or data from representative household surveys on children and families.

Epidemiological research often measures the direct association between inputs to health, such as nutrition and medical care, and health outcomes, such as child morbidity, disability, and mortality. Economic research, on the other hand, generally evaluates how the constraints on peoples' opportunities are associated with child health, presumably by affecting behaviorally some of the direct inputs. The purpose of this paper is to show why the former direct association between health inputs and an individual's health is a statistically biased and potentially misleading indicator of the corresponding causal effect. This bias arises because people are essentially different in their health endowments, and their use of health inputs tends to be affected by what they know about their endowments or heterogeneity.[1] A stochastic framework is proposed for studying jointly the biological determinants of health in the presence of such heterogeneity, and the economically constrained selection of health inputs. Within this integrated framework the requirements for merging several types of data and for maintaining various "structural" assumptions will become clear. The goal is to estimate without bias both the underlying biological and behavioral relationships that will allow one to assess the benefits of "technology-based health interventions" and the consequences of "socio-economic change" that affects the prospects for child survival by influencing people's opportunities and thereby their use of health-related inputs.

Table 1 classifies information used in the study of child health according to whether the variable is viewed here as independent/exogenous or dependent/ endogenous, whether a variable is unobserved by the researcher, and the appropriate level of aggregation, namely the household or community. There are two basic sources of data: (1) information from surveys or census records on a representative sample of households and individuals and (2) character- istics of regions where these individuals live, of markets in which they obtain and exchange goods and services, and of the physical environment that con- strains their health and productive opportunities. To implement a research design based on these data, it is necessary first to lay out the conceptual framework guiding the research. It is important then to specify the structure and source of statistical disturbances and unobserved factors that enter the central relationships, for these features of the problem suggest how to estimate without bias the parameters in some of these relationships.

TABLE 1   Parallel classifications of variables employed by Mosley/ Chen and by Schultz in the study of child mortality determinants

I. Independent or exogenous variables	II. Dependent or endogenous variables
a. Preferences or individual/family goals (unobserved by researcher) (P_i)	**a. Proximate (Mosley/Chen) or intermediate input (Schultz) variables** (I_i) related to the technical determination of child health, e.g.
b. Individual endowment variables (X_i) Economic endowments (E_i) Education-labor $\}$Adult lifetime wealth Nonhuman assets Biological endowments (unobserved by researcher and not controlled by individual) (B_i) Healthiness or frailty Fecundity	Nutrition, breastfeeding, and consumption patterns Hygiene and child care Water and sanitation environment Preventive and curative medical care Fertility and child spacing
c. Community or regional variables (X_r) Market exchange prices and wage rates Public programs—access, money, and time costs to use Availability of information Infrastructure for production—e.g., roads Climate and exposure to disease	**b. Child health outcomes or output** (Y_i) Child survival Child acute and chronic morbidity: incidence, severity, and duration of episode

General framework for estimating the determinants of child health

The relationship between child mortality or morbidity for the ith mother, Y_i, is assumed to be approximately a linear function of a vector of proximate biological inputs to child health, I_i, and a vector of persistent biological endow- ments of the child, B_i, and a random disturbance, e_{1i}, and is hereafter called a health "production function" (see Figure 1):

$$Y_i = c_o + c_1 I_i + c_2 B_i + e_{1i} \quad , \tag{1}$$

where the cs are the parameters of this linearized biological/technical rela- tionship.

FIGURE 1 Flow diagram of factors determining child health

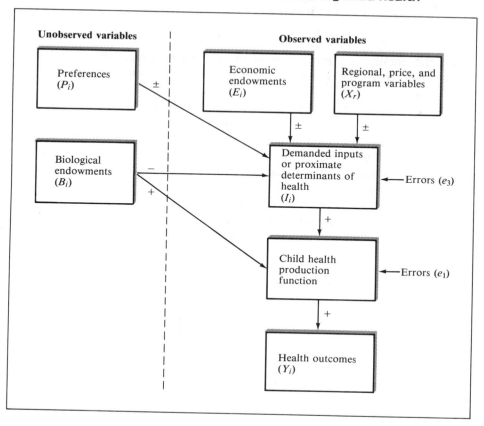

The I_i are chosen by the woman and her family to minimize Y_i, and to achieve other goals with her limited resources; B_i is again the child's health endowment, that component of child health due to either genetic or environmental conditions that cannot be influenced by the family's behavior, but that is partially known to it, called health heterogeneity; the economic endowments of the individuals, including human and nonhuman capital, E_i; the regional prices, programs, and environmental constraints, X_r; preferences, P_i, of the woman and her family; and e_{2i}, a stochastic disturbance that is independent of the exogenous variables in Table 1:

$$I_i = a_o + a_1 E_i + a_2 B_i + a_3 X_r + a_4 P_i + e_{2i} \quad . \qquad (2)$$

This relationship between the use of health inputs and all relevant exogenous variables is referred to as a reduced-form input demand function. The parameters, as, reflect behavioral responsiveness to socioeconomic and biological constraints, as well as the parents' understanding of the health production function.

Finally, there implicitly exist reduced-form equations for the health outcomes that have the same arguments as equation (2):

$$Y_i = b_o + b_1 E_i + b_2 B_i + b_3 X_r + b_4 P_i + e_{3i} \quad , \qquad (3)$$

where the parameters, bs, represent the combined effects of technological constraints and demand behavior, for example in this simple linear model, $b_1 = a_1 c_1$, and $b_3 = a_3 c_1$.

The parameters of these reduced-form equations (2) and (3) can be estimated consistently by standard statistical methods, such as ordinary least squares, if the dependent variable is continuous and normally distributed, since the inability of the researcher to observe preferences (P_i) or biological endowments (B_i) need not bias the remaining estimates. This follows from the conventional assumption that tastes and biological endowments are distributed independently of economic endowments, prices, programs, etc.—that is to say, P_i and B_i are uncorrelated with E_i and X_r.

The estimation problem is to obtain consistent estimates of the health production function (1). Because the unobserved biological variability in a child's health endowment, say its frailty, may both increase the likelihood of morbidity ($c_2 > 0$) and increase the use of beneficial health inputs ($a_2 c_1 < 0$), one expects compensating responses in observed health inputs for low (unobserved) health endowments. Direct estimation of the health production function by standard epidemiological methods is unsuitable in this case because input use, I_i, and health heterogeneity, B_i, are likely to be related. The estimation problem posed by heterogeneity in health endowments across a population is likely to be more serious in the evaluation of the effect of curative health inputs for acute conditions and less serious in evaluating the benefits of long-term preventive health measures. As in the conventional simultaneous equations model, some instrumental variable(s) is required that is independent of the biological endowment (B_i), but will account for some of the variation in health input demands. This exclusion restriction that is needed to identify statistically the production function parameters might be based on the economic expectation that regional prices and health programs influence health input demands, but do not enter directly as arguments in the production function.[2] In this paper, the identification restriction proposed is to assume that the input selection process (input demand equations) are conditional on regional prices, etc. (X_r), but that regional prices are not in the health production function. The mechanics of this two-stage instrumental variable estimation of the health production function are illustrated in the lower panel of Table 2. There are other methods for estimating the "structural" production function, such as by using panel data to estimate directly the role of the individually persistent biological endowments, that is, fixed or serially correlated individual effects. It is preferable to use qualitative structural model estimates if the dependent variable is discrete, such as mortality, or if the health outcome is disproportionately concentrated at particular points, such as zero episodes of illness in the last month (Manski and McFadden, 1981; Olsen and Wolpin, 1983).

TABLE 2 Alternative strategies for statistical study of merged household and regional variables defined in Table 1

Type of relationship represented	Linear approximation of relationship	Suitable statistical technique for estimating relationship
1. Unconditional or reduced-form demand functions determining		Single equation methods, such as ordinary least squares regression; for discrete dependent variables, logit or probit functions might be estimated
a. Proximate determinant or input to child health (I)	$I_i = a_0 + a_1 E_i + a_2 B_i + a_3 X_r + a_4 P_i + a_{2i}$	
b. Health outcomes (Y) with production and demand parameters not separately identified	$Y_i = b_0 + b_1 E_i + b_2 B_i + b_3 X_r + b_4 P_i + e_{3i}$	
2. Production functions determining health outcomes (Y), or a demand function conditional on the input choices (I) that are not systematically correlated with biological endowments (B) or preferences (P)	$Y_i = c_0 + c_1 \hat{I}_i + e_{1i}$ where $\hat{I}_i = \hat{a}_0 + \hat{a}_1 E_1 + \hat{a}_3 X_r$ and the as are estimated by standard methods as in 1a above.	Structural equation methods, such as instrumental variable simultaneous equation estimators

It may always be argued that important health inputs to the health production function are omitted from any empirical study and they might be correlated with the included inputs. This situation also leads to biased estimates of the effects of the subset of proximate health determinants that can be observed and jointly analyzed (Griliches, 1957). This omitted input problem may be serious in the case of child survival because the inputs that might reasonably exert an effect on child survival are numerous and difficult to quantify. The most one can do is try to measure and include all of the major determinants, particularly if those determinants covary with the policy interventions being evaluated. Only true randomized experimental design can free one entirely of this complication.

With this introduction to the general framework, the next section outlines how the microeconomic approach to household behavior helps one specify the regional constraints and individual economic endowments. The following sections show how interactions between mother's education and regional program activity may be used to evaluate distributional implications of policy. Subsequent sections consider data requirements and report the empirical application of the methodology to the study of infant health determinants in the United States. The final section recapitulates the main points of the paper.

The microeconomic model
of the family

Microeconomic analysis of family economic and demographic behavior rests on the hypothesis that people allocate their time and other economic resources in response to the value of the time of each family member, the amount of the family's nonhuman capital endowments, and the relative prices of the family's market inputs and outputs. The marketplace sets wage rates for various types of labor, and thereby determines the value of the time of persons working in the market or hiring additional labor to supplement their own efforts within the family's productive activities. Despite the diversity in family and market structures and the different degrees of coordination in production, consumption, and reproduction within the family/household in different societies, this greatly simplified economic approach to the interrelated labor market, demographic, and demand behavior of family members has provided a useful framework for much empirical research in high- and low-income countries.

This economic framework suggests that families are likely to respond differently to variation in male and female wages. The wage rate paid to women relative to men is emphasized in family time allocation studies as a relative price for household goods and services that are primarily produced by women. The care of children in many cultures consumes much of the time of their mothers, and therefore an increase in the opportunity value of women's time relative to men's is likely to increase the opportunity cost of children and child care and thus depress fertility, even though it provides the family with increased income opportunities. Consequently, this simplified model of household economic and demographic demands provides some suggestive predictions for how the labor market is likely to affect the long-run evolution of fertility and, possibly, child mortality.

While good data are not always available on market wage opportunities of men and women or the shadow value of time of household workers, women's education—a close correlate of women's wages—is associated with decreases in fertility and increases in child survival in both urban and rural areas at virtually all levels of development. Numerous studies also confirm the importance of a mother's education for understanding the survival rates of her children, even after the effect of husband's income or education is held constant (Caldwell, 1979; Schultz, 1980; Cochrane et al., 1981; Farah and Preston, 1982).[3] Moreover, education is a good predictor of the probability of interregional migration for women, as it is for men. Since most migration in low-income countries is from rural to urban areas, and rural conditions appear to favor higher child mortality, higher fertility, lower labor force participation by women, and lower school enrollment rates, the increased probability that an educated woman will migrate from a rural to an urban region reinforces the tendencies for her to give her fewer children better health and greater educational opportunities. All of these changes in behavior associated with increasing women's education lead to reinforcing improvements in the "quality" of the future population or the human capital embodied in the next generation (Schultz, 1983). Understanding how mother's education affects child mortality is a priority issue for research.

Mother's education

Economics suggests at least five distinct ways that mother's education might affect child health.[4] (1) Education may affect the productivity or effectiveness of the health inputs used in the production of child health, as hypothesized by Grossman (1972). Thus, more educated mothers may obtain greater benefits from a given use of health services; higher "productivity" would also increase their demand for health services, because the mother's resources are thereby effectively increased for allocation to any or all activities. (2) Education may affect perceptions about the best allocation of the health inputs. In this case, more educated mothers would have healthier children because they have better information on the optimal allocation of health resources, and thus are able to produce health at lower cost. Moreover, such mothers would be particularly advantaged where information on "best" input allocations is scarce or costly to acquire, as with new technologies. (3) Education may increase total family resources. Even where women tend not to work in the market, more educated women may have greater market resources because, due to assortative mating, they marry wealthier men. Such women might be expected to invest more resources in the production of child health and thus would have healthier children. (4) More educated women may assign a higher value to their own time, particularly, but not only, if they work in the market and receive a higher wage rate. If mother's time is an essential "input" in the production of child health, education could then be negatively related to the health of children. (5) Education may residually affect preferences for child health and family size, given total resources, prices, and technology.

To ascertain precisely how education affects child health, estimates are needed of the actual technology associated with the production of health. Such estimates require, as noted above, that all behavioral inputs be observed for each child—breastfeeding, nutrient intakes, use of medical services, and so on. In the presence of heterogeneity in health endowments, information would also be required on prices of all inputs and on the household environment. In the absence of such reasonably complete knowledge of the biological and behavioral determinants of child survival, it is still possible to learn about the effects of policy interventions and to explore the distributional implications of policies by interacting regional policy variables with educational variables in generalized reduced-form health equations (Table 2, row 1b).

Public program interventions and education interactions

In the jargon of economics, demand equations for health inputs are derived from the maximization of household utility, subject to the production functions and the budget constraint. The demands for health inputs are explained by the conventional types of exogenous variables—prices, income, education, age, the local environment, and the unobserved endowments of health. Public programs may play three distinct roles in affecting health, and related behavior, through the demand equations:

1 They may reduce the prices of the health inputs, directly through subsidization of the goods or services, or indirectly by increasing access to them, thereby reducing the time or travel costs to evaluate and use the service.

2 They may provide information on how to produce health more efficiently. This might include information on new inputs or on efficient practices with traditional inputs—how long to breastfeed, how to sterilize baby formula, etc.—that yield greater survival rates for a given expenditure.

3 They may alter the health environment, without directly affecting other opportunities available to people. The control of malaria and eradication of smallpox are often cited as examples of exogenously introduced change in health conditions or technology that occurred for all persons living in an area, regardless of their economic status and educational attainment.[5]

The behavioral framework suggests that programs which reduce the costs of health inputs will lead to greater investments in health and thus greater survival rates. An implication of the household framework is that any program that affects the cost of goods consumed, whether directly useful to the production of health or not, may influence the demand for health inputs and thus indirectly affect health or survival. Thus, prices of all major goods and certainly the prices of goods that are thought to be close complements to or substitutes for child health belong in the demand equations for child health inputs.

The effects of program interventions may differ depending on the mother's education, according to the relative importance of the (five) roles of education in affecting health, and on the predominance of (1) the user subsidy or (2) the productive information or (3) the disease eradication effects of the programs. Table 3 outlines the distributional consequences of these possibilities.[6]

TABLE 3   Who benefits more from health program interventions, according to the roles of the programs and of mother's education

	Roles of health programs		
Role of mother's education	Information raises technical efficiency (A)	Modern input subsidy encourages use (B)	Improvement in healthiness of environment (C)
1 Increase productivity of health inputs	Unknown	Unknown	Less educated
2 Reduce costs of information on technology	Less educated	More educated	Less educated
3 Increase family income	Unknown	More educated	Less educated
4 Increase mother's price of time	Unknown	Less educated	More educated
5 Affect preferences for health	Unknown	Unknown	Unknown

Estimates of the effects of education and public health programs on child health are likely to be misspecified, if the interactions between education and the health "infrastructure" are ignored. Moreover, while estimates of such interactions, in the absence of information on the characteristics of the health production function, cannot conclusively pin down the most important roles either of education or of the health programs in augmenting health, they can eliminate some possibilities.[7]

Implementation of the general framework

The general framework proposed here to structure study of child survival is primarily a way to classify relationships and variables, but this taxonomy has important implications for how variables should be measured. A distinction has been made between (1) technical or biological relationships that link inputs to the production of health outcomes and (2) demand relationships that translate individual preferences into the demand for consumption goods and intermediate inputs, conditional on the technological or biological relationships, the prices of inputs and outputs, and the initial factor endowments, education, and age of the individual. The production functions contain little information about economic or demographic behavior per se; they represent physical–technological limitations of the human environment and knowledge of how to use this environment. The demand functions contain the economic core of the model. Strong assumptions are usually made regarding the optimizing behavior of the individual or the family in choices of economic and demographic behavior, over a budget of given resources, whose exchange values (prices) are fixed in the marketplace, subject to technically fixed production possibilities. Household demand economics embeds the traditional consumer demands for market-produced goods into a household firm that also produces the basic commodities that satisfy individual needs. In our case, the household produces the commodity of child survival. The consumer's demands are thus extended to encompass demographic events that are quite different from market goods; since there is no direct market for children or for child health, the consumer must be her or his own producer.

Few researchers have given empirical content to this distinction between production technology and consumer demand. If the assumptions required to disentangle household technology and consumer demands by two-stage estimation procedures prove to be too restrictive, then another more limited approach to studying child survival can be pursued. The socioeconomic and environmental determinants of child survival can be directly estimated unconditional on production technology. These unconditional demand relationships are called reduced-form demand equations for health (Table 2, row 1b), and they mix together the underlying structural parameters that characterize the production functions and the conditional input demand functions discussed earlier.

Estimation of these reduced-form demand equations loses track, however, of the interesting linkages across input allocations and the specific details of household production processes. For example, what determines when an individual adopts a child survival input, such as oral rehydration therapy, or how effective it will be when it is adopted? On the other hand, these reduced-form health equations do indicate what many policymakers want to know. For instance, if the local wage rate for women increases in the labor market (i.e., there is a change in this market price), what will be the consequences for child survival? If a hospital bed is added per thousand persons in a locality, (i.e., the price of some forms of medical care is reduced), what will be the consequences for child survival in that region, and also for which groups of parents in that locality will the increase in child survival be greatest? Not only do reduced-form demand equations answer such questions, they can also be estimated without bias by standard multiple regression or multiple logit/hazard techniques. Consistent estimates are, thus, readily obtained at relatively low cost from commonly available data, if one can forgo the separation of technological from behavioral parameters.

The controversial aspect of this approach to studying the determinants of household economic and demographic behavior is in deciding precisely what types of behavior are appropriately viewed as demand determined (i.e., endogenous), and what variables are legitimately intepreted as predetermined market prices and individual endowments (Table 1).

In principle, all forms of behavior that are influenced or constrained by household production and consumption can be treated as partially determined by the equilibrium system of household demand behavior. It is largely an empirical question whether the degree of influence of the demand determinants is substantial or negligible.[8] Of course, an included explanatory variable may be capturing the effect due to an omitted explanatory variable; or joint and simultaneous effects may be present, clouding any causal insight; or any of a number of the other specification errors arise if the estimated model were wrong. But conditional on the specification of a model, empirical analysis may proceed to determine whether the factors emphasized by a theory are in fact helpful in explaining variation in behavioral outcomes.[9]

Specification and measurement of variables

One important insight of household economics is also a limitation to empirical analysis of variation in child survival. Many forms of household economic and demographic behavior are viewed as endogenous to the broader, longer term set of choices that include child health and survival. One endogenous choice cannot generally be used to ''explain'' another choice or related behavioral outcome.[10] First, a line must be drawn at some point in an individual's lifetime, before which events are treated as predetermined or exogenous for the purposes of looking at a specific set of subsequent outcomes. For understanding the determinants of a couple's choices with respect to labor supply, fertility, or child health, one might draw the line when the couple is married. But their timing of marriage could be closely related to the later events under study and probably reflects the heterogeneous unobserved biological characteristics and tastes of persons.

Alternatively, it may be more satisfactory to select one spouse, say the woman, and treat her characteristics as predetermined when she has completed her childhood and schooling. The argument for this specification is that parents play a dominant role in inducing or preventing their children from attending school, and consequently, the schooling decision reflects heavily the preferences of the family rather than that of the child. It then follows that, given what we know about the individual's characteristics on leaving school, the endogenous choices and behavior that are to be explained start with the woman's age at marriage or age at first birth, as well as the characteristics of the husband, if she is married.

Prices

What are appropriate variables to use to explain household demand behavior and outcomes related to child health? The first major class of factors is prices.

Prices are predetermined, if they are set by a market over which the individual has negligible control. These prices must not vary with the quantity demanded by the consumer, or they would thereby be contaminated by consumer choices and tastes.[11]

Market price data are unfortunately rarely collected by household demographic-economic surveys. The level of local wages may be available, and household demand theory emphasizes the relevance of wage rates for men, women, and children to the choice of activities people undertake, particularly market labor supply behavior. Other market prices are proxied by the availability of private and public services, where access is often a major part of "price" variation. For market prices to differ across a population at one point in time, there must be something separating markets, perhaps the costs of transporting goods to consumers or the costs of migrating to consume immobile services, or both. This suggests that the concept of market price implicitly relates to an aggregation of households in a market area. Cross-sectional studies require a sufficient number of market aggregates to provide a basis for estimating the effect of "market prices" on household demands across these local market areas. The appropriate level of aggregation to measure market prices depends on the good or service and what delimits its market. Clearly it is not apppropriate to measure the household's price by observing what the household pays, since this will embody the household's demand for "quality" in that good, which is unlikely to be independent of its demand for "quantity." For example, the family that spend a great deal per visit to a doctor for their children cannot be viewed as confronting a higher price for medical care than neighbors who spend much less per visit to a doctor for their children. Conversely, a household located in a town that spends more on public health programs than does the average town will actually confront a lower "market" price of medical services, presumably of quality-adjusted health care, that does not necessarily reflect the individual household's preferences. Market prices must be measured, then, at a level of aggregation above the household to assure that the prices are exogenous to the household's demands and behavioral outcomes that axiomatically depend also on the preferences of the household.[12]

Residential community characteristics may be particularly useful in estimating input demand relationships because they generally can be assumed to be exogenous from the household's point of view. Merging data on small community markets—their wages, prices, and service programs—is a natural step toward empirical application of the household production-demand approach to child survival. Extraction of "price-type" variables from regionally aggregated data—from a census or consumer expenditure survey, for example—to explain individual household behavior is increasingly common in economic demography.

Endowments

The second class of demand determinants is the household's ownership of factors of production. The prior discussion suggested why one might want to treat the individual's education as such a predetermined labor endowment. It may be useful to also treat vocational training as an exogenous determinant of demands. Inherited nonhuman wealth may, by the same logic, be viewed as given to the individual or at least as largely outside of the individual's control. Although the ownership of land and reproducible capital is generally viewed as exogenous to short-run household consumer behavior and to producer input allocation decisions, these stocks of nonhuman wealth reflect lifetime accumulation behavior and may not be predetermined from the point of view of long-term demographic behavior. Again, drawing the line between exogenous constraints and endogenous choices becomes a critical matter of model specification. In this case, the characterization of an individual's initial endowments might be inferred from family history questionnaires that seek to distinguish among sources of inherited wealth and subsequent accumulation over the individual's adult lifetime. Clearly, one should distinguish between inherited wealth brought to the household by husband and wife and that brought by other members.

Environment

The third and final determinant of household demands is the productive environment that lies outside the behavioral control of the individual or household. A local climate conducive to malaria, for example, may increase child mortality. The area may benefit from a public irrigation project that alters cropping possibilities and raises the market value of land, but spreads schistosomiasis. Resulting changes in cropping patterns may then affect women's employment opportunities, through encouraging, for example, rice or cotton cultivation that assigns greater value to the tasks that women appear to have a comparative advantage in performing. These technological characteristics of the productive environment are related to geographical and administrative aggregates that need to be specified for each productive process or outcome. There are likely to be many ramifications of a change in the local productive environment, and the net effect of these on child survival may not always be clarified by theoretical insights but may simply require extensive empirical study.

Health inputs

Another tier of data required to estimate the structural model relates to child health inputs. The standard medical care inputs must be summarily measured, for the statistical inefficiency of the two-stage estimation approach argues against the evaluation of a very long list of inputs, particularly when the prices of the inputs and the income elasticities of their demand are similar. In addition to medical care inputs, birth order of the child, spacing, number of siblings, and age of mother at birth are relevant data. All of these aspects of the timing of family formation are thought to influence the parent time and market resources available for child care and other consumption needs. Duration and extent of breastfeeding and nutritional inputs should be summarized, perhaps by anthropometic measures, such as height, weight, and skinfolds. Time inputs of mothers and other persons performing child care functions should be quantified, and the educational attainment of these individuals recorded. Household consumption patterns that may affect child survival include whether the family has a protected water supply or modern sanitation facilities, and various aspects of quality of housing. The productive activities engaged in by household members, including the mother and child, may affect the provision of child care or exposure to particular diseases or occupational hazards.

All of these potential inputs to child survival are to some degree choice variables, even though these household choices may not be strongly affected by their consequences for child survival. Occupational choices, for example, may be determined primarily by other factors (e.g., wage rates), even though they often entail exposure to different health risks. The income effects associated with the occupational choices may neutralize these differences in risks to child survival, or they may not. Direct correlational evidence is not likely to clarify these issues, just as we have slowly learned that the simple correlation of fertility and child mortality is not necessarily a satisfactory estimate of a causal relationship.

The third type of health programs, those that alter the exogenous health environment, can be treated as an input at the community level eradicating or controlling a local disease and thereby reducing child mortality risks for all persons. As suggested in Table 3, however, one has reason to expect such programs to benefit differentially the population according to their preprogram capacity to protect themselves through other inputs, such as mother's education, or father's wages, or household nonhuman wealth. The production function should be specified to include interactions between inputs in these cases where it is hypothesized that inputs are substitutes or complements for one another. The earlier discussion of mother's education and program effects could be generalized to many pairs of inputs. Empirical study of such potential interactions is possible whenever more than one of the inputs is measured at the household level. However, where both inputs are measured at the community level, multicollinearity across regions in various inputs and input prices may make it difficult to observe sufficient independent variation in the inputs so as to test empirically for cross-substitution effects in the production function. Experimental design may ultimately be needed in the implementation of public programs across regions to introduce independent variation in the mix of programs that would permit one to confidently measure synergistic effects among policy inputs of this form. Nothing in the approach precludes, however, estimating cross-substitution effects among program inputs in the reduced-form child survival equation.[13]

An empirical example: US infant
health determinants

Experience in estimating "structural" health production functions is still very limited. Only one study of infant health determinants has dealt with the statistical problem of health heterogeneity (Rosenzweig and Schultz, 1982a). The timing and extent of prenatal medical care is not consistently associated with infant health outcomes in large random samples of US births (Eisen, 1979). This finding could be interpreted to suggest that prenatal medical care does not systematically increase birth weight or improve prospects for child survival. However, heterogeneity in health endowments could lead women with difficult pregnancies to secure earlier prenatal medical care and yet report below-average child health outcomes. If this form of "adverse selection" of compensatory early prenatal medical care were widespread, health heterogeneity would bias downward direct estimates of the "benefits" due to prenatal care.

To test this reasoning and apply the estimation strategy outlined in this paper, Table 4 reports the simple linear determinants of birth weight, gestation,

TABLE 4 Proximate determinants of infant health indicators: United States, 1967–69

| | Dependent variable | | | | | |
| | Birth weight (grams) | | Gestation (weeks) | | Infant mortality (1 = died) | |
Explanatory variable	OLS (1)	IV (2)	OLS (3)	IV (4)	OLS (5)	IV (6)
Delay in prenatal medical care (months)[a]	−1.96 (3.11)	−23.6 (4.16)	−.0091 (3.21)	−.0512 (2.18)	−.00015 (.81)	.0043 (2.49)
Smoking while pregnant (cigarettes per day)[a]	−10.0 (15.3)	−20.0 (3.84)	−.0082 (2.83)	−.0159 (.74)	.0000 (.04)	.0043 (2.74)
Age at birth (years)[a]	3.05 (2.41)	.486 (.12)	−.0085 (1.52)	.0080 (.48)	−.0015 (3.12)	.0017 (1.37)
Parity at birth[a]	22.9 (3.85)	67.0 (4.15)	.0044 (.26)	.0734 (1.10)	.0159 (13.4)	.0051 (1.05)
Black	−250.0 (16.6)	−242.0 (10.1)	−.725 (10.9)	−.639 (6.46)	.0235 (5.06)	.0297 (4.12)
1967	16.8 (1.21)	13.7 (.86)	.540 (8.89)	.522 (8.00)	−.0084 (1.98)	−.0097 (2.04)
1968	13.2 (.95)	13.5 (.90)	.110 (1.81)	.119 (1.91)	−.0011 (.27)	−.0017 (.39)
Intercept	3,245.0 (110.0)	3,323.0 (31.2)	39.2 (302.0)	38.8 (88.1)	.0282 (3.12)	.0612 (1.91)
R^2	.0540	—	.0242	—	.0287	—
F	78.39	32.37	34.12	30.13	40.52	14.73
Sample size = 9,484						
Dependent variable mean	3,288.0		39.06		.0306	
Standard deviation	568.0		2.47		.172	

NOTE: The absolute value of t ratios is reported in parentheses beneath the regression coefficients. Note that in the case of columns 5 and 6 the t ratios are not unbiased, because the dependent variable is a binary variable (infant mortality).
[a] Endogenous variables estimated by the instrumental variable (IV) method. Instruments include those cited in Rosenzweig and Schultz (1982a), plus husband's education by five discrete levels; milk prices; share of labor force in manufacturing, government, agriculture, and construction; unemployment rate; population per ob-gyn; sex of child; part-time share of jobs; ease of divorce laws; AFDC payment average; whether Medicaid includes family planning services.

and infant mortality for a representative sample of nearly 9,500 legitimate births in the United States from 1967 to 1969. Columns (1), (3), and (5) report ordinary least squares (OLS) estimates of the child health production functions that would be biased by the hypothesized form of health heterogeneity and self-selection of health inputs; the inputs analyzed are the mother's delay in seeking prenatal care, smoking while pregnant, age, and parity. Columns (2), (4), and (6) report the instrumental variable (IV) estimates of the same child health production functions that are statistically consistent in the presence of health heterogeneity. The following variables are selected as instruments: education of mother and father, father's income, and merged characteristics of the residential area such as prices, health and family planning programs, and labor force characteristics.

Health heterogeneity appears to mask almost completely the significant beneficial impact of early prenatal medical care on these three infant health indicators. The child health effect of postponing prenatal care is increased twelvefold on birth weight and fivefold on gestation, and the sign of the effect on infant mortality is reversed and becomes statistically significant when the appropriate IV estimates replace the standard OLS estimates. A mother who delays one month in obtaining prenatal care raises her expected infant mortality in this sample by 14 percent, according to the instrumental variable estimates (col. 6) that allow for health heterogeneity.

The strong effects of smoking on birth weight that are noted in many direct epidemiological studies of birth outcomes are also evident in this sample (see col. 1). But allowing for health heterogeneity doubles the estimated effects of smoking while pregnant on birth weight, while the effect on infant mortality is also increased substantially.

Although the age and parity of the mother exhibit a strong linear (and nonlinear) association with birth weight and infant survival in this sample, the instrumental variable estimates suggest relatively little linear biological effect of mother's age on birth weight, gestation, or infant mortality, although parity continues to contribute to greater birth weight. Interactions of age and smoking, however, are deleterious to the child's birth weight (Rosenzweig and Schultz, 1982b).

This empirical analysis of a probability sample of US births matched to residential regional characteristics suggests that inferences drawn regarding the child health effects of health inputs can be sensitive to whether or not heterogeneity in health endowments is present and correlated with health input behavior. In this empirical example, child health effects of early prenatal care are obscured by standard epidemiological methods, as has been the case in past studies based on individual data. Allowing for the self-selection of health inputs and the interactive role of health heterogeneity, one obtains strong evidence that early prenatal medical care is beneficial in this US population.

Summary and conclusions

Empirical study of the biological and behavioral determinants of child survival may proceed in two directions: either to estimate the reduced-form unconditional relationships between child survival and individual- and community-level variables that are assumed to be exogenous to the many demographic, consumer, and producer choices a household makes over time (Table 2, row 1b); or to estimate both the demand equations for health inputs (Table 2, row 1a) and the production function linking health inputs to child survival by simultaneous structural equation methods (Table 2, row 2).

The reduced-form equation for child survival may be estimated without imposing a great deal of structure on the problem, although specifying which variables are exogenous and which are endogenous to child survival may prove controversial. The approach proposed here is that all events after the woman reaches economic independence of her parents and completes her schooling are reasonably treated as endogenous; in particular, the timing of her first birth may be seen as the first life-cycle decision that may subsequently be an important endogenous input to the health of her children.

The biological production function for child survival can only be estimated after more structure is imposed on the problem, because in the presence of health heterogeneity self-selected health inputs will tend to be correlated with the child's unobserved biological health endowment. To eliminate the bias due to self-selected inputs and heterogeneity, a two-stage estimation procedure is outlined that first estimates the health input demand equations and then estimates indirectly the health production function (Table 2).

In the estimation of either the reduced-form equation or the health input and production relationships, it is valuable to have data collected both for individuals from a representative sample of households and on prices, programs, and characteristics of the communities in which these households are located. Since the health inputs are often household choice variables, they are not independent of the health endowments of the children, or of the preferences of household members. Consequently, the community aggregate variables on prices, wages, programs, and environmental conditions are essential for the analysis, because they are outside the control of individuals in the household, and hence, they are legitimately treated as exogenous instruments. This merger of micro and macro variables facilitates both types of empirical research strategies and draws the line more distinctly between endogenous and exogenous variables for the purposes of studying the determinants of child health. The joint analysis of micro and macro variables also permits the study of plausible interactions between the two levels, such as that illustrated above between the mother's education and the community level of program activity. Microlevel observations on child survival, observed for the individual child or averaged for each mother over all her children, also provide a firmer basis to explore nonlinear response patterns than is feasible when analysis relies on aggregate measures of child mortality across regions.[14] On the other hand, market prices and certain forms of variation in the productive environment are conceived in terms of aggregates over geographic and administrative regions. Other aggregates of individuals might also be considered, where it is hypothesized that group identification influences the productive possibilities available to individuals, such as their membership in a certain caste, class, racial, or religious group. The absence of individual data, however, might conceal the interactive structure and nonlinear form of relationships, and confound simultaneous relationships and feedbacks.

If the general hypothesis of health heterogeneity is accepted, as I think it must be, the widely cited evidence of direct associations between proximate health inputs and child health outcomes cannot be accepted at face value as evidence of causal relationships. The bias embodied in these associations may be minimal, but I suspect it is frequently substantial. The problem of evaluating health inputs may be particularly serious when it comes to policy interventions that subsidize the self-selected curative medical services for acute illness.

More generally, if social and biological scientists are to apply convergent research strategies in their analyses of the determinants of child survival, they must move toward a common framework. This framework needs to draw clearly the stochastic distinction between independent or exogenous variables and dependent or endogenous variables. Child survival should be viewed as one among many endogenous household variables that are modified by economic and demographic choices. Child survival may be usefully interpreted as directly conditioned on exogenous constraints and environmental conditions, such as regional public programs, prices, wages, and individual biological and economic endowments. To estimate the structure that links these exogenous variables to child survival will require added information about the problem. This paper has outlined one possible estimation strategy for clarifying this structure.

Notes

This research was supported in part by grants from NIH, Center for Population Research HD-12172, and from the Hewlett Foundation to the Yale Economic Demography Program. I appreciate the comments of E. Churchill and D. Feeny.

1 Examples abound of this form of bias misleading the researcher who tries to characterize health technology from nonexperimental evidence. Efforts to estimate the effect of vaccinations on child survival, for example, are bedeviled by the tendency for children who "naturally" get vaccinated to be otherwise different from nonvaccinated children.

2 It is possible to identify the selection correction solely on the basis of functional form assumptions (Heckman, 1979), but this seems to place excessive reliance on nonlinear specification choices, such as implied by the probit or logit formulation.

3 Mark Rosenzweig and I have examined the possibility that education of the mother may achieve an increase in birth weight by three means: altering the measurable mix of inputs to child health, enhancing the productivity of specific inputs differentially, and exerting a neutral productivity-enhancing effect on all inputs. Thus far we have found that most of the effect of education on birth weight in the United States can be attributed to education's effect on the mix of inputs used by mothers, although the exception may be in the timing of the first visit to the doctor for prenatal care, which is of enhanced value for more educated mothers.

4 This section draws on the joint research the author has been engaged in with Mark Rosenzweig over several years (summarized in Rosenzweig and Schultz, 1982b).

5 For further discussion with respect to mortality, see Schultz (1980).

6 Column A, row 2 (i.e., A.2) indicates that if the informational roles of both public health and family planning programs and maternal education are predominant, such programs are likely to have a greater effect on child health in families with less educated women, compared with families in which the mother has a higher level of schooling. This difference reflects the fact that the availability of information is only of value to households that have not already acquired the information, namely, to those who face higher costs of information acquisition. If programs mainly lower the user cost of modern health inputs (column B), however, higher educated families, who are already more aware of the "benefits" of such inputs, will be the ones benefiting most, given the informational role of education (B.2). With respect to the four other roles of mother's education, it cannot be established a priori who will benefit more from the public provision of technological information (A) relating to the production of health, because the effects will depend on the type of information generated and on unknown differential income effects by mother's educational level.

Programs that cause the remission or eradication of disease from the community environment, without otherwise affecting the regimen of people (column C), have the potential for narrowing mortality differentials by educational class, assuming that before the program, disease is more common among the least educated. Broadly based eradication campaigns are, therefore, likely to benefit most the least educated, since it is implicitly assumed that education's effect on the preprogram incidence of disease through roles 1, 2, 3, and 5 outweighs any effect arising from role 4.

7 For example, if it is found that the effects of health programs on child survival are greater in families with less educated mothers, the joint hypotheses that the programs reduce input costs and that more educated mothers are more able and willing to take advantage of such subsidized health services (B.2) can be rejected. This is, incidentally, a widely accepted view of the process by which public health services benefit disproportionately the more educated (Caldwell, 1979). It may be a valid hypothesis at very low levels of income and average education, such as in sub-Saharan Africa, but may also be rejected by data from higher income populations, such as in Latin America.

8 In this context, it is not the size of an R^2 (or the portion of variation in individual behavior that one explains) that is the appropriate criterion for judging the "importance" of behavioral demands in the study of child survival. The importance of this relation is better evaluated in terms of the magnitude of "slope" coefficients in conjunction with the range of changes that might reasonably occur in the conditioning variables. Also the size of the slope coefficients relative to their standard error (i.e., t ratio) provides a useful indicator of the precision of the slope coefficients.

9 Ideally, the theoretical structure will also imply the direction of some effects (one-tailed tests may then be applied) and restrictions across coefficients in a single or a group of demand equations. This stronger level of confirmation of theory, however, is uncommon where unconditional demand relationships are being estimated, since the demand and production parameters cannot generally be separately identified. If the estimated slope of the relationship does not exceed 2.4 times its standard error (two-tailed test, sample size exceeding 60), one cannot be confident that in even 99 percent of the random samples would the slope coefficient be different from zero. In this case, where that ratio is less than 2.4, the relationship can be viewed as suggestive, but not confirmed with much confidence. In the case of mutually exclusive and exhaustive discrete variables conditioning an outcome (e.g., racial groups), the joint F test may be employed, since the suppressed category is arbitrary and hence the magnitude of the individual class coefficient and associated t ratios are meaningful only relative to the (arbitrarily) suppressed class.

10 For instance, this framework is not designed to help interpret the inverse partial correlation between ownership of consumer durables (e.g., toilets) and child survival, even though child survival may be affected by sanitation facilities. Neither can one interpret causally the simple association between women's employment behavior and their fertility.

Both outcomes are jointly determined choices, just as the quantities of apples and oranges purchased by the consumer are joint decisions, to some degree, linked through the budget constraint and probably related in the utility function. We would not expect a regression of apples on oranges to be interpreted as suggesting that apple purchases have the associated effect on the purchases of oranges. They are both outcomes of a system of demand equations determined by prices, endowments, and preferences.

11 The shadow prices of the final commodities produced in the home are not identical with market prices, for they are an amalgam of the prices of time and goods inputs; and since the individual's time may be valued differently depending on what the individual does, the shadow prices reflect consumption and labor supply choices of the individual. Thus, the commodity prices discussed by Becker (1965) and later by Willis (1974) with regard to the household's time allocation or choice of fertility do not satisfy the criteria for market prices that are appropriately treated as exogenous determinants of demand.

12 This assumes explicitly that people do not migrate to a community where the available mix of public services fits their tastes. Once it is admitted that interregional migration is heavily determined by people's preferences for child survival (or closely related household commodities such as fertility), then regional characteristics are not a suitable basis for purging the input demand equations of the effect of health heterogeneity. Conversely, if governments locate health programs in regions that have an unusual average level of health endowment—say, areas where malaria is still uncontrolled—then care must be exercised in interpreting the "effect" of such programs on child survival. In this example, the regional health program becomes itself a response to "endowments" and must be explained by the more basic governmental priorities in conjunction with regional characteristics (see Schultz, 1983).

13 For example, Schultz (1971) estimated across 361 regions of Taiwan the cross-substitution effects on fertility of different types of fieldworkers in the family planning program. Thus, in a locality that had already received much attention by "prepregnancy health workers," the "village health education workers" were notably less effective in reducing birth rates among older women. This conclusion was derived from a reduced-form specification of a fertility equation that assumed child mortality as predetermined.

14 Categorical or higher order polynomials in the explanatory variables might be introduced. Box–Cox (1964) power transformations might also discriminate among alternative functional forms for the dependent variable, as well as those for the explanatory variables.

References

Becker, G. S. 1965. "A theory of the allocation of time," *Economic Journal* 75, no. 299 (December): 493–517.

Box, G. E. P., and D. R. Cox. 1964. "An analysis of transformations," *Journal of the Royal Statistical Society,* Ser. B 26: 211–243.

Butz, W. P., J. DaVanzo, and J. P. Habicht. 1981. *Improving Infant Nutrition, Health, and Survival,* R-2924-AID, June. Santa Monica: The Rand Corporation.

Caldwell, J. C. 1979. "Education as a factor in mortality decline," *Population Studies* 33, no. 3 (November): 395–413.

Cochrane, S. H., J. Leslie, and D. J. O'Hara. 1981. "Parental education and child health." Paper presented at symposium on "Literacy, Education and Health Development," Ann Arbor, Michigan.

Eisner, V., J. V. Brazie, M. W. Pratt, and A. C. Hexter. 1979. "The risk of low birth weight," *American Journal of Public Health* 68: 887–893.

Farah, A.-A., and S. H. Preston. 1982. "Child mortality differentials in Sudan," *Population and Development Review* 8, no. 2 (June): 365–383.

Griliches, Z. 1957. "Specification bias in estimates of production functions," *Journal of Farm Economics* 39: 8–20.

Grossman, M. 1972. "On the concept of health capital and the demand for health," *Journal of Political Economy* 80 (March/April): 223–255.

Heckman, J. 1979. "Sample selection as a specification error," *Econometrica* 47, no. 1 (January): 153–161.

Manski, C. F., and D. McFadden. 1981. *Structural Analysis and Discrete Data with Econometric Applications.* Cambridge, Mass.: MIT Press.

Mincer, J. 1963. "Market prices, opportunity costs and income effect," in *Measurement in Economics,* ed. C. Christ, et al. Stanford: Stanford University Press.

Olsen, R. J., and K. I. Wolpin. 1983. "The impact of exogenous child mortality on fertility," *Econometrica* 51, no. 2 (May): 731–750.

Rosenzweig, M. R., and T. P. Schultz. 1982a. "The behavior of mother as inputs to child health," in *Economic Aspects of Health,* ed. V. Fuchs. Chicago: University of Chicago Press.

———, and T. P. Schultz. 1982b. "Child mortality and fertility in Colombia: Individual and community effect," *Health Policy and Education,* Vol. 2, pp. 305–348.

Schultz, T. P. 1971. *Evaluation of Population Policies: A Framework for Analysis and Its Application to Taiwan's Family Planning Programs,* R-643-AID, June. Santa Monica: The Rand Corporation.

———. 1980. "Interpretation of relations among mortality, economics of the household, and the health environment," in *Proceedings of the Meeting on Socioeconomic Determinants and Consequences of Mortality.* New York and Geneva: United Nations and World Health Organization.

———. 1983. "Migrant behavior and the effects of regional prices: Aspects of migrant selection in Colombia," Yale University Economic Growth Center Discussion Paper No. 443, New Haven, August.

Willis, R. J. 1974. "Economic theory of fertility behavior," in *The Economics of the Family,* ed. T. W. Schultz. Chicago: University of Chicago Press.

Technology and Child Survival: The Example of Sanitary Engineering

John Briscoe

This paper focuses attention on conceptual models in a specific sector, namely, water supply and sanitation, that has played a fundamental role in reducing infant mortality in industrialized countries (McKeown, Brown, and Record, 1972), and from which a similar contribution is expected in underdeveloped countries. The analysis has two major objectives. First, it is intended to demonstrate how conceptual frameworks arise in response to specific challenges, how they are modified to meet different challenges, and how such modifications and revisions must continue to be made when facing relatively new challenges such as those posed in underdeveloped countries. Second, through discussion of specific examples, a general methodology is presented for determining priority research needs when there is uncertainty about the values of many relevant parameters. Although concerned with the field of sanitary science, the paper illustrates how the neglect of socioeconomic dimensions of a problem can greatly compromise the effectiveness of a health intervention.

Sanitary engineering in industrialized countries

The modern history of sanitary engineering begins with the Industrial Revolution and, in particular, with three facets of that revolution. First, urban settlements of unprecedented size and concentration were created in a short space of time. In London, for instance, the size of the land area supporting 10 persons per acre expanded from 43 square miles in 1837 to 75 square miles in 1858. Second, a central tenet of the Industrial Revolution was that practical material problems could be solved through the development and application of scientific principles. And third, the wave of unrest that swept Europe in the late 1840s and culminated in the revolutions of 1848 led to an increasing concern with the economic and social conditions of the working class.

The development of sanitary engineering, in direct response to the challenges arising from these three factors, arose out of a world view formed by both social and natural scientists. Engels (1845), Virchow (see Ackerknecht, 1953), Chadwick (1842), and other social reformers of the nineteenth century drew attention to the critical role of environmental conditions in mediating the relationship between social and economic factors, on the one hand, and morbidity and mortality, on the other. Through the development of the "germ theory" by Pasteur, Koch, and others and the imaginative collection and analysis of epidemiological data on cholera in London by Snow (1854), and on typhoid in the Elbe Valley by Koch (1894) the biological link between water, sanitation, and health was established. In short, the conceptual framework of sanitary engineering was originally holistic, taking account of the social and economic antecedents of environmental conditions, of the engineering problems of facilities' design, and of the biological mechanisms linking exposure to disease.

Guided by this conceptual framework, sanitary engineers first tackled the development and testing of technologies to reduce the number of bacteria in drinking water. While sand filters had been used for centuries to improve the aesthetic quality of drinking water, the role of filtration in improving bacteriological quality had never been recognized. A number of experiments demonstrated that the number of bacteria in drinking water could be reduced by one or two orders of magnitude through slow-sand filtration.

A particular problem not solved by slow-sand filtration was the treatment of highly turbid waters. Building on the chemical-coagulation process (patented in 1884), the Louisville, Kentucky, Experiment Station demonstrated that so-called mechnical filters, preceded by coagulation and sedimentation, could solve the problems posed by these waters.

By the early twentieth century engineers were confident that good quality water could be produced by pretreatment followed by filtration. The most significant advances in water treatment, however, came with the introduction of chlorination in 1908. Not only was calcium hypochlorite a cheap and widely available chemical, but chlorination consistently eliminated pathogenic bacteria in drinking water.

Accompanying these scientific advances were simple but convincing demonstrations that use of these technologies resulted in the anticipated effects on public health. For example, a study in the Ohio River Valley recorded typhoid death rates per 100,000 of 76.8 and 74.5 in 1906 and 1914 respectively in 11 cities with untreated water supplies. By contrast, typhoid death rates dropped from 90.5 in 1906 to 15.3 in 1914 in 16 cities with untreated water supplies in the former year and treatment in the latter year (Maxcy, 1941). The Mills–Reinke Theorem, postulated in 1910, held that, for every death from waterborne typhoid, there were several deaths from other diseases for which the causative agents were transmitted by water (Sedgewick and MacNutt, 1910).

The founders of sanitary engineering realized that the benefits of these advances could be enjoyed by everyone only if appropriate design rules and standards were developed for the guidance of engineers. In commenting on water quality standards in 1914, Alan Hazen reflected the comprehensive grasp that these pioneers had of the economic, engineering, and epidemiological factors that must underlie such design criteria:

> There is no final reason for such standards. They have been adopted by consent because they represent a purification that is reasonably satisfactory and that can be reached at a cost which is not burdensome to those who have to pay for it. . . . There is no evidence that the germs so left in water are in any way injurious.

This early period of modern sanitary engineering was thus one of dramatic advances. Indeed, by the early part of the twentieth century the scientific bases of all of the processes of conventional modern water treatment—coagulation, sedimentation, filtration, and disinfection—were understood, and technologies were developed for the practical application of these principles.

This success meant that the initial conceptual framework rapidly became outdated. It was modified in two fundamental ways. First, the study of the relationship between water and infectious diseases was no longer of much practical interest to design engineers, and, second, the achievement of anything but the complete elimination of bacteria from water became unsatisfactory. From its original broad conceptual framework sanitary engineering was thus rapidly reduced to the narrow technical dimensions characteristic of the ''mature'' profession. However, since the sanitary revolution was as much a social as a scientific revolution, this task was not simply a technical one, but was simultaneously an economic one, for water treatment had not only to be effective, but also to be sufficiently inexpensive so that high quality water could be supplied to and paid for by all urban residents in industrialized countries.

The effective and inexpensive preparation of water for disinfection has been the single most important water treatment challenge facing the mature sanitary engineering profession. Indeed, any textbook on water treatment is predominantly a book on water clarification; the bulk of the capital and operating expenses of a water treatment plant are those connected with clarification; and for a water treatment plant operator ''good'' water is equivalent to ''low turbidity'' water.

Simultaneously, developments were proceeding on the treatment of sewage. In the present context it is unnecessary to trace the history of this enterprise in similar detail. Suffice it to note that, as the conceptual framework of water treatment engineers was narrowed to concern with preparing water for disinfection, so the conceptual framework of sewage engineers was narrowed to the dominant concern of reduction of the Biochemical Oxygen Demand (BOD) of treated wastewater.

The ''mature'' conceptual model of the sanitary engineering profession thus represents a drastic simplification of the holistic perspective that characterized the original conceptual model. With this loss of holistic perspective, the discipline has undergone a process akin to the "involution" described by anthropologists in which human cultures, after developing a pattern for responding to an initial challenge, meet all new challenges by ever-increasing internal sophistication and differentiation rather than by developing creative new systemic responses (Geertz, 1966). In sanitary engineering the pre-World War I period was one of creative response and rapid fundamental progress, but in the subsequent 70 years there have been, in the words of the National Academy of Sciences (1977), "many refinements in engineering techniques but no basic changes in concepts of water and wastewater purification."

The objective of the application of scientific principles to any frequently encountered problem is the development of a set of simple "rules" that may be applied easily by someone with only a rudimentary understanding of the process by which the rules were developed. The degree to which such an objective has been achieved is a measure of the "maturity" of that particular application of scientific principles. Familiar examples in medicine would be the use of oral rehydration therapy for the treatment of diarrhea, or the use of penicillin for the treatment of pneumonia. In environmental engineering, such "maturity" was reached in the early part of this century with the development of simple design rules for deciding on the quality of water to be supplied and the price to be charged for it.

In the following paragraphs we outline what these water supply "design rules" are, how they were developed, and how their validity is dependent on the specific behavioral and epidemiological conditions prevailing in the industrialized countries.

In the design of a water supply system, the quantity, or "design flow," required by a population is simply determined by multiplying the population to be served by an "average per capita requirement" (in liters per capita per day) and multiplying this figure, in turn, by a factor that accounts for the fact that peak flows (which the system has to be able to provide) exceed the average quantity of water required. Once the capacity of the system is specified, the engineer is free to devote his attention to the detailed hydrologic and hydraulic design of the reservoirs, pipelines, and other components of the water supply system.

The second major system decision, the price to be charged for water, plays no part in determining the capacity. This is because the demand for water for domestic purposes in industrialized countries changes little as the price of water changes—in the economist's jargon, the demand for water is inelastic with respect to price (Howe and Linaweaver, 1967). Given this fact and the fact that utilities typically face no competition in providing water in a certain area, utilities could make enormous profits by setting prices very high. For this reason the prices that utilities can charge are usually regulated.

Finally, it should be noted that although public water supplies are considered a cornerstone to the maintenance of public health, consumers demand levels of service that far exceed those required for public health purposes, and thus the engineer and economist can make their decisions on capacity and price without concerning themselves with the epidemiological consequences of their decisions.

To the water supply engineer in an industrialized country these "golden rules" specifying the quantity of water to be supplied and the price to be charged for the water are entirely satisfactory. They have served the profession well for many years, and the engineer correctly feels little need or desire to explore their behavioral, epidemiological, or economic underpinnings. Indeed, paradoxically, the "maturity" of the science of water supply may be measured by the degree to which practitioners can remain ignorant of these underpinnings and yet continue to design (more or less) satisfactory systems.

Sanitary engineering in underdeveloped countries

What of the sanitary engineering response to the challenge of reducing water-related diseases through the provision of improved water supplies and sanitation facilities in underdeveloped countries?

First, consider the outlook inculcated during the training of the sanitary engineers who practice in these countries. Many of them are expatriates, recommending, where they are conscientious, "exactly what I would recommend for my own home city (in North America or Europe)." Where there are local sanitary engineers, they have virtually all been trained either in industrialized countries, or by teachers trained in industrialized countries. The textbooks used are those written for industrialized countries, the curricula are similar, and thus the conceptual framework drawn on in addressing the problems of underdeveloped countries is that of the "mature" sanitary engineering profession in industrialized countries.

Second, consider the challenge faced by sanitary engineers in underdeveloped countries. From a bacteriological point of view this challenge is different from that in an industrialized country not only because of the much lower proportion of the population served by adequate facilities, but also because a typical person in an underdeveloped country excretes many orders of magnitude more pathogenic organisms than a person in an industrialized country (Feachem et al., 1981). Economically, too, the situation is different. While paying off the capital cost of a multiple-tap piped water supply (typically about $700 per household) and a waterborne sewerage system (about $1200 per household) may not impose an intolerable burden in an industrialized country, the ability to pay is drastically different in an underdeveloped country, where annual household income often is less than $500. Finally, the demographic situation is different, since the underdeveloped world is still predominantly rural, while most people in industrialized countries live in towns and cities.

A hint of the inadequacy of the conventional sanitary engineering response to this challenge is evident in the fact that in the rural United States, where people are often poor by national standards but wealthy in international terms, many households—200,000 in North Carolina alone—have inadequate water supply and sanitation facilities, and outbreaks of waterborne diseases are not uncommon (National Demonstration Water Project, 1978; Craun and McCabe, 1973). In the underdeveloped countries conditions are a great deal worse, with water-related diseases endemic. WHO estimates that 23 percent of urban and 78 percent of rural inhabitants in the Third World do not have access to water supplies of adequate quality within easy walking distance, while far fewer have access to adequate sanitation facilities (McJunkin, 1983).

The anomalies arising from the application of the "mature" conceptual framework to this set of problems are numerous and can be illustrated by the following example. In Kenya, just 2 percent of the population are served by waterborne sewers (Mara, 1976). The majority of the wastewater treatment units are either trickling filter or activated sludge plants, that is, plants using a technology designed for use in industrialized countries. Few of these plants operate effectively. These simple facts notwithstanding, an enormous effort has gone into the drawing up of entirely unrealistic "master plans" for providing waterborne sewers and wastewater treatment plants to serve every urban inhabitant in Kenya.

It is thus no exaggeration to describe this situation as a crisis, since the contrast is so great between the magnitude and characteristics of the problem, on the one hand, and the conceptual models and tools available to address the problem, on the other hand.

The history of science shows that in impasses of this sort it is often from outsiders, and usually outsiders not deeply schooled in the techniques and ideologies of the "relevant" profession, that fundamentally new approaches may be expected.[1] It was thus surprising to engineers (but not to historians) that it was a biomedical scientist and not a sanitary engineer who stood back from the accepted "mature" sanitary engineering conceptual framework and asked, afresh, about the relationship between sanitary engineering and health in a rural Third World setting. As with many revelations of this sort, David J. Bradley's classification scheme, published first in 1968 (with Emurwon), at first appeared to simply systematize what was already widely known. In fact, however, Bradley's scheme for classifying water-related diseases raised questions that were quite different from those considered by the sanitary engineers who design water supply schemes in underdeveloped countries. In particular the classification scheme brought to the fore questions of behavior ("How does the quantity of water used vary as distance to the source increases?"; "How can people be induced to change the habit of bathing in schistosomiasis-infected streams?"); questions of economics ("What is the cost of achieving supplies of a given quality and quantity?"); and questions of epidemiology ("What are the effects of improving drinking water quality?"; "What are the health effects of increasing the quantity of water used for domestic purposes?"). While questions of technology ("What are appropriate supply and treatment technologies under Third World conditions?'') were by no means dismissed as unimportant, the classification scheme showed that the "new sanitary engineering" had to draw on four conceptual bases—behavioral sciences, economics, epidemiology and technology— rather than on the one—technology—on which the "mature" profession of sanitary engineering had come to rely.

Bradley's scheme has become familiar to most engineers working in underdeveloped countries and has already had an impact on the design of water supply schemes in these countries. As this paper will show, however, it still remains unclear exactly how to translate the concepts embodied in the classification system into practical design rules.

The conventional design procedure in underdeveloped countries

As indicated earlier, in industrialized countries it is possible to consider the fundamental engineering decision (viz., the capacity of the system) and the fundamental economic decision (viz., the price to be charged for the water) independently, and it is possible to ignore health considerations. In underdeveloped countries the situation is different.

First, because of the economic realities of these countries, the level of service, which is not a decision variable in industrialized countries, becomes a critical decision variable. In particular, the distance between the home and the point to which water is delivered both determines the monetary cost (and thus the price) of the supply, and affects, over a certain range at least, the quantity of water that will be used. Furthermore, the quantities of water used are such that there are generally increased health benefits to be reaped if increased quantities of water are used for domestic purposes. It is thus evident that in underdeveloped countries the engineering and economic decisions relating to water supplies and the health aspects have to be considered jointly. For instance, the price levied for water will affect the demand for water (and thus the capacity that the engineer should design for) as well as the health of the people because price will affect both choice of source (and thus choice of water quality) and the quantity of water used in the home.

The convention in designing a rural water supply scheme in an underdeveloped country, however, is to follow precisely the procedure developed for use in industrialized countries, ignoring these major systemic differences. Thus, for instance, the engineer just assumes some arbitrary figure to be the "requirement" for water. (WHO recommends 30 liters per capita per day as the minimum, while others have recommended 50 liters per capita per day; McJunkin, 1983.) No account is taken of the fact that demand may not reach, or alternatively may exceed, this "requirement," and no systematic account is taken of the fact that by increasing the quantity of water that will be used, health may be improved.

Incorporating household behavior into the design process

Data from around the world suggest that the quantities of water used for domestic purposes vary considerably from culture to culture and from group to group within any particular society. Furthermore, field studies in rural Africa suggest that the demand for water is inelastic with respect to distance over a certain range, but elastic when the distance is greater than about 1 kilometer (White et al., 1972; Feachem et al., 1978).

It is thus incorrect to assume, in any particular setting, that there is a "standard requirement" for water. The critical policy question, however, is not whether the conventional procedure is correct or not, but whether the cost of being incorrect is sufficiently great to justify the collection and analysis of additional data and the modification of conventional design procedures.

To indicate how one might go about specifying this cost of using incorrect demand information, consider the following simple didactic model for the design of a rural water supply project.

The objective of the rural water supply project is to maximize health benefits. It is assumed that there is a monotonic relationship between health benefits and the quantity of water used by the population for domestic purposes, a reasonable assumption in many rural communities (White et al., 1972). A limited sum of money is available for constructing the project. The source works are already in existence, and the source is capable of providing more water than can be used by the community to be served.

The dilemma faced by the engineer is that there is a direct trade-off between the design capacity of the system and the distance at which water can be supplied. That is, if the engineer chooses to build a system that is capable of supplying large quantities of water, the standposts are going to be far from the homes of the villagers, while if he chooses to build a system that delivers less water, the water can be provided closer to the home.

The problem can be formulated in a mathematical model:[2]

Objective: Maximize Q
Subject to:

> (1) behavior constraint: $Q = \alpha_1 S^{\beta_1}$; and
> (2) budget constraint: $K \geq \alpha_2 S^{\beta_2} Q^{\beta_3}$

where

> Q = total consumption of water,
> S = distance from household to standpost,
> K = available resources,

and the αs and βs are parameters estimated from field data.

If complete and precise information is available on both behavioral and cost relationships, the "optimal" values of the design parameters can be calculated and two different types of "sensitivity analyses" carried out. First, the effect of including behavioral information in the design procedure can be assessed by calculating the quantity of water actually used when the design procedure takes account of the information on the relationship between distance and demand for water, and comparing this quantity with the quantity of water used when the conventional method is applied. Second, assuming that detailed demand information is to be incorporated into the design process, the model can be used to determine the sensitivity of the quantity of water actually used to errors in the parameters of the behavioral and cost relationships. In this way, information is gleaned on the value of collecting additional data on each of the parameters. Where the output is insensitive to a particular parameter, a coarse estimate of that parameter will suffice; where particularly sensitive parameters are identified, subsequent research efforts and data collection exercises should concentrate on obtaining precise estimates of these particular parameters.

For a range of "standard water requirements" (all of which have been advocated in the technical literature) the inefficiencies due to neglect of the actual demand information are presented in Table 1. The usefulness of collecting detailed demand data and incorporating these into the design process obviously cannot be assessed definitively with so simple a model. Nevertheless, the model suggests that incorporating such demand information leads to substantially higher estimates of the quantities of water used by the population than if such data are ignored. That is, the model suggests that the validity of design decisions is seriously impaired by the conventional practice of ignoring the elasticity of demand with respect to distance.

TABLE 1 The effect of simple demand assumptions on water use

	Optimal design	Assumed requirement[a]		
		15	30	50
Distance to standpost	1,430	1,170	2,680	4,950
Liters of water used per capita per day	17.9	15.0	14.8	12.3
Percent reduction in consumption due to inefficient design	0	16	17	31

[a] Liters per capita per day.

Assuming that demand information is to be incorporated into the design procedure, the question arises as to the amount of effort that should be expended on estimating the parameters of the behavior and cost functions. To answer this question, the second sensitivity analysis is carried out as follows.

The value of more precise information on any particular parameter, say

β_1, may be determined by comparing the quantity of water that will be consumed when the system is designed using the true value of β_1 with the quantity of water that will be consumed when the system is designed using an estimated value of β_1, namely, $\hat{\beta}_1$. That is:

$$\text{Loss of efficiency} = \frac{Q(\beta_1) - Q(\hat{\beta}_1)}{Q(\beta_1)}$$

In Table 2 the inefficiencies due to 10 percent over- and underestimates of each parameter value are presented.[3] As before, no definitive conclusions on the relative importance of information on the different parameters can be drawn from so simple a model. Nevertheless, it appears that the inefficiencies due to errors in estimates of some behavioral and cost parameters can be serious, and, second, precise estimates of the parameters in the exponents of the behavioral and economic functions (i.e., the βs) appear to be more important than precise estimates of the scaling parameters (i.e., the αs). Since engineers have devoted a great deal of attention to the estimate of cost functions, the errors in the cost parameters are likely to be relatively small. The errors in the behavioral parameters, however, are likely to be much larger and much more serious.

TABLE 2   Reduction in quantity of water actually used due to errors in parameter estimates

Parameter	Percent reduction if parameter value is	
	Underestimated by 10 percent	Overestimated by 10 percent
Behavioral		
α_1	8	3
β_1	6	14
Cost		
α_2	2	4
β_2	16	6
β_3	9	22

This example has several implications. First, the model strongly suggests that the validity of decisions made in designing rural water supply projects is seriously affected by the conventional engineering approach toward estimating required system capacity. Specifically, the model suggests that "standard water requirements" should not be used in designing these systems, but that detailed information should be collected on the effect of distance on demand and such information incorporated into the design procedure.

Second, the model indicates that the inefficiencies resulting from errors in the parameter estimates can be substantial, implying that detailed data should be collected on actual water demand functions in any specific area in which a water supply program is planned. The cost of such data collection is not likely to be great, while the benefits of incorporating such information into the design procedure appear to be substantial.

Incorporating epidemiological considerations into the design procedure

Bradley's classification scheme, by directing attention to the relationship between quantity of water used and health, demanded that health considerations be restored to a central role in the design process. Over the past ten years some attention has been given to ways of doing this. The emphasis has been on trying to define "threshold values" beyond which further increases in the quantity of water used have little impact on health, and in using such values to define "targets" for water use.

Several problems have arisen in the course of this work. Different analysts have arrived at quite different target requirements, varying from 15 liters per capita per day (lcd), to 20–30 lcd, to 50 and even 60 lcd (Cuny, 1983; Hughes, 1983; McJunkin, 1983; Bannaga et al., 1978, respectively).

There are serious problems, moreover, not just with the definition of a "magic number," but with the behavioral, epidemiological, and decision-making assumptions implicit in such efforts. Because of the great importance of finding ways of translating this epidemiological knowledge into practical and appropriate guidelines for the design of water supply systems, these problems and some tentative steps toward solving them are outlined.

First, the behavioral problem. As indicated earlier, it is insufficient to simply specify that the capacity of a system should be such that the population served can draw a "target" amount of water from the system each day, even if that target is based on sound epidemiological data. It is essential that the determinants of water usage by any particular population be understood, and that such knowledge be used in designing the water supply system.

Second, the epidemiological problem. The most obvious difficulty with operationalizing the water quantity–health concept in any particular area is that it is prohibitively expensive and difficult to carry out the required epidemiological studies in every such area. For this reason there have been attempts to define, using existing epidemiological studies, "target" water use figures at which water-washed diseases (i.e., those diseases the prevalence of which is affected by the quantity of water used for personal hygiene) are greatly reduced. Yet, of all of the epidemiological studies on this issue, not one has collected data on the quantities of water used for personal hygiene, the explanatory variable in Bradley's scheme. Rather, surrogates have been used—most commonly, distance to the water source and total quantity of water used for domestic purposes. This use of surrogates without validation of the relationship between the surrogate and the explanatory variable may well account for the large variation observed in the overall levels of water usage necessary to reduce the incidence of water-washed diseases. Because water-use habits are an integral part of an overall pattern of culture, the quantity of water used for hygienic purposes by, for example, a family that uses 15 lcd in the New Guinea Highlands may be quite different from the quantity of water used for hygienic purposes by a Bengali family that uses the same overall amount of water.

Third, there are decision-theoretic problems with the present method of incorporating epidemiological considerations into the procedures for allocating resources in the water sector. As indicated earlier, the consensus of analysts interested in this problem is that water supplies should be designed to provide water to a threshold level beyond which there are no further reductions in water-washed diseases. Indeed it has been argued that it may be better to supply fewer people at the threshold level than to spread resources around so that more people can be supplied at a lower level (Shuval et al., 1981). This decision-making process is examined using Figure 1, which shows the hypothetical relationship between investment in water supply and health benefits.

FIGURE 1

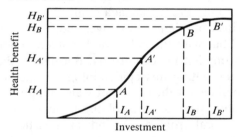

A quantity of money is available either to improve the water supply to a community from level A to level A', or to ensure that a second community's supply is improved from level B to the "threshold level," B'. The proponents of the threshold theory would argue that the effectiveness of the investment, measured in health terms, would be maximized by ensuring that community B was moved to the threshold level. Given the relationships shown in Figure 1, this would be an incorrect decision, since $(H_{A'} - H_A) > (H_{B'} - H_B)$. In more general terms this example suggests that the whole notion that supplies must be built so that at least the threshold level of supply is available to the communities served is incorrect, and that the correct decision rule is rather the economist's rule, namely of targeting investments to those communities where the marginal benefit of the investment is greatest.

The fact of the matter, then, is that while most water supply planners in underdeveloped countries recognize the desirability of including epidemiological factors into the resource allocation and design procedures, in the absence of sound practical methods for doing so, these considerations are largely ignored in practice. In light of these many difficulties is there any way to transform the conceptual framework implicit in the above discussion into a set of practical procedures to be used by planners and designers?

One procedure might be to develop detailed information on the effect of investments in water supply programs on health in each of the potential project areas. However, there are serious methodological difficulties with such an approach (Briscoe, 1984). Measurement of the direct effect of the investment ignores the degree to which the investment affects the health impact of subsequent, complementary programs. Furthermore, the scale and complexity of the required field studies make this option impractical.

A feasible alternative is to try to operationalize Bradley's explanatory variable, "the quantity of water used for hygienic purposes." It is more difficult to measure this disaggregated variable than to measure the total quantity of water used for domestic purposes. Upon closer examination, however, this does not appear to be an insuperable difficulty, and the following is proposed as a first step in developing a practical operational procedure.

In any area in which water supply programs are being considered, two baseline behavioral studies would be carried out. First, the relationship between the quantity of water used for hygienic purposes and the total quantity of water used for domestic purposes would be specified (as in Panel 1 of Figure 2). Second, the relationship between distance to the source and the total quantity of water used would be specified (Panel 2). Using the infor-

FIGURE 2 Conceptual model for measurement of investment decisions related to water supply programs

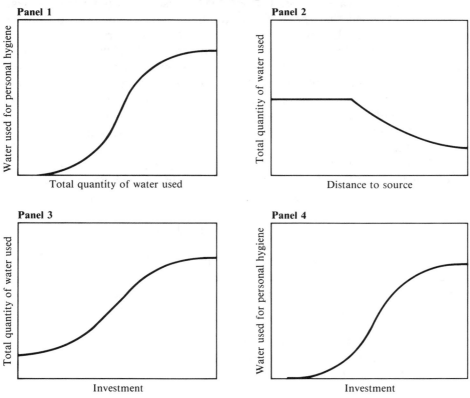

mation in Panel 2, the engineer would determine the relationship between the level of investment and the total quantity of water used (as in Panel 3). Then, combining the information of Panels 1 and 3, the engineer would develop a curve relating the quantity of water used for personal hygiene to the level of investment (as in Panel 4). Then, rather than trying to compare investment opportunities by comparing the marginal effect of investments on health, the marginal effect of investments on the quantity of water used for hygienic purposes may be used.

The use of this surrogate appears to be defensible on both theoretical and practical grounds, and the procedure outlined would appear to represent a reasonable first step in incorporating epidemiological considerations into the planning and design of water supply projects in underdeveloped countries. In the medium and long run, of course, it is essential that the validity of the choice and use of this surrogate be tested in several settings and that the necessary procedural adjustments be made as the findings of such research become available.

Conclusions

This paper illustrates some generic concerns with the conceptual frameworks used in research on child survival by examining these concerns in a specific sector, namely the water sector. This analysis is based on two major premises. First, it is assumed that the water sector has a significant role to play in reducing child and other mortality in underdeveloped countries. Second, it is assumed that this role can be carried out efficiently only if the resource allocation and design procedures used in underdeveloped countries are based on an assessment of the problems faced in these countries, and not by adopting willy-nilly the procedures developed to deal with sanitary engineering problems in the quite different setting of the industrialized countries.

A striking general conclusion from the analysis presented in this paper is that, if the effectiveness of water supplies in enhancing health in underdeveloped countries is to be maximized, the priority area of research is the development of methods for collecting and analyzing data on water-use behavior and on methods for incorporating this information into planning and design procedures.

This research must necessarily be carried out by an interdisciplinary team. Anthropologists, social psychologists, and other behavioral scientists will play an important role in identifying the factors that affect water-related behavior. Economists will play a central role, for the major objective of the research would be to collect data on behavior and to deduce, from these data, the effect of each factor that affects choice. Sanitary engineers, too, would play a central role, since the ultimate product of such research must be a set of planning and design procedures that will be implemented primarily by these professionals, who have traditionally been encharged with these tasks. And, finally, health educators would play a central role given their task of developing the "software" components of water supply projects.

Although the analysis in this paper has focused on the need to expand the conceptual framework used by sanitary engineers, similar analyses could be undertaken for many other areas that are likely to play a role in increasing child survival in developing countries. In developing expanded immunization programs, for instance, the critical constraints are not strictly problems of medical technology but are those that deal with the effectiveness of the delivery systems and the utilization of the available services by the population (Foster, 1984). In sum, as stated by Tekçe and Shorter (1984), a critical task in formulating effective strategies for improving child survival in developing countries is "to recapture and reformulate the early concerns with the social aspects of health and disease" in light of the conditions prevailing in the developing countries of today.

Notes

1 An outstanding example of this occurrence is Darwin, a man who had no more than a rudimentary understanding of physical and chemical principles but who was, nevertheless, able to produce a new and higher level of understanding of material phenomena. This understanding had eluded those much better schooled than he in the physical and chemical principles that biology both incorporated and transcended.

2 Solution of the model: Since both constraints will be binding, the optimization problem can be solved using Lagrange's method, i.e.,

$$L(Q,S,\lambda_1,\lambda_2) = Q + \lambda_1(Q - \alpha_1 S^{\beta_1}) + \lambda_2(K - \alpha_2 S^{\beta_2} Q^{\beta_3})$$

and

$$\frac{\partial L}{\partial Q} = 1 + \lambda_1 - \beta_3 \lambda_2 \alpha_2 S^{\beta_2} Q^{\beta_3 - 1} = 0$$

$$\frac{\partial L}{\partial S} = -\beta_1 \lambda_1 \alpha_1 S^{\beta_1 - 1} - \beta_2 \lambda_2 \alpha_2 S^{\beta_2 - 1} Q^{\beta_3} = 0$$

$$\frac{\partial L}{\partial \lambda_1} = Q - \alpha_1 S^{\beta_1} = 0$$

$$\frac{\partial L}{\partial \lambda_2} = K - \alpha_2 S^{\beta_2} Q^{\beta_3} = 0$$

Solving the 4 simultaneous equations in 4 unknowns, the optimal values of the design variables are found to be:

$$S^* = \left(\frac{K}{\alpha_1^{\beta_3} \alpha_2}\right)^{\frac{1}{\beta_2 + \beta_1 \beta_3}}$$

and

$$Q^* = \alpha_1 \left(\frac{K}{\alpha_1^{\beta_3} \alpha_2}\right)^{\frac{\beta_1}{\beta_2 + \beta_1 \beta_3}}$$

It is assumed that the supply will serve 1000 people, that $15,000 is available for the project, and that the parameter values are

$$\alpha_1 = 158 \times 10^3$$
$$\beta_1 = -0.30$$
$$\alpha_2 = 1600$$
$$\beta_2 = -0.5$$
$$\beta_3 = 0.6$$

For these values, $S^* = 1430$ meters and $Q^* = 17,900$ liters/day $= 17.9$ lcd

Some typical values for calibrating the mathematical model are:

Behavior Empirical data from East Africa (White et al., 1972) suggest that the effect of distance on water use is of the form shown in Figure 2. It is assumed that for the 1000 people: $Q = 20 \times 10^3$ l/d for $S \leq 1000$ m and $Q = 158 \times 10^3 S^{-0.3}$ l/d for $S > 1000$ m (whence $Q = 10 \times 10^3$ l/d at $S = 10,000$ m).

Costs (a) The effect of scale: For water distribution systems a typical scaling factor is $\beta_3 = 0.6$ (Thomas, 1971). (b) The effect of density of standposts: Under a set of simplifying assumptions it can be shown that a reasonable value for $\beta_2 = -0.5$, which implies that, for a given supply, as the average distance to a standpost is halved the cost of the distribution network increases by 41 percent.

Average cost A representative cost for a rural water supply delivering 20 lcd is $20 per capita (Saunders and Warford, 1976). Calibrating the cost equation thus yields a value of $\alpha_2 = 1600$.

3 Procedure for determining the cost of incorrect parameter estimates:

(a) Using the incorrect value of the estimated parameter and the correct values of all other parameters, values of S_{design} and Q_{design} are estimated from:

$$S_{design} = \left(\frac{K}{\alpha_1{}^{\beta_3}\alpha_2} \right)^{\frac{1}{\beta_2 + \beta_1\beta_3}}$$

and

$$Q_{design} = \alpha_1 S^{\beta_1}$$

These are the design parameters on which the system design is based.

(b) When the system is actually constructed, however, it is found that after the system of capacity Q_{design} is laid to S_{actual} the funds are exhausted, where

$$S_{actual} = \left(\frac{K}{\alpha_2 \hat{Q}^{\beta_3}} \right)^{\frac{1}{\beta_2}}$$

calculated with the true parameter values.

(c) At this actual distance, S_{actual}, the demand for water will be

$$Q_{demand} = \alpha_1 S_{actual}^{\beta_1}$$

calculated with the true parameter values.

(d) The amount of water actually used will be the lesser of the design flow (Q_{design}) and the demand (Q_{demand}).

References

Ackerknecht, E. H. 1953. *Rudolf Virchow*. Madison: University of Wisconsin Press.

Bannaga, S. E. I., and J. Pickford. 1978. "Water-health relationships in Sudan," *Effluent and Water Treatment Journal* 18: 559–569.

Bradley, D. J., and P. Emurwon. 1968. "Predicting the epidemiological effects of changing water sources," *East African Medical Journal* 45: 284–291.

Briscoe, J. 1984. "Intervention studies and the definition of dominant transmission routes," *American Journal of Epidemiology* (in press).

Chadwick, E. H. 1982. *Report of the Sanitary Condition of the Labouring Population of Great Britain,* 1965 edition. Edinburgh: Edinburgh University Press.

Craun, G. F., and L. J. McCabe. 1973. "Review of the causes of water-borne disease outbreaks," *Journal of the American Water Works Association* 65: 74.

Cuny, F. C. 1983. "Development of water supply standards for refugee camps." Dallas: Intertect.

Engels, F. 1845. *The Condition of the Working Class in England in 1844*. Palo Alto: Stanford University Press.

Feachem, R. G., E. Burns, S. Cairncross, A. Cronin, P. Cross, D. Curtis, M. K. Khan, D. Lamb, and H. Southall. 1978. *Water, Health and Development: An Interdisciplinary Evaluation*. London: Tri-Med.

———, D. J. Bradley, H. Garelick, and D. Mara. 1981. *Health Aspects of Excreta and Sullage Management—A State of the Art Review,* No. 3 in series on Appropriate Technology for Water Supply and Sanitation. Washington, D.C.: World Bank.

Foster, S. O. 1984. "Immunizable and respiratory diseases and child mortality," in this volume.

Geertz, G. C. 1966. *Agricultural Involution: The Process of Ecological Change in Indonesia*. Berkeley: University of California Press.

Hazen, A. 1914. *Clean Water and How to Get It,* 2nd ed. New York: Wiley.

Howe, C. W., and F. P. Linaweaver, Jr. 1967. ''The impact of price on residential water demand and its relation to system design and price structure,'' *Water Resources Research* 3, no. 1: 13–32.

Hughes, J. M. 1983. ''Potential impacts of improved water supply and excreta disposal on diarrheal disease morbidity: An assessment based on a review of published studies,'' draft manuscript for publication. Atlanta: Centers for Disease Control.

Koch, R. 1894. *Professor Koch on the Bacteriological Diagnosis of Cholera, Water Filtration and Cholera, and the Cholera in Germany during the Winter of 1892–3.* Edinburgh: David Douglas, Publisher.

McJunkin, F. E. 1983. *Water and Human Health,* 2nd ed. Washington, D.C.: National Demonstration Water Project.

McKeown, T., R. G. Brown, and R. G. Record. 1972. ''An interpretation of the modern rise of population in Europe,'' *Population Studies* 26, no. 3: 345–382.

Mara, D. D. 1976. *Sewage Treatment in Hot Climates.* New York: Wiley.

Maxcy, K. F., ed. 1941. *Papers of Wade Hampton Frost, M.D., A Contribution to Epidemiological Methods.* New York: Commonwealth Fund.

National Academy of Sciences. 1977. *Drinking Water and Health,* Vol. I. Washington, D.C.: National Academy of Sciences.

National Demonstration Water Project. 1978. *Drinking Water Supplies in Rural America.* Washington, D.C.: National Demonstration Water Project.

Saunders, R. J., and J. J. Warford. 1976. *Village Water Supply: Economics and Policy in the Developing World.* Washington, D.C. and Baltimore: World Bank and Johns Hopkins University.

Sedgewick, W. T., and J. S. MacNutt. 1910. ''On the Mills-Reinke Phenomenon and Hazen's Theorem concerning the decrease in mortality from diseases other than typhoid fever following the quantification of public water supplies,'' *Journal of Infectious Diseases* 7, no. 4: 489–564.

Shuval, H. I., R. L. Tilden, B. H. Perry, and R. N. Grosse. 1981. ''Effect of investments in water supply and sanitation on health status: A threshold-saturation theory,'' *Bulletin of the World Health Organization* 59, no. 2: 243–248.

Snow, J. 1854. *On the Mode of Communication of Cholera,* ''Second edition, much enlarged.'' London: Churchill. Reprinted by the Commonwealth Fund, New York, 1936.

Tekçe, B., and F. C. Shorter. 1984. ''Determinants of child mortality: A study of squatter settlements in Jordan,'' in this volume.

Thomas, H. A., Jr. 1971. ''Sensitivity analysis of design parameters of water resource systems.'' Cambridge, Mass.: Division of Applied Sciences, Harvard University.

White, G. F., D. J. Bradley, and A. U. White. 1972. *Drawers of Water, Domestic Water Use in Africa.* Chicago: University of Chicago.

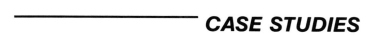 **CASE STUDIES**

Determinants of Child Mortality: A Study of Squatter Settlements in Jordan

Belgin Tekçe

Frederic C. Shorter

The Amman study was born of two overlapping interests. One was to investigate the determinants of child health and mortality; the other, to assess the potential for health benefits of an urban upgrading project in Jordan.[1] While each of these goals has its own complexity in terms of conceptualization and research strategy, the association is not fortuitous. Their conjunction is a somewhat ambitious attempt to reestablish the link between health and urban planning that prevailed in the nineteenth century. To a considerable extent the history of public health legislation and services is also the history of modern urban planning; both originated in efforts to meet serious problems of survival created by the growth of industrial cities (Benevolo, 1971; DuBos, 1979).

In order to create a new unified approach to the problems generated by institutions and conditions of today's cities, two important tasks need to be undertaken. One is to recapture and reformulate the early concerns with the social aspects of health and disease. The idea of a social etiology of disease and death needs to be made the subject of systematic thinking and empirical investigation. The objective is to formulate, with greater precision and clarity, the social determinants of health and mortality in the light of progress made in understanding the biological mechanisms of disease causation. Second, the health consequences of social policy, particularly those that follow from the major modes of urban planning, need to become an integral part of problem definition and evaluation. The monopoly of financial and physical criteria over the process of urban development planning may be eroded usefully by making concerns with health an explicit component of such planning. The second task presumes that some progress is made in conceptualizing the processes that determine health.

This presentation discusses one particular conceptualization of the social determinants of health and mortality, and reports findings from its application in a particular setting.

The Amman upgrading project

The East Bank of Jordan had a population of approximately 2.15 million in 1979.[2] Two-thirds of the inhabitants live in urban areas, and over three-quarters of all city dwellers live in the capital city of Amman. The census enumerated a population in the conurbation of Amman of 1,084,940.[3]

Amman is a city stacked in two-storied profusion up and down several hills, sprawling into the plain and desert fringes surrounding the center. Until 1948, it was a small city serving as a trading center for the farmlands of the plateau and was the governmental seat for the Kingdom of Jordan. Beginning in 1948 each of the Arab–Israeli wars was followed by large influxes of refugees and displaced persons into Amman. These surges of population increase were compounded by high fertility in the urban population. Meanwhile, Amman has also attracted commercial and service activities that serve the whole region. Today it is a dynamic, rapidly expanding economic center.

The setting of the Amman upgrading project is five squatter settlements that lie along the fringe of the urban zone that existed in 1948. As a result of urban sprawl, the squatter areas are located well within the central urban area of the Amman municipality. The areas are defined as squatter settlements because an overwhelming proportion of households, 98 percent, have no legally recognized property right to the land they live on. At the time of the study, winter 1980–81, almost all of the land was privately owned by a few persons. Only some small sections were public land belonging to the municipality.

The upgrading project is concerned primarily with legalization of tenure and physical improvements, but also includes action in a number of areas of social and economic development. Specifically, upgrading inputs include physical infrastructure in the form of water, sewerage, electricity, footpaths, and community buildings for various functions (e.g., small shops to be rented out). The plans also include long-term financing for land-tenure acquisition, dwelling improvement loans, construction of perimeter walls for each plot, and provision of standard sanitary cores (flush toilet and piped water with sewage connection).

The project implementation agency is the Urban Development Department (UDD), established in late 1980 and responsible to the Municipality of Amman. The particular upgrading project discussed here was planned to benefit approximately 1,660 households in five squatter settlements. The UDD is responsible for other projects as well, and has considerable independence in plan preparation, implementation, and disbursal of funds.

Urban projects need a sound data base to assist decision-making and as a benchmark to assess effects following implementation. It was recognized at the outset that information would have to be collected by a survey to make detailed physical plans for the project and to gauge the capacity of the beneficiaries to contribute to the costs. To prepare for the tenure regularization process, every family had to be registered. Such inquiries are generally recognized as a routine part of urban project implementation. The decision by the UDD to expand the scope of inquiry to include information on the health status and population structure of the upgrading areas is the unique aspect of the Amman project. It is useful to discuss briefly the reasoning underlying this decision.

Urban development and health

The general question is whether the health of poor urban dwellers is improved by projects to upgrade housing quality and associated infrastructure. The question is not usually asked explicitly in urban project planning because the answer is assumed to be positive. Decisions to invest in physical redevelopment projects typically depend upon financial feasibility. If the community is willing to summon the resources, their commitment is taken as proof that the residents expect value in return. In advance of project investments, studies usually focus, therefore, on prospective affordability and cost recovery.

The market test of success, while necessary, is not sufficient to demonstrate that the maximal effectiveness of investment has been realized. The degree and level of satisfaction remain unmeasured. Reliance on the test of affordability also tends to mask the existence of alternatives. An additional and important test of success is how much better people's lives are made by the investment of resources. Among the benefits, a principal one that would make people willing to bear the costs is health.

The present study looks into that prospect in the particular setting of the squatter settlements. It was carried out with two basic objectives: first, to provide a baseline assessment of health conditions; and second, to define how existing living conditions and family behavior operate as determinants of child health and mortality. The first objective provides a point of reference for assessing the magnitude of improvement in health conditions that may follow the upgrading activities, while the latter objective permits the explanation or interpretation of why improvements in child health and survival have, or have not, occurred as a result of specific project activities. More importantly, we anticipated that the identification of major social and economic determinants of health, as well as investigation of how these are related to family behavior and its biological implications for health, would lead to formulation of more effective health and urban planning strategies.

Demonstration of health benefits in a specific project setting could be a powerful argument for communities and their financial supporters to proceed with upgrading projects in general. Choices within particular plans also could be made in a more informed manner, balancing one type of investment against another. For the UDD and for health policy planners, it would be of interest to show that specific institutional and physical interventions can improve health. If demonstrated, appropriate community upgrading would be seen as a health intervention additional to (some would say alternative to) more conventional health care interventions based on medical technology.

To answer the general question, the process that determines the health status of a community must be understood generally, but also reduced to relatively simple statements of cause and effect so that statistical description and partitioning of the role of different variables is feasible. This paper sets forth a general framework, and then selects specific relationships that are believed to be causally important and suitable for statistical description. The study makes simultaneous use of variables that measure household-level socioeconomic conditions, family behavior, disease and nutritional factors, and their outcomes in terms of health status and mortality.[4]

Conceptual framework

The focus of the health study is on infants and young children up to the age of 3 years. While many reasons can be given for directing attention to this group, the primary one is that it is by far the most vulnerable to adverse health risks within the immediate family and community environment. It is also a large group in any high fertility population. Differentials and changes over time in the health status of children correlate with the overall health conditions and mortality rates of populations as a whole, even though the processes of disease and morbidity differ importantly by age.

The ability to survive the first few years of life and the quality of that survival is a function of many environmental and social stresses that impinge upon the individual child beginning during pregnancy and continuing through infancy and childhood. The complexity of this process may be simplified conceptually by formulating a general framework that identifies and orders its determinants in terms of their causal proximity to the biological outcomes of disease and death.[5]

The framework is based on the premise that the social conditions of life are major determinants of child survival, and that these determinants make their impact through a set of intermediate mechanisms that can be decomposed analytically. Within this multilayered framework, disease and death are direct consequences of a set of factors originating in the social conditions of life and behavior of families.

The present analysis examines the relationship of determinants at different levels of proximity to health outcomes and mortality in three steps: first, following the traditional way of identifying and estimating the socioeconomic determinants of mortality, the statistical relationships are described without indicating how the intermediate mechanisms are involved. Then the direct relationship of socioeconomic determinants to the intermediate mechanisms is considered. Finally, a simple demonstration is given to show the linkage between health outcomes of the intermediate process and levels of child mortality.

Socioeconomic determinants

For multivariate analysis of the determinants of child mortality, diversity in the study population is necessary. An idea of the range of variability between settlement areas on a few key aspects of life is given in Table 1. In the analysis below, variation among households is studied without regard to areal location, and variation at the household level is, of course, much greater. Four factors were selected from the socioeconomic layer of determinants: mother's education, quality of housing, household income, and occupation of head of household. Sex of child was included as an additional factor at this level, as explained later.

TABLE 1 Selected characteristics of the five areas prior to tenure regularization

	East Wahdat	Jofeh	Wadi Er Rimam	Wadi Haddadah	Nuzha	All
History of settlement						
Year begun	1967	1948	1948	1948	1955	
Years that current heads have lived here (mean)	9	18	17	15	12	14
Origin of current heads (percent of all heads)						
Amman and East Bank	56	27	49	50	64	49
Palestine	43	70	47	45	31	47
Other	1	3	4	5	5	3
Demographic						
Households registered	390	335	387	224	330	1,666
Population living at home	2,712	2,337	2,599	1,485	2,101	11,234
Children under age 3	328	237	295	153	256	1,269
Total fertility per woman	—	—	—	—	—	7.4
Life expectation at birth (years)	—	—	—	—	—	60.5
Crude birth rate (per 1,000)	—	—	—	—	—	38.4
Crude death rate (per 1,000)	—	—	—	—	—	9.2
Tenure of households						
Land owned and registered (percent)	0	2	0	13	0	2
Dwelling "owned" (percent)	90	94	68	79	63	79
Housing (in percent of households)						
Walls of cement or concrete	34	80	87	96	98	77
Roofs of cement or concrete	2	54	81	39	95	54
Sewer connection	1	4	1	20	6	5
Watermain connection	1	44	77	61	74	50
Electricity connection (own or via neighbor)	3	92	97	98	99	75
Residential density						
Persons per household	7.1	7.0	6.7	6.6	6.4	6.7
Persons per room[a]	4.7	4.2	4.2	4.2	3.6	4.2

— = Data insufficient to make separate area estimates.
[a] Excludes kitchen, toilet, and rooms shared with other households, if any.
SOURCE: 100 percent survey of households.

The resources of the mother influence greatly the quality of care the child receives from conception through the early years of life. Ranging from biological assets such as physical stature to social assets such as education, these resources represent also an important dimension of intergenerational transfers in health. Education of the mother is used in this study as a measure of the mother's resources for nurturing her children.

Investigations in many countries have consistently shown a strong inverse relationship between mother's education and child mortality (Behm, 1979; Caldwell, 1979; Caldwell and McDonald, 1981). Mother's education has been found to be important in its own right and not merely a reflection of the living standards of the family. The explanation of its major role relates to the skills and knowledge that a more educated woman may have about appropriate measures for prevention and treatment of diseases; it also reflects a change in her status in the family and in the community that permits her to act more effectively on that knowledge.

It is also known that short birth intervals contribute to higher child survival risks due both to biological disadvantages of maternal depletion (low birth weight) and to between-child competition for care (Mata, 1983; WFS, 1983). Since mother's education typically encourages longer birth intervals, it may produce better child survival by this route as well.

For mother's education, a dichotomy between literate and illiterate was adopted. Overall, 49 percent of the mothers under age 50 in this population are literate. Female education has been changing rapidly in Jordan in the past two decades, so that younger women are far better educated than older ones: 89 percent of females in the age range 15–30 are literate, compared with 31 percent among those aged 30–50.

Housing is typically the family's single most important capital asset, usually owned though in some instances rented (Table 1). Housing is defined as the dwelling unit and associated physical infrastructure. The quality of the immediate physical environment strongly influences the child's risk of exposure to infectious diseases and to injury (Moore et al., 1965; Puffer and Serrano, 1973). In assessing the factors associated with these risks, it is useful to distinguish between standards of personal hygiene and standards of physical environment in the home. The higher the quality of the physical environment, the smaller the burden of daily cooperation of individual household members to minimize the risks of exposure.

The quality of housing is defined by stratifying households into three classes on the basis of materials used in roof and wall construction: first class consists of houses with both walls and roofs of cement (or concrete); second class houses have cement walls but other kinds of roofing, mostly corrugated iron sheets finished with zinc; and third class dwellings are constructed of less permanent materials such as zinc sheets, tin, mud, and canvas tenting for both the walls and the roof (Table 1). While this is a relatively simple categorization, it largely captures differences in physical shelter, infrastructure, and specialization in use of living space that are associated with housing quality. For example, 75 percent of first class houses have watermain connections, while only 9 percent of third class houses have them. All but 2 percent of first class houses have sanitary facilities (pit latrines and sewerage connections), whereas 21 percent of third class houses lack these arrangements.

Household income is a measure of the current flow of economic resources to the family. It indicates the family's capacity to purchase health through market inputs such as food, medical services, and household amenities. Household income was measured by a set of questions on income from earnings, rent, and remittances that were then summed up. Actual levels of income were probably underreported, particularly nonearned income. In our analysis, the relative position of households with respect to income was used by grouping them into two categories of above and below the median.

Occupation of the head of household is a measure of the work status and environment of the head. These factors may affect organization of home life and resourcefulness of the household to obtain better health care. Information on occupation was collected in great detail in the Amman survey to evaluate financial strength of households, and as a clue to their capacity to carry responsibility for home improvement activities. In the present analysis, occupation of the household head, usually a male, was categorized into three broad groups: white collar, laborer in the formal sector, and informal laborer.[6] A small group of heads who had no occupation was included in the informal laborer category because that category has the lowest access to resources, which is also true of the nonworking heads.

Sex of child is not itself a socioeconomic variable, but a physiological attribute. The study found evidence, however, that family behavior in rearing of children varied depending on their sex (see Chen et al., 1981). Therefore, sex of the child is included to identify this behavioral response to the child's needs.

Measures of child mortality

Child mortality refers to death rates among children, perhaps best summarized by standard indexes of the life table. Since this study is concerned with mortality up to age 3, the appropriate life-table index would be the proportion dying between birth and age 3. All child experience, however, including exposure up to 5 years or more, can be used to estimate the index.[7]

Estimates of child mortality are based on information collected from women during the household survey concerning the number of children they have ever borne and the number of children who subsequently died. The proportion of child deaths to children ever born, classified by age (or marital duration) of women, is a crude measure of the level of child mortality in the recent past. Methods developed by William Brass (1968) and refined by others (UN Manual X, 1983) are used to convert these crude measures into precisely defined life-table indexes. In this application of the method, mortality rates were estimated separately for the children of three age groups of mothers, 20–24, 25–29, and 30–34. In order to increase the robustness of the estimates, the results for the three groups were expressed in terms of the proportion dying up to age 3 and then averaged. This procedure gave satisfactory numbers of cases when the children were subdivided by categories of the socioeconomic variables.

To avoid too great a disjuncture between the time reference periods of the independent and dependent variables, the children of women aged 35 and over were excluded from this part of the analysis. This decision involved a sacrifice, because some of the older women also had recent births, though not many. The tradeoff was between some loss of child survival experience and better (though not complete) control over the recency of births. The cutoff at age 35 also helped to limit the number of children who were born prior to their family's move to Amman and who had lived, therefore, under different conditions. Taking women for the mortality estimates from the age range 20–34 produces a general estimate for child mortality in the recent past—averaging between three and four years prior to the survey.

Estimates of child mortality for categories of the socioeconomic variables are presented in Table 2. The differences in levels by categories within each of the variables suggest that the socioeconomic determinants do, indeed, have a considerable impact on child mortality. Since there is some association among the variables, one cannot evaluate the separate effects of different variables without further investigation.

TABLE 2   Child mortality rates by socioeconomic
variables (children of women aged 20—34)

Socioeconomic variable	Children ever born	Child deaths	Proportion dead[a]	Proportion dying up to age 3[a]
Mother's education				
Literate	1,743	124	71	72.9
Illiterate	943	104	110	111.6
Housing quality				
First class	1,351	100	74	73.4
Second class	705	63	89	92.9
Third class	564	55	98	109.8
Household income				
Above median	1,354	104	77	73.7
Below median	1,314	121	92	99.1
Head's occupation				
White collar worker	336	19	57	54.1
Formal laborer	503	41	82	90.4
Informal laborer and other	1,836	169	92	94.8
Sex of child[b]				
Male	444	40	90	79.8
Female	404	35	87	79.5
Total population	2,697[c]	229	85	86.1

[a] Per 1,000 births.

[b] Based on one-third sample of households. Child mortality in the sample was somewhat lower than in the whole population. However, the questions on children ever born and dead were asked by sex in the sample, which was not done in the main survey.

[c] Missing data cause the deletion of some cases when estimates are made by categories of the population, rather than for the whole population.

Socioeconomic determinants
of child mortality

To separate the effect of each variable on child mortality, a suitable multi-variate model may be selected to describe the data. To reduce the data to an interpretable form, some simplifying assumptions must be made. An assumption consistent with the approach of this study is that the effects of each variable separately can be added to the effects of the other variables to give total effects. Expressed in terms of cross-tabulations, the dependent variable is assumed to have row and column effects, but no cell effects in addition. This is the assumption of additivity and leads one to choose multiple classification analysis (MCA), which is based on that assumption. As long as the reality is not very different, the MCA model allows one to obtain a clear and precise description of the separate effects of the different variables on the dependent variable (Blau and Duncan, 1967; Sonquist, 1970).[8]

Unlike standard regression models, MCA imposes no assumption about the form of the relationship (whether linear or nonlinear) of the dependent variable to each of the independent variables. It is particularly suited, therefore, to analyzing the effect of classificatory variables such as those in the present study. In addition, it tolerates association among the independent variables and uses data economically.

The economy feature is important for studies that do not have large amounts of data. The Brass-type mortality estimates use data rapidly because each estimate is made from a group of women, and numbers must be large enough to yield robust estimates. The data in the present study are sufficient to estimate mortality for a small number of categories of an independent variable, regrouping the same data for each independent variable in turn, but not for many cross-classifications. To estimate net effects in an MCA model, one needs only the values of the dependent variable for each category (marginals), not the mortality values for inner cells. The latter are estimated by solving the equations of the model.[9]

The effect of the socioeconomic determinants on child mortality is evaluated by the MCA model in Table 3. All of the variables have substantial and theoretically plausible effects. In rank order, the size of the effects puts mother's education first, followed closely by housing quality, head's occupation, and household income. The large net effect of being a white collar worker is valid, but the spread of the effects for occupation is partly the result of a small number of children in the white collar category. Partitioning variables into more categories generally increases the spread, but uses data rapidly and has to be avoided for that reason.

The gross or total effect of any factor is a composite of its own net effect, plus the additional effects of other factors associated with it. To illustrate, the gross effect for housing quality is decomposed in Table 4. This shows how the overlapping positive effects of associated variables make the net effect of housing less than its gross effect. When there is independence

TABLE 3   Gross and net effects of socioeconomic variables on child mortality

Socioeconomic variable	Children ever born	Proportion dying up to age 3[a]	
		Gross effects	Net effects
Mother's education			
Literate	1,702	− 13.3	− 10.8
Illiterate	899	+ 25.3	+ 20.4
Housing quality			
First class	1,332	− 13.1	− 8.3
Second class	700	+ 6.3	+ 2.8
Third class	569	+ 23.1	+ 15.9
Head's occupation			
White collar worker	331	− 33.7	− 23.7
Formal laborer	476	+ 1.5	− 1.0
Informal laborer and other	1,794	+ 5.8	+ 4.6
Household income			
Above median	1,323	− 12.5	− 7.5
Below median	1,278	+ 12.9	+ 7.8

Grand mean[b] = 86.1

[a] Per 1,000 births.
[b] Of the proportion dying up to age 3.

between variables, as between mother's education and income, housing, and occupation of the head, the net effects (for education) are almost as large as the gross effects.

Another way of looking at the additive effects of the four social and

TABLE 4   Decomposition of gross effect of housing quality on child mortality (proportion dying up to age 3, per 1,000 births)

	Gross effect	Net effect
Housing quality		
Third class	+ 23.1	+ 15.9
First class	− 13.1	− 8.3
Difference	36.2	24.2
Effects of other factors associated with housing		
Household income		5.6
Mother's education		4.2
Head's occupation		2.2
Total (gross effect of housing		36.2

economic variables on mortality is depicted in Figure 1. At one extreme, among the children born into households with illiterate mothers, with the poorest quality of housing, and the household head working in the informal sector with below-median household income, 135 per thousand die before age 3. At the other extreme, where the head of household is a white collar worker and all other conditions are most favorable, the mortality rate is 36 per thousand births before age 3.

FIGURE 1   Net effects of social and economic variables on child mortality (proportion dying up to age 3, per 1,000 births)

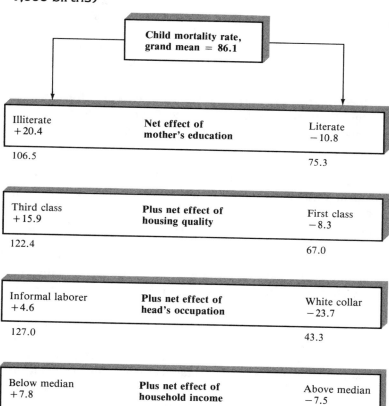

Child mortality rate, grand mean = 86.1

| Illiterate +20.4 | Net effect of mother's education | Literate −10.8 |
| 106.5 | | 75.3 |

| Third class +15.9 | Plus net effect of housing quality | First class −8.3 |
| 122.4 | | 67.0 |

| Informal laborer +4.6 | Plus net effect of head's occupation | White collar −23.7 |
| 127.0 | | 43.3 |

| Below median +7.8 | Plus net effect of household income | Above median −7.5 |
| 134.8 | | 35.8 |

Statistical questions

The results so far obtained may be examined from the standpoint of two statistical questions. The first asks whether the model provides a reasonable representation of reality without taking interaction among variables into account. This is the issue of additivity. The second question asks whether the mortality effects could be due to chance. This is the issue of replicability: Could we expect to find the same pattern of mortality effects in another squatter population or in the same population at another time?

One way to address these questions is to reformulate the dependent mortality variable at an individual level of observation, so that a method of multivariate analysis may be selected that provides standard statistical tests. An approach developed by Trussell and Preston (1982) and used in a number of recent studies is appropriate. The method is based on the idea that the proportion of deaths among children ever born to an individual woman may be used as a "death rate" for the dependent variable after suitable transformation. The "death rate" is adjusted for the effect of differing time periods of exposure on the risk of dying—children born recently are less likely to have died than those born further in the past. The age of the mother is used to make this adjustment.

For the application of this technique, the data are restricted to the same age range of mothers as before, namely 20–34. The new dependent variable is a ratio: the actual proportion of children that have died for a particular woman, divided by the proportion that would be expected for mothers of her age in the population as a whole. The expected proportions were based on a model life table with a proportion dying up to age 3 of 86.1 per thousand births.

A multiple classification analysis using the new dependent variable is presented in Table 5. The results are interpreted by noting that the grand mean of the dependent variable is approximately 1.0, and that the effects are proportionate effects at the mean. The pattern of effects obtained by using the individual-level procedure is similar to that found earlier by using grouped data.[10]

To check the assumption about additivity, interaction terms were included in a classical analysis of variance, again using the individual-level dependent variable. These terms did not explain significant amounts of variance.

The question of replicability is usually approached as if one were interested in generalization of knowledge to all times and places, in which event the chance factor should be quite small before one states that an effect has been demonstrated.[11] However, when practical decisions are being made to select investments or make alternative plans, larger amounts of chance are acceptable. Projects usually have a substantial chance factor associated with them, and decisions are made in an environment of uncertainty.

Based on statistical tests alone, the mother's personal resources, measured in this study by her education, have a strong effect on child mortality. The family's dwelling assets, represented by the variable for housing quality, have a less certain effect. The large spread of net effects and the distribution of cases suggest, however, an impact that is not much less than that of the significant literacy variable. Trichotomous definition of the variable uses more degrees of freedom and probably obscures the mortality effect between first and third class housing.

TABLE 5   Multiple classification
analysis using the Trussell–Preston
dependent variable for mortality[a]

Socioeconomic variable	N[b]	Gross effect	Net effect
Mother's education			
Literate	376	−.13	−.11
Illiterate	198	+.25	+.21
Housing quality			
First class	294	−.14	−.10
Second class	155	+.06	+.03
Third class	126	+.25	+.19
Head's occupation			
White collar worker	73	−.32	−.22
Formal laborer	105	−.03	−.05
Informal laborer and other	396	+.07	+.05
Household income			
Above median	292	−.09	−.04
Below median	282	+.10	+.04

[a] Ratio of actual to expected proportion dead among children
ever born. The grand mean is 1.0.
[b] Observations (women) were weighted by their number of
children ever born and normalized. The Ns refer to normalized
numbers of women.

The variables for household income and for head's occupation do not
show as much statistical reliability as the other determinants. Yet in the specific Amman situation at the time of the survey they were of interest, and
their relevance will be shown below.

Intermediate mechanisms

The second part of the analysis considers the causal relationship between the
socioeconomic determinants of child mortality and the intermediate mechanisms. The social conditions of life are associated with patterns of family
behavior that (a) create and favor disposition to disease (susceptibility), (b)
transmit agents of disease (exposure), and (c) influence the course of disease
(therapy). In the Amman study a distinction is made between an outer layer
of behavioral factors and their immediate health outcomes. The latter are the
major biological processes of concern for child survival: malnutrition, infection, and injury.

The behavioral factors are arranged in five groups as follows: (1) maternal reproductive behavior, (2) diet and feeding practices, (3) standards of
personal hygiene, (4) immunizations, and (5) sickness care practices. These
clusters of behavioral factors were observed by selecting specific elements of
each for data collection and measurement.

The same selective approach was adopted for the health outcomes. Malnutrition was evaluated by weighing each child and relating its current weight

to a standard for growth by age and sex. Disease and injury were measured by asking about episodes during two weeks preceding the survey (a winter season). Finally, a stool sample was taken for each child and examined for parasites.[12]

The independent variables are the four socioeconomic factors introduced earlier. In addition, the effect of child's sex is examined whenever causally relevant. The dependent variables are measures of the five behavioral factors and one of the intermediate health outcomes.

As each dependent variable is described below, the pattern of presentation is to define the dependent measure, consider which independent variables are causally relevant, and comment on the statistical description. The relationship between socioeconomic variables and intermediate mechanisms is examined by using multiple classification analysis.[13] The basic results are presented in Table 6. One should note that the net effects shown in the table are additive, so that the total effects for particular classes of families can be sizable. When necessary, the discussion is extended to include other types of data and analysis. One of the behavioral factors, diet and feeding practices, has to be analyzed with a detailed age control, so it could not be included in the multiple classification analysis. It is treated separately below.

TABLE 6   Net effects of socioeconomic determinants on behavioral factors and nutritional status

Socioeconomic determinant	Reproductive behavior (birth attendant)	Personal hygiene (soap)	Immunizations (DPT)	Sickness care (professional)	Nutritional status (90% + of weight-for-age)
Number of cases	411	395	264	144	397
Mean percent	72	17	85	73	63
Mother's education					
Literate	+4[b]	+2	+6[a]	+7[b]	+5[a]
Illiterate	−5	−3	−8	−7	−7
Housing quality					
First class	NCR	+6[a]	NCR	NCR	+4[b]
Second class	NCR	−5	NCR	NCR	−1
Third class	NCR	−11	NCR	NCR	−10
Household income					
Above median	+5[a]	+3[b]	+0	+0	+1
Below median	−5	−3	−0	−0	−1
Head's occupation					
White collar worker	+2	+18[b]	−2	+11	+4[c]
Formal laborer	−0	+4	+5	−2	+7
Informal laborer and other	−0	−5	−2	−0	−4
Sex of child					
Male	NCR	NCR	+5[a]	+3	+8[a]
Female	NCR	NCR	−4	−4	−8

NCR = Not causally relevant and hence excluded from the MCA.
a,b,c = The F test for significance in a classical analysis of variance shows the probability of the result being due to chance: a < .05; b < .10; c < .20. The test refers to the variable and not to each category separately.

Maternal reproductive behavior

Care of the mother during pregnancy and delivery as well as her birth spacing pattern have substantial effects on fetal life, pregnancy outcome, and survival of the newborn. For natal care, the survey collected information on the type of birth attendant for the delivery of the child. The question of antenatal care was not addressed, but this was likely to be correlated closely with the use of trained professional care at childbirth.

The causally relevant determinants include the mother's education, household income, and head's occupation. Neither sex of the child (not known until the delivery was completed) nor the physical organization of the environment expressed by housing quality is considered a factor in the choice of an attendant. As shown in Table 6, the use of a trained birth attendant (physician or trained midwife) is favored by mother's education and household income. The head's occupation is not important.

Short birth intervals of the mother can affect the health and survival prospects of the living children adversely through low birth weights, if there is a depletion syndrome, through competition among children for care, or by greater density of habitation with its effects on disease transmission.

The Amman squatter population has high fertility (total fertility rate of 7.4 children per woman) and little contraceptive practice (14 percent of married women, confined mostly to older women). In these circumstances, breastfeeding has a major effect on birth spacing, because its duration regulates the natural spacing of children. Breastfeeding is moderately long (Table 7), even for young women in the literate category. However, shortening of breastfeeding, which is associated with education, does exert an upward pressure on fertility by shortening birth intervals, and that is a negative factor for child health. At the existing low levels of contraception, there is no indication that educated young mothers have begun to control fertility by contraception, although behavior as the cohort grows older remains to be seen.

TABLE 7   Estimated average duration of breastfeeding (in months) by mother's age and level of education

Age in years	Illiterate	Literate
Under 30	11	9
30 and over	17	14

NOTE: Duration of breastfeeding in months $= 12 \times$ (women currently breastfeeding/women who gave birth during past year).
SOURCE: Married women under age 50 in the one-third sample. Birth rates were estimated for the four cells from the 100 percent survey.

Personal hygiene

Standards of personal hygiene were evaluated by observing whether soap was available near the toilet for washing hands. Since it requires considerable personal effort to use soap and water in poor housing where supply of abundant water is a problem, one expects housing quality to be a major determinant of this hygienic practice. The other socioeconomic variables are also causally relevant. Sex of the child is not. Using soap for hand washing is a general practice for the whole family, not a response to a particular child under age 3 in the household.

As expected, housing quality is a major determinant. The importance of the availability of water as the relevant dimension of housing quality becomes evident when the existence of a watermain connection to the house is substituted for housing quality as an independent variable. Results were quantitatively almost identical.

The large net effect of the head's occupation is due to the influence of being a white collar worker and the habits that implies. White collar heads of household number only 38 in the sample, so their large positive net effect is balanced by a much smaller negative effect for the more numerous laborers in the sample (247 laborers in the informal sector) to produce the grand mean. The use of soap for washing hands thus appears to depend not only on physical arrangements, but also on social factors. Income and education of the mother appear to be less important.

Immunizations

Immunizations provide protection to the individual against specific and serious infectious diseases. The level of immunization in a population of children may be used not only to assess the prevalence of specific disease protection but also to provide an indicator of the parental attention given to children to protect their health and welfare.

The survey included information about a number of immunizations. Here the vaccine for diphtheria-pertussis-tetanus (DPT) is selected for statistical analysis. Given the recommended time schedule for shots, all children should complete the series by age 12 months. In this study, 85 percent of children had at least one shot by 12 months. If reliable information were available to show how many completed the whole series, the proportion undoubtedly would be lower, and the discriminating effect of the socioeconomic determinants would be stronger. Nevertheless, the study shows that mother's education favors immunization and that more parental concern is shown for boys than for girls. The other potentially relevant factors (income and head's occupation) do not show significant effects.

Sickness care

Just as socioeconomic differentials are found in the provision of preventive care to healthy infants, differences are also likely to be found in the provision of medical care to the sick child. This issue was examined by asking questions concerning how many children had been sick with any of a short list of illnesses during the two weeks immediately prior to the survey. For those who had respiratory or diarrheal illnesses, the survey asked who, if anyone, was consulted for the provision of care. An analysis of the respiratory and diarrheal cases combined gives the results in Table 6, where the professional practitioner is a physician, pharmacist, or nurse.

All the causally relevant determinants except income appear to affect sickness care, although the small number of cases of illness (144) makes the statistical significance of each one less clear. With regard to the sex factor, there was an opportunity to look into this question with data from another source as well. An examination of the records of Bashir Hospital, which serves the squatter areas and other areas in Amman, was made referring to 438 children seen and weighed at its diarrheal treatment center during a specified period. Male children were brought to the hospital substantially more often than female children, and female children were significantly more seriously ill than male children when brought for treatment (UDD, 1982: Appendix C).

Diet and feeding practices

For an examination of diet and feeding practices, three questions are used from the survey: (1) whether the child is currently receiving breastmilk; (2) whether it is receiving any other form of milk; and (3) whether the child has begun to receive solid or semisolid food. The study did not make detailed observations over time, as would be necessary for an accurate evaluation of the nutritional adequacy of the diet.

The data were arranged by current age of the living child, and charted to show the proportion of children at each age receiving breastmilk, other milk, or solids. Some combinations were also examined by this simple procedure. Since the number of children at each age was small, moving averages were used to increase the strength of the proportions and to smooth the curves. Cross-classification of the children by sex was feasible, but small numbers of cases limited exploration of multiple socioeconomic determinants.

Findings are compared with recommended regimes for diet and feeding in order to make statements about the effects of socioeconomic variables on child health and survival. Nutritional status is directly influenced by diet and feeding practices, as well as by a number of other factors, particularly the frequency of infectious disease. In this evaluation it is assumed to be recommended that the child be breastfed (unless the mother's health does not permit) for at least the first six months and, with appropriate and necessary supplementation, for as long as possible thereafter. Breastmilk continues to be an excellent food for children as long as it can be supplied by the mother— provided other sources of nourishment, especially protein foods, have been introduced beyond the sixth month.

In the study population, 25 percent of children were not receiving any breastmilk by the third month, with no important difference by sex. There was great variation in duration of breastfeeding, with 20 percent of children still on breastmilk after 18 months. Girls were taken off breastmilk earlier than boys. By the ninth month, more than half the girls were receiving no breastmilk; for boys, this was true by the fourteenth month. (The mean duration of breastfeeding for all mothers in the sample was 11.5 months, referring to their most recent birth whether still alive or not.)

Corresponding to shorter breastfeeding for girls than boys, the curve of proportions receiving other milk and no breastmilk shows that more than 50 percent of girls received other milk as their sole source of milk by the ninth month. For boys the proportion is only 25 percent by the ninth month. With growth, increasing proportions of boys are given other milk, and there is no detectable sex differential after 15 months of age. By then, the proportion of both sexes receiving other milk as their sole source of milk approaches 60 percent, and declines soon after, as weaning is completed for increasing proportions of children.

Supplementation by the sixth month is critical for healthy growth. The data show that solid or semisolid food of some type is given to 75 percent of children by this age, with no important difference by sex. A qualitative evaluation of the solids was not made, however. While details are not reported here, the Amman data show that those groups of children not receiving food according to the recommended regime are generally of lower weight-for-age and weight-for-sex than the others.

Investigation of socioeconomic determinants other than sex suggests that mother's education not only reduces mean duration of breastfeeding (Table 7), but does so significantly more for girls than boys as judged by charting proportions breastfeeding by age by education. The same relationship is found for household income. Both relationships are controlled by sex but not by each other. In a population in which the care of boys is favored over that of girls, women continue to breastfeed boys on demand longer than girls. When pressures to stop breastfeeding are increased by higher education and income, that pressure is translated into earlier decisions for girls than boys. Whether earlier termination is actually detrimental to the health of girls depends upon the alternatives adopted, including the quality of other milk that is given and of solids, neither of which could be evaluated in this study.

Nutritional status

One of the simplest indications of a child's overall health status is the child's pattern of growth. In this study, health status was evaluated by comparing each child's weight to the expected median weight for that age and sex group in the reference growth tables known as the Harvard standard. Results for males and females are shown in Figure 2.[14] Note that in a healthy population there is some variation, so that there is an expected distribution above and below the standard, as shown in the following table:

Percent of reference weight-for-age	Percent of children
90+	85
80–89	13
70–79	2
Under 70	0

FIGURE 2   Weights of male and female children compared with a weight-for-age standard

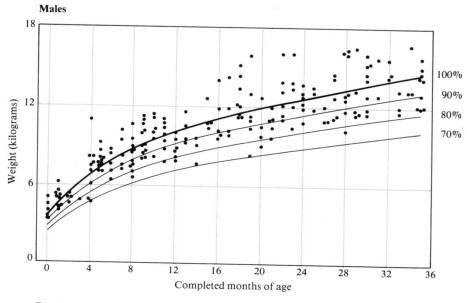

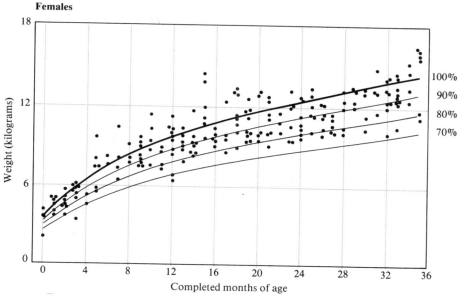

The Amman study population contains a higher than expected proportion of males and females at less than 90 percent of the reference weight-for-age, with a great differential between the two sexes. Overall, 29 percent of males and 45 percent of females are below 90 percent of the standard level. Not all of these individual children are actually malnourished, since one might expect 15 percent of a healthy population to fall in this 70–89 percent range.

Most children below 80 percent of the standard, however, are probably mal-nourished. Note that 6 percent of males and 13 percent of females fall below this level. Nutritional status for both sexes appears to decline with age, indi-cating an inadequate diet for these young children combined with frequent infections.

Nutritional status as an outcome reflects the effects of all the socioeco-nomic determinants, because its proximate determinants include not only diet and feeding practices, but also the factors that determine experience with infectious diseases. Consequently, all the factors in this study are considered to be causally relevant.

In rank order, the determinants of overall child growth, as measured by the proportion exceeding 90 percent of standard weight, are sex of the child, housing quality, and maternal education. Sex operates principally through its social impact on diet and feeding practices and on preventive and sickness care. Housing quality presumably operates through hygienic practices and physical control of exposure to disease. Mother's education operates through multiple paths, some of which have been identified above. Household income and the head's occupation are more marginal in their net effects on nutritional status.

Nutritional status and mortality

The final link in the causal sequence of health outcomes is from poor health to death. In a survey of living children, there is an opportunity to examine relationships between socioeconomic factors and the intermediate mechanisms as observed among those who are alive. But what of those who died? Were their deaths the result of demonstrably negative prior conditions? Or, to state the problem from the standpoint of the living children, is there any way to demonstrate that those whose growth has already faltered have heightened risks of death? Normally, these questions are approached by longitudinal stud-ies, following individuals over time to determine which current conditions predict subsequent mortality outcomes.

In a single survey, the link between current health status and future mortality rates can be examined by making an assumption about the continuity over time of family behavior patterns. If successive children in the same family are subject to these same patterns, then the living children will have the same general risks of death as children born into the same families in the past. This relationship is examined by grouping children who are above and below 90 percent of standard weight-for-age, and computing the mortality rates in the recent past of their families (Table 8). Because of differences by sex in nutri-tional status, this factor is controlled separately.

The association of low nutritional status for the living children with high mortality in the family is striking. Indeed, children of low nutritional status (below 90 percent of standard) appear to be at approximately double the risk of dying compared with other children, given the continuity assumption.

TABLE 8   Child mortality rate of families by the nutritional status of current child up to age 3

Percent of standard weight-for-age	Number of mothers	Children ever born	Child deaths	Proportion dead[a]	Proportion dying up to age 3[a]
Current child: male					
Under 90	40	214	23	107	103
90 and over	88	351	20	57	53
Current child: female					
Under 90	55	258	24	93	86
90 and over	75	363	23	63	57
Current child: both sexes					
Under 90	95	472	47	100	94
90 and over	163	714	43	60	53

[a] Per 1,000 births.
SOURCE: Reports of women aged 20–34 on children ever born and weights of current children from the one-third sample of households.

Discussion

Drawing the findings of this study together, one notes that whenever physical housing quality was causally relevant as a determinant (Tables 3, 5 and 6), the statistical descriptions show that it has a substantial effect on health and child mortality. Despite the narrow empirical base of the present study, one can hazard a guess that urban development planners will find support in the Amman study for the idea that community upgrading, even when chiefly physical, will have favorable effects on health and child survival. If behavioral factors are also addressed by programs, their modification can make additional positive contributions. Since the organization of the physical environment is less well described and its effects less well documented in most studies, it is of interest to a wider audience that strong effects on child mortality could be shown.

The results of the study predict that the children of these squatter areas will have better health in the future simply because almost all Jordanian women are now receiving an education. An educated generation will have lower child mortality, other things equal, than the uneducated generation that is now reaching the end of its childbearing years. The study suggests a few of the mechanisms by which this happens. It demonstrates that specific child care practices are more likely to be found in families with literate as compared with illiterate mothers, holding some of the other determinants constant.

The study did not directly examine the differential roles and power relations of women within the family. As mentioned earlier, however, one theorizes that education favors women's ability to utilize their knowledge more effectively and to gain access to resources that benefit child health.

While head's occupation and, to a lesser extent, household income appear to play a role in child health in the squatter population, it is not a consistently strong one. An interesting point suggested by the results is that the critical distinction in survival chances is between children of white collar workers and children of the rest of the urban labor force. This inference is offered tentatively, however, because the white collar category contains relatively few cases.

It was shown earlier (Table 2) that the child mortality rate by sex, estimated from the one-third sample, was the same for boys and girls—80 per thousand up to age 3. In most large populations where accurate mortality data are available, both historical and current, female child mortality is lower than male. This is commonly thought to be due to biological advantages of girls over boys. The difference has never been measured in a pure state, independent of differences in exposure to disease, family care, and therapy for boys and girls.

For historical comparison, one may use the West group of Coale–Demeny model life tables, which are based on actual populations in the past. They show that when boys have a probability of dying by age 3 of 80 per thousand births, the level for girls averages 66 per thousand. Thus, the mortality measurements of the one-third sample suggest that girls in the squatter population have higher death rates than is "normal" compared with boys.

Historical comparisons have one serious limitation. Social and biological factors were intertwined in the past as they are today. In order to demonstrate that there is a difference in social response to boys and girls that causes a difference in their risks of death, two points must be documented. The family behavior that determines health status, and consequently mortality rates, should be identified. Second, differences by sex of the child in family behavior of the type identified should be shown. To an extent, both points are addressed in the Amman study. They indicate that whatever the biological differences in survival risks for boys and girls, a layer of social differences is added. Families may know that they care for boys and girls differently in many details, but they may not realize that these differences in behavior result in differential health consequences.

Notes

1 Participants were Leila Bisharat, W. Henry Mosley, Frederic Shorter, and Belgin Tekçe. The director of the Urban Development Department of Amman, Dr. Hisham Zagha, provided continuous support and valuable suggestions throughout the study. His staff was responsible for field work, with advice and guidance from Dr. Bisharat.

2 The West Bank of Jordan is under Israeli military occupation and thus could not be enumerated in the 1979 census.

3 In addition to the municipality of Amman, this includes Zarqa, Ruseifa, Wadi Zeir, and a number of adjoining settlements.

4 Data for the study were collected both by a survey of all households and by a one-third sample. The socioeconomic and demographic information was collected from all households. This survey included a detailed physical description of every dwelling and its water and sanitary arrangements. The one-third sample of households was used to interview ever-married women of reproductive age and to collect information on current health status and care of all children under age 3. Intermediate mechanisms (discussed below) were defined on the basis of data collected from the one-third sample of households. Child mortality was assessed both for the one-

third sample and the 100 percent survey by using data on children ever born and surviving. The approach was a single survey, not longitudinal data collection.

5 The conceptual formulation used here was influenced by the work of W. Henry Mosley, who presented his approach at a regional workshop prior to the Amman study and subsequently reformulated it in considerable detail (Mosley, 1980, 1983).

6 According to the specification used in the survey, occupations were classified as belonging to the informal sector if the work activity had one of the following characteristics: place of work had fewer than five workers or was at home, or transient or mobile; no municipal license; no social security or medical benefits.

7 Formally, one assumes that a family of model life tables, in this instance the West models of Coale and Demeny, represents the age pattern of child mortality in Jordan.

8 Interaction (nonadditivity of effects) is discussed in a later section, and a reasonable case is made for regarding it as unimportant to the present study.

9 The model is a set of linear equations, one for each category of each independent variable. In each equation the net effects (unknowns) weighted by the number of children are summed across the pairwise cross-classification of the independent variables. The system is normalized so that the sum of the effects is zero at the grand mean, which is why the unknowns become net differences, or effects, from the mean. To solve the system, the sum of weighted effects for one category for each variable is set to zero, and the others adjusted to it. For x categories there are x equations and x net effects (unknowns). Robert Hodge suggested this way of using the MCA model when the marginals of the dependent variable are known.

10 Exact correspondence between results of the two methods is not expected, because the Trussell–Preston procedure makes a number of assumptions additional to those made for the mortality measurements above. Most notable is the assumption of "proportionality" of mortality relationships, which simplifies the assumed life-table relationships and facilitates transformation of the dependent variable into a ratio of actual proportion dead to expected proportion dead for the women in question. The original article must be consulted for a discussion of this point (Trussell and Preston, 1982). For a justification of OLS procedures see the comments of Trussell and Preston and those of Goodman (1976).

11 The use of F tests to examine statistical significance for problems like the present one is a matter of discussion in the profession. A classical analysis of variance with the individual-level dependent variable using the F test produces the following probabilities: all effects .08; mother's education .04; housing quality .34; head's occupation .47; and household income .59.

12 For a description of data collection procedures, see note 4.

13 Cross tables with all dimensions of the relevant independent variables were examined, and it was found that the simplifying assumption of additivity of effects (row and column differences generally stable across categories) is acceptable for these data. Thus, multiple classification analysis is appropriate.

14 The maximum weight that could be measured accurately by the beam scale used in this study was 16 kilograms. There were seven boys and two girls who weighed 16 kilograms or more. For classification these children were simply grouped with others who exceeded the weight-for-age standard. In Figure 2 those cases are plotted at 16 kilograms or slightly higher in order to give a complete picture.

References

Behm, Hugo. 1979. "Socio-economic determinants of mortality in Latin America." Paper presented at the Meeting on Socio-economic Determinants and Consequences of Mortality, World Health Organization, Mexico City, June.

Benevolo, Leonardo. 1971. *Origins of Modern Town Planning*. Cambridge, Mass.: MIT Press.

Blau, Peter M., and Otis Dudley Duncan. 1967. *The American Occupational Structure.* New York: Wiley, pp. 128–140.

Brass, William, et al. 1968. *The Demography of Tropical Africa.* Princeton: Princeton University Press.

Caldwell, J. C. 1979. "Education as a factor in mortality decline: An examination of Nigerian data," *Population Studies* 33, no. 3: 395–413.

———, and P. McDonald. 1981. "Influence of maternal education on infant and child mortality: Levels and causes," *International Population Conference, Manila,* Vol. 2. Liège: IUSSP.

Chen, Lincoln C., Emdadul Huq, and Stan D'Souza. 1981. "Sex bias in the family allocation of food and health care in rural Bangladesh," *Population and Development Review* 7, no. 1: 55–70.

Dubos, Rene. 1979. *Mirage of Health: Utopias, Progress, and Biological Change.* New York: Harper and Row.

Goodman, John L. 1976. "Is ordinary least squares estimation with a dichotomous dependent variable really that bad?" *Working Papers* 216–223. Washington, D.C.: The Urban Institute.

Mata, Leonardo. 1983. "Evolution of diarrheal diseases and malnutrition in Costa Rica and role of interventions," *Seminar on Social Policy, Health Policy, and Mortality Prospects.* Paris: IUSSP-INED.

Moore, H. A., E. du la Cruz, and O. Vargas Mendez. 1965. "Diarrheal disease studies in Costa Rica: The influence of sanitation upon the prevalence of intestinal infections and diarrheal disease," *American Journal of Epidemiology* 82, no. 2: 162–184.

Mosley, W. Henry. 1980. "Social determinants of infant and child mortality: Some considerations for an analytical framework," in *Health and Mortality in Infancy and Early Childhood: Report of a Study Group.* Cairo: *Regional Papers* of the Population Council.

———. 1983. "Will primary health care reduce infant and child mortality? A critique of some current strategies, with special reference to Africa and Asia." Paper presented at *Seminar on Social Policy, Health Policy, and Mortality Prospects.* Paris: IUSSP-INED.

Puffer, R. R., and C. V. Serrano. 1973. *Patterns of Mortality in Childhood.* Washington, D.C.: Pan American Health Organization, pp. 309–324.

Sonquist, John. 1970. *Multivariable Model Building.* Ann Arbor: Institute for Social Research, University of Michigan.

Trussell, James, and Samuel Preston. 1982. "Estimating the covariates of childhood mortality from retrospective reports of mothers," in *Health Policy and Education,* Vol. 3, pp. 1–36. New York: Elsevier.

United Nations Department of International Economic and Social Affairs. 1983. *Manual X: Indirect Techniques for Demographic Estimation.* Population Studies, No. 81. New York.

Urban Development Department. 1982. *A Baseline Health and Population Assessment for the Upgrading Areas of Amman.* A report to the UDD by the Population Council (L. Bisharat, W. H. Mosley, F. C. Shorter, B. Tekçe). Municipality of Amman, Hashemite Kingdom of Jordan.

World Fertility Survey. 1983. "Findings of the World Fertility Survey on trends, differentials and determinants of mortality in developing countries." Meeting of *Expert Group on Mortality and Health Policy,* International Conference on Population 1984, U.N. Population Division, Rome, 30 May–3 June.

Intervention Projects and the Study of Socioeconomic Determinants of Mortality

Anne R. Pebley

Much of the evidence on the relationship of social, economic, and cultural factors to child mortality in developing countries comes from analyses of surveys, vital statistics, and censuses.[1] A central finding of these studies has been the importance of maternal, and sometimes paternal, education in reducing a child's risk of dying, even when other socioeconomic and environmental variables are held constant. This result suggests that a well-educated mother may care for her child differently than a more poorly educated mother, even if both have the same economic resources. Higher income or occupational status, better housing conditions, and longer child spacing have also been shown to be related to lower child mortality.

These studies have been valuable in documenting the magnitudes of mortality differentials and in disentangling the relative importance of various socioeconomic variables in "explaining" child mortality. They have been less successful in determining the mechanisms through which these factors affect mortality. The conclusion that maternal education or longer child spacing reduces child mortality, for example, poses more questions than it answers. Is maternal education associated with lower child mortality because more educated women distribute food differently within the family, are more likely to seek medical care for a sick child, live under more sanitary conditions, or are more likely to follow sanitary practices, such as hand washing? Caldwell (1979) suggests that education changes a woman's position within her family, giving her more control over resources that she can use to care for her children. But how do more educated women use this greater control, and which of their actions are most effective?

One reason for the limited scope of current demographic and social research on mortality is the lack of a theoretical framework describing the relationship between socioeconomic factors and more proximate determinants of mortality. The paper by Mosley and Chen, in this volume, is an attempt to develop such a framework.

Another limitation is the types of data usually employed in studies of socioeconomic determinants of mortality. While surveys, censuses, and vital statistics have the advantage of yielding nationally (or regionally) representative results, they are usually unsatisfactory for collecting accurate data on factors through which socioeconomic variables affect mortality, such as diet and feeding practices, morbidity and treatment, immunization, and use of medical services. Since mortality in developing countries is usually the result of repeated insults to a child's system, such data should ideally be collected repeatedly over the course of a young child's life.[2] Because of the expense of continuous data collection on a sufficiently large sample and the ethical problems associated with a surveillance program not accompanied by treatment of health problems detected, attempts to collect these data in nonintervention settings have been rare. However, such data are often collected as part of a longitudinal nutrition or health intervention project. Over the past 20 years a large number of longitudinal intervention studies have been carried out in developing countries (for a review, see Gwatkin, Wilcox, and Wray, 1980). The intent of these projects has usually been either to test a set of hypotheses about the effect of the intervention or to demonstrate the feasibility of a particular type of public health program. While not all of these studies collected data adequate for analyses of child mortality determinants, several have produced detailed and reliable data on both biological and socioeconomic factors.

This paper examines the potential role of data from longitudinal public health intervention projects in attempts to test and quantify the relationship between socioeconomic and biological determinants of mortality, using models such as those described by Mosley (1980, 1983) and Chen (1981). As examples, I discuss three projects with different research designs and objectives. One of the projects was carried out by the Department of International Health at the Johns Hopkins University in ten villages in Narangwal, Punjab, India. The second was a study by the Instituto de Nutricion de Centroamerica y Panama (INCAP) in four villages in the departamento of El Progreso in eastern Guatemala. The third project is being conducted by the International Centre for Diarrhoeal Disease Research, Bangladesh (ICDDR,B) in Matlab Thana, Bangladesh. This paper is not a comprehensive review of these projects and their results. Rather, the objectives are to discuss: (1) the types of data these studies have collected; (2) analytical approaches and problems related to the study of socioeconomic determinants of child mortality using data of this type; and (3) the ways in which the design of such projects may affect the usefulness of the data generated. In the next section, each project and study population are briefly described. Then, I review analyses that have used these data to investigate socioeconomic determinants of child mortality. In the final section, I outline cautions required in generalizing from research that uses data from intervention studies.

Project design and data collection

All of the projects considered here were originally designed to answer questions about public health interventions, not socioeconomic differentials or changes. Both the Narangwal and El Progreso projects were intended to be experimental studies in the sense of having randomly assigned treatment and control groups. In each case, however, the designs were eventually modified because of practical considerations. The Matlab project is really a series of studies, each with its own design, carried out in one area. Schematic diagrams of the experimental designs employed in the Narangwal and El Progreso projects are shown in Figure 1. Table 1 summarizes the types of data collected in each of the three projects.

The Narangwal project

The Narangwal Nutrition Project examined the effects of different combinations of health and nutritional services on child mortality, growth, and morbidity. It was carried out between 1968 and 1973 simultaneously by the same team of researchers with the Narangwal Population Project, which focused on integrated family planning and health care. As shown in Figure 1, one treatment group was shared between the population project and the nutrition project. The investigators also used data from the population project control villages to augment those from the nutrition project control villages.

Two types of services were offered. Nutrition care consisted of monitoring of growth, nutrition education (with a special emphasis on prolonged breastfeeding), and food supplementation for malnourished children less than 3 years old. Medical service included efforts to immunize regularly all children under age 3, and weekly surveillance for and treatment of illness by family health workers, with referral of severe cases to a physician. As shown in Figure 1, one group of villages in the nutrition project received no services, a second received only nutrition care, a third received only medical care, and a fourth received both medical and nutrition care. Complicating the design, however, is the fact that the fourth group also received family planning services. Since an effort was made throughout the project to keep the number of personnel and their hours equivalent in each treatment group regardless of the range of services provided (Kielmann et al., 1977: paper I, p. 5), the need for family health workers to provide family planning services is likely to have decreased the amount of time available for nutrition and medical care. Thus, the addition of family planning to the family health worker's responsibilities may account in part for the poorer performance in reducing mortality in the combined nutrition and medical care villages, as discussed below. In all nutrition project villages, morbidity surveys were conducted weekly, and anthropometry, diet, vital statistics, and fertility updates were collected at regular intervals. In the population project control villages, only vital statistics were regularly recorded.

TABLE 1 Characteristics of the three health intervention projects

	Narangwal	El Progreso	Matlab
Organization conducting fieldwork	Department of International Health, Johns Hopkins University	Division of Human Development, Instituto de Nutricion de Centroamerica y Panama (INCAP)	International Centre for Diarrhoeal Disease Research, Bangladesh (ICDDR,B) (formerly Cholera Research Laboratory)
Period of study	October 1968–May 1973 (Services started 1/70)	2 rural villages: 1/69–9/77 2 rural villages: 5/69–9/77	Beginning in 1963 up to present
Original research objective	1. Relative impact of nutrition care and illness care on child growth, morbidity, and mortality 2. Demonstrate auxiliary-based nutrition and health care program	Impact of mild to moderate malnutrition on physical growth and mental development	Originally to provide population for cholera vaccine field trials; now a wide range of health-related studies
Location	Narangwal, Punjab, India	El Progreso, Guatemala	Matlab Thana, Bangladesh
Age group studied	0–3-year-olds	0–7-year-olds	All ages
Sample	All children in chosen villages	All children aged 0–7 in villages between 1/69 and 3/73	Total population; different subsamples used for individual studies
Approximate sample size	2,900 children observed by the end of the project	1,623 children observed for at least 1/4 time	1982 total population 180,000
Experimental design	Villages divided into four groups: 1. nutrition care only 2. medical care only 3. combined nutrition and medical care (plus family planning) 4. no services except for emergencies	All villages had medical clinic staffed by auxiliary nurse and visited weekly by doctor; two villages received high-protein/high-calorie supplement; two received low-calorie supplement	Dependent on individual study
Anthropometry for children	Weight and height collected monthly from 0–9 months; every 2 months from 10–21 months; every 3 months from 22–36 months; other measures less frequently	Weight, height, and 16 other measures collected at specific ages	Dependent on individual study
Maternal anthropometry	Weighed and measured at time pregnancy was detected	Several measures taken during each trimester of pregnancy (except for first pregnancy)	Dependent on individual study
Biochemical and clinical	Periodic cross-sectional biochemical surveys	Regular clinical checkups and biochemical tests	Dependent on individual study

Dietary	Dietary survey every 2 months	24-hour recall once every 3 months from 0–36 months; every 6 months from 37–60 months; yearly until 84 months	Dependent on individual study
Nutritional supplementation	Supplementation quantities recorded (nutrition villages only)	Supplementation quantity recorded	None
Morbidity	Weekly visits for children up to 3 years of age; list of 44 clinical symptoms checked during illness	Fortnightly home visits for households with preschool children	Dependent on individual study
Births and deaths	Collected by resident family health workers, specially appointed vital statistics investigators, and the traditional village chowdikar	Collected by morbidity interviewers and through continuous updates of INCAP census	Recorded for all children as part of the Matlab demographic surveillance system
Social and economic data	Cross-sectional socioeconomic surveys; longitudinal fertility survey at 2-month intervals; frequent census	Biennial census asked questions on education, housing quality, and ownership of durable goods; battery of cross-sectional socioeconomic and demographic surveys between 1974 and 1976	Regular census

FIGURE 1 Experimental design of the Narangwal and El Progreso projects

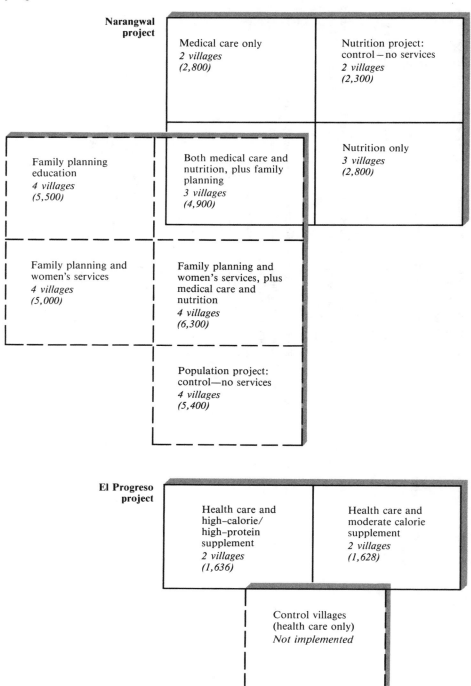

Narangwal project

| Medical care only
2 villages
(2,800) | Nutrition project:
control – no services
2 villages
(2,300) |

| Family planning education
4 villages
(5,500) | Both medical care and nutrition, plus family planning
3 villages
(4,900) | Nutrition only
3 villages
(2,800) |

| Family planning and women's services
4 villages
(5,000) | Family planning and women's services, plus medical care and nutrition
4 villages
(6,300) |

| | Population project:
control—no services
4 villages
(5,400) |

El Progreso project

| Health care and high–calorie/high–protein supplement
2 villages
(1,636) | Health care and moderate calorie supplement
2 villages
(1,628) |

| Control villages (health care only)
Not implemented |

NOTE: Figures in parentheses indicate approximate 1972 village populations.
SOURCES: Narangwal project: Taylor et al. (1975), Figure 1.A.2; El Progreso project: Klein et al. (1975: 2).

As Table 1 shows, a variety of cross-sectional surveys were also taken in the study villages. From them, information for each family is available on income and wealth, land ownership, educational attainment and literacy, ownership of durable goods, housing quality, water supply, and utilization of health services.

The El Progreso project

The objectives of INCAP's El Progreso study, conducted between 1969 and 1977, were quite different. The project was originally designed to investigate the impact of mild to moderate malnutrition on mental development and physical growth during childhood (Klein et al., 1975). Thus, the aim of the experimental design was to produce sufficient variation in nutritional status between experimental groups and among individual children to determine whether there were developmental differences. The original design called for three pairs of villages, one in which a high-protein/high-calorie supplement (called "atole") was to be provided, one in which a placebo supplement (called "fresco") containing no food value was available, and a third in which no supplement was given (Klein et al., 1975). Comprehensive medical care was to be provided in all six villages through a central clinic located in each village.[3]

Two important changes were made in the experimental design before the start of the project. First, due to limited funding, the control group that was to receive no supplementation was eliminated. Second, the contents of fresco, the placebo supplement, were changed. The original plan was to use an artificial sweetener rather than sugar in fresco. Because of concern over the potential dangers of cyclamates, the investigators decided instead to develop a supplement containing approximately one-third of the calories of atole (the high-protein/high-calorie supplement), but no protein. Commenting on the impact of this change, Klein et al. (1975) point out that "had cyclamates or some other artificial sweetener been used in the fresco it would have been impossible to separate [the effect of] calories from proteins and the most likely interpretation, given the original biases of the investigators, would have been that protein was the important factor in physical growth and psychological test performance." In fact, the results indicate that in this population lack of calories, not of protein, seems to be the factor limiting growth. As the investigators recognize, this conclusion makes the absence of a control group that received no caloric supplementation an even more unfortunate omission.

As in the Narangwal nutrition care villages, supplements were available *ad libitum* to children and their families at feeding centers located in each village, and quantities consumed were recorded for children 0–7 years old and for pregnant and lactating women. A morbidity survey was taken every two weeks in each village, and anthropometry and dietary surveys were conducted at regular intervals. Social and economic information was collected both in biennial censuses and in a series of cross-sectional surveys conducted between 1974 and 1976 in collaboration with the Rand Corporation. The types of social and economic data available for the El Progreso study population are quite similar to those for the Narangwal population.

The Matlab project

Unlike the Narangwal and El Progreso projects, the Matlab project, carried out by ICDDR,B in Matlab Thana in the Comilla district of Bangladesh, has a broad range of objectives that have changed over time. The initial purpose was to carry out field trials of cholera vaccines on a large population in which the disease is endemic. In connection with these trials the Cholera Research Laboratory (which subsequently became the ICDDR,B) in 1966 established a demographic surveillance system and a central diarrheal hospital for the study population. In that year, the surveillance system covered approximately 110,000 residents of 132 villages. Between 1968 and 1978 changes were made in the area included in surveillance, and the 1982 population of the study area was reported as 180,000 (D'Souza, 1982). The surveillance monitors births, deaths, migrations, and, since 1975, marriages and divorces. In addition, censuses are taken at regular intervals. The ICDDR,B hospital is located in the village of Matlab, and its services—primarily emergency treatment of severe diarrhea—are available to all residents of the Matlab region.

Within the larger framework provided by demographic surveillance and emergency treatment, a variety of research projects have been carried out on subsets of the Matlab population. These projects have generally been of two types: (1) those concerned primarily with either improved methods of service delivery or a new method of prevention or treatment; and (2) those concerned primarily with investigation of demographic, social, or physiological processes in a poor, rural population. In 1977, the study area was divided into two groups with populations of roughly equal size. One group receives village-based maternal and child health/family planning (MCH-FP) services, while the other serves as a control, continuing to receive emergency diarrheal treatment at the central hospital. MCH-FP services include family planning, tetanus immunization, oral rehydration therapy, and nutrition education (Chen et al., 1983). The impact of the MCH-FP program has been monitored principally through the surveillance system and a program of lay diagnosis of cause of death.

Mortality in the study populations

How successful was each of these interventions in reducing levels of infant and child mortality in their study populations? Tables 2, 3, and 4 show estimates of infant and child mortality rates during the course of each project.

In Table 2, infant and 1–3-year-old mortality rates are shown for treatment and control groups in the Narangwal project. The infant mortality figures come from the final report of the Narangwal Population Project, since reports from the nutrition project do not show mortality rates for different time peri-

TABLE 2 Infant and child mortality rates (per 1,000 births) in the Narangwal project, 1970–73

Treatment group	Neonatal mortality		Postneonatal mortality		Infant mortality		1–3-year-old mortality
	1970/71	1972/73	1970/71	1972/73	1970/71	1972/73	1970–73
Controls (nutrition and population studies)	71	56	35	52	107	108[a]	26
Nutrition	61	34	40	44	101	77	7
Medical care	60	48	32	13	91	63	7
Nutrition and medical care, plus family planning	49	55	35	28	83	82	16

[a] Kielmann et al. (1978: 33), however, give a 1970–73 average infant mortality rate of 129 from the combined population and nutrition study control villages.

SOURCES: Neonatal, postneonatal, and infant mortality rate: Taylor et al. (1975: Table IV.D.4). Mortality rates for 1–3-year-olds: Kielmann et al. (1978: 3).

ods. Infant mortality appears to have declined considerably in the nutrition and the medical care villages between 1970/71[4] and 1972/73. In the nutrition villages, the improvements seemed to occur entirely in the neonatal period, while in the medical care villages rates in both the neonatal and postneonatal periods declined. The combined nutrition and medical care villages surprisingly do not appear to have experienced a mortality decline, although in 1970/71 they had the lowest overall levels of infant mortality recorded. The 1–3-year-old mortality rate in these villages was higher than in the other treatment groups, although substantially lower than in the control group. As previously indicated, the addition of family planning activities to the responsibilities of the family health workers in the combined service villages resulted in a lower level of child nutrition and medical care in these villages than in the other two treatment groups.

Estimates of trends in infant and child mortality for the El Progreso villages are presented in Table 3. The rates show a decline in infant mortality preceding the intervention in 1969, and a substantial decline after the intervention.[5] The decline occurs about equally in atole and fresco villages. This result is not surprising given the conclusion that protein intake—the only difference between the experimental groups—was not a factor in children's diets limiting their growth.

Infant and child mortality rates are shown in Table 4 both for the entire Matlab study area[6] since 1967, and for the MCH-FP treatment and control areas between 1979—when the MCH-FP program was fully implemented—and 1981. Except for the periods of disruption associated with the war of liberation (1971–72) and the severe Bangladesh famine (1974–75), infant mortality rates appear to have declined in the Matlab study area. Table 4 also

TABLE 3   Estimated trends in infant
mortality rates (per 1,000 births) in the
El Progreso project

| Period | Infant mortality rate | | |
	Total	Atole villages	Fresco villages
1963–65	141	152	128
1966–68	112	120	102
1969–71[a]	45	51	39
1972–74[a]	64	63	66

[a] Project in progress during these years.
SOURCE: Lechtig and Klein (1979), Figures 1–4.

shows that the MCH-FP program produced a significant reduction in both
neonatal and postneonatal mortality in the treatment area.

While mortality declines can be documented in all three study populations, it is more difficult to determine how much of each decline can be
attributed to the intervention. In the case of the Matlab MCH-FP study, the
evidence is fairly clear that the intervention reduced infant and child mortality
rates in comparison to what they would otherwise have been.[7] One important

TABLE 4   Trends in infant and child mortality rates (per
1,000 births) in Matlab, Bangladesh: entire study area,
1967–80, and MCH-FP treatment and control
areas, 1979–81

Period	Neonatal mortality	Postneonatal mortality	Infant mortality	1–4-year-old mortality
		Entire study area		
1967–68	67.8	57.6	125.4	
1968–69	83.1	41.0	124.1	
1969–70	87.5	40.0	127.6	
1970–71	89.9	41.3	131.3	
1971–72	83.2	63.6	146.8	
1972–73	70.9	56.2	126.8	
1974	78.1	59.8	137.9	23.2
1975	79.9	111.9	191.3	38.4
1976	65.2	37.6	102.8	32.1
1977	71.3	42.4	113.7	22.2
1978	74.1	46.3	120.4	22.3
1979	73.0	43.5	116.0	21.6
1980	66.6	37.3	103.9	22.1
		Treatment area		
1979	70.9	43.5		
1980	59.3	32.6		
1981	65.8	37.7		
		Control area		
1979	74.6	43.3		
1980	72.7	41.3		
1981	69.0	46.3		

SOURCES: For entire study area: D'Souza (1982); Chowdhury et al. (1981, 1982a,
1982b). For treatment and control areas: Chen et al. (1983).

reason for this clear-cut result is that the study involved a comparison over time between a treatment group and a true control group. A second reason is that the sample size was sufficiently large to avoid a common problem, namely, that sampling variability resulting in small numbers of deaths and children can hinder comparisons between mortality rates. Furthermore, the large sample and the random assignment of villages to experimental groups meant that differences in the social and economic characteristics of villages in the control and treatment groups were minimized. The cost of including a large sample is that the data available for each child are less detailed than those collected in the Narangwal and El Progreso projects.

The rates for the Narangwal and El Progreso projects are based on small numbers of deaths and child-years of exposure and are, therefore, subject to large sampling variability. Even if these figures are accepted at face value, however, it is difficult to determine what portion of the mortality change in these two study populations should be attributed to the intervention because child mortality was already declining before the studies began, and there is scant information about mortality in similar villages in which no intervention took place. In the El Progreso study, there were no control villages that could be used for comparison. The Narangwal Nutrition Project included two control villages, but after the study began it was apparent that one of these villages was quite different from the experimental villages in terms of income and employment. Fortunately, the population study control villages were available to provide an idea of the course of mortality in that area during the same period. The investigators repeatedly warn, however, that differences in social organization and economic resources between the study villages are important and may explain at least part of the differences in mortality. Thus, in the case of the El Progreso and Narangwal projects, we cannot adequately determine how much of the mortality decline resulted from the intervention.

Research on socioeconomic determinants of mortality

All three projects produced publications and reports on a wide variety of public health issues. Some of these reports address the association between socioeconomic factors and child mortality, although few employ a comprehensive framework relating socioeconomic variables to the biological processes determining mortality. Many of these analyses are based solely on bivariate statistical methods—such as correlation or cross-tabulation—making inference about the magnitude and causality of relationships difficult. The objective of most of these reports was description rather than explanation.

Both the Narangwal and El Progreso data, however, have been used in more carefully conceived, multivariate analyses of socioeconomic and biological determinants of growth in children. Although these studies are only indirectly concerned with child mortality, they are included in the following discussion to illustrate potentially more fruitful uses of intervention study data in mortality analysis.

The Narangwal project

Three papers from the Narangwal project examined the association between socioeconomic or demographic characteristics and child mortality determinants. In the first, Kielmann and his colleagues (1978a) calculated child mortality rates separately by caste, sex, and season. They found that both lower caste children (*Ramdasias*)[8] and girls die more frequently, especially in the postneonatal period. Postneonatal mortality rates are also higher during May and June. This last result demonstrates the difficulty of drawing conclusions about mortality causation—or developing action programs to reduce mortality—from simple comparisons of mortality rates between groups. May and June are the hot, dry months in the Punjab, during which the incidence of diarrhea is highest. These are also the months when the spring wheat harvest takes place and child care becomes more haphazard, since all able-bodied adults participate in the harvest. If we assume that a large part of the increased mortality during this season is due to diarrheal deaths, does the increased incidence of diarrhea result from environmental conditions affecting children's susceptibility, poorer child care, some other seasonal factor, or all three?

A second study, by Kielmann, Uberoi, and Bhatia (1977), compared children who died before their third birthday with all children in the population under age 3, by frequency distributions of their characteristics. They found that children who died were more likely to have had one of their siblings die, to be a seventh or higher order child, and to be more seriously malnourished. All three differentials were statistically significant. Again, these results tell us relatively little about mortality determinants. Whether or not a previous sibling died, for example, reflects a variety of attributes related to a family's ability to produce and maintain a healthy child, and thus its relationship with the mortality of the index child is difficult to interpret.

Of the three studies of determinants of growth from the Narangwal project, only the paper by Taylor et al. (1978) employed data for the entire population of children. This paper examined the relationship of socioeconomic and fertility-related factors, experimental group membership, and season with weight and height. A set of 13 multiple regressions was estimated for height, and a second set for weight. Within each set, a separate equation was estimated for each age at which anthropometry was measured.[9] The sheer number of coefficients generated by these 26 equations complicates interpretation of the results.[10] The results presented by Taylor et al. do, however, show several consistent patterns.

As we might expect from the results of Narangwal mortality analyses, Taylor et al. found that both sex and caste were consistently and significantly related to weight and height at each age. The number and composition of siblings[11] was also consistently related to weight and height. The season in which the anthropometric measurement was taken was significantly related only to weight—a measure of current rather than long-term nutritional status. Weight at a given age was highest in the cold season and lowest in the wet season. Above the age of 17 months (the average age at weaning for Narangwal study village children) differences in weight and height among experimental groups were statistically significant even when the other independent variables were held constant. In general, children in villages receiving nutritional care, whether alone or in combination with medical care, had the highest weights and heights, those in the medical care villages the next highest, and those in the control villages the lowest. Finally, the coefficients of maternal age were sometimes statistically significant, but their direction was inconsistent.

To look more directly at the reasons for differential growth, Kielmann, Kielmann, and Arora (undated) analyzed data on dietary intake from a sample of 170 Narangwal village children aged 6 to 36 months using both 24-hour recall and an observation and weighing technique.[12] They cross-tabulated nutrient intake by sex and by caste and found that an important reason for more frequent growth failure among girls and lower caste children was simply lower nutrient intake. From ages 6 to 36 months, girls received only 86 percent of calories, 84 percent of protein, 69 percent of calcium, 88 percent of iron, and 78 percent of vitamin A received by boys. Lower caste children (Ramdasias) also received fewer nutrients than upper caste children (Jats). However, part of this difference may result from differences between boys and girls in size. The investigators also report finding no statistically significant correlations between dietary intake of children and birth order or maternal age, suggesting that Taylor et al.'s birth order result must have some other explanation.

Chernikovsky and Kielmann (1977) employed Kielmann, Kielmann, and Arora's data to analyze child growth determinants, using multivariate techniques. Unlike the study by Taylor et al. (1978), Chernikovsky and Kielmann's analysis was based on a specific conceptual model of the process of child growth and its determinants. As a result, the authors were able to make more concrete inferences about the determinants of child growth from their results. First, they examined the effect of a household's socioeconomic status both on growth in terms of weight and height and on dietary intake in the form of calories and calcium. In each case, multiple regression was used. Some of the results are shown in columns (1)–(3) in Table 5. Two measures of socioeconomic status were included: paternal occupation and acres of land cultivated by the family. Occupation is roughly equivalent to the caste variable used in other analyses. When the amount of land cultivated was substituted in the equation for paternal occupation, the results were roughly the same, suggesting that the impact of caste reported in other Narangwal analyses is economic. Only the equations including paternal occupation are shown in Table 5.

Age and age-squared are included in the equation as control variables reflecting the well-known curvilinear relationship of growth with age. Sex is

TABLE 5   Selected regression results from Chernikovsky and Kielmann's analysis of growth determinants using data from the Narangwal villages

	Single equations			Simultaneous equations	
	Dependent variable			Dependent variable	
Variable	Weight (1)	Height (2)	Calories (3)	Weight (4)	Calories (5)
Age	0.342*	1.233*	47.540*	0.112	
Age^2	−0.003*	−0.012	−0.751*	0.000	
Sex (1 = boy)	0.929*	1.922	171.869*	0.169	
Maternal height		0.353*			
Paternal occupation					
Landowner	0.946*	4.519*	180.499*		78.43
Civil servant	0.495	0.910	−80.198		−212.42*
Prevalence of diarrhea		−1.989			
Weight					99.885*
Calories				0.004*	
Constant	2.647	1.501	268.071	1.788	120.727
R^2	0.54	0.48	19	0.59	0.19
F	37.2	8.10	7.9	45.6	12.3
N	167	58	173		

* Coefficient is statistically different from zero at or below the .05 level.
SOURCE: Chernikovsky and Kielmann (1977), Tables 2, 3, and 4.

included because even in well-nourished populations, girls are shorter and lighter than boys. Maternal height is intended as an indicator of genetic potential.[13] The authors recognize, however, that it also reflects the socioeconomic status of a woman as she was growing up. The prevalence of diarrhea, a variable also known to be related to growth, is included only in the height equation for reasons the authors do not discuss.

The results clearly show that landowners (and those cultivating more land) have taller and heavier children and that these children consume more calories than the children of agricultural laborers. To determine how much of the difference in growth by socioeconomic status could be explained by differences in dietary intake, Chernikovsky and Kielmann estimated a second model. They hypothesized that while dietary intake would be an important determinant of weight, weight would also affect intake by determining appetite. Thus, a simultaneous equations model was estimated, with results shown in columns (4) and (5) of Table 5.

The coefficients indicate that calories are strongly and significantly related to weight at any given age, and further, that weight is significantly associated with calorie intake. The children of landowners appear to consume more calories than those of agricultural laborers, although the relationship is not statistically significant, perhaps due to the small sample size. However, children of civil servants consume significantly fewer calories than the other two groups. Since these children have the same growth curve in weight-for-age as children of agricultural laborers, it appears that they need fewer calories to maintain the same level of growth, either because their activity level is lower (they do not work in the fields) or because they experience less disease.

Thus, Chernikovsky and Kielmann's results suggest that caloric intake is associated with a family's economic resources. They also indicate, however, that there are differences other than caloric intake between families at different socioeconomic levels that influence growth. There is also evidence of discrimination by sex within families in the distribution of available food, suggesting that the higher mortality of girls is the result of deliberate differences in child feeding practices.

There are several problems with Chernikovsky and Kielmann's analysis. First, the lack of a statistically significant difference between the calorie intake of children of laborers and landowners in the simultaneous equations model may be due to a longer term relationship between weight and socioeconomic status. Current weight, while reflecting recent nutrient intake, also results from calorie intake over a longer period of time, which is related to past socioeconomic status. Thus, current weight in this model may also represent past socioeconomic status—which in turn is closely associated with current socioeconomic status—and confounding isolation of the total effect of the paternal occupation variable. Second, the investigators chose to test a very limited model of child growth determinants. For example, maternal education was not included in this analysis, despite its apparent importance as a determinant of child mortality and, presumably, of child growth. The lack of a significant difference in calorie intake between laborers and landowners, despite the important difference in weight, may result partly from superior child care given by more educated mothers, who may be more common in landowning families. Also excluded are variables reflecting other resource constraints within the household, such as Clark (1981) used in an analysis of INCAP data described below. Despite its weaknesses, this analysis indicates the importance of a conceptual model and multivariate methods for understanding socioeconomic determinants of mortality.

The El Progreso project

Most of the papers from the El Progreso project relating to child mortality concern the association between maternal supplementation during pregnancy, supplementation of children during infancy, birth weight, and infant mortality. A summary of these results can be found in Lechtig and Klein (1979).[14] Lechtig et al. (1978) investigated the relationship between socioeconomic status and infant mortality, using a bivariate analysis. The investigators employed a socioeconomic scale originally developed for INCAP's analysis of nutritional status and mental development. This scale is "a composite indicator reflecting the physical conditions of the family house, the mother's clothing and the reported extent of teaching various skills and tasks to preschool children by family members" (Lechtig et al., 1978: 154). The authors divided scores on this scale into two categories and compared infant mortality rates between the categories. The results indicate that children from families scoring low on this scale had an infant mortality rate of 59, compared with a rate of 47 for children from high-scoring families. Unfortunately, this result is very difficult to interpret because of the composite nature of this index.

In contrast to these analyses of mortality differentials, Clark (1981) investigated determinants of infant growth in the El Progreso project, using a comprehensive version of Chernikovsky and Kielmann's conceptual model (1977) and multiple regression. As shown in Table 6, Clark hypothesized that four groups of factors determine child growth: the availability of food and medical inputs; maternal health; the availability of child care time; and environmental, genetic, and socioeconomic variables.[15] Her dependent variable was weight at the end of a period, and she estimated separate equations for

TABLE 6 Clark's multiple regression results for change in child weight between birth and 12 months of age

Variable	Coefficient
Availability of food and medical inputs	
Household income	.0002*
Calories of atole	.0031**
Calories of fresco	.0003
Length of breastfeeding	.0115**
Residence in	
Village 3	−.4898**
Village 6	.0269
Village 8	−.2026
Maternal health	
Mother's weight (end of 3rd trimester)	.0208*
Number of live births	−.0765*
Number of stillbirths	.2354
Mother's age	.0002
Short last birth interval	−.3804**
Availability of child care time	
Number of preschoolers	−.2012**
Number of 7–10-year-olds	.0688
Number of 11–14-year-olds	.0231
Number of 15+-year-olds	−.0340
Environmental, genetic, and socioeconomic variables	
Number of rooms	.1546**
Birth weight	−.3966**
Child's sex	.5487**
Mother's height	.0394**
Constant	−1.9882
R^2	.37
F	6.34
N	270

* significant at <.10.
** significant at <.05.
SOURCE: Clark (1981: 29).

three periods: birth to 6 months, 6 to 12 months, and birth to 12 months. Only the results for the entire birth-to-12-month period are presented in Table 6.

Several of the variables related to availability of food and medical inputs are significantly related to growth. The coefficient for household income, which includes income from both monetary and nonmonetary sources and is used as an indicator of total food resources in the family, is marginally significant but very small.[16] The number of calories of atole consumed and length of breastfeeding have larger and more significant effects on growth. Clark (1981: 36) cautions that "care must be taken in attributing all of this relation [between atole consumption and growth] to supplementary food intake since supplementary food intake may be correlated somewhat with the use of the medical clinic for curative and preventative care." Both length of breastfeeding and calories of atole consumed have their greatest impact on growth between 6 and 12 months of life.

Among maternal health factors, a mother's weight at the end of the third trimester of pregnancy is positively related to child growth (note that the child's birth weight is held constant) and negatively related to the number of previous live births and to a short last birth interval. These factors have their greatest impact on growth of the infant during the first 6 months of life. The large and significant coefficient for the last birth interval variable, when various potentially confounding variables are held constant, suggests that birth interval length may deplete a mother's resources or affect her health in a way that influences her child's growth. Unfortunately, Clark did not control for whether or not the last child died, which is likely to affect birth interval length through the duration of breastfeeding. Thus it is impossible to determine how much of the apparent effect of childspacing results from a genetic predisposition to high mortality in the family, or from family characteristics not captured by other variables that increase the risk of mortality of all children in the family.

Among variables affecting availability of child care time, only the number of preschoolers in the household is statistically significant in this equation, and it has a large and negative effect on child growth. This result suggests that with a given level of household resources, an increase in the number of preschool children (less than 7 years old) in a family increases the competition for child care time and/or increases exposure to infectious disease.

Finally, all environmental, genetic, and socioeconomic variables were statistically significant. The number of rooms in a family's house was positively related to growth. Clark explains that this variable may either measure the degree of crowding or serve as a better indicator of the family's long-term economic circumstances than income. A child's sex is an important determinant of growth, with boys growing faster than girls. However, the differences between girls' and boys' growth in the El Progreso villages are no larger than those in the National Center for Health Statistics standards for the United States, suggesting that discrimination by sex as is seen in the Narangwal and Matlab studies is negligible in Guatemala. Somewhat surprisingly, birth weight is negatively related to growth. Clark suggests that this may result from catch-up growth by low birth weight babies and from the fact that the lowest birth weight babies often die and are therefore excluded from the analysis.

Had Clark used child mortality (rather than child weight change) as a dependent variable, her results may have been similar, since growth failure seems to be an important predictor of mortality. One of her more important findings is that fertility-related factors seem to be related to physical growth in several distinct ways. The number of other preschoolers in a household appears to increase competition for child care time and other family resources, such as available food supply. At the same time, close spacing of the last birth seems to be related to growth even when the number of preschool children, availability of resources, and length of time that the child was breastfed are controlled. This result is consistent with the notion that close birth spacing alone may deplete a mother's physiological resources regardless of the number of other small children she must care for. Clark's analysis also reaffirms the importance of breastfeeding for child health even in a setting where a safe and nutritious supplemental food is available.

The Matlab project

As discussed earlier, the Matlab project is quite different in design and scope from the other two projects. Over the years, papers on mortality-related topics have been generated by a number of projects in the Matlab area. Only a few of these are discussed here.

Cross-tabulating data from the census and other sources, D'Souza and Bhuiya (1982) describe socioeconomic and environmental differentials in child mortality, between 1 and 4 years of age, in Matlab by calculating child mortality rates for different categories of these variables. Their findings indicate that child mortality rates are substantially higher in households whose members are poorly educated and in lower status occupations. They confirm that maternal education is especially closely associated with child mortality: children of mothers with no education experienced 5.3 times the rate of children whose mothers had completed seven or more years of school.[17] As in the Narangwal study villages, children of agricultural laborers experienced the highest mortality rates, followed by children whose parents farmed both their own and other people's land,[18] and then by landowners' children.

D'Souza and Bhuiya also considered three variables that may represent both socioeconomic status and environmental factors—the area of dwelling space in the household, the number of cows owned by the family, and whether the family used a latrine. As might be expected, children living in smaller houses, in families with fewer cows, and in families not using latrines had significantly higher risks of dying. As the authors recognize, many of these variables are likely to be correlated, and a multivariate analysis would be required to sort out their relations with mortality. In particular, the highest educational level attained by a household member seems to be highly correlated with dwelling size and use of a fixed latrine, and these latter two variables are correlated with each other (D'Souza and Bhuiya, 1982: 796).

Chowdhury (1982) analyzed infant mortality using data from a smaller sample of women and their infants from the Determinants of Natural Fertility Study in 14 Matlab villages. Using multivariate analysis, Chowdhury estimated two equations—one for the neonatal period and another for the post-neonatal period. Variables in each equation included maternal age, parity, education, height, and weight; number of boats owned (a useful measure of socioeconomic status in this riverine area); and gestational age of the child at birth. The second equation also included infant's weight in the second month of life.[19] The sex of the child was, unfortunately, not included; nor was any indication of whether the child was being fully breastfed. However, in rural Bangladesh women tend to breastfeed their children well past the first year of life. Chowdhury's results indicate that once other factors were held constant, maternal education was not statistically significantly related to either neonatal or postneonatal mortality. In the neonatal period only gestational age at birth and maternal height were significantly related to mortality, while in the post-neonatal period the coefficients for maternal height and the infant's weight were significant. Thus, Chowdhury's results suggest that any effect maternal education has on infant mortality in this population may operate through education's correlation with maternal height.

As in the Narangwal study population, mortality rates for girls in Matlab have been consistently higher than for boys after the neonatal period (D'Souza and Chen, 1980). Chen, Huq, and D'Souza (1981) used data from the Matlab Food and Nutrition Study to investigate sex differentials in child mortality with cross-tabulations. They found that the prevalence of malnutrition among children, as measured by growth failure, was substantially higher among girls than among boys, even when measurements were standardized using sex-specific schedules. The female deficiency in growth was observed in both weight-for-age and height-for-age, thought to measure acute (wasting) and chronic (stunting) malnutrition, respectively. Part of this growth differential is due to significantly lower calorie and protein intake by girls: Chen, Huq, and D'Souza show that even when caloric intake is standardized by body size, girls consumed substantially fewer calories than boys, between birth and age 5. Although the incidence of various diseases (including diarrhea) among children under age 5 did not vary substantially by sex, Chen, Huq and D'Souza's results show that boys are much more likely to receive treatment for diarrhea at ICDDR,B's Matlab Treatment Unit than are girls, even though the Centre provides free services and transportation to the facility. This analysis strongly suggests that sex differentials in child mortality in the Matlab study area result from discrimination against girls in the type of care given.

Unfortunately, Chen, Huq, and D'Souza do not attempt to determine whether discrimination in child care by sex varies between families in different social and economic circumstances. Evidence from D'Souza and Bhuiya (1982) indicates that significant sex differentials in child mortality remain even when maternal education and index of economic status are held constant. However, D'Souza and Chen (1980) show that in times of great stress, such as the 1975 Bangladesh famine, the excess in female mortality rates over male rates increased substantially. In view of the patchy evidence, it is difficult to determine how the pattern of neglect described by Chen, Huq, and D'Souza might change as, for example, female education becomes more common, or household income rises.

Discussion

I argued in the introduction that intervention projects, such as those described in this paper, provide a source of unusually detailed data on the relationship between socioeconomic variables and biological determinants of child mortality. Although important analyses of the association between socioeconomic factors and child mortality were produced by each project, much of the potential of these data for testing models including both socioeconomic and biological mortality determinants remains untapped. At least two problems limit the usefulness of many of these analyses. The first is the lack of a conceptual model or framework guiding the analysis that describes both the biological process of child mortality and the ways socioeconomic factors may affect this process. The second is reliance on simple bivariate statistical methods that are inadequate to the task of testing complex hypotheses. Despite their limitations, the studies of child growth determinants by Chernikovsky and Kielmann (1977) and by Clark (1981) show that is it possible to use these data far more effectively.

Inference from intervention study data

While data from intervention projects may be useful for testing models of socioeconomic and biological determinants of mortality, the projects are generally designed for other purposes. This final section considers how the design of intervention studies may affect the results of both the analyses described in the previous section and future research on this topic. To what extent can conclusions reached from these data on socioeconomic determinants of mortality be generalized to other populations?

First, the samples chosen for these and other intervention projects are not, in any statistical sense, samples of a larger population. In the case of the Narangwal and El Progreso studies, the investigators chose communities thought to be "representative" of rural villages in the region. Other factors, however, such as accessibility of the village and receptivity of community leaders, must also have figured in the choice.

Second, the design and implementation of the intervention may have altered the patterns of variance and covariance within the study population. In the El Progreso and Narangwal projects, investigators attempted to *minimize* intervillage socioeconomic and cultural differences in the process of village selection in order to achieve comparability between the experimental groups. Thus, the variance in social, economic, and cultural characteristics among villages within the study population is likely to be substantially less than among villages of a region or country. The selection process, however, is less likely to have affected the variation in these characteristics among families within a village.

Health intervention projects also alter the usual pattern of variation in nutritional status and morbidity within a given population. In experimental designs, like those in the Narangwal, El Progreso, and Matlab MCH-FP projects, the distribution of health services is likely to increase the intervillage variance in health status, while decreasing intravillage variance. Increasing intervillage variance in health status was the *objective* of the experimental design. Decreasing intravillage variance in health status resulted from the fact that health services were made available to all village families regardless of ability to pay. The net effect is likely to be an increase in variance in health status variables in the entire study population, but an attenuation in the treatment village of the commonly observed association between income and children's nutritional status or use of health care facilities. Thus, analyses using data from intervention projects are less likely to find significant relations between socioeconomic variables and health status than studies using data from other sources. This may be the explanation, for example, for Clark's (1981) finding that family income played a relatively unimportant role in children's physical growth in the El Progreso project.

Another problem with intervention data is sample selection bias within the study population. Although intervention studies may weaken the relationship between a family's economic resources and children's health status by offering services free of charge, those who use the available services will still be a select sample of the village population, since ethical considerations dictate that participation in all aspects of the intervention be voluntary. It is clear, for example, from Chen, Huq, and D'Souza's (1981) results that even though services and transportation are free, Matlab families seek diarrheal treatment for boys more often than for girls, despite equal incidence of diarrheal disease. Results from field trials of tetanus toxoid immunization in Matlab also indicate that only certain segments of the population were willing to be immunized and that some families seem to be more willing than others to accept any type of medical innovation (Rahman, 1981). From the El Progreso study, Lechtig and Klein (1979) offer evidence that utilization of clinic services is selective, based on whether an older sibling had died: families that had already experienced a child death were more likely to take advantage of services for a surviving child.

Selection bias also results from differential willingness or ability of families to participate in data collection throughout the project. In the Narangwal project, for example, mothers were very reluctant to permit staff to weigh babies just after birth, especially if the baby was small or not healthy. Kielmann et al. (1978) report that this reluctance was gradually overcome in the villages receiving child care services, but never entirely overcome in the control villages. Migration into and out of the communities, especially common in the El Progreso villages, exerts another type of selection effect, since data can only be collected on children while they are in the villages and migration is highly selective.

In summary, while almost all data sources have limitations, the biases created by the design and implementation of a health intervention project are potentially more severe and complex than, for example, in a cross-sectional survey. Nevertheless, the gain in accuracy and frequency of measurement by the continuous surveillance of a population during an intervention program is likely to make analysis worthwhile. The conclusion to draw from this discussion is that results from analyses of socioeconomic determinants of mortality using health intervention project data must be interpreted cautiously.

Notes

1 See, for example, Behm et al., 1976–79; Carvahal and Burgess, 1978; Schultz, 1979; Caldwell, 1979; Chackiel, 1982; Trussell and Hammerslough, 1983; Nag, 1983; Haines, Avery, and Strong, 1983; Martin et al., 1983; Mensch et al., 1983; Hobcraft, McDonald, and Rutstein, 1983; Rosenzweig and Schultz, 1982.

2 One-time measurements of, for example, anthropometry tell us about a child's current health status, and perhaps whether a health problem is chronic or acute, but they say little about the causes of reaching the current state.

3 Presumably, the objective of providing medical care in all villages was to minimize the effect of disease on a child's appetite and nutrient absorption, and to maximize the differences in growth due to nutrient availability and intake alone. It also appears that the investigators felt an ethical obligation to provide treatment for children in the communities.

4 The Khanna Study, carried out in other villages in the Ludhiana District, reported a probability of dying by age 2 ($_2q_0$) of 140 per thousand live births for 1966–67 and a probability of dying by age 1 ($_1q_0$) of 115, from retrospective survey data (Wyon and Gordon, 1971: 302). Other sources report estimates of $_2q_0$ for 1970–72 of between 136 and 143 (NAS, Panel on India, 1983). Even an IMR of 129 in the control villages indicates a substantial drop in mortality prior to the study, since

the Khanna Study reported a $_2q_0$ of 230 for 1956–58 (Wyon and Gordon, 1971) and a survey of Hindu households in the Punjab produced an estimate of 168 for 1965–66 (NAS Panel on India, 1983).

5 Lechtig and Klein's rates for the preintervention period are roughly equivalent to those from other sources. Haines, Avery, and Strong (1983), for example, estimated a $_2q_0$ of roughly 160 for 1968 for all of rural eastern Guatemala using census data, implying an approximate $_1q_0$ of 129 using a West model Coale–Demeny life table.

6 Although the surveillance area changed during the project, the rates for the early period (from the old surveillance area) probably adequately represent the experience of the new area during the same period.

7 Even though mortality was clearly reduced, Chen et al. (1983) are still unable to determine exactly how the reduction occurred.

8 *Ramdasias* are primarily agricultural laborers, while *Jats,* who have lower mortality, cultivate their own land.

9 In this summary, the results of the first equation with birth weight as the dependent variable are ignored, since birth weight measurements are available only for a biased sample (Taylor et al., 1978: 9–10).

10 Using methods such as hazards models, which explicity incorporate time (in this case, age), might have resulted in a more par-

simonious summary of the relationships in the data. These methods were unavailable to the investigators when the analysis was done.

11 The variable was coded as follows: 1 = 1 male and 0–1 female sibs; 2 = 0 or 1 male sibs and 2 female sibs; 3 = 2 male sibs and 0–1 female sibs; 4 = 2 male sibs and 2 female sibs. The results indicate that growth was greater among groups 1 and 2 than among 3 and 4, suggesting that the number of siblings alone may have been the important consideration and not their sex composition.

12 The authors do not say whether they included breastmilk intake in their calculations. Their sample included weaned and partially weaned children.

13 The results for sex and maternal height should be interpreted with caution since Chernikovsky and Kielmann found an unusually high correlation (.31) between maternal height and being a boy. They suggest that this is evidence of underreporting of girls by Jats, who have a strong preference for boys and are also taller. Underreporting may have affected this sample more than the entire Narangwal study population. The sex ratio at birth for the entire population was 110 (Kielmann et al., 1978: 28), which is higher than normally observed but not totally improbable for a sample of 2,984 births.

14 Results from Lechtig and Klein (1979) should be interpreted cautiously. Although parts of the anlaysis are not fully described, it appears that some of the results may be due to the way the data were coded. For example, the authors find a statistically significant correlation between total supplement intake by a child during his/her first year of life and infant mortality. Depending on the coding of the supplement variable, a correlation of the size observed might be generated simply because infants who died had less time to consume the supplement.

15 Clark also included literacy of child's mother in a separate set of equations not shown in Table 6. She found that the coefficient of literacy was small and not statistically significant.

16 Clark measured income in *quetzales* (Q1 = $1). Estimates of annual income in the villages average Q502.

17 It is important to note that very few women complete seven or more years of school in the Matlab study area. In this sample only about 3 percent had, compared with 12 percent of household heads.

18 This group comprises the majority of the sample and also includes self-employed workers such as fishermen, fish vendors, boatmen, and businessmen (D'Souza and Bhuiya, 1982: 760).

19 Chowdhury does not indicate how this variable was coded if the infant died before he was weighed in the second month.

References

Behm, Hugo, et al. 1976, 1979. *La Mortalidad en los Primeros Años de Vida en Países de la America Latina*. Individual Country Volumes. San Jose, Costa Rica: Centro Latinoamericano de Demografía.

Butz, W. P., Julie Da Vanzo, and Jean-Pierre Habicht. 1982. *Biological and Behavioral Influences on the Mortality of Malaysian Infants*. Rand Corporation Note N-1638-AID.

Caldwell, J. C. 1979. "Education as a factor in mortality decline: An examination of Nigerian data," *Population Studies* 33: 295–414.

Carvahal, Miguel, and Paul Burgess. 1978. "Socioeconomic determinants of fetal and child deaths in Latin America: A comparative study of Bogota, Caracas, and Rio de Janeiro," *Social Science and Medicine* 12: 89–98.

Chackiel, Juan. 1982. "Niveles y tendencias de la mortalidad infantil en basé a la encuesta mundial de fecundidad: Factores que afectan a la mortalidad en la niñez," *Notas de Población* 28: 43–87.

Chen, Lincoln. 1981. "Child survival: Levels, trends and determinants," in *Determinants of Fertility in Developing Countries: A Summary of Knowledge*. Panel on Fertility Determinants, Committee on Population and Demography, National Academy of Sciences.

———, Emadual Huq, and Stan D'Souza. 1981. "Sex bias in the family allocation of food and health care in rural Bangladesh," *Population and Development Review* 7, no. 1 (March): 55–70.

————, et al. 1983. "Mortality impact of an MCH-FP program in Matlab, Bangladesh," *Studies in Family Planning* 14, no. 8/9 (August/September): 199–209.

Chernikovsky, Dov, and A. A. Kielmann. 1977. "Correlates of preschool child growth in rural Punjab," in *The Narangwal Nutrition Study*, ed. A. A. Kielmann et al., mimeo.

Chowdhury, A. K. M. A. 1982. "Education and infant survival in rural Bangladesh," *Health Policy and Education* 2: 369–374.

Chowdhury, M. K., et al. 1981. *Demographic Surveillance System-Matlab*, Vol. 7: Vital Events and Migration, 1978. ICDDR,B Scientific Report No. 47.

————, et al. 1982a. *Demographic Surveillance System-Matlab*, Vol. 9: Vital Events and Migration Tables, 1979. ICDDR,B Scientific Report No. 56.

————, et al. 1982b. *Demographic Surveillance System-Matlab*, Vol. 10: Vital Events and Migration Tables, 1980. ICDDR,B Scientific Report No. 58.

Clark, Carol A. M. 1981. *Demographic and Socioeconomic Correlates of Infant Growth in Guatemala*. Rand Corporation No. N-1702-AID/RF.

D'Souza, Stan. 1982. "Mortality case study: Matlab, Bangladesh." Paper prepared for the United Nations/World Health Organization, Third Project Collaborators' Meeting on Case Studies of Determinants of Mortality Change and Differentials, Geneva.

————, and Lincoln Chen. 1980. "Sex differentials in mortality in rural Bangladesh," *Population and Development Review* 6 no. 2 (June): 257–270.

————, and Abbas Bhuiya. 1982. "Socioeconomic mortality differentials in a rural area of Bangladesh," *Population and Development Review* 8, no. 4 (December): 753–769.

Gwatkin, Davidson, Janet R. Wilcox, and Joe D. Wray. 1980. *Can Health and Nutrition Interventions Make a Difference?* Washington, D.C.: Overseas Development Council, Monograph No. 13.

Haines, Michael R., Roger C. Avery, and Michael A. Strong. 1983. "Differentials in infant and child mortality and their change over time: Guatemala, 1959–1973," *Demography*, 20, no. 4: 607–621.

Hobcraft, John, John McDonald, and Shea Rutstein. 1983. "Child spacing effects on infant and early child mortality," *Population Index*, 49, no. 4: 585–618.

Holland, Bart. 1983. "Breastfeeding and infant mortality: A hazards model analysis of the case of Malaysia," Ph.D. thesis, Princeton University.

Islam, M. Shafiqul, and Stan Becker. 1981. "Interrelationships among certain socioeconomic variables in a rural population of Bangladesh," ICDDR,B Working Paper No. 18.

Kielmann, A. A., et al., 1977. "The Narangwal Nutrition Study: Report to the World Bank. Baltimore: Johns Hopkins University, Department of International Health, mimeo."

————, and Colin McCord. 1977. "Home treatment of childhood diarrhea in Punjab villages," *Environmental Child Health* (August): 197–210.

————, Inder S. Uberoi, and Shushum Bhatia. 1977. "Child mortality in rural Punjab: Level and causes of child deaths." Baltimore: Johns Hopkins University, Department of International Nutrition, mimeo.

————, et al. 1978a. "The Narangwal experiment on interactions of nutrition and infections: II. Morbidity and mortality effects," *Indian Journal of Medical Research* 68 (suppl.).

————, Carl E. Taylor, and Robert L. Parker. 1978b. "The Narangwal Nutrition Study: A summary review," *The American Journal of Clinical Nutrition* 31: 2040–2052.

————, and Colin McCord. 1978. "Weight-for-age as an index of risk of death in children," *The Lancet* (10 June): 1247–1254.

Kielmann, Nandita S., A. A. Kielmann, and Bimla D. Arora. Undated. "Diet and growth in rural preschool children: I. Levels of dietary intakes." Baltimore: Johns Hopkins University, Department of International Health, mimeo.

Klein, Robert E., et al. 1975. "Malnutrition and human behavior: A backward glance at an ongoing longitudinal study." Paper presented at the Conference on Malnutrition and Behavior, Cornell University, 6–8 November.

Lechtig, A., et al. 1978. "Effect of maternal nutrition on infant mortality," in *Nutrition and Human Reproduction,* ed. W. H. Mosley. New York: Plenum Press.

——, and Robert E. Klein. 1979. "Effects of food supplementation during pregnancy and lactation on infant mortality, morbidity, and physical growth," *Archivos Latinoamericanos de Nutrición* 29, no. 4, Supplement 1: 99–142.

Martin, Linda G., et al. 1983. "Covariates of child mortality in the Philippines, Indonesia and Pakistan: An analysis based on hazards models," *Population Studies* 37, no. 3 (November): 417–432.

Martorell, Reynaldo, et al. 1975. "Acute morbidity and physical growth in rural Guatemalan children," *American Journal of Diseases of Children* 129: 1296–1301.

——, et al. 1979. "Interrelationships between diet, infectious disease and nutritional status," in *Social and Biological Predictors of Nutritional Status, Physical Growth, and Neurological Development,* ed. Lawrence S. Green. New York: Academic Press.

Mejía Pivaral, Víctor. 1972. *Caracteristicas Economicas y Socioculturales de Cuatro Aldeas Ladinas de Guatemala.* Guatemala Indigena 7, no. 3.

Mensch, Barbara, et al. 1983. "Comparative patterns and child mortality differentials in developing countries." Paper presented at the Annual Meeting of the Population Association of America, Pittsburgh.

Mosley, W. H. 1980. "Social determinants of infant and child mortality: Some considerations for an analytical framework." Discussion Paper for a conference on Health and Mortality in Infancy and Early Childhood, Cairo, 18–20 May, the Population Council.

——. 1983. "Will primary health care reduce infant and child mortality? A critique of some current strategies, with special reference to Africa and Asia." Paper prepared for the IUSSP Seminar on Social Policy, Health Policy and Mortality Prospects, Paris, 28 February–4 March.

Nag, Moni. 1983. "Impact of social and economic development on mortality: Comparative study of Kerala and West Bengal," *Economic and Political Weekly* (Bombay) 18, nos. 19–21, Annual Issue (May): 877–900.

Nerlove, Sara B., et al. 1974. "Natural indicators of cognitive development: An observational study of rural Guatemalan children," *Ethos,* 2: 265–295.

Panel on India, Committee on Population and Demography, U.S. National Academy of Sciences. 1983. "Vital rates in India, 1961–1981," mimeo.

Rahman, Makhlisur. 1981. *Factors Related to Acceptance of Tetanus Toxoid Immunization Among Pregnant Women in a Maternal-Child Health Programme in Rural Bangladesh.* ICDDR,B Scientific Report No. 43.

Rosenzweig, Mark R., and T. Paul Schultz. 1982. "Market opportunities, genetic endowments, and interfamily resource distribution: Child survival in rural India," *American Economic Review* 72, no. 4: 803–815.

Schultz, T. Paul. 1979. "Interpretation of relations among mortality, economics of the household and the health environment." Proceedings of the Meeting on Socioeconomic Determinants and Consequences of Mortality, United Nations and World Health Organization, El Colegio de Mexico, Mexico City, 19–25 June.

Taylor, Carl E., et al. 1975. *The Narangwal Population Study: Integrated Health and Family Planning Services.* Narangwal, Punjab, India: Rural Health Research Center.

——, et al. 1978. "The Narangwal experiment on interaction of nutrition and infections: I. Project design and effects upon growth," *Indian Journal of Medical Research* 68 (suppl.): 1–20.

Trussell, James, and Charles Hammerslough. 1983. "An illustrative analysis of the covariates of infant and child mortality in Sri Lanka," *Demography* 20, no. 1: 1–26.

Wilson, Alan B. 1981. "Longitudinal analysis of diet, physical growth, verbal development, and school performance," in *Malnourished Children of the Rural Poor,* ed. J. B. Balderston, A. B. Wilson, M. E. Freire, and M. S. Simonen. Boston: Auburn House Publishing Company.

Wyon, John B., and John E. Gordon. 1971. *The Khanna Study.* Cambridge, Mass.: Harvard University Press.

A Household Survey
of Child Mortality
Determinants
in Malaysia

Julie DaVanzo

This paper reports on a series of ongoing studies of infant and child mortality in Malaysia that have been conducted at the Rand Corporation. They are based on data from a household survey known as the Malaysian Family Life Survey (MFLS). The research has been performed by a team of social and biomedical scientists.[1] This paper reviews unique features of the MFLS and of the Rand analyses of infant and child mortality, and illustrates some of the findings that have resulted.

Malaysia is a very interesting setting for a study of infant and childhood mortality. Mortality rates there have declined dramatically since World War II. For example, the infant mortality rate fell from around 100 infant deaths per thousand live births in the 1940s to around 30 in the 1970s. Malaysia has also experienced rapid economic growth and profound social and demographic change in recent decades. Our data document both child mortality and socioeconomic variables over this period, thereby providing insights into possible reasons for the mortality decline. Furthermore, it has been possible to collect high-quality survey data in Malaysia, including good retrospective data. The country has capable survey organizations, and respondents are able to provide accurate answers. For example, many respondents to the MFLS had birth and death certificates in their homes that could be used to verify dates.

The survey and the data

The Malaysian Family Life Survey

The Malaysian Family Life Survey consisted of 11 questionnaires that were fielded in three rounds, each four months apart, between August 1976 and August 1977. It used a population-based probability sample consisting of randomly selected private households that each contained at least one ever-married woman less than 50 years old at the initial visit. A total of 1,262 households (88 percent of the eligible probability sample) completed Round 1 of the survey. These households are contained in 52 primary sampling areas in Peninsular Malaysia, 49 of which were randomly selected; the other three were purposely selected to give additional representation to Indian households and households in fishing communities.

The initial purpose of the MFLS was to provide data for estimating the magnitude of key economic and biomedical relationships affecting families' infant mortality, birth spacing, and breastfeeding patterns. A goal was to identify factors amenable to public policy influence that directly or indirectly affect these outcomes. We have also sought to identify screening characteristics of populations at high risk of infant mortality to whom interventions could be effectively targeted. These aims led to several features of the survey that taken together make it unique: The data document both socioeconomic and biomedical variables in considerable detail. They also document community characteristics (e.g., distances to medical care) in order to provide information on factors that policymakers might be able to affect.[2]

Data used in the mortality analyses

The key questionnaire for the mortality analyses is the Round-1 Female Retrospective Life History questionnaire, which includes life events as early as the mid-1940s for some respondents. It includes a complete life history of a woman's pregnancies and related events. For each pregnancy the woman was asked the date and type of outcome (live birth, stillbirth, miscarriage, or abortion). For each live birth, information was collected on birth weight, lengths of full (unsupplemented) and supplemented breastfeeding, whether the child died and, if so, the date of death.[3] The retrospective data also contain a residential history, including characteristics of houses where respondents have lived (such as type of toilet, with whom lived). Hence explanatory variables can be defined to be specific to each child and to refer to the time of his or her birth. This contrasts, for example, with the World Fertility Surveys, which also document trends in infant mortality over a similar period, but lack corresponding historical information on most of its correlates.

The MFLS data include most of the influences commonly cited as affecting mortality (e.g., Klein, 1980; United Nations, 1973)—maternal education, socioeconomic class (income), age, parity, prior reproductive loss, availability of health services, and infant sex and birth weight—as well as others considered in some recent studies, for example, birth spacing (reviewed in Wray, 1971), breastfeeding and type of weaning food (reviewed in Jelliffe and Jelliffe, 1978), and desire for having this baby (Scrimshaw, 1978).[4] Maternal smoking and illegitimacy were not examined because both are rare in Malaysia, and data on them were not collected. Maternal nutrition is not included, although its contribution to birth weight in these data is discussed in detail in a related paper (DaVanzo, Habicht, and Butz, 1984). Only crude measures of use of medical care are available. Some key variables—for example, respiratory and gastrointestinal morbidity—were not measured directly, and proxies were used.

Two rather unusual data items in the retrospective life history have added some interesting features to the analyses: (1) When breastfeeding was absent or lasted less than three months, mothers were asked the reasons. This information enables us to identify cases where breastfeeding was short because the baby died or was ill-unto-death, and hence to attempt to control for this potential bias in estimating the influence of breastfeeding on mortality. (2) As a prelude to the question about the survival of each live-born child, mothers were asked: "Where is this child now?" In 46 cases, the answer was that the child was given away. If women tend to give away children because they are unwanted (rather than explicitly producing them for sale), a comparison of the correlates of which children are given away and which children die should shed some light on the extent to which some mortality relationships are due to the neglect of unwanted children (Scrimshaw, 1978).

Quality of the data

The reliability and validity of retrospectively reported data on infant and child mortality and associated life events are usually open to serious question. In this case, however, Haaga (1983) has investigated important aspects of these issues for the MFLS. He finds that the secular trends in infant mortality in the MFLS data and the mortality differences between Chinese and Malays are generally similar to those indicated by Malaysian vital statistics (which are regarded to be of very high quality).[5] The comparisons of trends show no evidence for decreased reporting of mortality events that occurred in the distant past. For babies born in the late 1960s, Haaga also compares the distributions of ages at death within the first year of life with vital statistics for that period and finds that both the shapes of the survival curves and the differences between Malays and Chinese in the MFLS are very similar to those in the vital statistics. The apparent good quality of these retrospective mortality data probably stems, in part, from their having been collected as part of an entire life history of salient events in which respondents and interviewers used the occurrence of one type of event to prompt memory of the occurrences of others. Furthermore, the dates of probably the most salient of those events—birth dates of children—were verified with documents (birth certificates or identity cards) for over 70 percent of the live births.

DaVanzo, Habicht, and Butz (1984) have investigated the quality of the MFLS recall data on birth weight and have found their distributions and relationships with well-established correlates to be remarkably similar to those in other studies, including clinical investigations.

As is true in many surveys, the self-reported breastfeeding data exhibit considerable heaping at lengths of 6, 12, 18, and 24 months. Haaga (1983) shows that the source is in the reporting rather than actual breastfeeding norms. Removing these heaped observations from the sample, however, does not notably change the breastfeeding coefficients or their statistical significance in this analysis. Haaga has also investigated the quality of several other parts of the data used in this analysis, finding most of them to be adequate to support multivariate analysis.

Conceptual framework and empirical model

Our conceptual framework for analyzing infant and child mortality resembles those proposed by Chen (1983) and Mosley (1982), and elaborated by Mosley and Chen in this volume. Our analyses are based on the premise that, although the ultimate cause of death is biological, the determinants of the fatal biological factor may be a chain of biological and behavioral factors (Butz and Habicht, 1976). A corollary is that behavioral factors do not affect mortality directly, but rather indirectly, through more proximate biological correlates.

Our framework derives partly from models in economic demography that view parents as deriving utility, or well-being, from child services and other goods and services (e.g., Willis, 1974). The quantity of child services depends on how many children survive and on the quality (e.g., health, education) of each. By investing in their children's health (with inputs of their own time, money spent on medical care, etc.), parents can affect both survival rates and health quality per child, subject to the biomedical relationships between these inputs and children's health and survival. A child's health and survival prospects also depend on the stock of "health capital" (e.g., birth weight, birth defects) with which he is initially endowed, which in turn is influenced by his mother's health capital (e.g., her nutritional status).

This approach emphasizes that much of the behavior, and hence many of the socioeconomic factors, that affect children's survival prospects may not be exogenous, but may be purposely chosen to promote survival, in light of the expected benefits and costs of a surviving child.

The empirical analyses consider the effect on infant and child survival of a variety of biological and behavioral variables—although certainly not all that are pertinent—and attempt to determine some of the avenues through which the behavioral factors exert their effect. The empirical analyses have used data on individual children, with supporting information on their mothers, households, and communities. This approach is consistent with the notion that "socioeconomic and environmental determinants at the family, community, and national levels operate through the proximate determinants at the individual level" (Chen, 1983:208). Furthermore, since the causes of death and their determinants change as an infant ages, the analyses of infant and childhood mortality are disaggregated over subperiods of the first 5 years of life.

Explanatory variables considered

We have divided the explanatory variables available in our data into two main categories, distinguishing those that are most likely to influence mortality through known biological mechanisms from those whose influence is more indirect and is likely to operate through some more proximate variable.[6] All explanatory variables are specific to the child in question and refer to the time of his or her birth.

The variables exerting proximate biological influences are the following.

Birth weight (treated as nonlinear to allow the strongest effects of very low birth weight and the possibility of increased mortality risk for very heavy birth weight). Birth weight reflects intrauterine pathology, prematurity, and ability to survive illnesses immediately after birth. It is also related to size later in infancy and hence to ability to survive infectious illnesses in post-neonatal infancy.

Mother's age at child's birth (treated as nonlinear to allow very young (<18) and very old (>40) mothers to exhibit different mortality risks than mothers in prime childbearing years). Young age reflects maternal immaturity, while old age is associated with increased likelihood of birth defects. Age may also measure mother's experience with child care and may be related to likelihood that the child is wanted.

Short pregnancy intervals and prior reproductive loss We have included variables indicating whether the preceding interval is short (<15 months), the proportion of other intervals that are short,[7] and the proportion of all births that are stillbirths. These variables measure gestational prematurity and nutritional depletion of the mother, which may, for example, impair her lactational performance. A short interval may measure competition of a previous young and surviving child for the mother's attention and could also be negatively correlated with likelihood the child was wanted.

Sex of child Gender reflects inherent biological differences in survival probabilities. It will also reflect differential treatment of boys and girls, say, in light of their different values in particular households or societies.

Birth order This variable is often treated as reflecting a biological mechanism. It may also reflect likelihood the child was wanted and the degree of competition for family resources.

Duration of unsupplemented and supplemented breastfeeding and type of supplemental or weaning food (adjusted for the possible reverse causation that death or illness-unto-death can curtail breastfeeding.)[8] Duration of breastfeeding may measure nutritional intake. The extent of supplementation or substitution reflects the likelihood of ingestion of pathogens with breastmilk supplements or substitutes. The latter influence should depend on the quality of water and sanitation. To allow for this in the analysis, the breastfeeding variables are interacted with the water and sanitation variables.

Types of household water and sanitation[9] These measure likelihood of exposure to gastrointestinal disease through contaminated water. They are interacted with type and duration of breastfeeding in the analysis, since breastfeeding, especially if not supplemented, reduces exposure to contaminated water.

House density (persons per room) This is a proxy for degree of contagion of respiratory infection and for likelihood of contact and fomite transfer of orally ingested pathogens. House density may also reflect pressure on household resources.

Year of child's birth This is a proxy for other influences accompanying socioeconomic development, for example, public health improvements.

The variables exerting indirect family influences are as follows.

Mother's education A mother's education is probably related to her knowledge of how to care for children and the quality of time she spends with them. It also affects the opportunity cost of time that mothers spend with children, and hence may affect the quantity of that time.

Household income This is a likely correlate of the mother's and child's nutritional intake and use of medical care.

Household composition We have considered the number of young children (<2 years old), of grandparents, and of other relatives in the household. On the one hand, the more members there are, the greater the competing demands on family resources—as children, for example, compete for the mother's attention. On the other hand, grandparents and other relatives can substitute for parents in child care. Furthermore, the fact that grandparents are alive could reflect a low-mortality environment or genetic stock.

Infant's institution of birth Particular types of birth institutions may be better able to handle birth complications or to identify conditions at birth that may increase mortality risk later. However, type of birth institution may also represent self-selection of mothers who give babies better care or who expect birth complications.

Ethnicity This variable captures the influence of unobserved factors that vary among ethnic groups.

Rurality scale This measures the influence of unobserved factors that vary with degree of rurality.[10]

Research strategy

One of our goals was to assess the extent to which family characteristics and behavior exert their effects indirectly through the more proximate factors we are able to measure. We do this by comparing regression equations that include either the proximate biological factors or the less proximate family variables with regressions that contain both sets of variables. Our intent, however, is not to trace all avenues through which the less proximate family variables affect mortality (in which case path analysis might have been preferable), but rather to investigate the overall extent to which their effects are mediated through the more proximate determinants we consider.

We have investigated mortality determinants in successive subperiods of infancy and childhood, using a life table approach. For each subperiod we use a sample of those who survived until the beginning of the subperiod and who could have survived until the end of the subperiod.[11] Given the distribution of ages at death in our sample, we have disaggregated the most at the beginning of life: we treat separately the first week and the remainder of the first month. Thereafter, we examine the probabilities of infant deaths in two periods: months 2 through 6, and months 7 through 12. These disaggregations are probably compatible with the speed of change in the structure of mortality determinants. In work in progress (Khairuddin et al.), we are extending the analysis to the childhood period.

For each subperiod and each set of explanatory variables, we have estimated a linear probability model by ordinary least squares (OLS). This approach allows the coefficients of the mortality determinants to differ in each subperiod. We have also estimated logit regressions explaining overall infant mortality for the most complete specification of variables and in an analysis that allows influences to differ for births before and after 1960 (DaVanzo and Habicht, 1984).[12] Almost all inferences about the relative strengths of association among determinants of infant mortality are the same in the OLS and logit estimates.[13]

The conceptual framework implies that parents choose the amount of time and resources to invest in children's health and survival prospects in light of the value to parents of the expected return on the investment. Hence, investments should be more likely where additional healthy surviving children are valued and where the investments are perceived as increasing health and survival prospects. The OLS estimation procedure, however, yields unbiased estimates only if all explanatory variables are exogenous, or predetermined, in terms of their influence on mortality. This assumption is satisfied if the explanatory variables are not affected directly by the mortality of the child under consideration (e.g., death curtailing breastfeeding) or by unobserved (at least to the researcher) factors that affect the mortality of this child or of all children in a family.[14]

Illustrative findings

To illustrate our approach, we present several findings from the Rand research, focusing on those that are new and have potential implications for programs and policies.

Babies born to very young mothers (less than 19 years old) are much more likely to die in the first month of life (Figure 1). Various biomedical factors could lead to this association, but the effects of environmental and behavioral factors that might cause infant deaths to very young mothers would not normally show up until later in infancy. Therefore, we infer from this pattern of very early mortality, and from the fact that this association between mothers' young age and babies' deaths is unchanged when indirect socioeconomic influences are controlled (see Figure 1), that the relationship is due primarily to biological causes.

Babies born to mothers older than 40 are also more likely to die in infancy (Figure 1). Some die in the neonatal period. Other deaths are concentrated in the second six months of infancy. No known biological mechanism

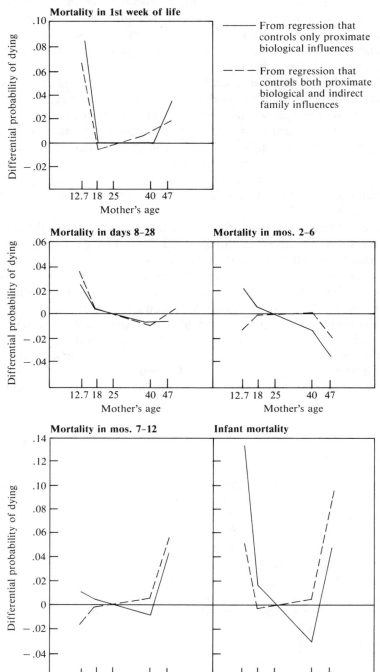

FIGURE 1   Maternal-age splines for each subperiod of the first year of life

SOURCE: DaVanzo, Butz, and Habicht (1983).

would produce this pattern of late infant mortality, but several behavioral factors associated with older motherhood could cause it.

These two infant mortality patterns, which were discovered because of our consideration of subperiods of infancy, our nonlinear treatment of mothers' age, and our distinction between direct and indirect influences, have several important implications for programs and policies. They imply that family planning programs should focus on very young and much older mothers for reasons of babies' health and survival, apart from the usual reasons of reducing fertility and improving mothers' health and well-being. The first finding also implies that policies that raise women's marriage age will reduce infant mortality. Furthermore, these results imply that programs should provide health care early in infancy for babies of very young mothers, but should monitor the condition of babies of older mothers throughout infancy.

The absence of modern toilet sanitation and piped water is strongly associated with mortality for babies who breastfeed little or not at all; however, the presence of these facilities makes no significant difference for the mortality of babies who breastfeed without supplementation (Table 1). Presumably, the reason is that babies who do not breastfeed usually have other foods mixed with water, which may be contaminated. Fortunately, Malaysian babies who do not breastfeed are considerably more likely to live in homes with modern facilities and thus escape pernicious effects. The task for public health officials, then, is to identify localities where breastfeeding is uncommon or is at risk of becoming so and where water and sanitation are poor, for those are the areas where the introduction of good water and sanitation is most likely to matter.

TABLE 1   Association of mortality with sanitation and type of water, depending on breastfeeding[15]

Type of breastfeeding[a]	Changes in mortality in		
	Days 8–28	Months 2–6	Months 7–12
	Modern toilet sanitation		
None	− 26.5***	− 59.7***	− 15.0*
Supplemented	2.1	− 14.8**	− 7.5*
Unsupplemented[b]	1.5	8.3	2.8
	Piped water		
None	− 8.1*	− 7.3	− 10.7**
Supplemented	− 12.1***	− 0.3	0.5
Unsupplemented[b]	− 1.7	7.4	3.3

[a] The duration of unsupplemented or supplemented breastfeeding is 1 week in the 8–28-day sample, 28 days in the 2–6-month sample, and 6 months in the 7–12-month sample.
[b] No other food or drink, including water.
SOURCE: Butz, Habicht, and DaVanzo (1984b), Table 3.

A corollary implication is that the beneficial influence of breastfeeding is greatest where water and sanitation are poor (Table 2), and that the promotion of breastfeeding will have its greatest effect in such places. Current

TABLE 2   Mortality effects of reduced breastfeeding, depending on sanitation and water

Toilet	Piped water	Changes in mortality in		
		Days 8–28	Months 2–6	Months 7–12
		Unsupplemented breastfeeding reduced to zero from		
		1 week	28 days	6 months
No	No	43.6***	90.2***	43.0***
No	Yes	37.1***	75.5***	29.0*
Yes	No	16.0***	22.1***	25.2***
Yes	Yes	9.6**	7.5	11.2*
		Supplemented breastfeeding reduced to zero from		
		1 week	28 days	6 months
No	No	29.7***	55.6***	22.2**
No	Yes	33.6***	48.6***	11.0
Yes	No	1.0	10.7	14.8***
Yes	Yes	5.0	3.7	3.6

NOTE: Table entries are differences in the mortality rate (deaths per thousand infants alive at the beginning of the period) associated with reductions in breastfeeding. See notes to Table 1.
SOURCE: Butz, Habicht, and DaVanzo (1984b), Table 4.

theory expects some benefit from breastfeeding even in infants with access to pure water, but our estimates strongly indicate that these benefits are small.

Breastfeeding reduces infant mortality less than previous estimates indicate. The effect is nonetheless substantial and important, at least where water and sanitation are poor, but it is considerably less than implied by most other studies. Most of these studies have attributed to short breastfeeding many infant deaths that were probably due to other causes. Prevalent diseases, for example, frequently weaken the child so that he stops nursing; then the disease kills him. The halt in breastfeeding is not responsible for the death, though most studies have treated it as such. The MFLS information on reasons for not breastfeeding or for ceasing breastfeeding have helped us disentangle these relationships. Table 3 illustrates the sensitivity of estimates of the association between breastfeeding and infant mortality to methods of treating this potential bias.

Policies concerned with infant health and mortality should take account of this finding. Previous estimates suggesting a substantial breastfeeding–mortality link may have incorrectly implied that principal priority should be given to policies to increase breastfeeding. Our findings suggest that policies to reduce mortality by other means are also worth pursuing. The fostering of breastfeeding is important, at least under some conditions, but should be accompanied by other measures (e.g., improved maternal education, improved sanitation) to reduce infant mortality.

TABLE 3 Estimates of association between infant mortality and breastfeeding: sensitivity to treatment of possible reverse-causation bias[a]

A Effects of ever breastfeeding

	Difference in infant mortality rate between nonbreastfed and breastfed babies
Sample	
1 All live births (n = 5,357)	74.7***
2 Excluding cases where breastfeeding was not begun because baby died on first day (n = 5,298)[b]	16.0**
3 Also excluding those who were too ill to breastfeed (n = 5,275)[c]	3.9

B Effects of duration of breastfeeding in months[d]

	Reduction in deaths per 1,000 live births for each month of breastfeeding	
	Full	**Partial**
Actual breastfeeding duration for infants who died		
4 All live births (n = 5,357)	11.9***	9.5***
5 Excluding cases where length of breastfeeding = length of life (n = 5,214)	4.7***	3.7***
6 Also excluding cases where breastfeeding stopped because of illness-unto-death (n = 5,134)[e]	3.4***	2.8***
Imputed breastfeeding duration for infants who died[f]		
7 All live births (n = 5,357)	5.5***	0.8*

[a] The regressions control for child's year of birth to make results comparable with those in the literature, which usually use cross-sectional data. Asterisks indicate whether differences are significantly different from zero at the 10 percent (*), 5 percent (**), or 1 percent (***) level (one-tail test).

[b] Babies who did not breastfeed and who died the first day.

[c] Babies who did not breastfeed, who died, and whose mothers said they were not breastfed because they died or were too ill or were in incubators.

[d] Total breastfeeding duration truncated at 12 months for infants who breastfed longer.

[e] Babies who died and whose mothers said they stopped breastfeeding because the baby was about to die or was too ill and those who stopped breastfeeding within the last 12.5 percent of their life span just before dying. More infants than expected stopped breastfeeding within the last 12.5 percent of their life span. (See Butz, DaVanzo, and Habicht, 1982, pp. 61–63.)

[f] Breastfeeding of babies excluded in rows 5 and 6 is imputed to be equal to the average length of breastfeeding (after truncation) of the other babies, who had the same breastfeeding experience up to the point where the former babies' breastfeeding was interrupted.

SOURCE: Habicht, DaVanzo, and Butz (1984), Table 1.

Lessons for future research

Researchers conducting future studies of infant and childhood mortality may wish to include several features of the Malaysian Family Life Survey and of the Rand analyses that have proved useful.

Retrospective data on births and deaths The MFLS experience suggests that, at least in Malaysia, women are able to report these events accurately and that important findings can be drawn from the resulting data on mortality trends.[16]

Retrospective data on mortality determinants Such information permits analysis of influences on mortality and of determinants of mortality trends, since explanatory variables can be defined to be specific to each child (and not merely to refer to the time of the survey). Furthermore, a life history matrix, in which retrospective information is collected at one time on a variety of life areas, undoubtedly provides more accurate information on each life area than if it were the only area being covered. (The sequencing of different types of events can help prompt recall of the timing of their occurrence.)

Data that document both behavioral and biomedical factors Respondents apparently can accurately report biomedical variables such as children's birth weights, duration of breastfeeding, and timing of first regular supplementary food or drink. Such information has been useful in understanding influences on mortality and in discovering the proximate determinants through which socioeconomic variables affect it.

Analysis of subperiods of infancy and childhood By identifying when particular influences are strongest during infancy and childhood, we have been able to understand better the reason for their effect and to identify the ages of children on which policies and programs should focus to be most effective.

Examination of interactions and of subgroups This has identified population subgroups on which particular programs and policies should focus to be most effective. For example, the promotion of breastfeeding holds the greatest promise in less developed areas and in households where water and sanitation are poor or absent.

Reasons for not breastfeeding or for stopping breastfeeding This information has been very useful in helping to estimate more accurately than before the effect of breastfeeding on infant mortality.

However, our understanding of the influences on infant and childhood mortality is still considerably short of being complete. The following would be extremely valuable in rounding out our knowledge.

Retrospective community data Community-level data on prices and the availability of medical care, nutritious foods, and water and sanitation are important for studying children's health and survival. These factors are largely outside families' control but may be amenable to influence by policymakers. In a setting where change is rapid, however, community data that only document conditions at the time of the survey will not be very useful in explaining past mortality. Future retrospective surveys of child mortality should document important community-level factors retrospectively, over the same period that they document mortality.[17]

Data on morbidity, diet, health practices, and use of medical care (both preventive and therapeutic) These are proximate determinants of mortality that are usually not well documented but that clearly can strongly affect children's survival prospects.

Modeling parent-choice inputs as endogenous We must understand why parents choose particular types of medical care or feeding patterns for their children if we are to assess accurately how these decisions affect their children's health and survival. Recent economic studies of choice of inputs and of the influence of ''unobserved heterogeneity'' (e.g., by Rosenzweig and Schultz, 1982, and Olsen and Wolpin, 1983) are useful first steps.

Notes

I want to acknowledge the contributions of my collaborators, William P. Butz, John Haaga, Jean-Pierre Habicht, and Khairuddin Yusof, who are coauthors of the reports on the research summarized here. The research on which this paper was based was funded by grants from the US Agency for International Development and the Ford and Rockefeller Foundations. Preparation of this paper was supported by the grant from the Ford and Rockefeller Foundations.

1 The team consisted of: William P. Butz, economist, previously at Rand, currently associate director of the US Bureau of the Census; Julie DaVanzo, economist at Rand; John Haaga, policy analyst, formerly at Rand, currently deputy director of the Nutritional Surveillance Program at Cornell University; Jean-Pierre Habicht, M.D., M.P.H., Ph.D., a nutritional epidemiologist at Cornell University; and Khairuddin Yusof, M.D., an obstetrician-gynecologist who is chairman of the Department of Social Obstetrics and Gynecology at the University of Malaya.

2 For more information about the MFLS see Butz and DaVanzo (1978).

3 Some mothers were unable to report the exact death dates of their deceased children. Using other information in the survey, we were able to place all of these deaths within the age intervals examined in this study.

4 The MFLS, however, only documented the last item for the time of the survey. Husbands and wives were each asked how many children they would have were they to start their married life all over again. We attempted to use this information to construct a retrospective measure of whether a child was wanted, but found that there were serious problems in doing so for children who had died. For example, if the respondent said she would like four children if she started again, had four at the time of the survey, but had had a fifth child who died before the survey, we inferred that the fifth child was ''unwanted.'' This procedure led to inferring that many children who had died were unwanted and to a very high correlation between mortality and ''being unwanted.'' However, we believe most of this relationship is spurious, because many parents reported that they wanted the number of living children they had at the time of the survey. Accordingly we did not include the variable indicating whether the child was wanted in most of our analyses.

5 The United Nations classifies Malaysia's vital registration system as ''virtually complete.'' An exception to the agreement with vital statistics is for Indians in the MFLS sample, whose infant mortality is higher than that indicated by vital statistics for the entire population of Malaysian Indians. The MFLS Indian sample is relatively small.

6 Although conceptually useful, the division of variables into proximate biological influences and indirect family influences is necessarily arbitrary, as will be obvious from the multiplicity of possible avenues of influence for some of the variables listed below. In DaVanzo, Butz, and Habicht (1983), we distinguish three categories of influences, subdividing the biological influences into those present at the time of birth (e.g., mother's age, child's birth weight) and those that can be affected by subsequent parental behavior (e.g., breastfeeding).

7 Excluding the intervals immediately before and after the birth in question.

8 See Habicht, DaVanzo, and Butz (1984) for a discussion of the methods we used to do this.

9 Because the relationship between sanitation and infant mortality is probably mediated through water quality, the sanitation variables are probably more appropriately measured at the community level than at the household level. This data set does contain information on community prevalence of the different sanitation systems, but this information describes conditions only at the time of the survey, in 1976–77. We attempted to use these variables for births after 1970 that occurred in the same community in which the mother was interviewed, since the community characteristics should be most accurate for these observations. However, the household-level sanitation variables give consistently stronger estimates. In the year of the interview these are highly correlated with community prevalence of toilet systems.

10 In addition to the variables listed here, we investigated the roles of other factors that were never statistically significant in the analysis of infant mortality and hence not listed. These were: the mother's hours of work (other than housework) in the child's first year of life, the occupation of that job, and its distance from her home; other dimensions of household composition (presence of other children by sex and age, presence of servants); incidence of epidemics during the child's first year of life; the type of health care the people in the community generally seek when sick; and community types of sanitation, prices and availability of infant foods, and access to various types of medical care. Proximity to medical care was found to be significantly related to birth weight, an important correlate of infant mortality, but not to infant mortality when birth weight is controlled. Most of the MFLS community data, like community data in most other surveys, refer to the time of the survey (1976–77) and hence are most applicable to births that occurred within a few years of the survey. However, there are not many infant deaths in this period, and this is probably why we find no significant relationships with these community data in the mortality analysis.

11 For example, in the regression explaining mortality in the seventh through twelfth months of infancy, we exclude from the sample babies born in the 12 months prior to the survey.

12 Our small samples of mortality events, combined with relatively large numbers of variables and concentrations of mortality events at particular values of some variables, make logit estimation impossible for subperiods of infancy and childhood.

13 There are some interesting differences between the OLS and logit estimates in which effects differ between the 1946–1960 and 1961–75 periods (DaVanzo and Habicht, 1984). An alternative technique would have been to use a hazard model, which is currently very popular in demographic studies. However, the hazard model tends to become cumbersome when one wishes to allow relationships to vary over subperiods of infancy and childhood. An important advantage of hazard models is that they enable incorporation of truncated observations; for example, a child who was 4 months old at the time of the survey could be included in the analysis even though he or she had not yet experienced all of childhood (and, say, might die at age 9 months). Our subperiod approach enabled us to include many such observations. (For example, the child in this illustration could be included in our analyses of mortality in the first week and the remainder of the first month, but would not be included, as it implicitly would be in a hazard model, in explaining mortality after the second month.)

14 However, if, for example, a woman chooses to give birth in a hospital or to breast-feed because she has an otherwise above-average mortality risk, our estimates of the beneficial effect on survival of hospital birth or of breastfeeding will be biased downward. (Alternatively, she may choose these behaviors because she is the type of mother who values child health highly and takes excellent care of her children in all possible ways. In this case we would overestimate the influences of these variables on survival prospects.) If, however, breastfeeding and hospital birth are affected by observable socioeconomic factors that also affect mortality, say mother's education, but not by unobserved factors that also affect mortality, then we can obtain unbiased estimates of their influence if we control in the mortality analyses for these observable factors. For example, Malaysian women who breastfeed more tend to have characteristics such as less education and Malay ethnicity

(Butz and DaVanzo, 1981) that are associated with higher infant mortality, other things the same. Not controlling these factors in the mortality analyses would result in an underestimate of the beneficial effect of breastfeeding. In addition to breastfeeding and birth institution, such variables as birth order, mother's age at the child's birth, and the length of the preceding or subsequent birth interval may be endogenous in the sense that they reflect parents' decisions about the number of births to have and their timing and spacing—decisions that might be made jointly with those about "quality" of children. To date, we have not formally allowed for these possible endogeneities in our analyses of infant and childhood mortality, say, by using two-stage least squares. (Indeed, there are so many possible endogeneities that it is probably not feasible to allow for all of them.) We have, however, performed separate analyses of determinants for many of these variables—birth weight, birth in hospital, birth spacing, breastfeeding, and age at first birth—and these have informed our assessment of their effects on mortality. We have attempted to correct for the bias that could arise from death curtailing breastfeeding, using the method described in Habicht, DaVanzo, and Butz (1984).

15 Table entries are differences in mortality rates (deaths per thousand infants alive at beginning of the period) associated with presence of toilet sanitation or piped water compared with the rate in the absence of the feature. These derive from a multivariate analysis that controls the other variables discussed in the text. Asterisks indicate whether differences are significantly different from zero at the 10 percent (*), 5 percent (**), or 1 percent (***) level (one-tail test).

Mean mortality rates (deaths per thousand infants alive at the beginning of the period) for the three subperiods are: 6.0, 16.3, and 9.9, respectively. Seventy-nine percent of the entire MFLS sample of babies were born to households with toilet sanitation and 43 percent to households with piped water.

16 The relatively high level of development of Malaysia, and the fact that most women had records against which birth dates could be verified, probably made it easier to collect good retrospective information in Malaysia than it would be in many other developing countries. However, the World Fertility Survey experience also suggests that retrospective surveys can yield better information than was previously thought to be the case.

17 An additional complication is migration: some respondents will have lived in non-sample communities in the past.

References

Butz, W. P., and J. P. Habicht. 1976. "The effects of nutrition and health on fertility: Hypotheses, evidence, and interventions," in *Population and Development: The Search for Selective Interventions*, ed. R. G. Ridker. Baltimore and London: Johns Hopkins University Press.

———, and J. DaVanzo. 1978. *The Malaysian Family Life Survey: Summary Report*. R-2351-AID. The Rand Corporation.

———, and J. DaVanzo. 1981. "Determinants of breastfeeding and weaning patterns in Malaysia." WD-995-1-AID. The Rand Corporation.

———, J. DaVanzo, and J-P. Habicht. 1982. *Biological and Behavioral Influences on the Mortality of Malaysian Infants*. N-1638-AID. The Rand Corporation.

———, J-P. Habicht, and J. DaVanzo. 1984a. "Improving infant nutrition, health, and survival: Policy and program implications from the Malaysian Family Life Survey," *Malaysian Journal of Reproductive Health* 2, no. 1 (January).

———, J-P. Habicht, and J. DaVanzo. 1984b. "Environmental factors in the relationship between breastfeeding and infant mortality: The role of water and sanitation in Malaysia," *American Journal of Epidemiology* 119, no. 4: 516–525.

Chen, L. 1983. "Child survival: Levels, trends and determinants," in *Determinants of Fertility in Developing Countries: A Summary of Knowledge*. Washington, D.C.: National Academy of Sciences.

DaVanzo, J., W. P. Butz, and J-P. Habicht. 1983. "How biological and behavioural influences on mortality in Malaysia vary during the first year of life," *Population Studies* 37, no. 3 (November): 381–402.

———, J-P. Habicht, and W. P. Butz. 1984. "Assessing socioeconomic correlates of birthweight in Peninsular Malaysia: Ethnic differences and changes over time," *Social Science and Medicine* 18, no. 5: 387–404.

———, and J-P. Habicht. 1984. "What accounts for the decline in infant mortality in Peninsular Malaysia: 1946–1975?" Background paper for the *World Development Report*, World Bank.

Government of Malaysia. Various years. *Report of the Registrar-General on Population, Births, Deaths, Marriages, and Adoptions*. Kuala Lumpur.

Haaga, J. 1983. "Investigating the accuracy of retrospective life history data from the Malaysian Family Life Survey." The Rand Corporation.

Habicht, J-P., J. DaVanzo, and W. P. Butz. 1984. "Does breastfeeding really save lives?" The Rand Corporation.

Jelliffe, D. B., and E. F. P. Jelliffe. 1978. *Human Milk in the Modern World*. Oxford: Oxford University Press.

Khairuddin, Y., C. Peterson, J. DaVanzo, and J-P. Habicht. In progress. "Why are infant and child mortality rates in Peninsular Malaysia higher in Kedah, Kelantan, Perlis, and Trengganu?"

Klein, S. D. 1980. "Class, culture, and health," in *Public Health and Preventive Medicine*, ed. J. M. Last. New York: Appleton-Century-Crofts.

Mosley, W. H. 1982. "Considerations for a conceptual framework for the study of child survival."

———, and L. Chen. 1984. "An analytical framework for the study of child survival in developing countries," this volume.

Olsen, R. J., and K. I. Wolpin. 1983. "The impact of exogenous child mortality on fertility: A waiting-time regression with dynamic regressors," *Econometrica* 51: 731–749.

Rosenzweig, M., and T. P. Schultz. 1982. "Birth weight, the production of child health, and input demand," in *Economic Aspects of Health*, ed. V. R. Fuchs. Chicago: University of Chicago Press.

Scrimshaw, S. C. M. 1978. "Infant mortality and behavior in the regulation of family size," *Population and Development Review* 4, no. 3 (September): 383–403.

United Nations. 1973. *The Determinants and Consequences of Population Trends: New Summary of Findings on Interaction of Demographic, Economic and Social Factors*, Vols. I and II. Population Studies No. 50, pp. 115–137.

Waite, L., D. De Tray, and R. Rindfuss. 1983. "Mothers' expectations for children's schooling in Malaysia." N-1947-AID. The Rand Corporation.

Willis, R. J. 1974. "Economic theory of fertility behavior," in *Economics of the Family*, ed. T. W. Schultz. Chicago: University of Chicago Press.

Wray, J. D. 1971. "Population pressure on families: Family size and child spacing," in *Rapid Population Growth: Consequences and Policy Implications*. Baltimore: Johns Hopkins University Press.

ANALYTICAL METHODS

Estimating Levels, Trends, and Determinants of Child Mortality in Countries with Poor Statistics

James Trussell

Jane Menken

The estimation of levels, trends, and determinants of infant and child mortality in statistically poor countries has received intense attention from demographers during the past 15 years. The literature on this subject is vast, so our review is focused on the most commonly applicable methods of analysis. We approach this task as demographers, asking the types of questions demographers typically ask. It will prove convenient first to consider methods and data sources for estimating levels and trends and next to explore how these can be adapted to measure determinants. Although many pages of methodological development follow, we emphasize that the ultimate goal of our work is entirely practical. By concentrating on techniques of analysis, we provide tools for addressing such questions as why mortality has fallen in the past and what policy interventions are most cost-efficient for reducing mortality in the future. We close with a discussion of strategies for analyzing specific intervention programs.

Preliminary methodological considerations

Because death rates vary by age, indexes of mortality that do not control for the effects of age composition of a population can be seriously misleading. For example, in 1984 the crude death rate in the United States is 9 per thousand population, while that in Mexico is only 6 per thousand despite the fact that death rates are lower at every age in the United States. The reason is that the population of Mexico is concentrated in the younger age groups, in which mortality is lower. Although one could work directly with age-specific death rates, demographers find it more convenient to convert them into a life table, which shows the proportion of persons surviving to exact ages 1, 2, 3, etc. In this paper, we focus on techniques for estimating life table probabilities of dying between birth and some specific childhood age a. For several reasons, demographers have long searched for mathematical relationships that can describe well the life table of any population in terms of relatively few parameters. First, one could summarize an entire column of survivorship probabilities into just a few index numbers for easy storage. Second, one could easily compare the mortality experience of different populations and determine the range of human mortality experience by examining the index numbers. Finally, if mortality rates at different ages were related in some simple fashion, then by knowing reasonably accurately one or a few age-specific mortality rates, one could infer all the others and hence generate the entire life table for a population. The attempt to model age-specific mortality rates has been largely successful. Although there is no mathematical function that can represent the mortality experience of all populations, several sets of model life tables are essential to the demographer's tool kit. We mention these briefly here.

The first is a relational system proposed by William Brass (1971). Given an appropriate standard life table, Brass suggested that the life table l_x function for a particular population was related to the standard in the following way:

$$ ln\left(\frac{l_x}{1 - l_x}\right) = a + b\ ln\left(\frac{l_x^s}{1 - l_x^s}\right) \tag{1} $$

where l_x^s is the survivorship function of the standard. The parameters a and b determine roughly the overall level of mortality and the relation between levels of adult and child mortality, respectively. The relational system is often converted into a one-parameter system by setting b equal to 1. Although Brass proposed two standards (general and African), the standard can be borrowed from a population thought to have similar mortality conditions and more reliable data or chosen from a set of model tables.

The second set of models was developed by Coale and Demeny (1966, 1983). Using life tables from populations thought to have reliable data, they discovered four common patterns of mortality rates by age, which they denoted North, South, East, and West. Within each pattern or region, they developed two sets of model life tables, one for males and one for females, that are indexed by expectation of life. Hence, their models for a given sex have only one parameter (level) within each region but have four basic patterns to account for observed differences in the relation between child and adult mortality, patterns in infant and child mortality, and patterns in old-age mortality.

The United Nations (1982) recently prepared a third set of models specifically for developing countries. They identified five distinct patterns of mortality by age based on examination of age-specific mortality rates from populations thought to have reasonably reliable data: Latin America, South Asia, the Far East, Chile, and a (residual) general pattern. The model tables, published separately for each sex, are one-parameter tables indexed by expectation of life.

If these models were merely mathematical exercises in curve fitting, they would hardly warrant our attention here. Some familiarity with such models is essential for understanding later sections of our paper for two reasons. First, they form the basis of methods of estimating levels, trends, and covariates of mortality from the incomplete and defective data likely to be encountered in most statistically poor countries. Second, they provide a yardstick by which to judge the plausibility of any estimates obtained.

Estimation of levels and trends

Why should one be interested in estimating levels and trends in mortality? Levels of child mortality provide an index of the health and vigor of a population; trends give an indication of changes over time. But such information can be of far more value than mere description: it is essential for the formation of sensible policy. If mortality has fallen, why? If it has ceased to fall, why? Has a particular health intervention scheme reduced mortality?

We limit our attention here to two sources of data—retrospective maternity histories and retrospective reports of women on number of children ever born and surviving. We omit discussion of dual record systems (Carver, 1976) and postpone consideration of multiround prospective surveys until a later section.

Retrospective maternity histories

The work of the World Fertility Survey (WFS) has provided us with retrospective maternity histories in dozens of otherwise statistically poor countries. Included in these histories are date of birth of every child and dates of death (or age at death) for those who died. Given such information, it is a routine task to calculate directly probabilities of dying between birth and exact age of childhood. Rutstein (1983) provides a summary of estimates for many developing countries with WFS surveys. We hasten to add that just because such information was collected does not mean that it is accurate. Dates of birth may be misreported or guessed, children who have died may be omitted, and countless other defects may characterize the data.

The quality of many if not most WFS surveys has been evaluated either by WFS central staff or by analysts in the home country. Many evaluations have been published in the *Scientific Reports* series issued by WFS. Techniques of analysis include comparison of WFS data with data from censuses, other surveys, and vital registration, as well as comparison of data with models. Common sense also plays a large role. Implausible discontinuities in time trends, for example, signal defects in the data. Our judgment is that most evaluations have revealed WFS surveys to be of high quality, especially if attention is confined to the recent past.

Consider, as one example, the Republic of the Philippines Fertility Survey of 1978. Reyes (1981) concludes that the data on infant and child mortality appear to be accurate after comparing results on levels and trends with those of the 1973 National Demographic Survey and after examining sex differentials in mortality. Her estimates of infant and child mortality calculated directly from data on date of birth and age at death reveal that mortality essentially ceased to decline after 1960. Whatever defects are present in the data, this conclusion is very unlikely to be reversed. It spawns a host of questions. Why was the decline arrested? Why has child mortality remained essentially on a plateau for 15 years?

Brass-type estimates

William Brass (1968) developed a technique for estimating child mortality simply from information by women on children ever born and children surviving commonly collected in censuses and surveys. It has proved to be the most useful and robust technique of demographic analysis for statistically poor populations, since the requisite questions have been routinely asked in many censuses and surveys for decades.

   To understand how the technique works and its underlying logic, we first examine a later elaboration by Preston (Preston and Palloni, 1978).[1] Consider a cohort of women aged 25–29. In a census or demographic survey, ages of surviving children and their relationship to the head of the household are normally collected, as is the number of children ever born to each woman; extracting such data may require a special tabulation, and it is important to include only biological children of the female respondents. Children aged a were obviously born a years ago and represent the survivors of the entire birth cohort of own (biological) children; this relation is expressed in a formula

$$S(a) = {}_1L_a \, CEB \, (t - a) \tag{2}$$

where $S(a)$ is the number of surviving children aged a, $CEB(t-a)$ is the number of children ever born a years before the survey, and ${}_1L_a$ is the life table person-years lived between age a and $a+1$, a measure that is also the fraction of a life table one-year birth cohort who would be observed to be alive at age a (i.e., aged a to $a+1$). We do not typically know $CEB(t-a)$ but we do know the sum over all ages a, a quantity equal to the total number of births to women aged 25–29. Summing (2) over age and rearranging, we obtain

$$CEB = \sum_{a=0}^{w} S(a)/{}_1L_a \tag{3}$$

   In equation (3) we know CEB and $S(a)$; the goal is to estimate ${}_1L_a$ for all a. Without model life tables this task would be impossible, for there is but one equation and there are many unknowns. But for any set of one-parameter model life tables belonging to a particular family (say, Coale–Demeny model West), there is one and only one model life table that will satisfy equation (3). If the mortality level of the model is too low, the set of ${}_1L_a$ will be too high and the predicted number of children ever born will fall below the actual.

The opposite result obtains when the chosen life table represents a mortality level that is too high. Using this technique, Johansson and Preston (1978) were able to estimate that the probability of survival to age 5 (l_5) in 1900 for Hopi children was .490. Without the Brass technique, our knowledge of mortality among children of this American Indian tribe would be severely diminished.

Often, especially for historical data, the number of surviving own children by age was not tabulated. This is the situation Brass faced when examining the demography of tropical Africa in the early 1960s. What he did have was an abundance of data on total number of children ever born and children surviving by age group of mother. Such information can now be found routinely, for example, in the United Nations *Demographic Yearbook*. Brass reasoned that the proportion of children who have died must represent the probability of dying between birth and some exact age in childhood. Logically,[2] that age must lie between 0 and the age that the oldest child is (or would have been) at the time of the survey and should be roughly equivalent to the average age that all children would have been if all had survived to the time of the survey. The missing link is this hypothetical age distribution if all children had survived, which also provides the age distribution of childbearing of the mothers. To infer the age pattern of childbearing, Brass resorted to models of fertility. To pick the right model, he used an index of the "earliness" of childbearing, the ratio of children ever born for women 20–24 and 25–29. Later, Sullivan (1972) and Trussell (1975) refined the technique; the latest version appears in the new United Nations manual (Manual X) on demographic estimation from incomplete data (Hill, Zlotnik, and Trussell, 1983). It is relatively simple to use. One converts the proportion of children who have died into a life table probability of dying by multiplying the proportion dead by an adjustment factor:

$$\tilde{q}(a) = \tilde{K}(j) \cdot PD(j) \tag{4}$$

where the adjustment factor $\tilde{K}(j)$ depends on the fertility schedule of the population; as inferred from information on *CEB* at the young ages of childbearing:

$$\tilde{K}(j) = a_j + b_j \, CEB \, (20–24)/CEB(25–29) \tag{5}$$

In equations (4) and (5), $\tilde{q}(a)$ is the estimated probability of dying by exact age a, $PD(j)$ is the proportion of children who have died among women in age group j, and $\tilde{K}(j)$ is an adjustment factor for women aged j estimated from the ratio of *CEB* for women 20–24 and 25–29. The regression equation for the adjustment factor was based on model fertility and mortality schedules. Since in a one-parameter model life table knowledge of any age-specific death rate enables one to infer all such rates and hence the whole life table, reports of *CEB* and children surviving by women aged 25–29 could be used to estimate $q(a)$ for any age a. As Preston and Palloni (1978) have shown, however, for any age group of women there exists a particular age a such that the bias introduced in the estimation procedure by the improper choice of model life table family is minimized. Traditionally, information from women aged 20–24, 25–29, 30–34, and 35–39 is used to estimate $q(2)$, $q(3)$, $q(5)$, and $q(10)$, respectively.[3]

The Brass technique, though powerful, is not immune to defects in the data. In some cultures women may be reluctant to mention children who have died and in many populations women omit children who have grown up and moved away from home. Adherence to a protocol of six questions—three for each sex on the number of children who have died, surviving children living at home, and surviving children living elsewhere—seems to maximize the likelihood of obtaining correct responses. Ewbank (1982) reviewed the sources of error in Brass estimates of infant mortality in Bangladesh and concluded that errors introduced by changing age at marriage, annual fluctuation in mortality, and birth order differences are as important as errors introduced by secular trends in mortality and age misreporting of mother. One of these sources of bias, caused by changing age at marriage, can be reduced substantially by using information tabulated by duration of marriage rather than age of the woman. This strategy may also reduce bias caused by age misreporting, since women who do not know their age may well know their marriage duration. Tables of regression coefficients for equations similar in structure to (4) and (5), but based on marriage duration, are given in UN Manual X.

Two examples indicate the value of the Brass technique: China in the late 1920s and Afghanistan in the early 1970s. Without this technique (and similar techniques for the analysis of fertility and adult mortality), both populations would remain demographic mysteries. By good fortune, the demographic survey supervised by Lossing Buck in China in 1929 and the survey conducted by SUNY-Buffalo in Afghanistan in 1972–74 included questions suited for analysis by the latest techniques of indirect estimation. Both surveys reveal extremely high mortality when subjected to the Brass technique: the probability of dying by age 2 is estimated to have been .340 in China (Barclay et al., 1976) and .316 in rural areas and .239 in urban areas of Afghanistan (Trussell and Brown, 1979). In both populations, females had higher mortality relative to males than would be expected from model life tables; in China, females actually had a higher probability of dying by ages 2, 3, and 5 than did males. Hence demographic models and techniques of indirect estimation enable us to infer with some degree of confidence that mortality levels were extremely high and that females suffered higher mortality than would be expected if they had received care and feeding to the same degree as males.

The observant reader might well wonder how the Brass technique handles declining mortality. The answer is not so straightforward as one might wish. First, the simulations upon which the technique is based embody an assumption of constant mortality over time. Hence there is no distinction between period and cohort life tables. The real world is decidedly not so simple, and declining mortality at some periods in the recent past is nearly universal. Hence, it might appear that the Brass technique is an abstract tool of little use unless one can find populations, such as Afghanistan and China in the 1900s, characterized by nearly constant mortality. Feeney (1980) first tackled this problem by postulating a linear decline by period in the level of mortality. There are then two parameters that identify the time path of mortality—the rate of decline and the final level. Consider any two paths of decline, one faster than the other. In order for the actual proportion of children who have died to equal the estimated, the path with the higher rate of decline must have the lower final level. Hence the two paths must cross at some time in the past, when the period life table would be the same for both paths. Feeney found that *all* possible paths intersected at the same point in time, or at least the intersections are close enough to be considered identical. Preston and Palloni (1978) showed that if the linear decline takes place in cohort life table levels, then there is an exact analytical solution yielding the same point in the past for all paths. Coale and Trussell (1978) showed analytically that the result could not be exact but was approximately exact (duplicating Feeney's simulations) for a period decline. Techniques are available (Hill, Zlotnik, and Trussell, 1983) for "dating" the Brass mortality techniques: the reference point in the past can be estimated by

$$\tilde{t}_j^* = a_j + b_j \, CEB(20-24)/CEB(25-29) \qquad (6)$$

where $\tilde{t}_j^*$ is the estimated number of years before the survey to which the mortality estimate for women in age group j applies. The a_j and b_j are regression coefficients, different for each age group j of women, which can be found in published tables. Similar tables exist for estimates based on data tabulated by marriage duration.

Two problems remain. What if the mortality trend is not linear? It turns out that there will be an intersection at approximately the same point in time for paths that are not linear, but no simple dating techniques such as those given by equation (6) have been published. One can always find a solution from first principles, but the functional form of the time path would have to be assumed.[4] The second problem is what to do with the isolated estimates that emerge. For example, we might conclude that $q_2 = .051$, $q_3 = .065$, and $q_5 = .072$ for Panama at the exact times 1974.3, 1972.4, and 1970.1, respectively (Trussell and Hill, 1976). What we would like is an entire life table, or at least a life table for the childhood ages for each of these years, not just one $q(a)$ for each year. The only solution is to assign a whole life table from a one-parameter family on the basis of the single $q(a)$ for each year. Feeney (1980) adopts such an approach to estimate a common measure q_1 for each year. But assigning q_1 or (e_0) on the basis of a single $q(a)$ leaves the analyst terribly vulnerable to a wrong choice of model life table family. For example, a q_5 of .662 (Afghanistan rural females) implies a q_1 of .196 if the Coale–Demeny model family is North but .241 if the family is East.

Estimation of covariates

From a policy perspective, the most useful information about child mortality is its determinants. Hence, demographers have increasingly turned their attention to identifying factors associated with low mortality. Factors associated with mortality might be biological (e.g., breastfeeding, maternal age, nutritional status, disease environment) or more removed socioeconomic influences (e.g., maternal and paternal education, occupation, income). As in most socioeconomic research, the emphasis thus far has been on analyzing existing data sets that were not collected as a part of any true experiment. Given the quasi-experimental design, it is not possible to identify factors as determinants but only to identify covariates, those factors associated with low or high mortality. The objective of such studies is to suggest strategies for reducing mortality. In this section we describe the statistical and methodological procedure for estimating the quantitative association between background variables and the risk of death. In the next section we discuss evaluation of particular intervention strategies.

Life tables are routinely calculated separately for males and females, for residents of urban and rural areas, and for other such classifications of the population (see Arriaga, 1981, and Rutstein, 1983). These tables can be viewed as rough attempts to identify covariates. After such life tables have been constructed, one could examine mortality differentials by sex, by region of a country, or by race. We know, however, that it is important to examine such differentials simultaneously, not sequentially. Otherwise one can be led to the erroneous conclusion that a factor is associated with mortality when in fact it is not. One example is worth many words. Behm et al. (1977–79) examined mortality differentials by urban/rural residence and found, as have others, that mortality is lower in urban areas. Such lower mortality is often attributed to better facilities in urban areas. But when Behm examined differentials simultaneously by urban/rural residence and maternal education, the urban/rural differentials were narrowed, if not eliminated. Hence, in urban areas, mortality is lower because mothers have higher educational attainment.

But such exercises can seldom have a truly multivariate flavor since simultaneous cross-classification of several factors soon results in cell sizes too small for reliable estimation. For example, cross-classification by sex (two categories), education of mother (say, three categories), age of mother (say, three categories), breastfeeding status (two categories, ever and never), time period of birth (three categories), and type of water supply (say, three categories) results in $2 \times 3 \times 3 \times 2 \times 3 \times 3 = 324$ cells. In a typical WFS survey with 5,000 women and perhaps 20,000 births, there would on average be only 62 births per cell. Addition of another factor, say father's education with three categories, would cut average cell size to 20. Hence, demographers have increasingly turned to a technique, called the hazard model, specifically designed for multivariate analysis of life tables. This technique requires information on exposure to risk for each child; hence date of birth and date of death (or age at death) are needed. Trussell and Preston (1982) compared proportional hazard models to other techniques that require less detailed data. They examined how much precision in estimation is lost as various pieces of information such as dates of birth or death are discarded. Their conclusion is that even incomplete Brass-type mortality data routinely collected in household surveys or censuses can yield estimates of covariate effects that are very close to those based on the much richer wealth of data collected in detailed maternity histories. However, it should be emphasized that their conclusions apply only to *proportional* hazards models. They did not examine the possibility that the effects of covariates vary with age, and their alternative techniques do not allow such time-varying effects. These other techniques will not be described here; those interested are referred to their paper.[5]

A full discussion of hazard models in terms familiar to demographers can be found in Trussell and Hammerslough (1983). A hazard model can be described briefly as follows: let age be measured as time in months since birth. We assume that age can be broken into K categories (say, 0–2 months, 3–5 months, etc.) during which the risk of death is constant for individuals with the same values of the covariates. The simplest such model is the *proportional hazards* model with fixed covariates. Let r_{ik} be the risk of death (death rate or hazard) in age category k for individual i with vector of covariates X_i. Then, under the proportional hazards assumption:

$$ln(r_{ik}) = a_k + X_i'b \qquad k = 1, \ldots, K$$
$$= a_k + b_1 X_{i1} + b_2 X_{i2} \ldots + b_n X_{in} \qquad (7)$$

Note that the risk in duration category k is $e^{a_k} e^{X_i'b}$, where e^{a_k} may be considered an underlying age-specific risk. The covariates of individual i shift this risk up or down depending on whether $e^{X_i'b}$ is greater than or less than 1.0. Moreover, in a proportional hazards model this multiplicative factor is the same at every age, so that the ratio of hazards of any two individuals is the same at all ages. Individuals have different values of $X_i'b$ depending, of course, on the values of their covariates X_i.

In the next simplest model, the values of the covariates are allowed to change over time. For example, a child may be breastfed during the first three age intervals and then weaned. With *time-varying covariates*, the model for individual i with covariates vector W_{ik} in period k becomes:

$$ln(r_{ik}) = a_k + W_{ik}'c \qquad (8)$$

Note, however, that there is no age subscript on c, so the model is still a proportional hazards model in the sense that a given value of a covariate has the same effect at each age. W_{ik} varies with age, but its effect does not. When the covariate changes over age, then the ratio of hazards for two individuals will not necessarily stay constant.

Finally, the effect of a particular covariate on the hazard may change with age, even though the covariate itself stays the same. For example, suppose that we know that a child was born into a household with a clean water supply. Then we might expect the effect of a dummy variable indicating the presence of a clean water supply to change with age, as exogenous factors become more important. Under the *time-dependent effects* assumption, the model for individual i in age interval k with covariate vector Y_i becomes:

$$ln(r_{ik}) = a_i + Y_i'd_k \tag{9}$$

In this case, there is an age subscript on the coefficient (so that the effect changes across intervals), but not on the covariate. Note, however, that it is possible for a time-varying covariate to have time-dependent effects.

A general model can encompass all of these assumptions:

$$ln(r_{ik}) = a_k + X_i'b + W_{ik}'c + Y_i'd_k + Z_{ik}'e_k \tag{10}$$

where the term $Z_{ik}'e_k$ has been added to allow for the possibility of a time-varying covariate with time-dependent effects. The parameters are not estimated by regression. Instead, for each infant whose birth appears in the sample, the probability that he or she survived to the survey or died at a particular age is formed from equation (10), using the basic mathematics of the life table. The product of all such probabilities is the likelihood function; estimation of the unknown parameters is performed numerically by maximizing the likelihood function. Several computer packages are available for estimating hazard models; several of these are compared in the appendix.

Now that the logic of the technique has been presented, a simple example may illustrate its interpretation. Suppose we are interested in infant mortality. We divide the first year of life into four age categories: the first month, months 2–3, months 4–6, and months 7–12. These intervals were chosen because we think that mortality rates vary sharply by age during the first few months of life and less thereafter. Consider two covariates, time period of birth with three categories and education of mother with three categories. Assume a simple proportional hazards model

$$ln(r_{ijk}) = A_i + T_j + E_k \qquad \begin{aligned} i &= 1, \ldots, 4; \\ j &= 1, \ldots, 3; k = 1, \ldots, 3 \end{aligned} \tag{11}$$

where A_i, T_j, and E_k are the effects of being in age interval i, having been born in time period j, and having a mother in education group k.[6] Then the risk of death for those in the first month of life and in the first category of each of the two covariates is

$$r_{111} = \exp(A_1 + T_1 + E_1) \tag{12}$$

The risk for those in the first month of life, in time period 1 and education category 2, is

$$r_{112} = \exp(A_1 + T_1 + E_2) \qquad (13)$$

Hence, the *relative risk* of death for those whose mothers are in education category 1 compared with those whose mothers are in education category 2 is

$$r_{111}/r_{112} = \exp(E_1 - E_2) \qquad (14)$$

It can be seen that this relative risk applies at all ages, not merely the first age interval, and to all time periods. In a more complex model with interactions between education and age, the relative risk would be different for each age interval.

Holland (1983) estimated such a model to determine the impact of breastfeeding on mortality.[7] He postulated that the beneficial effect would decline with age of the child. Using data from Malaysia, he found a relative risk of 12.1 during the first month of life when those never breastfed were compared with those ever breastfed, even after the effects of other factors such as age and education of the mother, time period of birth, birth order, length of previous birth interval, sex, birth weight, ethnicity, and source of water supply were controlled. In the last age interval, 7–12 months, the relative risk fell to 1.9 when those never breastfed were compared with those breastfed until the start of the interval.

Hobcraft et al. (1983) analyzed the effect of child spacing on infant and early child mortality. Using data from World Fertility Surveys in 26 developing countries, they were able to document the adverse effects on an "index" child of rapid appearance of younger siblings and to show that these operate through direct competition for family resources. They also found that the occurrence of one birth during the period 0–2 years before the birth of the "index" child approximately doubled the risk of death, while the occurrence of two births in the two years beforehand approximately tripled the risk of death, when compared with a situation of no births in the previous two years.

Two other studies further illustrate the nature of results gleaned thus far from the application of hazard models.[8] In a large cross-national comparison of the effects of socioeconomic factors on infant and child mortality, Hobcraft et al. (1982) estimated a common five-factor model on WFS data for 29 countries. They found that the five factors considered—mother's education, mother's work status, father's education, father's occupation, and place of residence—were each important in some populations in some age intervals (<1 month, 1–11 months, 1–4 years). In general, the husband's characteristics played an important role in tropical Africa and parts of Southeast Asia, while mother's education seemed to affect survival chances in Latin America and Southeast Asia. Mother's work status proved to be a significant covariate less often than the other factors. Martin et al. (1983) examined a larger number of factors in a smaller number of countries. Using WFS data from the Philippines, Indonesia, and Pakistan, they examined the relative importance of mother's education, father's education, place of residence, time period of birth, region, mother's age at the birth, birth order, and sex of child. One of the results of interest is the effect of birth order. Conventional wisdom tells us that first births have higher mortality than second or third births. Indeed, in single-factor analyses of both Indonesia and Pakistan, this result held. But when mother's age at the time of the birth was added to the model, the result was reversed; first births had lower mortality. In the Philippines, the first-born child enjoyed an advantage over the second and third even when birth order was examined alone, but once age of the mother was controlled, this advantage increased substantially. Hence, they conclude that the adverse mortality typically observed for first borns is really caused by the fact that first births typically occur to young mothers, who impart much higher risks of dying to their children.

The first two analyses described above can be usefully contrasted with the second two. At first glance, there appears to be no logical difference between the two groups. Both employ hazard models with several covariates. The difference lies in the purpose for including covariates. Holland and Hobcraft et al. wished to focus on the effect of breastfeeding and child spacing, respectively. But they knew that effects estimated from examination of these factors alone would be contaminated because the effects of other factors known to influence mortality were not controlled. Hence, they included other factors merely as controls. In contrast, the latter two analyses were not so sharply focused; instead, several factors thought to be associated with mortality were included in order to determine their relative importance. The second strategy is essentially exploratory data analysis aimed at discovering those factors strongly associated with mortality levels, whereas the second focuses attention on a particular factor and employs covariates to control for the effects of confounding variables. The first strategy sounds ideal for assessing the effect of alternative schemes devised for mortality reduction. In our view, however, this use of the hazard model methodology is illegitimate, for we think that no statistical techniques, no matter how elaborate, can ever correct for the absence of a proper experimental design. In the following section we elaborate this point. We first discuss the difficulty in drawing inferences of cause and effect, next state the classical solution, and finally suggest contexts in which hazard models can nevertheless be very useful.

Evaluation of intervention schemes

The principle that association does not imply cause and effect is taught in every introductory statistics course. Yet it is violated nearly universally when evaluating the effects of public policy interventions. In order to illustrate the point, consider maternal education. In many populations, increased maternal education has been found to be associated with lower infant and child mortality, even when the effects of father's education and occupation, as well as other factors, are controlled. Do such findings mean that increasing female education would be an effective intervention strategy? The answer, in our minds, is not known. We suspect that raising levels of female education would lower mortality, but the negative association could reflect circumstances other than cause and effect. Female education, while itself not linked to mortality, could nevertheless be correlated with another variable that is. Introducing covariates other than female education in the hazards model analysis could eliminate this source of bias, provided that the analyst chooses the covariates with care; indeed, the work on breastfeeding and child spacing cited in the last section explicitly involves such controls.

But another source of bias is far more insidious—sample selection bias. When the intervention scheme (in this case education) is self-selected, the analyst loses the ability to assess cause and effect. The classic example is the initial design for evaluation of the Salk vaccine. This called for giving the vaccine to second graders who volunteered for the trials and then comparing the average outcome for the treated group with the average for first and third graders, none of whom were treated. Another control group was provided by second graders who did not volunteer. This research design yielded rates of poliomyelitis (per 100,000) of 17 for the treatment group, 46 for the first and third graders, and 35 for the second graders who did not volunteer. In contrast, a proper experimental design that included random assignment of volunteers to the vaccine or a placebo yielded rates of 16 and 57 (Meier, 1972: 11). What explains the difference? Polio, in contrast to most diseases, strikes primarily those in higher socioeconomic groups. But persons of higher socioeconomic status are far more likely to volunteer for experiments. Hence, volunteers are at much higher risk of contracting the disease. In the randomized trials, volunteers who were not vaccinated had a rate of 57, while nonvolunteers had a rate of only 36. In both sets of trials, those who volunteered and were vaccinated contracted the disease at the same rate (16–17/100,000). But the effectiveness of the vaccine would be underestimated in the nonrandomized trials, because those volunteering had the highest risk of getting the disease. Selection may be due to the investigator as well. In the famous Lanarkshire milk experiment, 10,000 children were given 3/4 pint of milk per day for four months while another 10,000 children served as controls. As Student (1931) pointed out, the conclusions of the study—beneficial effects of milk supplementation on height and weight gain, no sex or age differentials, and no differences between pasteurized and raw milk—were compromised by the tendency of head teachers to assign poor and hence relatively ill-nourished children to the treatment group.

That selection exists in mortality studies is quite likely. Consider an analysis of breastfeeding. Some infants are not breastfed because they are sick and die soon thereafter. Hence, an evaluation of the effects of breastfeeding on mortality, no matter how many socioeconomic or demographic factors are employed as controls, will overstate the relative risk of not breastfeeding. The only hope is to eliminate children who were reported to have been "too sick to breastfeed," a strategy employed by Holland. Is maternal education another example of selection? Possibly. But we will never know until a proper experiment is conducted—for example, by random assignment of girls/women to school and later follow-up. We hasten to add that we do not think that girls/women should cease to be educated until such a link can be proven. There are compelling reasons indeed to favor campaigns to raise female educational levels. But if the sole aim of female education were to lower mortality, we would definitely favor conducting a proper experiment before proceeding. The same reasoning applies to other intervention schemes. On grounds of efficiency this position seems nearly unassailable: a good field trial shows how a scheme works in practice, not on paper. Many people accept the efficiency argument but counter with an equity argument. How can one deliberately withhold the benefits of a promising intervention? While we understand the humanitarian spirit underlying this argument, we feel it is misguided. First, a scheme that does not work benefits no one. Often, however, we can feel fairly certain that an intervention scheme will have some beneficial effect. The question is how much of an effect. The answer needs to be known with some precision in order to allocate scarce resources efficiently.

Of what use, then, are methods of analysis such as hazards models? Proper randomization ensures that children are not selected into a treatment group on the basis of their characteristics. Hence differences in outcomes can be analyzed by far simpler statistical techniques.[9] This line of reasoning is true, but limited. It applies only to factors subject to policy intervention. If we followed the purist line we would never discover the effects of breastfeeding, age of mother, and birth spacing on mortality since these are not really subject to control. If we want a quantitative estimate of the effects of such factors, we have no choice but to rely on studies such as those described earlier. A similar reasoning applies to attempts to ferret out causes of mortality decline in the past. We either abandon the attempt because we cannot conduct a true experiment or do the best we can under the circumstances. We clearly favor the latter course.

Research priorities

Thus far, we have discussed advances in demographic methodology that permit examination of child mortality using relatively faulty or incomplete information or that, when more complete or better quality data are available, lead to more sophisticated and conceptually detailed studies of child survival. A particularly important methodological advance has been the recent application of hazard models to analyze the covariates of infant and child mortality. Difficult technical issues, however, remain to be resolved. In the analyses of child mortality reported earlier in this paper, investigators implicitly assumed: (1) that their models were correctly specified (e.g., that all determinants were explicitly included as covariates); (2) that variables subject to choice (endogenous variables), such as whether and how long to breastfeed, can be entered in the model in the same way as nonchoice (exogenous) variables, such as race or ethnicity; (3) that each birth is an independent observation so that survival of one child is unrelated to survival of another, even in the same family; and (4) that all observations were generated as a simple random sample. We consider these four assumptions briefly here, in order to give some idea of the added complexity when they are not true.

Unobserved heterogeneity

In complicated nonlinear models, such as hazard models, omission of a relevant variable distorts effects estimates for all variables included in the model, even if the omitted variable is uncorrelated with those included. Investigators have long recognized this problem and have even given it a name: omitted variables bias. The classical solution is to collect data on all variables likely to belong in the "true" model. Recent attention has focused on the recognition that some relevant variables might not be observable. An example in fertility analyses is the underlying fecundity of the woman (or couple), a condition not known to the analyst. In mortality analyses the corresponding variable has been dubbed frailty (Vaupel et al., 1979). The first attempts to control for the effects of unobserved heterogeneity involved specifying a distribution function for frailty and then mathematically "repairing" the model by integrating it out. More recent work (Heckman and Singer, 1982) has shown that the parameter estimates of interest in the model can vary widely depending on the particular functional form assumed for frailty (e.g., normal, lognormal, beta, gamma). But the investigator surely is unlikely to know the correct functional form of the distribution of frailty, when frailty is unobservable. Heckman and Singer do not leave this problem unaddressed; they propose a way to control for the effect of unobserved frailty without imposing a functional form on its distribution. To do so, however, they must impose a functional form on the age pattern of death rates. Trussell and Richards (1983) have shown that parameter estimates of interest vary widely with different choices of functional form of the age pattern of mortality, even when the Heckman–Singer procedure is used to correct for heterogeneity, and they argue that the analyst is just as unlikely to know the correct mortality pattern as the correct distribution of frailty. Unfortunately, they do not propose any way to solve this remaining problem, and it seems to us that new progress will not come with more sophisticated statistical techniques, but only with better demographic (or biological) theory that allows us to narrow the possible choices for distributional forms.

Endogeneity

Earlier we discussed the serious problems in interpreting the results of an experiment when participants self-select a particular treatment. This selection problem manifests itself in multivariate statistical analysis when choice variables appear as explanatory variables. There are two ways in which choice

variables plague statistical analysis, but we believe that only one is likely to
be important in studies of child mortality. The first case involves simultaneous
equations. In a simple example with only two equations, (1) Y depends on Z
and other covariates (W, X, etc.), and simultaneously (2) Z depends on Y and
other covariates (A, B, etc.). If the analyst ignores the simultaneity and estimates only equation (1), the parameter estimates will be biased and inconsistent. To avoid this problem, the technique of instrumental variables, described
by Schultz elsewhere in this volume, is used; all endogenous explanatory
variables are replaced by their predicted value based on all exogenous variables
in the system.

Consider a choice variable in the analysis of child mortality, such as
the decision to deliver in a hospital. While survival of the child may well
depend on hospital delivery, it seems extremely unlikely that hospital delivery
could depend on survival of the child (except possibly in a roundabout way
discussed below). If hospital delivery does not depend on survival of the child,
then entering it as an ordinary covariate in a hazard model is permissible,
even though it is a choice (or stochastic, or endogenous) variable.

Suppose, however, that we now reintroduce frailty, and that frailty of
her children is known to the woman but not to the investigator. Also suppose
that knowledge of her children's frailty affects a women's decision about
whether to deliver in a hospital. In this case both survival and hospital delivery
depend on a latent variable called frailty. The relationship is not simultaneous,
because hospital delivery is not determined by survival. In this circumstance
the technique of instrumental variables is useless; more complicated statistical
procedures are needed. We write down the distribution of survival times,
conditional on frailty and hospital delivery. We next write down the distribution of hospital delivery, conditional on frailty. The product of the two is
the joint distribution of survival times and hospital delivery, conditional on
the unobserved frailty. Finally, we mathematically purge frailty from the
model either by assuming a distribution of frailty and integrating it out or by
application of the Heckman–Singer procedure.[10]

Independence of observations

There is evidence that some families produce children with smaller survival
chances than others, even after the effects of covariates have been controlled
(see Cleland and Sathar, 1983). If this is so, the survival of each child in the
sample cannot be considered to be an independent event. The form of the
dependence must be built into the statistical model to be estimated.

Design effects

Almost all hypothesis tests for parameters in complex models are predicated
on the assumption that observations are drawn as a simple random sample. In
contrast, virtually no large survey is ever conducted under such a sampling
scheme. Instead, stratified and cluster samples are used. If the stochastic
structure of the model to be estimated were independent of the sample design,

then the design could be ignored and estimation and hypothesis testing could proceed as if there were a simple random sample. This observation is not very useful, however, because no simple tests for independence exist. It is theoretically possible, though usually very complex, to incorporate the sample design explicitly in the estimation scheme. Preliminary work in this area is encouraging, but not easily applicable to the complex models we are considering.

Concluding comments

There are, then, two final remarks we would like to offer regarding the methodology for studies of child survival. As reviewed here, recently developed techniques are available that have not yet received widespread attention outside the realm of technical demography and consequently have not been routinely applied. They require simple additions to data collection efforts to achieve large improvements in our ability to analyze mortality determinants. Analyses can be carried out simply by the use of standard computer packages (see appendix).

New lines of research in statistical theory and methodolgy have identified several remaining technical issues. The results to date have deepened our understanding of the problems involved and show promise of leading to practical solutions in terms of new and more powerful methodology. We think, however, that greater understanding of the determinants of infant and child mortality is more likely to come from increased attention to improving research design and data collection than from application of ever more sophisticated statistical analysis.

Appendix

The availability of computer software for estimating levels, trends, and determinants of mortality has greatly enhanced the ability of investigators to use more sophisticated techniques and to experiment widely by changing assumptions. This section is a summary of our own experience and should not be taken as a definitive or exhaustive evaluation of pros and cons of existing software.

Levels and trends

WFS central staff (Westlake, 1980) have written and distributed a program called FERTRATE that is designed to process WFS standard recode files and produce direct estimates of fertility rates as well as infant and child mortality rates. The program is fully documented and relatively easy to use. By far the best and most widely available software for obtaining Brass-type mortality estimates is that produced by the National Academy of Sciences (Zlotnik, 1981). The programs are intended as a supplement to UN Manual X, *Indirect Techniques for Demographic Estimation* (Hill, Zlotnik, and Trussell, 1983). Of the eight separate programs, two pertain to estimation of infant and child mortality. The only difference between the two is the form of input; information is based either on age of woman (Program AFEMO) or duration of marriage (Program DFEMO). The NAS programs do not have an option for using the Preston technique (equation 3 in the text).

Determinants

Options to estimate hazard models are now being included in standard statistical packages such as SAS and BMDP, but in our opinion they are not very flexible. We have used extensively three packages that are compared here in detail.

LOGLIN (Olivier and Neff, 1976), Version 1.0, was developed for the analysis of contingency tables. To use it to estimate hazard models, all covariates must be categorical. The package is *very* easy to use. The main disadvantages are cost and inflexibility. The cost would be equivalent to that of other packages except that effects estimates and their standard errors must be produced in separate runs, thus doubling the cost. There is no way to create variables or to collapse categories of variables within the program. Likewise, if one wishes to estimate interactions, there is no way to specify only partial interactions. For example, if one wants an interaction of time period (T) and age (A), one specifies $T*A$; there is no way to confine the interaction to, say, the *first* time period. In most analyses thus far, data have been prepared beforehand.[11] Essentially, two matrices, one containing numbers of deaths and the other numbers of months (or years) of exposure, are required. However, we recently learned of an option in LOGLIN, not described in the user's manual, whereby data can be prepared in a far easier way, as is true for RATE (see below); the requisite matrices are then constructed by user commands within LOGLIN.

GLIM (Baker and Nelder, 1978) is perhaps the most powerful statistical package ever written. It is claimed by GLIM addicts that there is no statistical problem that cannot be estimated with the package, though some ingenuity might be required. A newsletter provides users with details on the newest ways to trick GLIM into estimating ever more fancy statistical models. The package is easy to use, once the manual can be penetrated; its combination of statistical and computer jargon, written in the Queen's English, does not make for ready comprehension. Covariates can be declared to be continuous (VARIABLES) or categorical (FACTORS). Data may be prepared in two ways. If the covariates are categorical, the investigator can construct two matrices (of deaths and exposure). The other option, which must be used if covariates are continuous but may be used if they are categorical, is to construct a separate data card for each individual in each age interval; it must contain the termination status (died or cen-

sored), number of months (or years) of exposure, and values of the covariates. Once the data set is ready, the ability to manipulate it within GLIM is excellent; new variables can be created, categories can be collapsed or combined, etc.

RATE (Tuma, 1979) was created specifically for the analysis of hazard-type models. Its advantages are many. Data can be prepared very easily. For each individual, a duration of exposure and an indicator variable (died or censored) plus information on covariates are all that is needed; the age intervals are defined within the program and can be modified at will. Models with time-varying covariates and time-dependent effects are far easier to estimate than with other software. In addition, RATE allows more complicated models with multiple states.[12] The main disadvantage is an inability to create new variables. In particular, the estimation of interaction effects is made difficult because all such interaction variables must be created before invoking RATE.

As the above descriptions indicate, we have discovered no package that dominates all others in every respect. For those who wish to learn only one package for all their statistical needs (contingency tables, regressions, logit regressions, etc.), GLIM is the only choice. RATE is, in our minds, the package of choice for estimating hazard models, despite its drawbacks. LOGLIN is perhaps the easiest for the novice to learn.

One final warning is in order. When covariates are categorical, one can compare the number of nonempty cells in a covariate exposure matrix with the number of individuals. If the former is far smaller than the latter, it pays to collapse the data before using RATE. All individuals with the same covariate information, the same duration of exposure, and the same termination status can be combined and assigned a weight equal to the number of individuals with such characteristics. One example shows that cost savings can be substantial. In an analysis of mortality in Fiji (Fernandez, 1983) RATE was first run with data on 18,011 individual children. The cost was $600 for a single proportional hazards model. Then the data were collapsed, resulting in only 6404 distinct observations. The cost of estimating the same model was reduced to $50, while the cost of collapsing the data was minimal (less than $10).

Notes

1 The elaboration was independently proposed by Ansley Coale to Lee-Jay Cho for use in the own-children technique of fertility analysis (Cho and Feeney, 1978).

2 By the first mean value theorem of integral calculus.

3 Information from women aged 15–19 can be used to estimate $q(1)$, but the estimate so obtained usually indicates higher mortality than does the estimate of $q(2)$, $q(3)$, or $q(5)$. Many investigators (e.g., Feeney, 1980) attribute the cause of this bias to the fact that first births, concentrated among women aged 15–19, have higher mortality. Other evidence (Martin et al., 1983) suggests that it is the age of the mother, not birth order, that matters. It should be noted that Preston and Palloni showed that the "best" ages for estimating $q(a)$ corresponding to women 15–19 through 35–39 are actually 1, 2, 4 or 5, 6 or 7, and 9 rather than the "traditional" ages 1, 2, 3, 5, and 10.

4 See Palloni (1981) for an assumed quadratic decline.

5 While Trussell and Preston's substantive analysis was merely illustrative (Sri Lanka with three covariates—mother's education, father's education, and urban residence; and Korea with the same three covariates plus father's occupation), two other studies using their methodology have been much more exhaustive. Farah and Preston (1982) examined the effects of nine covariates in Sudan and of 13 covariates in Khartoum; one of their more interesting findings is that child mortality is 20 percent higher among children of women married to their cousins as compared with children whose parents are not related by blood. In a much larger study, Mensch et al. (1983) estimated similar structural models for 15 developing countries. They found that, after controlling for the effects of other variables, mother's education was an important predictor of child mortality in virtually all countries. Ethnic and religious differentials are large, particularly in rural areas. Urban/rural residence and features of the housing structure are not closely associated with mortality.

6 Note that we have changed notation slightly from equation (7) because all covariates are categorical. We could put equation (11) in the same form as (7) as follows:

$$ln(r_{ik}) = a_k + b_1 X_{i1} + b_2 X_{i2} + b_3 X_{i3} + b_4 X_{i4}$$

where $X_{i1} = 1$ if the child was born in time period 2 and 0 otherwise; $X_{i2} = 1$ if the child was born in time period 3 and 0 otherwise; $X_{i3} = 1$ if mother's education is category 2 and 0 otherwise; and $X_{i4} = 1$ if mother's education is category 3 and 0 otherwise. As is usual with dummy variables, the omitted category for each covariate (the first category for both) forms the base category.

7 Holland (1983) and Hobcraft et al. (1982, 1983) estimated separate equations for each age interval, and they do not call their models hazard models. Technically such models are equivalent to hazard models with interactions between all covariates and age intervals.

8 Those interested in substantive results should see Chackiel (1982) for an analysis of World Fertility Surveys in Costa Rica and Peru; Larson (1983) for a study based on WFS data from Jamaica, Trinidad and Tobago, Guyana, and Colombia; Fernandez (1983) for an analysis of the WFS in Fiji; and Frenzen and Hogan (1982) for a study using non-WFS survey data from two provinces in Thailand.

9 There are good reasons, however, for applying multivariate techniques to data from randomized trials. Comparison of mean outcomes does reflect the likely relative risk in a population with characteristics identical with those in the trial. To extrapolate to other sample compositions, one needs estimates of the effects of relevant characteristics.

10 Montgomery et al. (1983) have used this approach in a logit model. The mathematics and computation are simpler than in a hazards model, but the same logic could be applied.

11 Using programs written by the investigator. Some of our colleagues have found it easier to perform the required calculations in flexible statistical packages such as SAS than to write programs from scratch using traditional programming languages such as FORTRAN, PLI, or BASIC.

12 As an example, Montgomery (1983),

using Malaysian data, has estimated models in which children at birth are breastfed or not. Those breastfed have three possible exits— death, survival, and transition to a non-breastfed state. Those not breastfed either die or survive. Results indicate that while the death of a child does not affect the probability that the next child is breastfed, it does appear to lengthen the duration of breastfeeding among those that are breastfed.

References

Arriaga, Eduardo. 1981. "Direct estimates of infant mortality differentials from birth histories," in *World Fertility Conference 1980: A Record of Proceedings*. Voorburg: International Statistical Institute, pp. 435–466.

Baker, R. J., and J. Nelder. 1978. *The Glim Manual—Release 3*. Oxford: Numerical Algorithms Group.

Barclay, George, Ansley Coale, Michael Stoto, and James Trussell. 1976. "A reassessment of the demography of traditional rural China," *Population Index* 42, no. 4 (October): 606–635.

Behm, Hugo, et al. 1977–79. *La mortalidad en los primeros años en países de la America Latina*. 14 volumes. San José: Centro Latinamericano de Demografía.

Brass, William. 1971. "On the scale of mortality," In *Biological Aspects of Demography*, ed. William Brass, et al. London: Taylor and Francis, pp. 69–110.

———, and Ansley Coale. 1968. "Methods of analysis and estimation," in *The Demography of Tropical Africa*, ed. William Brass et al. Princeton: Princeton University Press, pp. 88–150.

Carver, Jane, ed. 1976. "Systems of demographic measurement, the dual record system: Bibliography on the dual record system," *Occasional Publications*. Chapel Hill: Laboratories for Population Statistics.

Chackiel, Juan. 1982. "Niveles y tendencias de la mortalidad infantil en base a la encuesta mundial de fecundidad: Factores que afectan a la mortalidad en la niñez," *Notas de Población* 28: 43–87.

Cho, Lee-Jay, and Griffith Feeney. 1978. "Fertility estimation by the own children method: A methodological elaboration," Reprint Series no. 20. Chapel Hill: Laboratories for Population Statistics.

Cleland, John, and Zeba Sathar. 1983. "The effect of birth spacing on childhood mortality in Pakistan," WFS/TECH 2163. London: World Fertility Survey.

Coale, Ansley, and Paul Demeny. 1966. *Regional Model Life Tables and Stable Populations*. Princeton: Princeton University Press.

———, and James Trussell. 1978. "Estimating the time to which Brass estimates apply," *Population Bulletin of the United Nations* 10: 87–88.

———, and Paul Demeny. 1983. *Regional Model Life Tables and Stable Populations*. Second edition. New York: Academic Press.

Ewbank, Douglas. 1982. "The sources of error in Brass' method for estimating child survival: The case of Bangladesh," *Population Studies* 36, no. 3 (November): 459–474.

Farah, Abdul-Aziz, and Samuel H. Preston. 1982. "Child mortality differentials in Sudan," *Population and Development Review* 8, no. 2 (June): 365–383.

Feeney, Griffith. 1980. "Estimating infant mortality trends from child survivorship rates," *Population Studies* 34, no. 1 (March): 109–128.

Fernandez, Marilyn. 1983. "Child mortality in Fiji: Results from a hazards analysis of covariates," unpublished manuscript. Honolulu: East West Population Institute.

Frenzen, Paul, and Dennis Hogan. 1982. "The impact of clan, education and health care on infant mortality in a developing society: The case of rural Thailand," *Demography* 19, no. 3 (August): 391–408.

Heckman, James, and Burton Singer. 1982. "Population heterogeneity in demographic models," in *Multidimensional Mathematical Demography,* ed. Kenneth Land and Andrei Rogers. New York: Academic Press, pp. 567–599.

Hill, Ken, Hania Zlotnik, and James Trussell. 1983. *Manual X: Indirect Techniques for Demographic Estimation.* New York: United Nations.

Hobcraft, John. 1981. "Strategies for comparative analysis of WFS data," in *World Fertility Conference 1980: A Record of Proceedings.* Voorburg: International Statistical Institute, pp. 509–574.

———, John McDonald, and Shea Rutstein. 1982. "Socieconomic factors in infant and child mortality: A cross-national comparison." Paper presented at the Annual Meeting of the Population Association of America, San Diego, May.

———, John McDonald, and Shea Rutstein. 1983. "Child spacing effects on infant and early child mortality," *Population Index* 49, no. 4 (Winter): 585–618.

Holland, Bart. 1983. "Breastfeeding and infant mortality: A hazards model analysis of the case of Malaysia," unpublished Ph.D. thesis, Princeton University. (Available from University Microfilms, Ann Arbor, Michigan.)

Johansson, Sheila Ryan, and Samuel Preston. 1978. "Tribal demography: The Hopi and Navaho populations as seen through manuscripts from the 1900 U.S. Census," *Social Science History* III, no. 1 (Fall): 1–33.

Larsen, Ulla. 1983. "A comparative analysis of the determinants of infant and child mortality," unpublished paper. Princeton: Office of Population Research, Princeton University.

Martin, Linda G., J. Trussell, Florentina Reyes Salvail, and Nasra M. Shah. 1983. "Co-variates of child mortality in the Philippines, Indonesia, and Pakistan: An analysis based on hazard models," *Population Studies* 37, no. 3 (November): 417–432.

Meier, Paul. 1972. "The biggest public health experiment ever: The 1954 field trial of the Salk poliomyelitis vaccine," in *Statistics: A Guide to the Unknown,* ed. J. M. Tanner et al. San Francisco: Holden-Day.

Mensch, Barbara, Harold Lentzner, Steve Taber, Michael Strong, and Nancy Denton. 1983. "Comparative patterns, child mortality, differentials in developing countries." Paper presented at the Annual Meeting of the Population Association of America, Pittsburgh, April.

Montgomery, Mark. 1983. "Child replacement effects, investment effects, and breastfeeding: Multiple state hazard models." Paper presented at the Annual Meeting of the Population Association of America, Pittsburgh, April.

———, Toni Richards, and Henry Braun. 1983. "Child health and survival in Malaysia: A random effects logit system," unpublished paper, Office of Population Research, Princeton University.

Olivier, Ronald, and Raymond Neff. 1976. *LOGLIN 1.0: User's Guide.* Cambridge, Mass.: Health Science Computing Facility, Harvard School of Public Health.

Palloni, Alberto. 1980. "Estimating infant and childhood mortality under conditions of changing mortality," *Population Studies* 34, no. 2 (March): 129–142.

———. 1981. "A review of infant mortality trends in selected under-developed countries: Some new estimates," *Population Studies* 35, no. 1 (March): 100–119.

Preston, Samuel. 1978. "Income, mortality, and morbidity," *Population Bulletin of the United Nations Economic Commission for Western Asia* 15: 63–75.

———, and Alberto Palloni. 1978. "Fine tuning Brass-type mortality estimates with data on ages of surviving children," *Population Bulletin of the United Nations* 10: 72–87.

Rutstein, Shea. 1983. "Infant and child mortality: Levels, trends and demographic differentials," *WFS Comparative Studies* no. 24.

Student. 1931. "The Lanarkshire mill experiment," *Biometrica* 23: 398–406.

Sullivan, Jeremiah. 1972. "Models for the estimation of the probability of dying between birth and exact ages of early childhood," *Population Studies* 26, no. 1: 79–98.

Trussell, James. 1975. "A reestimation of the multiplying factors for the Brass technique for determining childhood survivorship rates," *Population Studies* 29, no. 1 (March): 97–107.

————, and Eleanor Brown. 1979. "A close look at the demography of Afghanistan," *Demography* 16, no. 1 (February): 137–156.

————, and Ken Hill. 1980. "Fertility and mortality estimation from the Panama retrospective demographic survey, 1976," *Population Studies* 34, no. 3 (November): 551–563.

————, and Samuel Preston. 1982. "Estimating the covariates of childhood mortality from retrospective reports of mothers," *Health Policy and Education* 3: 1–36.

————, and Charles Hammerslough. 1983. "A hazards model analysis of the covariates of infant and child mortality in Sri Lanka," *Demography* 20, no. 1 (February): 1–26.

————, and Toni Richards, 1983. "Correcting for unobserved heterogeneity in hazards models: An application of the Heckman-Singer strategy to demographic data," in *Sociological Methodology 1985,* ed. Nancy Tuma. San Francisco: Jossey-Bass.

Tuma, Nancy. 1979. *Invoking Rate.* Stanford: Department of Sociology, Stanford University.

United Nations. 1982. *Model Life Tables for Developing Countries.* New York: United Nations.

Vaupel, James, Kenneth Manton, and Eric Stallard. 1979. "The impact of heterogeneity in individual frailty on the dynamics of mortality," *Demography* 16, no. 3 (August): 439–454.

Westlake, Andrew. 1980. *WFS Program Library: FERTRATE (Fertility Rate Program).* User Documentation. WFS TECH/1538. London: World Fertility Survey.

Zlotnik, Hania. 1981. *Computer Programs for Demographic Estimation: A User's Guide.* Washington: National Academy Press.

Mathematical Models of Infectious Diseases: Seeking New Tools for Planning and Evaluating Control Programs

Burton Singer

The problem of reduction of infant and child mortality rates in much of Africa, Asia, and Central and South America requires an understanding of dependent competing risks. The risk factors associated with infant and child mortality are a variety of infectious diseases—including measles, malaria, and diarrheal diseases—nutritional status, availability and quality of local medical facilities, and general socioeconomic conditions. Precise quantitative understanding of the interrelationships among these risk factors is almost nonexistent; however, a rather detailed picture—unfortunately still of limited practical value—can be put together about the dynamics of some of the principal risk factors.

The literature on mathematical models of transmission of infectious diseases is substantial. The question at issue concerning such models is whether they can play a central role in planning disease control and eradication programs so as to facilitate elimination or at least reduction of the impact of infectious diseases on infant and child mortality rates. Elimination of any one major infectious disease as a risk factor will not by itself solve the problem of high child mortality rates. Infectious disease control is a necessary but not sufficient condition for substantial reduction in child mortality rates. In this connection the review article by Molineaux (forthcoming) is particularly informative.

In this paper our focus is on the infectious disease portion of the overall set of competing risks. The principal question to be addressed is whether mathematical models can inform the process of planning programs of control and eradication. Especially important is the question of whether the information-organizing power of mathematical models can be focused sharply enough so as to provide accurate guidance about the potential consequences of disease control programs.

Despite a quite sophisticated mathematics literature on disease transmission, which suggests an affirmative answer to these questions, the record of useful application in evaluating the possible—and actual, in monitoring programs—consequences of public health interventions is exceedingly scanty. This situation is, in our opinion, a consequence of two features of the historical development of models of infectious diseases:

1 The ratio of the number of empirical tests of models to the number of mathematical theorems about them is very small.

2 The development of statistical methods for the specification of designs and for the analysis of data on the dynamics of infectious diseases has lagged far behind what is required.

This paper is in three parts. The first major section contains a discussion of both deterministic and stochastic process models of disease transmission, with the primary emphasis being on malaria models. Malaria provides an especially convenient setting in which to discuss next steps toward effective model development, because it has the most extensive history of modeling efforts among tropical parasitic diseases; and the issues which arise in that context are relevant for infectious disease modeling in general. In the next section we focus on an important theoretical and empirical program that seems essential if models are to guide the specification of interventions. In particular we describe some of the epidemiological and genetics issues associated with the increasing proliferation of malaria parasites resistant to antimalarial drugs. An uncharted area—the integration of genetics and transmission dynamics— is put forth as a major challenge to modelers that must be met if there is to be a smooth interface between the reality of drug resistance and the necessary simplifications of a mathematical theory. Again, the issues that arise with respect to malaria have their counterpart in the study of community drug-resistance generally. In the final section, we propose an agenda for developing rationally based designs for data collection aimed at estimating age-specific mortality rates, incidence and recovery rates, and basic reproduction rates. A schistosomiasis study aimed at estimating the human rate of elimination of egg-laying parasites—an important index of morbidity—provides the context for development of research plans.

We feel that there are ample grounds for optimism on the question of mathematical models playing a useful—if not always indispensable—role in planning and evaluating infectious disease control programs. Stipulation and clarification of the most important next steps is our goal in this paper.

Models of infectious diseases

The transmission models of infectious diseases developed to date are of two principal types: prevalence models and density models. Prevalence models are instances of compartment models in which individuals are classified into a discrete collection of states—for instance, infectious, susceptible, immune, and latent—and the dynamics are described by a system of ordinary differential equations (for prevalence in a general population) or by a system of partial differential equations for age-specific prevalence (see Dietz, 1982, for a concise review). Density models for parasitic diseases describe the dynamics of the number of parasites per host (via stochastic process models) and the mean number of parasites per individual (via differential equations).

Despite nearly 70 years of active research on mathematical theories of parasite–host interaction and disease transmission (see the reviews of much of this literature in Bailey, 1975, 1982), an understanding of the possible dynamics that are consistent with even moderately (biologically) plausible systems of transmission equations will require substantial mathematical efforts in the future. Countering the increasing sophistication and elaborate research agenda of the mathematical literature is the disconcerting fact that very few transmission models have been subjected to serious testing against actual field data (see in this connection Najera, 1974). Thus there seems to be a danger of the mathematical developments having a life of their own. Some important and notable exceptions to this situation are: (1) the preliminary assessments of a malaria transmission model by Dietz, Molineaux, and Thomas (1974, 1978), and the recent in-depth follow-up analysis of Nedelman (1983b); (2) the studies of rabies transmission by Bögel et al. (1976), Sayers et al. (1977), and Steck and Wandeler (1980); (3) the incorporation of heterogeneity of transmission potential and diagnostic error into models of gonorrhea dynamics by Yorke et al. (1978); and (4) the study of the incidence rate of congenital rubella syndrome and the incidence rate of rubella virus infection in a community by Knox (1980).

Among the tropical parasitic diseases only malaria has a modeling history that shows signs of coming to grips with the full transmission cycle in a unified manner and with testing against field data. The considerably more complicated schistosomiasis life cycle has only been modeled in a patchwork fashion (see Cohen, 1977) and has had rather little impact on control programs to date. However, more recent work by Anderson and May (1982) shows promise of changing this situation.

Both prevalence and density models are designed to describe the changes over time in population averages. Individual-level dynamics—for example, change over time in infection status or immune response—require description via stochastic processes and longitudinal data for estimation and testing. Proposed model specification to date focuses almost entirely on Markovian or semi-Markovian processes (Bailey, 1975). Furthermore, in the very limited use of stochastic process models with field data on tropical parasitic diseases— malaria, in particular—Markovian models are imposed for purposes of estimating quantities such as age-specific acquisition and recovery rates (Bekessy et al., 1976) from malaria infection without testing the basic Markovian assumption. Although this practice can lead to very biased estimates, there is no clear understanding at present of when such crude approximations to, for example, infection status dynamics are reasonable and when they are not.

In order to clarify the issues involved, consider the longitudinal infection status records from the WHO malaria surveys in the Garki district of northern Nigeria (Molineaux and Gramiccia, 1979). During the 18-month baseline period, from November 1970 to May 1972, a previously unprotected human population was studied without any attempt to interfere with malaria. Eight village clusters (follow-up units, each containing two or more villages or parts of villages) were surveyed every ten weeks. Eight of these surveys fell within the baseline period. Sixteen villages were included from survey 1; six more villages (or sections of villages) were added at survey 5. At that survey, the total set of 22 villages had 7,423 inhabitants. The surveys aimed at total coverage; however, only 2,785 individuals were present at all eight surveys. Considerably larger numbers—5–6,000 persons—were present at two, three, four, or five of the surveys.

At each survey, a thick blood film was collected from each individual; among the characteristics recorded from the blood film examination was presence or absence of malarial parasites of the species *Plasmodium falciparum* (*Pf*), *Plasmodium malariae* (*Pm*), and *Plasmodium ovale* (*Po*).

Focusing on *Pf* infections, with the aim of estimating age-specific acquisition and recovery rates, it is useful first to consider what actual infection histories are like and then contrast this complete information with the data available for estimation. Figure 1 shows two actual infection histories as they would be observed if blood samples were collected daily and without false-negative errors (see Aron, 1982, and Singer and Cohen, 1980, pp. 297–299, and 1982 for a discussion of the impact of measurement error on modeling infection histories; see Boyd, 1949, for an example of a measured (*Pf*) infection history based on daily blood samples).

FIGURE 1   Two prototypical *Pf* infection status histories (successive surveys spaced 10 weeks apart)

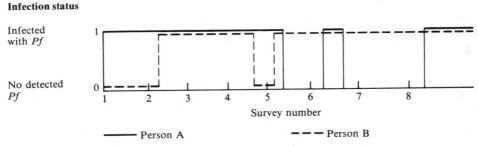

Both individuals are present for all eight surveys and have, respectively, the following observed longitudinal data on (*Pf*) infection status (as defined in Figure 1):

	Survey							
	1	2	3	4	5	6	7	8
Person A	1	1	1	1	1	0	0	0
Person B	0	0	1	1	0	1	1	1

Notice that the timing of transitions between statuses is unobserved as a consequence of the observation plan. Furthermore, person A has an unobserved spell of infection between surveys 6 and 7. The observation plan with data collected every ten weeks classifies this individual as uninfected at surveys 6 and 7 and cannot distinguish an uninterrupted spell of noninfection from the actual history, which contains a spell of infection between two surveys. Persons who are not present at all eight surveys have data records analogous to those shown above but with the additional troublesome feature that information on infection status is available only for those surveys for which the person was present. Finally, spells of infection and noninfection are censored on the left prior to 1970 and on the right for spells that continue beyond survey 8.

Calendar time (t)- and age (a)-dependent rates of onset (or acquisition) $h(t,a)$ and termination (or recovery) $r(t,a)$ can be estimated only within a defensible stochastic process model that describes the complete infection histories but uses only the observed sequences of 0s and 1s for the computations. The interpretations of $h(t,a)$ and $r(t,a)$ are, respectively: $h(t,a)$ = expected number of acquisitions of new Pf infections per day for individuals in age class a who are at risk of such an acquisition at time t; and $r(t,a)$ = expected number of recoveries from Pf infections per day for individuals in age class a who are at risk of such a recovery at time t. Standard practice (Bekessy et al., 1976; Singer and Cohen, 1980) has been to propose a sequence of continuous-time homogeneous Markov chains as candidates to describe the unobserved dynamics between successive pairs of surveys and to have a separate such sequence for each of (in the Garki study) seven age classes defined as of November 1970.

With this specification $h(t,a)$ and $r(t,a)$ will each be constant over the 70-day (10-week) interval between a pair of successive surveys. They can, however, vary across different pairs of consecutive surveys. To illustrate estimation and testing models, consider the transitions between surveys 4 and 5 for persons aged 9–18 years at survey 1. The possible infection statuses and their frequency of occurrence for this age class at the consecutive surveys (4 and 5) are as follows (Bekessy et al., 1976):

Infection status		Frequency of
Survey 4	Survey 5	occurrence
0	0	$N_{00} = 102$
0	1	$N_{01} = 135$
1	0	$N_{10} = 65$
1	1	$N_{11} = 375$

N_{ij} = number of persons in status i at survey 4 and status j at survey 5, $i = 0,1; j = 0,1$.

Associated with the observed counts $\{N_{ij}\}$ are estimated conditional probabilities $\hat{p}_{ij} = N_{ij}/(N_{i0} + N_{i1}) =$ (probability of an individual being in infection status j at the second survey—i.e., survey 5—given that the same individual was in infection status i at the first survey—i.e., survey 4). Incidence and recovery rates estimated from these conditional probabilities within any class of models could be subject to substantial bias as a result of neglecting false-negative errors. In the Garki study, a lower bound on the average—across surveys and people—probability of classifying a positive individual negative is approximately 0.15. This point estimate is based on examination of blood smears from individuals of very different ages and taken in both wet and dry seasons. Thus in some age classes and seasons, the false-negative rate can be 1 percent or less while in others it can be as high as 25 percent. For an initial assessment of the impact of false-negative errors on $\hat{p}_{ij}$ and on the rates, h and r, we take the error rate to be $\pi = 0.1$. We also assume that there are no false-positive classifications. Then the "error-free" estimated probabilities are given by

$$\tilde{p}_{11} = \hat{p}_{11}/(1 - \pi) \tag{1}$$

and

$$\tilde{p}_{00} = \frac{\hat{p}_{00} - (\pi/z)[1 - (1 - z)\tilde{p}_{11}]}{1 - (\pi/z)} \tag{2}$$

$z =$ proportion of individuals at initial survey who are observed to be uninfected.

See Singer and Cohen (1982) for further details about equations (1) and (2).

Now in terms of $\tilde{p}_{ii}$, $i = 0,1$, the estimated incidence and recovery rates—within the class of time-homogeneous Markov chains—are given by

$$\bar{h}(t,a) = \frac{(1 - \tilde{p}_{00})ln(\tilde{p}_{00} + \tilde{p}_{11} - 1)}{\tilde{p}_{00} + \tilde{p}_{11} - 2} \cdot \frac{1}{\text{(number of days between consecutive surveys)}}$$

and

$$\bar{r}(t,a) = \frac{(1 - \tilde{p}_{11})ln(\tilde{p}_{00} + \tilde{p}_{11} - 1)}{\tilde{p}_{00} + \tilde{p}_{11} - 2} \cdot \frac{1}{\text{(number of days between consecutive surveys)}}$$

The error-adjusted data $\{\tilde{p}_{ii}\}$ are compatible with the presumed Markovian model if and only if $\tilde{p}_{00} + \tilde{p}_{11} > 1$, a relation that holds for all pairs of consecutive baseline surveys in Garki. For the data presented above on age class 9–18 years at surveys 4 and 5, 210 days $\leq t \leq$ 280 days and 9 years $\leq a \leq$ 18 years. The estimated daily rates are $\bar{h}(t,a) = .0125$ and $\bar{r}(t,a) =$

.0011. The set of crude—i.e, $\pi = 0$—and error-adjusted incidence and recovery rates for age class 9–18 from survey 3 through survey 8 are shown in Table 1.

TABLE 1   Crude and error-adjusted incidence and recovery rates for age class 9–18 years

Surveys	Crude rates: $\pi = 0$		Error-adjusted rates: $\pi = .1$	
	$\bar{h}$	$\bar{r}$	$\bar{h}$	$\bar{r}$
3–4[a]	.0090	.0057	.0063	.0032
4–5[b]	.0129	.0033	.0125	.0011
5–6[b]	.0123	.0053	.0083	.0026
6–7[a]	.0093	.0063	.0060	.0037
7–8[a]	.0071	.0054	.0046	.0031

[a] Dry season.
[b] Wet season.

Based on similar calculations for seven age classes—<1, 1–4, 5–8, 9–18, 19–28, 29–43, ≥44—we find that:

— Within each age class, recovery rates per positive individual exhibit seasonal variation. The minimum occurs in the early part of the wet season. The maximum occurs toward the middle of the dry season.

— The seasonal patterns are parallel across age classes, and the recovery rates increase with increasing age. (Infants <1 year are an exception, exhibiting higher incidence and recovery rates than among children aged 1–4.) Increase in $\hat{r}$ and $\bar{r}$ with age can be attributed to a corresponding increase in immunity.

— Incidence rates are also roughly parallel across age classes. Above age 9, these rates tend to decrease with increasing age.

— The error-adjusted rates tend to be smaller than the crude rates, frequently by a factor of two or more.

The troublesome aspects of the above strategy and the numbers and interpretations produced from it are:

1 The time series of Markovian models do not take account of the fact that there are decidedly non-Markovian dependencies (Cohen and Singer, unpublished) in the infection status sequences of lengths 3, 4, . . . , 8.

2 These rates neglect the fact that there are three species of parasite present in Garki, two of which (*Pf* and *Pm*) are frequently present in the same individual. Furthermore, the bivariate infection status process (*Pf* status, *Pm* status) is also non-Markovian (Cohen and Singer, 1979); and transition rates for *Pf* should be marginal rates from the bivariate process.

Points 1 and 2 are the initial basis of a research agenda for developing models of individual-level infection dynamics of malaria, in particular, and of tropical parasitic diseases generally. Connected with this effort is a further important, but almost totally unexplored, topic. Namely, a system of differential (or differential-delay) equations that describe prevalence dynamics should be deducible from a stochastic process model of individual-level infection histories by averaging across the individual trajectories at each point in time. A mathematical result of this character, coupled with empirical evidence that both the micro-level and macro-level models account for observed field data, would provide the first systematic link between a description of disease transmission via gross trends and the much more refined detail of individual infection histories. No such systematic link exists between the ad hoc time series of Markovian models utilized, for example, to estimate rates of acquisition and recovery from *Pf* malaria infections and the differential- (or difference-)delay equations of Dietz, Molineaux, and Thomas that have been put forth to describe prevalence dynamics. This is all the more troublesome since rates produced from longitudinal micro-data by the estimation strategy described earlier are routinely used to constrain parameter estimation in a macro-level model of transmission. In particular, Dietz, Molineaux, and Thomas have the option of leaving recovery rates $r(t,a)$ free, as time- and age-dependent parameters, to be estimated from prevalence data in their difference-delay equations for *Pf* transmission. Alternatively they can substitute $\bar{r}(t,a)$ from the longitudinal estimation into their transmission equations, thereby reducing the number of parameters to be estimated from prevalence data. In their published analyses the second strategy is used. This raises the question: Do the two strategies lead to comparable estimates despite the fact that the Markovian models used to estimate $r(t,a)$ are not compatible with the macro-level transmission model? In particular, prevalence in the Dietz, Molineaux, and Thomas transmission model does not arise by averaging over trajectories in the underlying Markovian model. This question is another research agenda item; the answer would have far-reaching ramifications for effective use of mathematical models to assess the possible outcomes of control programs for infectious diseases generally.

Another facet of quantitative modeling of infectious disease transmission has been the recent extensive discussion of basic reproductive rates (Anderson and May, 1982). For microparasitic diseases, such as malaria, the basic reproductive rate R_0 is defined to be the average number of secondary infections generated by a single individual in a population of susceptibles. This quantity is of fundamental interest since the condition $R_0 < 1$ implies that the disease cannot maintain itself in the host population, while $R_0 > 1$ implies that transmission will persist. Direct estimation of R_0 by counting secondary infections is virtually impossible. Thus guidance about its estimation is achieved by asking how R_0 can be represented in terms of parameters—for example, in malaria: recovery rates, mosquito mortality rates, man-biting rates, and incubation delays—in prevalence models. For example, in the basic Ross–Macdonald model of malaria transmission, the basic reproductive rate is

$$R_0 = \frac{m\alpha^2 b}{\mu r}$$

where:

m = number of female anopheles mosquitoes per human host
α = rate of biting on man per unit time
b = proportion of infected bites on man that produce an infection
r = per capita recovery rate for humans
μ = per capita mortality rate for mosquitoes

This representation played an important role in Macdonald's (1956, 1957) effective arguments about alternative malaria eradication plans, despite the extreme oversimplification in the equation system on which it is based. Especially, the proportion, $x(t)$, of the human population infected at time t and the proportion, $y(t)$, of the female mosquito population infected at time t were modeled as solutions of the system of differential equations

$$\dot{x} = \alpha bmy(1 - x) - rx$$
$$\dot{y} = \alpha x(1 - y) - \mu y$$

with all parameters, as defined above, treated as though they were time-invariant. Assuming for the moment that these equations—and hence the above formulas—are an adequate representation of R_0, a major and largely uncharted area of research concerns the variability to be attributed to R_0. As the recent work of Nedelman (1983a) clarifies, man-biting rates exhibit enormous variation even within a given village and season of the year; and the effect on R_0 of this variation when combined with variation in r (as exhibited in Bekessy et al., 1976 and Singer and Cohen, 1980), variation in μ, and variation in indicators of m remains to be ascertained.

Although the natural next step in acquiring a deeper understanding of variability of R_0 might appear to be an analysis of variance based on the representation from the Ross–Macdonald model, it is our view that some alternative directions would be more productive. In particular the functional form of R_0 is sensitive to the structure of the transmission equations from which it is derived. Thus it is important to develop a representation of R_0, at least in terms of time-dependent man-biting rates, time- and age-dependent recovery rates, and incubation delays that are incorporated in a transmission model that can describe observed prevalence patterns with some accuracy and that is biologically defensible. Despite the exemplary model development in this direction by Dietz, Molineaux, and Thomas, the recent in-depth analysis of the Garki malaria models, both mathematically and empirically by Nedelman (1983b), indicates that a substantial research agenda may be necessary in order to produce valid estimates of R_0.

In order to clarify the principal issues, we first note that the transmission model of Dietz, Molineaux, and Thomas contained two important innovations beyond previous models: (1) the incidence rates $h(t,a)$ were parameterized to depend on the mosquito population dynamics through the time-dependent vectorial capacity, and (2) immune response in the human population was directly incorporated into the equations for prevalence dynamics. We focus here on the first innovation.

Dietz, Molineaux, and Thomas interpret vectorial capacity, $C(t)$—a notion introduced by Garrett-Jones (1964)—to mean the number of infective contacts a single person makes through the vector population per unit time. Then within an age class, a, they define $h(t)$ according to the formula

$$h(t) = C(t - N)y_1(t - N) \qquad (3)$$

where:

$N =$ incubation delay in the mosquito
$y_1 =$ proportion of the human population who are positive and infectious

Furthermore, $C(t)$ is represented in terms of parameters quantifying mosquito behavior as

$$C(t) = m(t)\alpha^2 bc[\exp(-N\mu)/\mu]$$

where:

$m(t) =$ number of mosquitoes present per person
$\alpha =$ mosquito's rate of biting people
$\mu =$ mosquito mortality rate
$b =$ proportion of uninfected people who become infected when bitten by an infectious mosquito
$c =$ proportion of uninfected mosquitoes that become infected after biting an infectious person

As clarified by Nedelman (1983b), the seemingly ad hoc specification (3) is derivable as an approximation to

$$h(t) = m^*(t)\alpha b \qquad (4)$$

where:

$m^*(t) =$ proportion of mosquitoes that are infectious.

The quantity $m^*(t)$ appears in a full differential equation system for the mosquito and human infection dynamics that contains the Dietz, Molineaux, and Thomas model with (3) as a limiting case. Thus (3) may be interpreted as a vectorial capacity approximation to (4), which is valid provided the mean lifetime of mosquitoes is much smaller than the expected time until a mosquito becomes infected—which is to say, few mosquitoes become infected.

Nedelman's equation system also contains a mathematically correct specification of Macdonald's verbal description of superinfection. This embedding of the model of Dietz, Molineaux, and Thomas in a biologically more realistic framework only served to clarify new questions about the process of fitting equations to data and testing models in the field. In particular, the following curious properties of their and Nedelman's formulations occur when both sets of models are tested in terms of their ability to reproduce baseline prevalence dynamics:

— Using $G^2 = 2\Sigma$ (observed) log $\left(\dfrac{\text{observed}}{[\text{expected under a given model}]} \right)$

   as a goodness-of-fit criterion, the model of Dietz, Molineaux, and Thomas did approximately as well as Nedelman's more general formulation when superinfection was ignored.

— Nedelman's full superinfection–mosquito dynamics model, but with parameters such as c in the vectorial capacity estimated directly from data on sporozoite rates and with gametocyte rates used to estimate proportions infectious, did not predict—in the sense of G^2—observed prevalence as well as the simpler models. On the other hand, parameters estimated in the simpler models by optimizing G^2 or fixed in advance, based on a priori plausibility arguments, were often substantially different and not epidemiologically as defensible as the corresponding values that were estimated directly.

This raises the following questions concerning the testing both of malaria models and of infectious disease transmission models generally:

1 How seriously should goodness-of-fit criteria such as G^2, which have nothing to do with the phenomena being modeled, be taken in testing overall compatibility of models with observed data?

2 How should biological and epidemiological "acceptability" of direct parameter estimates be quantified when the estimates are subsequently incorporated in a transmission model with further parameters to be estimated by optimizing a goodness-of-fit criterion? The importance of this question arises immediately from Nedelman's experience since a full superinfection specification with some key parameters estimated directly and then inserted in a biologically more realistic model leads to a complete set of parameters that are more "acceptable" than those used by

Dietz, Molineaux, and Thomas. Nevertheless, their specification with some less defensible parameter values constraining the G^2 optimization does a better—in the sense of G^2—job of describing observed prevalence.

This kind of tradeoff, suggesting fresh consideration of what one should mean by problem-dependent goodness-of-fit criteria, is in serious need of examination in many settings beside the Garki baseline data. Unfortunately, to date, the analogue of Nedelman's analysis still remains to be carried out with field data on a diversity of infectious diseases.

To conclude this overview of model development, which has focused heavily on malaria, it is important to observe that the issues we have raised are prototypical for the modeling of infectious diseases generally. Among the tropical parasitic diseases, malaria has received the lion's share of attention from people with extensive mathematical skill coupled with basic biological and epidemiological insight. Nevertheless, even the effective modeling of malaria prevalence dynamics—to say nothing of density dynamics in schistosomiasis or any dynamic modeling of other parasitic diseases—lies on the far side of the research agenda we have started to outline.

Models guiding intervention

With the exception of Macdonald's (1956) analysis of the impact on the basic reproduction rate for malaria of changes in its components—the man-biting rate, mosquito longevity, and so on—and, more recently, the Yorke et al. (1978) analysis of gonorrhea transmission, formal mathematical models have played a minimal role in the design of control or eradication campaigns. Further elaboration of this point appears in Dietz and Schenzle (1984). In our opinion, a fundamental reason for this state of affairs is that for a model to give believable predictions about the outcomes of possible interventions it is necessary to show that the model at least reproduces baseline prevalence patterns with some fidelity. As indicated in the previous section, such success lies in the future for virtually all of the tropical parasitic diseases. Nevertheless some important attempts are currently in progress to examine the possible impacts of malaria vector control programs and/or mass drug administration, via the transmission model developed and first calibrated in Garki. In this connection the simulations presented in Thomas and Molineaux (1982) are illuminating. See also the brief discussion in Bailey (1982) of use of the Garki model to plan control programs in China.

Despite the difficulty of modeling prevalence dynamics in a pristine endemic setting such as Garki, the increasingly widespread detection of drug-resistant parasites (Bruce-Chwatt, 1982)—to say nothing of mosquitoes resistant to chemical sprays—poses a new and fundamental challenge for modelers.

The basic idea behind the term "drug resistance" is simply that when the dose of a drug that is required to control an infection reaches or exceeds that which is fully tolerated by the host, one may say that the pathogen under investigation is "drug resistant." Although there has been an awareness of the phenomenon of drug resistance by *P. falciparum* and *P. vivax* even in the oldest antimalarial, quinine, since 1908–10 (see Peters, 1970, for a superb historical account) it was only with the mass drug administration programs in South America, South East Asia and the Pacific, and Africa beginning in the 1950s that serious attention has focused on its implications for malaria control programs. The most systematic and carefully conducted field studies of the development of drug resistance in human populations have been the studies of pyrimethamine resistance in *P. falciparum* in Tanzania by David Clyde and colleagues (see, in particular, Clyde, 1967).

Illustrative of the pyrimethamine resistance situation is the Clyde and Shute (1957) study in the Mkuzi area of Tanzania, where malaria was holo-endemic. Following initial drug sensitivity tests indicating that a dose of 50 mg of pyrimethamine for adults, with lower doses for young children, was successful in clearing *P. falciparum* from parasite carriers, 2–3,000 villagers began to receive the standard dose at weekly intervals. Administration continued for 18 months, at the end of which time 400 persons were still under regular treatment. Five months after the beginning of the program, *P. falciparum* appeared at low density in some of the regularly treated individuals. Under continuing drug pressure on this population, the *P. falciparum* prevalence increased from 0 percent initially to a stable 10–20 percent. This resistant parasite rate was substantially lower than the drug-sensitive parasite rate seen in villages under study prior to initiation of the program. Despite competition with drug-sensitive strains, the drug-resistant parasites spread rapidly to people in the test area who were not receiving pyrimethamine. The degree of resistance was such that the dosage required for parasite clearance was between 8 and 15 times the original standard. In many subjects this was the threshold of toxicity.

Much more fearsome but requiring a much longer time to become established is chloroquine resistance. Once established, however, it spreads rapidly across contiguous geographical areas while increasing in severity. For a dramatic example of spreading chloroquine resistance in India, see the discussion and references in Peters (1982). Fancidar resistance is now also established, thereby raising new doubts about what has been viewed as one of the best hopes for prevention and treatment of multiple-drug-resistant *P. falciparum* infections. This deteriorating epidemiological situation raises a host of new questions about the genetics of drug resistance, the precise nature of antimalarial drug action, and the new strategies that must be formulated for malaria control programs.

Although the epidemiological patterns of emergence of resistance in *P. falciparum* and *P. vivax* are becoming increasingly well documented, details of the underlying mechanisms are still poorly understood. In the case of pyrimethamine, however, there is experimental evidence (see Beale, 1980) indicating that abrupt shifts from sensitivity to resistance occur in single clones of parasites, that the resistance is stably inherited, and that segregation and recombination occur only during mosquito passage. Hence it seems appropriate to conclude that nuclear gene mutation is the cause of pyrimethamine resistance. It is currently assumed—although verification is still necessary—that the mutations are spontaneous. Concerning drug action, pyrimethamine acts on the enzyme dihydrofolate reductase that is essential for both host and parasite, but binding of the drug to the parasite enzyme is much stronger than to the host enzyme.

Unlike pyrimethamine, chloroquine resistance via mutation at a single step in cloned material has not been achieved. Genetic studies, as reviewed by Beale (1980), suggest that prolonged drug pressure is necessary to generate resistance, and that it is the result of the combined action of several mutant genes at different chromosomal loci. Also, chloroquine acts more powerfully on the parasites than on host cells because of the selective uptake of the drugs in parasitized cells.

In addition to the selection of resistant over sensitive parasites under drug pressure, it is important to understand whether resistant parasites also have a selective advantage in the absence of drugs. Limited experiments with *P. chabaudi* suggest such a selective advantage for chloroquine-resistant parasites. However, in the field, environmental conditions somehow compensate for the laboratory advantage of resistant parasites, suggesting that more elaborate investigations aimed at understanding the mechanisms of environmental influences are essential.

The challenge to the modeler posed by the diversity of mechanisms for development of drug resistance is the specification of models governing the genetics of the parasite within both an infected human host and the mosquito and then integrating the microprocess with a description of malaria transmission in a community. Such hybrid micro–macro models have had virtually no development in the literature on tropical parasitic diseases. A cryptic and interesting outline of how one might proceed appears in Rvachev (1967) but with the discussion confined entirely to directly communicable viral and bacterial infections. Diseases such as malaria, which require an insect vector for transmission and a treatment of microprocesses—that is, evolution of the parasites—in both the human and the insect vector, must now be reconsidered from scratch in terms of realistic description of the epidemiological and genetic aspects of drug resistance.

In our view, a systematic integration of parasite genetics, the reaction of parasites to drugs, and the dynamics of transmission is essential if mathematical models are to play a useful role in planning control programs. The basic problem is then reduced to asking which combinations of drugs, administered with what frequency and dosages, are adequate to reduce prevalence to prescribed target levels and to maintain them. Within an integrated model of transmission—incorporating the parasite genetics—this is a problem of optimal control theory that remains to be addressed. It also cannot be over-emphasized that assessing ability of such integrated models to describe field data on the development of drug resistance is a critical prior step to placing any trust in model predictions about the outcome of a control program. Here lies the central challenge.

Monitoring and data collection designs

The best kind of data for estimating age-specific mortality rates, incidence and recovery rates, basic reproduction rates, and (in malaria studies) vectorial capacity is a continuous record of individual infection status, together with contact rates between the human population and an animal population involved in the transmission process if the disease(s) in question is not directly communicable or between persons in the case of diseases such as gonorrhea. Data of this kind are virtually nonexistent on large populations, and it is impractical to even attempt to collect them. However, there are some small studies—for instance, stool samples from a select subsample in the Bocqueron schistosomiasis project (Vermund, Bradley, and Ruiz-Tiben, 1983)—in which very detailed fine-grained data can be used to gain insight about effective data collection designs which minimize the biases that arise when rates are estimated from data with gaps. Since rate estimation is a fundamental aspect of disease monitoring generally, we describe two lines of inquiry that can facilitate the development of relatively inexpensive but effective data collection plans for large populations.

(1) An important index of morbidity due to schistosomiasis is the human rate of elimination of egg-laying parasites. Estimation of such rates is usually constrained by assuming a constant elimination rate and estimating it from synthetic cohort data. The Bocqueron study contains a sample of 27 individuals from each of whom the number of eggs per gram was tabulated from ten consecutive stool samples collected in 1973, 1976, and 1977. The data collection was initiated *after* water in Bocqueron was cleared of all snails by use of a molluscicide in three major streams that run through the community. Thus there is an opportunity to directly estimate egg output and its variability from replicate measurements within the same individual in each of three years, as well as to compare these estimates across individuals. With estimates based on ten consecutive stool samples as a standard, one can address the question of which subsets of size two, or at most three, of the ten measurements, when averaged, best approximate the average of ten measurements. This issue is important since collection of ten consecutive stool samples is exceedingly difficult on a large population, whereas the first and last stool in a 10–15-day period may represent a design yielding reasonably accurate estimates of egg output. Thus, by imposing alternative designs yielding fragmentary data relative to the ten consecutive stool samples, we can directly assess which of the less expensive designs yield egg output estimates with minimum bias and variability relative to the more complete data.

This kind of study can play a key role in developing simple and efficient data collection designs for monitoring purposes. In the context of the Bocqueron data, an investigation of the efficiency of alternative designs—that is, replication patterns within years and over time—is currently under way (Singer and Vermund, in progress). Despite the restricted focus of these data, the general strategy outlined above could be, but to our knowledge has not been, a major source of guidance about efficient data collection for rate estimation in infectious diseases generally.

(2) Once it is recognized that rate estimation based on continuous observation in a population is intractable, then one requires guidance about which data collection designs involving gaps relative to a continuously evolving process are most informative about the rates of interest. To address the question using models of individual-level dynamics, there must first be some agreement about a restricted class of models—for example, the continuous-time Markovian or semi-Markovian models—that are reasonable candidates to account for the evolution of infection status histories. For purposes of illustration, suppose that we agree that continuous-time nonstationary Markovian processes are a plausible class of models. In addition, suppose that economic considerations dictate that infection status can be ascertained prospectively no more than four times per year. We are now confronted with the problem of optimal allocation of survey dates to facilitate rate estimation within a restricted class of nonstationary Markovian models. Even at the simplistic level of Markovian models, this is a largely uncharted subject. Nevertheless, it is a topic of central importance if longitudinal data collection is to provide adequate information for rate estimates and for testing the compatibility of stochastic process models with censored individual histories.

An additional facet of this question arises if we consider the modeling of bivariate processes, such as infection status and immune response histories. Precisely this kind of process is relevant for an understanding of malaria morbidity and mortality. Considering the Garki data, however, we find that serological information is collected less frequently than parasitological data. Thus the degree of detail obtained about the bivariate process is different for each coordinate. The design question, however, is to designate an optimal allocation in time of parasitological and serological surveys if, for example, cost considerations impose a constraint of six parasitological and four serological surveys within a 12-month period. There is virtually no literature on this obviously important topic.

Summary

The important admonition "Rubber boots come in model builders' sizes" (J. E. Cohen, c. 1975) has a complementary side: Numerical output from mathematical models need not be viewed as numerology by designers of public health programs.

To facilitate the integration of mathematical models of infectious diseases into the process of planning and evaluating disease control programs, a diverse range of research activities is necessary. The most important of these, as stressed in this paper, are the following:

— The development of statistical methods for estimating incidence and recovery rates and basic reproduction rates from fragmentary longitudinal data. The analytical methods should include adjustments for measurement error and take account of various facets of population heterogeneity.

— An integration of micro- and macro-level models of transmission and the development of strategies for testing them against field data.

— The need for formulations of transmission models that explicitly account for the development of drug resistance by parasites and resistance to toxic chemicals by insect vectors.

— The specification of inexpensive yet efficient designs for data collection to facilitate rate estimation and the testing of models. This topic is particularly important for monitoring and surveillance programs.

The agenda has many challenges for model builders. Optimistically, it will lead to new and very practical tools to aid the development of effective public health programs. These programs, in turn, can reduce the deleterious impact of infectious diseases as risk factors influencing current high rates of infant and child mortality.

Note

The research reported herein was completed with the assistance of fellowship support from the John Simon Guggenheim Memorial Foundation. Special thanks are due David Bradley for stimulating discussions, comments, and criticism of an earlier draft.

References

Anderson, R. M., and R. M. May. 1982a. "Population dynamics of human helminth infections: Control by chemotherapy," *Nature* 297 (June): 557–563.

———, and R. M. May (eds.). 1982b. *Population Dynamics of Infectious Diseases.* New York: Springer Verlag.

Aron, J. L. 1982. "Malaria epidemiology and detectability," *Transactions of the Royal Society of Tropical Medicine and Hygiene* 76, no. 5: 595–601.

———, and R. M. May. 1979. "Population dynamics of malaria," in *Population Dynamics of Infectious Diseases: Theory and Applications,* ed. R. M. Anderson. London: Chapman and Hall.

Bailey, N. T. J. 1975. *The Mathematical Theory of Infectious Diseases* (2nd ed.). New York: Macmillan.

———. 1982. *The Biomathematics of Malaria,* London: Charles Griffin and Co.

Beale, G. H. 1980. "The genetics of drug resistance in malaria parasites," *Bulletin, World Health Organization* 58, no. 5: 799–804.

Bekessy, A., L. Molineaux, and J. Storey. 1976. "Estimation of incidence and recovery rates of *Plasmodium falciparum* parasitemia from longitudinal data," *Bulletin, World Health Organization* 54: 685–691.

Bögel, K., H. Moegle, F. Knorp, A. Arata, K. Dietz, and P. Diethelm. 1976. "Characteristics of the spread of a wildlife rabies epidemic in Europe," *Bulletin, World Health Organization* 54: 433–447.

Boyd, M. F. (ed.). 1949. *Malariology*. Philadelphia: Saunders.

Bruce-Chwatt, L. J. (ed.). 1981. *Chemotherapy of Malaria*. Geneva: World Health Organization.

Clyde, D. F. 1967. *Malaria in Tanzania*. London: Oxford University Press.

———, and G. T. Shute. 1957. "Resistance of *Plasmodium falciparum* in Tanganyika to pyrimethamine administered at weekly intervals," *Transactions of the Royal Society of Tropical Medicine and Hygiene* 51, no. 6: 505–513.

Cohen, Joel E. 1977. "Mathematical models of schistosomiasis," *Annual Review of Ecology and Systematics* 8: 209–233.

———, and Burton Singer. 1979. "Malaria in Nigeria: Constrained continuous-time Markov models for discrete-time longitudinal data on human mixed-species infections," in *Lectures on Mathematics in the Life Sciences* 12: 69–133, ed. S. Levin. Providence: American Mathematical Society.

Dietz, K. 1982. "Overall population patterns in the transmission cycle of infectious disease agents," in *Population Biology of Infectious Diseases*, ed. R. M. Anderson and R. M. May. New York: Springer-Verlag, pp. 87–102.

———, L. Molineaux, and A. Thomas. 1974. "A malaria model tested in the African savannah," *Bulletin, World Health Organization* 50: 347–357.

———, L. Molineaux, and A. Thomas. 1978. "Further epidemiological evaluation of a malaria model," *Bulletin, World Health Organization* 56, no. 4: 565–571.

———, and D. Schenzle. 1985. "Mathematical models for infectious disease statistics," in *ISI Centenary volume—A Celebration of Statistics*, ed. A. Atkinson and S. Fienberg. New York: Springer-Verlag.

Garrett-Jones, C. 1964. "The human blood index of malaria vectors in relation to epidemiological assessment," *Bulletin, World Health Organization* 30: 241–261.

Knox, E. G. 1980. "Strategy for rubella vaccination," *International Journal of Epidemiology* 9: 13–23.

Macdonald. 1956. "Theory of the eradication of malaria," *Bulletin, World Health Organization* 15: 369–387.

———. 1957. *The Epidemiology and Control of Malaria*. London: Oxford University Press.

Molineaux, L. Forthcoming. "The impact of parasitic diseases and their control on mortality, with emphasis on malaria and Africa," in *Social Policy, Health Policy, and Mortality Prospects*, ed. Jacques Vallin. IUSSP Publication.

———, and G. Gramiccia. 1980. *The Garki Project*. Geneva: World Health Organization.

Najera, J. A. 1974. "A critical review of the field application of a mathematical model of malaria eradication," *Bulletin, World Health Organization* 50: 449–457.

Nedelman, J. 1983a. "A negative binomial model for sampling mosquitoes in a malaria survey," *Biometrics* 39: 1009–1020.

———. 1983b. "Inoculation and recovery rates in the malaria model of Dietz, Molineaux, and Thomas," *Mathematical Biosciences* (in press).

Peters, W. 1970. *Chemotherapy and Drug Resistance in Malaria*. London: Academic Press.

———. 1982. "Antimalarial drug resistance: An increasing problem," *British Medical Bulletin* 38, no. 2: 187–192.

Rvachev, L. A. 1967. "A model of the connection between processes in an organism and the structure of an epidemic," *Kibernetika* 3, no. 3: 75–78.

Sayers, B. McA., B. G. Mansourian, Phan Tan, and K. Bögel. 1977. "A pattern-analysis study of a wild-life rabies epizootic," *Medical Informatics* 2: 11–34.

Singer, B., and J. E. Cohen. 1980. "Estimating malaria incidence and recovery rates from panel surveys." *Mathematical Biosciences* 49: 273–305.

———, and J. E. Cohen. 1982. "Erratum," *Mathematical Biosciences* 62: 151–152.

Steck, F., and A. Wandeler. 1980. "The epidemiology of fox rabies in Europe," *Epidemiological Review* 2: 71–96.

Thomas, A., and L. Molineaux. 1982. *The Epidemiology and Control of Malaria: Simulations Using the Garki Malaria Model*. Geneva: World Health Organization (draft manuscript, December).

Vermund, S., D. J. Bradley, and E. Ruiz-Tiben. 1983. "Survival of *Schistosoma mansoni* in the human host: Estimates from a community-based prospective study in Puerto Rico," *American Journal of Tropical Medicine and Hygiene* 32, no. 5: 1040–1048.

Yorke, J. A., H. N. Heathcote, and A. Nold. 1978. "Dynamics and control of the transmission of gonorrhea," *Sexually Transmitted Diseases* 5: 51–56.

Modeling Resource Allocation for Child Survival

Howard N. Barnum

Robin Barlow

High rates of infant and child mortality are one of the heavier burdens borne by the populations of the less developed world. Yet, rarely are the minimal resources devoted to primary health care carefully marshaled to deal efficiently with the most pressing health and medical problems of children. One partial explanation for the inadequacy of current efforts has been the failure of policy analysts to devise an integrated and cost-effective approach to the alleviation of those community health problems that underlie high infant mortality rates.

The objective of the research reported here is to provide policymakers with an analytical framework to facilitate the efficient allocation of resources to programs intended to reduce the rate of child mortality. As a heuristic device, the framework is used to provide a direct assessment of health interventions designed to raise the probability of child survival in a hypothetical community.[1] The techniques developed are intended to have general application to an analysis of the cost-effectiveness of alternative health programs.

An important belief underlying the analysis is that direct interventions are a practicable means of improving the rate of child survival in less developed countries. Economic development is obviously the major requirement for the ultimate achievement of a fully satisfactory nutritional and health status. But development is a slow process, and there is growing evidence that the use of direct health and environmental interventions can bring about a substantial improvement in health status, especially in infants and young children, before development has occurred. The technical feasibility of alternative interventions has been demonstrated in numerous projects involving, for instance, nutritional programs, the improvement of water quantity and quality, the provision of preventive services, and the provision of curative clinical care.

In spite of technical feasibility, resource constraints restrict the adoption

of projects, and for this reason health programs must also be examined with
respect to economic feasibility. The binding resource constraints are not
always funds; the constraints may involve, depending on the time and place,
financial restrictions, limited administrative capacity, a shortage of skilled
personnel, or limits on the size of physical facilities. Often programs compete
for the same set of resources so that, for example, a prenatal care program
may use scarce registered nurse administrative time also needed for a child
immunization program. As a result the effectiveness of both programs is cut
by faulty administration. Thus, as the example illustrates, health programs
need to be coordinated and a careful choice must be made among alternative
programs competing for the limited resources available.

    The best health policy will, of course, consist of the set of interventions
bringing about the greatest improvement in child survival for a given level of
resource expenditures. If any other set of interventions is chosen there will be
an unnecessary waste of resources and an unnecessarily high level of child
mortality. In a high-income country the penalty for an incorrect choice of
resources is likely to be low. But in a poor country, with a high initial level
of child mortality and an acute scarcity of resources, the penalty for a subop-
timum choice of interventions is likely to be high. If scarce money, manpower,
and facilities are to be used to the best effect, then interventions must be
chosen carefully with tandem concern for program effects and costs.

Policy issues

The choice of interventions raises several policy issues that are broader in
scope than the detailed examination of the cost-effectiveness of individual
health measures. These are issues of emphasis on broad classes of interventions, program organization, and choice of target population subgroups.
Although the analysis in our study is designed to answer questions about the
optimum use of resources for specific interventions, the results also provide
tentative answers to questions that arise in considering several of the broader
issues. Among these are the following.

Curative versus preventive care

Is curative care cost-effective?

    The use of large-scale physical facilities (hospitals and clinics) to pro-
vide capital-intensive curative care for limited population subgroups has fallen
into justified disrepute. It is clearly recognized that these facilities do not
represent a cost-effective use of resources. The continued construction of
large-scale curative facilities is attributable to political processes and decisions
and not to an erroneous assessment of the cost-effectiveness of these programs
on the part of health planners. But the possible use of smaller scale curative
facilities, especially for outpatient care, remains an important ongoing question. Low-technology therapies, such as oral rehydration of diarrhea patients,
can be administered at the level of small health clinics and health posts. The

question of cost-effectiveness of low-technology curative care versus preventive care remains of interest.

A closely related question is that of mode of birth delivery. The demand for institutional delivery has in many areas caused a substantial allocation of health resources to delivery clinics. Many health planners feel that midwife-attended home deliveries would allow a more efficient distribution of health resources in resource-poor communities. The model applied in this study allows a comparison of alternative modes of birth delivery, as well as a comparison of curative versus preventive use.

Promotion versus services

How should resources be divided between health promotion and the actual provision of services?

The question of access versus usage remains important for both preventive care and curative care programs. In the promotional programs considered in this study, health workers with only a low level of education visit households and track the health status of children and women, encourage the consistent use of breastfeeding throughout infancy, and convey information about available health services. Recent experiments with health promotion programs in Candelaria, Colombia, and elsewhere demonstrate that the effectiveness of health services can be raised through early detection of pregnancy, the tracking of child growth progress, and the identification of high-risk children.[2]

Water and sanitation versus health services

Are water and sanitary interventions cost-effective in comparison with direct health services?

The cost-effectiveness of water and sanitation is expected to vary greatly over communities. The programs vary greatly in cost depending on the community's location and population density. In the water and sanitation programs examined here, the community population density is high, water resources are available, and an existing urban water and sewage infrastructure provides economies of scale so that the cost of extending the programs to the study community is relatively low. In this respect the results may not be of broader application. In general, however, water and sanitation programs do not rely heavily on continuing inputs of skilled manpower. Thus, if the important constraint on health programs is the availability of skilled manpower, water and sanitation programs may be competitive alternatives to other health programs.

Population target groups

What are the appropriate population targets?

Even though the ultimate objective of the policies to be considered is the lowering of child mortality, the appropriate population targets are not obvious. Is it the prenatal, neonatal, infant, or early childhood period that should receive the most attention? The answer depends not only on the relative mortality in each population group but also on the relative costs and effects of interventions aimed at the mortality problems of each group.

A second problem in the choice of population group is that of screening for high-risk targets. Is it cheaper to first incur the cost of examinations and tests for screening or to provide treatment to a larger group without attempting to identify high-risk individuals? For example, is it more cost-effective to provide nutritional supplements to all pregnant women or to first screen pregnant women by risk group and then provide nutritional supplements only to those evaluated as high risks of having low birth weight children? The answer is not obvious without analysis. It depends on the costs of screening, the proportion of pregnant women who are high risks, the cost of nutritional programs, and the relative effectiveness of the alternative nutritional programs.

Role of nutrition interventions

What is the relative importance of nutrition intervention efforts?

The importance of malnutrition as a contributing cause of mortality and the interaction of malnutrition with other diseases have emerged as clearly established findings from the Puffer and Serrano PAHO study, the Candelaria project, and research carried out at INCAP and elsewhere.[3] However, the implications of these findings for resource allocation need to be clarified. Leaving aside the question of agricultural productivity and marketing programs and looking only at the design of primary health care programs, is the best use of health funds for direct nutritional rehabilitation, nutritional supplements, or indirect nutrition-related activities such as oral rehydration and breastfeeding? The answers are related to the costs of interventions, the incidence of malnutrition, and the extent of interaction between malnutrition and other diseases.

Resource constraints

What are the binding constraints?

Interventions use differing proportions of different resources. Some health activities draw heavily on the use of physical facilities; other activities draw heavily on the time of skilled personnel; still other activities draw heavily on budgeted funds. Are the effective restrictions on the adoption of health programs to improve child survival primarily limits in budgets, personnel, or physical facilities? The answer to this question has important implications for long-term manpower planning, building programs, and budgeting. The resource allocation model developed below allows the identification of constraining resources and estimates the benefits to be derived from additional resources.

The child mortality model

The evaluation of alternative interventions is carried out through the application of a nonlinear optimization model that, given the epidemiological characteristics of the population, the availability of resources, and the effectiveness of health interventions, chooses the set of intervention activity levels lying within the resource constraints that maximizes the probability of child survival.

Salient features of the model include the use of interactive simultaneous equations to model the causes of death in a setting of multiple diseases, the clear distinction between preventive activities affecting morbidity and curative activities affecting case fatality rates, and the separation of the early childhood period into age subgroups with distinct morbidity characteristics. The optimization model also distinguishes between program use (which an economist might view as the demand side of the market for health services) and program availability (which can be viewed as supply), and operates in such a manner as to set intervention levels that tend to equilibrate use and availability.

Figure 1 provides an overview of the model. The basic relationship, shown at the bottom of the diagram, is the calculation of mortality rates as

FIGURE 1   The child mortality model

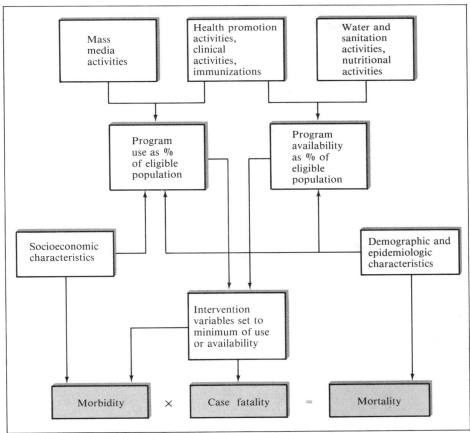

NOTE: In successive computer runs, the program is repeated for each age group using survivors from the preceding group as the population base.

the product of morbidity (the morbidity rate measures the incidence of disease
in the reference population) and case fatality (the fatality rate measures the
incidence of death in the diseased population).

Use versus availability of interventions

The boxes at the top of Figure 1 represent intervention activities, parti-
tioned into three groups: mass media; health promotion activities, clinical
activities, and immunizations; and water, sanitation, and nutritional activities.
The level of such activities is first measured in terms of an absolute number
of visits or other appropriate units and then recalculated as a percent of the
eligible population, given the demographic and epidemiological characteristics
of the population. For some interventions, such as water and sanitation, this
yields program availability directly. Other interventions, such as mass media,
act together with socioeconomic characteristics to determine the level of program use. Still other interventions, such as health promoters who visit the
household, both provide services and encourage program use.

Because a health intervention, in order to be effective, must not only
be available but also be used, the model selects the minimum of use or availability, expressed as a percent of the eligible population, to represent the
effective level of intervention activities in the determination of morbidity and
case fatality rates. Thus, for instance, if clinic capacity is 70 percent, but it
is calculated that only 60 percent of the eligible population used the clinics,
the morbidity and fatality rates would be calculated using 60 percent as the
effective level of the clinical interventions. On the other hand, if program use
were 100 percent, but the available capacity is only 70 percent, the calculation
of morbidity and fatality rates is based on the 70 percent figure.

Age groups

The model consists of three submodels covering different age groups between
birth and 5 years of age: (1) the neonatal period (the first month of life), (2)
infancy (2–12 months of life), and (3) postinfancy (13–60 months). These
three periods are distinguished from one another by large differences in mortality associated with distinct physiological characteristics in the development
of the child.

Individual age groups are linked in that the survivors of younger age
groups become the demographic basis for intervention coverage and morbidity
rates in the older age groups. Given the effective level of intervention activities, the socioeconomic characteristics of the population, and estimates of the
impact of these variables on morbidity and fatality rates, a mortality rate is
calculated for each age group. Because the survivors from each age group
become the population base for the next older age group, the age-specific
mortality rates for younger ages affect the flow of population into the box
labeled "Demographic and epidemiologic characteristics" for older age
groups. Repeating the process outlined in Figure 1 over all age groups considered in the model allows the derivation of an overall mortality rate for a

baseline number of births over the first 60 months of life and for a given selection of intervention levels.

Disease categories

The selection of diseases used in the model is guided by three criteria. First, an objective is to include a minimum number of morbidity states for simplicity but to account for at least 75 percent of childhood mortality. Second, diseases that have well-known and obvious interventions that might be thought cost-effective prior to a formal analysis are included. The final criterion is that the disease categories selected be those that show the most potential for mortality reduction as evidenced by the difference in mortality rates by cause and age of death between developed and less developed regions, or by the decline in disease-specific mortality rates for developed countries over time. This was the focus of the monumental study by Puffer and Serrano (see note 3) and is perhaps the most important criterion because it identifies a very few diseases with a large effect on health.

Using these three criteria, the diseases included in the model, summarized in Figure 2, account for 75–80 percent of childhood mortality in developing countries. The arrows connecting the diseases indicate the direction of a potential causal flow; these interdisease causal flows are included in the model in the form of a nonzero interaction coefficient (for the disease identified by the arrow) in equations generating the disease rates. Only the most signif-

FIGURE 2   Morbidity segment of the infant mortality model (showing interdisease causal flows), in the three age groups

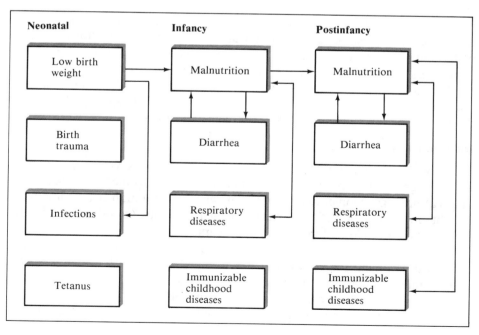

icant disease interactions are included. The importance of the disease inter-relationships is that they allow for indirect effects of interventions that, if not included, might cause the effectiveness of particular interventions to be under-estimated. For instance, malnutrition is not a significant direct cause of mor-tality; it is, however, an important contributor to higher morbidity rates for other diseases. Thus a nutritional supplement may be potentially cost-effective in mortality reduction even though direct deaths through starvation or nutri-tional deficiencies are small in number. Similarly, because of the interrela-tionship between diarrhea and malnutrition, interventions such as water and sanitation that reduce diarrhea will have secondary effects that act through lowered rates of malnutrition to reduce mortality from respiratory and immun-izable childhood diseases.

Marginal versus joint morbidity rates

The morbidity rates, that is, the marginal disease rates, are derived from functions analogous to marginal probability functions. These functions gen-erate the incidence of given diseases, including cases where other diseases are present as well as less complicated disease states. Using these functions and a set of assumptions regarding the degree of independence between diseases, together with a set of probability relationships, mutually exclusive joint dis-ease rates are generated.[4] These rates can be used to calculate the distribution of the population among the disease states representing the various possible combinations of the individual diseases considered. Fatality rates for each of the mutually exclusive joint disease states are then used to calculate the state-specific mortality rate. The overall mortality rate is obtained by summing over all disease states.

Generating the morbidity structure of the model from marginal disease functions, rather than directly through the use of separate functions for each of the mutually exclusive disease states, substantially reduces the number of parameters needed to specify the model. Whereas n structural equations are needed for a model of n diseases if the model is specified using marginal morbidity rates, $2^n - 1$ equations would be needed to specify the model directly at the level of the mutually exclusive disease states.

Interventions

The model includes 36 interventions and 7 socioeconomic variables. In terms of target groups the interventions are aimed at (1) all women of childbearing age, (2) pregnant women, (3) women known to have a high risk of low birth weight children or of birth trauma, (4) neonatal infants, (5) infants during the first year of life, (6) children aged 1–5 years.

Interventions for all women of childbearing age include examinations, tests, and treatment for venereal disease, other genitourinary tract infections, and anemia. Similarly for pregnant women, interventions consist of exami-nations, tests, and treatment for infections, hypertension, diabetes, toxemia, and anemia; tetanus immunization; and a nutritional program. An additional intervention is designed to promote early detection of pregnancy. For women with a high risk of low birth weight children or of birth trauma, there is a nutritional supplement. Interventions acting directly on neonatal infants are hospital or health center delivery, home delivery attended by a midwife, outpatient neonatal care, and inpatient neonatal care.

Interventions acting on infants and young children include DPT, polio, and measles immunizations; checkups and maternal education in well-baby clinics; nutritional supplement for breastfeeding mothers; nutritional supplement for the child; outpatient care, inpatient care, and intensive care for malnourished children.

Water and sanitation interventions affecting all population subgroups include public fountains, in-home piped water, latrines, in-house toilet facilities, and garbage and rubbish pickup. There are also the promotional interventions, mentioned earlier, which affect the level of intervention use.

An especially important intervention activity included in the model is the use of a nonprofessional health worker or health promoter who is given specific messages and assigned limited services to deliver in regular periodic visits to the household. The actions of the health promoter are differentiated within the model according to whether or not they promote the use of other health services or provide a direct service themselves. Specifically the health promoter provides information about personal and child hygiene and the proper use of sanitary services; gives nutritional advice, including the management of breastfeeding and growth monitoring; and teaches the mother to look for signs of morbidity and to care for mild illness, including the use of oral rehydration therapy for diarrhea.

Structural equations

The three types of structural equations in the model generate the rates for (1) intervention use, (2) marginal disease incidence, and (3) fatality. The role of the three types of equations can be reviewed referring to Figure 1. As the arrows indicate, the use rates (or alternatively, participation rates), u, are calculated as a function of socioeconomic variables and intervention activities:

$$u_l = u_l (C_l) \qquad l = 1 \dots L \qquad (1)$$

where C_l is a vector of appropriate socioeconomic variables and activities, and L is the total number of use functions calculated. In actuality the extent of program participation would be somewhat different for each intervention, since participation varies with the perceived utility of each program as compared with the perceived costs. However, to keep the number of intervention use equations manageable, we have collected interventions into nine groups that might reasonably be expected to have similar participation characteristics and have specified individual use functions for each group. The nine use equations are: (1) use of prenatal care by all women, (2) use of prenatal care by pregnant women, (3) use of curative care, (4) practice of breastfeeding, (5) proportion of prenatal care commenced in first trimester, (6) use of preventive care in the infancy group, (7) use of curative care in the infancy group, (8) use of preventive care in the postinfancy group, and (9) use of curative care in the postinfancy group.

The functional form employed for the use equations is the logit,

$$u_l = \frac{1}{1 + e^{-U_l}} \qquad l = 1 \ldots 9 \tag{2}$$

where the U_l are linear functions of the socioeconomic and intervention variables. The choice of functional form was arbitrary; the logit was chosen because of its convenient algebraic characteristics and because of the function's asymptotic properties.

The appropriate use rates are compared with the available level of intervention programs per capita, x_i, and the minimum is selected to represent the effective level of intervention, I_i, used in the calculation or morbidity and fatality rates; that is,

$$I_i = min \begin{Bmatrix} u \\ x_i \end{Bmatrix} \tag{3}$$

Given A_i, a vector of the socioeconomic variables and the effective level of the interventions, the age-specific morbidity rates can be calculated from marginal morbidity rate functions for each disease:

$$P_i = P_i(A_i, P_j) \qquad \begin{matrix} i, j = 1 \ldots n \\ i \neq j \end{matrix} \tag{4}$$

The functional form chosen for the morbidity functions is a modified logit, and the structural equations can be written as

$$P_{ia} = a_{ia} \frac{\alpha_{iU}}{1 + e^{-Z_{ia}}} + \alpha_{iL} + \sum_{j=1}^{n} b_{ija} P_{ja} + c_{ia} P_{i,a-1} \qquad \begin{matrix} i = 1 \ldots 4 \text{ (diseases)} \\ a = 1 \ldots 3 \text{ (age groups)} \end{matrix} \tag{5}$$

where $P_{i,a-1}$ represents the morbidity rate in the prior age group, Z_{ia} is a linear function of the various socioeconomic and intervention variables, a_{ia}, b_{ija}, and c_{ia} are coefficients, and α_{iU} and α_{iL} are parameters setting upper and lower limits to the function.

The malnutrition equations for the last two age groups are the only morbidity functions given a lagged specification; thus c_{ia} is assumed to equal zero for all morbidity functions except P_{12}, P_{13}. In general, the choice of functional form is arbitrary since there is no precedent for this type of model. We have chosen the logit form as appropriately reflecting the behavior of many biological processes. As experience with this type of model increases, other nonlinear forms may be found that provide a more accurate approximation of the processes involved; or, conversely, it may be found that linear functions are sufficient approximations of reality over the range of morbidity rates involved in specific problems.

Probability relationships (see note 4) are used to derive the mutually exclusive joint disease rates, c_k, from the marginal morbidity rates,

$$c_k = c_k (p_i), \qquad k = 1 \ldots K \tag{6}$$

Finally, fatality rates are calculated as functions of the proportion of cases receiving no care, outpatient care, or inpatient care,

$$f_k = \delta_{ko} (1 - I_{IN} - I_{OUT}) + \delta_{k1} I_{OUT} + \delta_{k2} I_{IN} \qquad k = 1 \ldots K \tag{7}$$

and the mortality rate is obtained as the product of case fatality rates and disease rates,

$$D = \sum_k f_k c_k \qquad k = 1 \ldots K \tag{8}$$

Specification of the structural parameters

The model just described is intended to involve the minimum number of relationships necessary for specifying a quantitative planning model for evaluating policy choices affecting child mortality. An effort was made to include only the most important disease relationships and the most feasible interventions from among the host of interrelationships and interventions that might be identified. The goal was to keep the model tractable, while still being large enough to provide a practical illustration of the construction of a disease model for cost-effectiveness analysis. This effort notwithstanding, there are still 221 parameters (coefficients) that need to be specified before the model can be applied. Potentially the parameters could be specified statistically, using data from field studies and clinical research. In fact, the parameters provide a catalogue of the separate problem areas that have been the focus of medical and health research on child mortality in developing regions over the last 20 to 30 years. However, in spite of the substantial body of operational and theoretical research on the treatment and prevention of childhood disease, the current literature does not allow the complete specification of the quantitative relationships required by even the modest dimensions of the child mortality simulation model.

To provide an illustration of how the model would work in an actual situation, we decided to specify the parameters through the use of a set of survey questions designed for the purpose. Respondents were medical and health practitioners with considerable experience in the problems of delivering health services in less developed countries.[5]

The survey consisted of four sets of questions covering intervention use, morbidity, fatality, and disease interactions. Respondents were asked questions appropriate to their expertise, with no respondent asked the total of all four sets of questions. Respondents were given a description of the baseline state of the hypothetical community, including baseline levels of the variables, and were asked to estimate the percentage change in one variable in response to a percentage change in another.[6] In most cases, the questions were phrased to obtain the percentage change in morbidity, case fatality, or use that might be expected from the adoption of an intervention in a reference population. For example, "In a reference population with an infant mortality rate of 100 per thousand births, a diarrheal morbidity rate of 2 cases per year per infant, and not previously practicing breastfeeding, what percentage reduction in the diarrhea rate would occur with the adoption of universal breastfeeding?" The responses were related by straightforward algebraic formulas to the coefficients of the relevant structural equation.[7]

Clearly, statistical estimation of the parameters based on data derived from a specific real setting would be a desirable next step. In the future, estimation of simultaneous equation models may yield interaction coefficients for the morbidity functions, especially for diarrhea and malnutrition. Additionally, some of the coefficients, such as those giving the effect of socioeconomic status and selected information and communication activities on intervention use, may be derived from local health programs. Nevertheless, major empirical gaps will remain. One advantage of the modeling procedure described here is that it is amenable to piecewise replacement of some parameters with empirically derived estimates while retaining the subjective specification for other parameters where statistical estimates remain impractical.

Resource requirements, resource availability, and demographic constraints

Differences in costs are perhaps the most important reason that specific quantitative results and policy conclusions obtained from an application of a resource allocation model in one region or country cannot be readily applied to another region. The costs of the activities considered are affected by the mode of delivery, the organization of health institutions, the availability of related technology, and the state of local resource markets, all of which vary greatly among regions. In deriving the resource costs for the hypothetical community modeled here, we have worked with local budgets and taken institutions, technology, and prices from the five *barrios* comprising the area of the PRIMOPS project in Cali, Colombia.

Resource constraints

The potential resource constraints are (1) total costs, (2) total cost of supplies, (3) physician time, (4) registered nurse time, (5) auxiliary nurse time, (6) bed days available, and (7) capacity of physical facilities. Total monetary costs include expenditures for administration, salaries, depreciation on capital equipment and buildings, and supplies. The costs of supplies and expendable equipment are analyzed separately because budget items in this category can be regarded by administrators as more easily changed over a planning period than are the other items in total costs, such as salaries and depreciation. Physician time includes both administrative and service uses of time. The same is true of registered nurse time (which, for most of the programs considered, is almost entirely administrative time) and to some extent of auxiliary nurse time. Both bed days and physical capacity represent the use of physical facilities, but a distinction is made between bed capacity, which is primarily a constraint on the number of inpatients, and the use of other forms of physical capital.[8] Inpatient and outpatient care for children, examinations and treatment of women, institutional deliveries, and visits to the well-baby clinic all make use of health center and hospital physical facilities apart from bed capacity. Physical capacity is measured in monetary units only as a convenience and could, conceptually, have been measured in other units, such as square meters. The total use of each of the seven resources by all activities is constrained to be less than or equal to the total resource availability,

$$\sum_{i=1}^{32} r_{ij} X_i \leq R_j \qquad j = 1 \ldots 7 \qquad (9)$$

where r_{ij} is the amount of resource j used per unit of activity i, R_j is the total availability of resource j, and X_i is used to denote the absolute level of an activity (as opposed to x_i, used in equation 3 to denote the per capita level of interventions) that gives the applicable demographic constraint, N_k, for each activity.

Epidemiologic and demographic constraints

All activities are also constrained by the size of epidemiologic and demographic groups.[9] Resources would, of course, be wasted if the scale of activities were allowed to be greater than the potential target populations. For example, the total number of households covered by a health promoter cannot be greater than the number of households in the modeled community. The population constraints can be summarized by

$$X_i \leq N_k \qquad \begin{array}{l} i = 1 \ldots 31 \\[6pt] k = f(i) \end{array} \qquad (10)$$

Epidemiologic and demographic constraints also enter the model as denominators in the calculation of the proportional coverage of the activities,

$$x_i = X_i/N_k \qquad \begin{array}{l} i = 1 \ldots 31 \\[6pt] k = f(i) \end{array} \qquad (11)$$

In the calculation of the per capita level of activities for the infancy and postinfancy age groups, the actual size of the demographic group varies with the success of earlier health activities (among the neonatal age group), and is obtained after the number of survivors for the earlier age group is computed.

Additional restrictions

In addition to the resource and demographic constraints, there are also a number of restrictions on the relationships between activities. These constraints restrict (1) the sum of institutional deliveries, midwife deliveries, and unattended deliveries followed by health promoter visits to be less than or equal to the total number of births; (2) the total of home and public water outlets to be less than or equal to the number of households; (3) the total of latrines and toilets to be less than or equal to the number of households; and (4) the total of inpatient and outpatient caseload to be less than or equal to the number of cases requiring treatment. Other restrictions require that the proportional coverage of treatments for pregnant women and all women be less than the proportional coverage of examinations for each group, and that the proportional coverage of nutritional programs for children and the iron supplement program for women be less than the proportional coverage of households by the health promoters. In all there are 16 additional restrictions of this type.

Optimization with the model

The model outlined above allows simulation of the patterns of morbidity and mortality that are the consequence of given sets of activity levels. Using a nonlinear computer optimization program to provide a systematic sorting of repeated simulations, an optimum set of activity levels can be selected for given levels of resource constraints.[10] Table 1 gives the results of alternative optimizations as the availability of all resources—budgets, physicians' and nurses' time, and capacity of facilities—increases from two to five times an initially specified baseline level.[11] Because the absolute level of the activities (for instance, health promoter visits to 10,500 households) has no intuitive meaning, the results are presented as a percentage of the relevant population that is covered by and using the intervention. Thus, Table 1 reports that at the lowest resource level, 85 percent (10,500 of the 12,300 households with women of childbearing age) of the eligible population receives visits from health promoters.

The fall in mortality rates with increased resources is indicated at the bottom of the table. Although the results are too extensive to reproduce here, a comparison of the morbidity and mortality rates for a low-resource community with the simulated rates for higher resource communities revealed that a substantial part of the reduction in mortality comes from the large decrease in morbidity associated with diarrhea and malnutrition.[12] Mortality is also decreased by lowering case fatality rates. The reduction in malnutrition has the important effect of shifting remaining morbidity into joint disease cate-

TABLE 1   Percent of eligible population using or covered by designated interventions with optimum resource allocation at alternative resource levels[a]

Intervention	Resource level[d]				
	1R	2R	3R	4R	5R
Promoter visits	85	98	90	89	89
All women					
Treat infection				12	22
Iron supplement	47	50	67	71	71
Iron-deficient women—iron supplement	2	17		11	22
Pregnant women[b]					
Treat infection			74	70	85
Nutritional supp.—LBW[c] risk			74	64	76
Tetanus immunization	20	90	93	94	94
Health center counseling			19	62	77
Nutritional supplement			75	66	81
Delivery					
Hospital, LBW[c] risk				28	31
Hospital					
Home, midwife		10	57	33	47
Unattended, with follow-up		41	23	38	35
Water					
In home	13	32	30	73	73
100-meter walk	23	29	70	27	27
Sanitation					
Toilet		12	13	38	44
Latrine	99	88	87	44	44
Mass media	72	78	99	99	100
Neonatal care					
Outpatient	26	94	98		
Inpatient				97	99
Immunization (DPT, polio, measles)		1	50	93	100
Infant					
Well-baby clinic	52	90	91	91	91
Nutritional supplement			45	10	11
Breastfeeding, with supp. for mother					
Breastfeeding, no supp.	73	78	78	78	78
Outpatient care	1	99	99	80	7
Inpatient care				20	92
Young child					
Well-baby clinic	77	82	78	77	77
Nutritional supplement	17	47	60	48	47
Outpatient care		42	98	98	97
Inpatient care					1
Age group mortality rates					
0–1 months	.035	.030	.022	.016	.015
2–12 months	.040	.022	.020	.017	.015
13–60 months	.039	.026	.020	.019	.019

[a] Zero entries are shown as blanks. Lack of uniformity in the progression of percentages from low to high resource levels in the table is attributable to the interaction of diseases and multiple effects of interventions.
[b] Interventions for pregnancies were evaluated with and without early detection of pregnancy. Separate results by trimester of pregnancy have been omitted to simplify the table, but early detection of pregnancy through use of the health promoter was found to be cost-effective at all resource levels.
[c] LBW = low birth weight.
[d] See note 11 at end of text for an explanation of the resource level.

gories with lower fatality rates. In addition, the reduction in morbidity with higher resources makes it feasible to treat essentially all morbidity using outpatient care. This leads to still further reduction in the fatality rates.

At all resource levels, the health promoter and mass media activities play a central role in motivating the use of other health activities and in encouraging breastfeeding and early prenatal care. Although examinations, treatment, nutritional programs, and tetanus immunization for pregnant women are among the more costly alternatives considered, these activities are selected at high participation levels, especially in combination with early detection of pregnancy.

The interventions selected for a resource-poor community ($1R$) are promotion, breastfeeding, latrines, water, well-baby clinics, tetanus immunization, iron fortification tablets for all women, and outpatient services for infants in the first 28 days. Except for tetanus immunization, outpatient clinic facilities, and water services, these activities are low in unit resource cost. Also, the epidemiologic population, and therefore the total number of units needed, is relatively small for tetanus immunization and outpatient services.

As resources increase to $2R$, the level of activities selected under $1R$ increases and health worker visits after delivery, outpatient care, and a nutritional program for children aged 13–60 months are added. An effect of the visit by the health promoter after delivery is to identify conditions of neonatal morbidity. This activity works in conjunction with the expanded use of neonatal outpatient care to reduce fatality rates. With the resource level at $1R$, breastfeeding provides a large decrease in malnutrition in the infant age group and the rate for the 13–60-month group is lowered from .15 to .05 by the indirect effects of the health promoter, latrines, and water. With the increase in available resources to $2R$, the nutritional program for children in the 13–60-month age group is selected, and the rate of malnutrition in this age group falls still further to .03.

Optimum allocations above $3R$ include the addition of higher cost activities, especially immunizations, institutional delivery of mothers at risk of low birth weight babies, and inpatient care for the neonatal and infant age groups. A notable feature of the change in allocations above $3R$ is an upgrading of alternative activities. Boundary conditions in the computer program restrict the sum of all delivery activities to be less than or equal to the total number of births, the sum of all inpatient and outpatient treatments to be less than or equal to the number of cases of morbidity, and the sum of households served by water and sanitation interventions to be less than or equal to the number of households. As resources increase, there is an upgrading of services within these boundaries—toilets replace latrines, water in the home replaces public fountains, midwife and institutional deliveries replace unattended deliveries, and inpatient care replaces outpatient care.

The payoff from upgrading becomes successively less, however, as resource levels increase. Figure 3 shows the tapering off of the number of additional births (in a five-year period) that can be expected to survive to the age of 60 months as resource availability increases. Shown somewhat differently, Figure 4 reveals the rapidly diminishing returns to increases in resources. In interpreting these two figures, it should be noted that although the percentage change in the number of survivors is small, the percentage change in the mortality rate may be large. Thus, an increase in resources from $4R$ to $5R$ increases the number of survivors by only .04 percent, but decreases the mortality rate by nearly 10 percent.

Experiments demonstrate that the shape of the survival curve is sensitive to responses on the morbidity survey. The reported results are based on the unaltered average survey responses. If, as may be psychologically plausible, the respondents uniformly overestimate the impacts of the alternative activities, the true coefficients would be much lower, although the relative emphasis on alternative activities would not change. In a sensitivity test using responses

FIGURE 3   Number of survivors to age 60 months at optimum activity levels, as a function of resource level

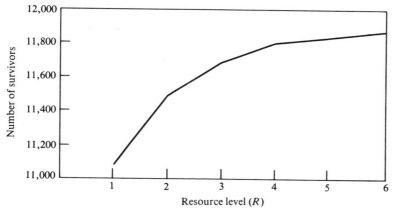

FIGURE 4   Illustration of the diminishing returns to increases in health resources

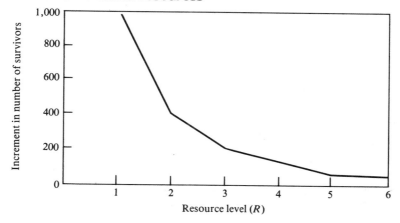

diminished by a constant proportion, the point of rapidly diminishing returns comes at higher resource levels.

Considering these cautionary observations, the response in number of survivors to increases in the level of health resources does not imply that further investment in this sector should cease after $6R$ or some other given resource level, but it does imply that the dramatic decreases in mortality come at fairly low resource levels through health promotion, education, water and sanitation, breastfeeding, and tetanus immunization. At higher resource levels the payoff to additional health resources is not as dramatic, and should be compared carefully with other priority areas competing for the use of community resources.

Seven resource categories are included in the allocation problem. Not all resource categories are exhausted at the optimal solution. The proportion of available resources in each category used at the optimum activity levels as the general availability of resources increases from $1R$ to $5R$ is reported in Table 2. The constraining resources at all levels are registered nurse time and either the supplies budget or the total budget. Hospital beds, physicians' time, and institutional facilities remain far below constraining levels and only come into use as the level of all community resources grows larger and an upgrading of services becomes involved in the optimal solution. To some extent the levels of physicians' and institutional resources may be unrealistically high because of the presence in the baseline community of a teaching hospital, although an effort was made to correct for this problem in tallying the available resources. But even making allowances for the possibility of such an overestimate, it is apparent that at low resource levels the important constraints are funds and nurses' time.

TABLE 2 Proportion of total resources used at optimum levels of activities

Resource level	Total budget	Supplies budget	Physician time	Registered nurse time	Auxiliary nurse time	Bed days	Capital capacity
$1R$	.90	1.00	.16	1.00	.63	.00	.02
$2R$	.97	1.00	.22	1.00	.84	.00	.01
$3R$	.88	1.00	.23	1.00	.90	.00	.01
$4R$	1.00	.99	.39	1.00	.68	.40	.04
$5R$	1.00	.99	.58	1.00	.72	.84	.07

Conclusion

For the modeled community, answers to the policy questions raised at the outset can be summarized briefly. With regard to curative care it is found that inpatient care and hospital deliveries are not cost-effective, and are not adopted by the optimization program until community resources reach high levels. But it is found that neonatal and infant outpatient care are chosen at low to middle resource levels.

Promotion, both the use of home visits by health workers and the use of mass media, is given strong emphasis by the allocation model. Simulations demonstrate that an important reason for the emphasis is the reduction in diarrhea and increase in nutritional status that is assumed (according to the subjective estimates given by respondents) to accompany the promotion of breastfeeding and hygienic education related to neonatal and infant diarrhea. The simulations also suggest that other important effects of the health promoter at low resource levels are to encourage the use of prenatal tetanus immunization and the use of neonatal outpatient services.

Low-technology water and sanitation interventions play an important role at low resource levels. As noted earlier, this is partly attributable to the relatively low monetary cost of the programs and to the fact that they do not draw on the time of skilled personnel. The effectiveness of the programs is enhanced by the fact that they are not age-group-specific and have strong effects on diarrhea in all age groups.

Looking at the question of target age groups, no clear pattern of emphasis on any age appears. The interventions chosen would provide a mix of coverage over all age groups and the prenatal period. The use of examinations for screening before treatment of iron or nutritional deficiencies in women of childbearing age or pregnant women is not demonstrated to be cost-effective until middle resource levels. Similarly, screening and institutional deliveries for women with high risk of low birth weight infants or birth trauma is not shown to be cost-effective until high resource levels.

Among the findings of the study, the importance of nutrition and nutrition-related interventions emerges as deserving special emphasis. Interaction of nutritional status with diseases affects case fatality and increased susceptibility to morbidity and bears heavily on the choice of interventions. In spite of the increased complexity and practical difficulty in modeling introduced by the malnutrition interactions, these relationships, especially the malnutrition–diarrhea interaction, are shown through simulation sensitivity tests as critical to include in future models. Broad nutrition supplements and nutritional rehabilitation are not confirmed as cost-effective at low resource levels. Instead the results underscore the importance of simple nutrition-related interventions—delivered through low-level health workers, backed up by well-baby clinics and neonatal outpatient care, and promoted through mass media and household contact—including nutrition education for mothers, growth monitoring, oral rehydration therapy, and breastfeeding. Iron supplements are also found to be cost-effective and this, together with findings in other studies, suggests that other low-cost, disease-specific supplements not included in the model (such as vitamin A or iodine) may be cost-effective even though broader nutritional supplements are not. Prenatal counseling for the mother was also revealed by the simulations as cost-effective at middle-level resource availability. Timing is crucial to the cost-effectiveness of prenatal care, and the optimization results emphasize the importance of early detection of pregnancy to reduce low birth weight deliveries.

Finally with regard to resource constraints, the optimization experiments indicate that the reduction in child mortality with the optimum use of resources is dramatic at low resource levels and diminishes as resources become more abundant. Similarly, the value of the constraining resources falls as the general level of resources increases. Registered nurse time and financial budgets are found to be the binding constraints, and a high proportion of available auxiliary nurse time is used in most of the optimization experiments. An implication is that manpower training programs should place more emphasis on the training of nurses.

The mathematical optimization model developed in this study is intended to exemplify a general approach to analyses of the cost-effectiveness of health projects designed to reduce child mortality. But the specific results of the application carried out in this study cannot be extrapolated directly to other communities. Before other projects can be analyzed in the framework provided by the model, the intervention impacts, costs, and baseline data for the specific setting must be assembled. Also, the diseases chosen for inclusion in the study may differ for other communities. In addition, the specific functional forms and relationships between activities contained in the present model are only some of many possibilities. Other forms and estimation procedures need to be explored as multiple disease optimization models are developed further.

Notes

The authors are grateful to Luis Fajardo and Alberto Pradilla, who collaborated in conducting the professional survey and in the selection of interventions and diseases for analysis. They wish to thank Peter Heller, who first suggested this area for research.

1 Our hypothetical community is modeled after the locale of the PRIMOPS project in Cali, Colombia—Programa de Investigación en Modelos de Prestación de Servicios de Salud, carried out by the Universidad del Valle and Tulane University. The results reported here are discussed more fully in H. N. Barnum, R. Barlow, L. Fajardo, and A. Pradilla, *A Resource Allocation Model for Child Survival* (Boston: Oelgeschlager, Gunn and Hain, 1980).

2 W. D. Drake and L. J. Fajardo, "The promotora program in Candelaria: A Colombian attempt to control malnutrition and disease 1968–1974," Cali, Colombia: Community Systems Foundation, 1976, mimeo.

3 R. Puffer and C. Serrano (eds.), *Patterns of Mortality in Childhood* (Washington,

D.C.: PAHO, Scientific Publication, No. 262, 1973); P. S. Heller and W. D. Drake, "Malnutrition, child morbidity and the family decision process," *Journal of Development Economics* (Amsterdam: North Holland Publishing Company, 1979); A. Rashmi, D. K. Guha, and P. C. Khandu, "Postmeasles pulmonary complications in children," *Indian Pediatrics* 8 (1971): 834–838; J. D. Wray, "Direct nutrition intervention and the control of diarrheal diseases in pre school children" (mimeo., 1978); J. B. Salomon, J. E. Gordon, and N. Scrimshaw, "Associated chickenpox, diarrhea and kwashiorkor in a highland Guatemalan village," *American Journal of Tropical Medicine and Hygiene* 15, no. 6 (1966): 997–1002; J. E. Gordon, M. A. Guzman, W. Ascoli, and N. Scrimshaw, "Patterns of epidemiological behavior in rural Guatemelan villages," *Bulletin of the World Health Organization* (1964): 9–20.

4 A derivation of the probability relationships and a mathematical specification of the model is given in chapters 2 and 3 of Barnum et al., cited in note 1.

5 Survey participants were selected from a number of fields—maternal and perinatal health, nutrition, environmental sanitation, pediatrics, and epidemiology. The participants also differed from the point of view of institutional affiliation and experience and included medical doctors, public health specialists, and scientists engaged in the selection and administration of government or institutional health policies, the actual delivery of medical and health services, and research related to the estimation of health intervention effectiveness and interdisease relationships. The results reported here do not necessarily represent the opinion of any participant individually. It is also emphasized that participation does not imply any agreement with the results of this study.

6 All questions assumed that the program or activity being considered has been operating for a long enough period to achieve a stable (or equilibrium) impact on the population in question. Also, all questions assumed that all programs and conditions remain unchanged except for the activity under consideration.

7 Four steps are involved in the conversion of the responses to impact coefficients. (1) The responses are reinterpreted as partial derivatives giving the change in the morbidity rate with a change in an intervention. (2) The morbidity functions are differentiated partially with respect to each intervention. This results in an expression containing the baseline morbidity, use, and intervention rates as well as the coefficient of unknown value. (3) The partial derivatives from the two sources—the survey responses and the morbidity equations—are set equal and solved for the unknown coefficient. (4) The coefficient is calculated as a point estimate using the survey responses and baseline levels of the interventions and morbidity rates.

8 The allocation of physical capacity should not be confused with depreciation, which represents the prorated cost of the capital equipment and buildings used over the planning period and which is included in total costs.

9 The demographic and epidemiologic groups distinguished are (1) families, (2) women aged 15–49 years, (3) pregnancies per month, (4) infected women per month, and (5) low birth weight and birth trauma risk births per month. The number of units of the interventions available is restricted to be less than the size of the appropriate group.

10 The computer program used, EXPLORE, was written by Byron S. Gottfried. The optimization technique is detailed in D. L. Reefer and B. S. Gottfried, "Differential constraint scaling in penalty function optimization," *American Institute of Industrial Engineers Transactions* 2 (1970): 281–291. See also R. Fletcher and M. J. D. Powell, "A rapidly convergent descent method for minimization," *Computer Journal* (British) 6 (1962–63). Operational qualifications to the possible optimum discovered by the computer program are: (1) the program may stop on a plateau after experiment shows that improvement greater than E is not possible, and (2) local optima may exist that preclude the discovery of the global solution. As a matter of mathematical rigor, the solution is called a "possible" optimum because it cannot rigorously be established that the program has indeed turned up the very best allocation of resources. But as a practical matter the allocation produced by the program is probably capable of only small improvement.

11 The baseline level, designated $1R$ in Table 1, is arbitrarily specified as 25 percent of the level of resources inventoried for a five-barrio area in Cali, Colombia. Increasing quantities of the resources are represented as a multiple of R. Thus, $2R$ represents a doubling of all resources—nurses' and physicians' time, capacity of facilities, and monetary budgets. The optimization search does not consider variations in the relative proportions of resources. Extension of the model to consider the optimum resource mix would lead to dynamic programming.

12 For purposes of the model, malnutrition is defined as Gómez classification II or above, i.e., less than 75 percent of the reference standard for age.

Authors

Robin Barlow is Professor of Economics and Director, Center for Research on Economic Development, University of Michigan, Ann Arbor.

Howard N. Barnum is Economist, The World Bank, Washington, D.C.

Robert E. Black is Chief, Epidemiology Section, Center for Vaccine Development, School of Medicine, University of Maryland, Baltimore.

David J. Bradley is Professor of Tropical Hygiene and Director of The Ross Institute, London School of Hygiene and Tropical Medicine.

John Briscoe is Assistant Professor, Department of Environmental Sciences and Engineering, University of North Carolina at Chapel Hill.

Kenneth H. Brown is Assistant Professor, Department of Pediatrics, The Johns Hopkins University, Baltimore, and Visiting Scientist, Instituto de Investigación Nutricional, Lima, Peru.

Lincoln C. Chen is Representative, The Ford Foundation, New Delhi, India.

Julie DaVanzo is Senior Economist, The Rand Corporation, Santa Monica, California.

Stanley O. Foster is Assistant Director, International Health Program Office, Centers for Disease Control, Atlanta, Georgia.

Teresa J. Ho is Economist, Population, Health and Nutrition Department, The World Bank, Washington, D.C.

Sandra L. Huffman is Associate Professor, Department of International Health, The Johns Hopkins University School of Hygiene and Public Health, Baltimore, Maryland.

Anne Keymer is Royal Society Research Fellow, Department of Zoology, Oxford University.

Barbara B. Lamphere is Staff Associate, International Division, John Snow Public Health Group, Inc., Boston, Massachusetts.

Reynaldo Martorell is Associate Professor of Nutrition, Food Research Institute, Stanford University.

Jane Menken is Professor of Sociology and Public Affairs and Assistant Director, Office of Population Research, Princeton University.

W. Henry Mosley is Program Officer, The Ford Foundation, Jakarta, Indonesia.

Anne R. Pebley is Research Demographer, Office of Population Research, Princeton University.

T. Paul Schultz is Director, Economic Growth Center, Department of Economics, Yale University.

Frederic C. Shorter is Senior Associate and Senior Representative, The Population Council, Cairo, Egypt.

Burton Singer is Adjunct Professor, Laboratory of Population, Rockefeller University, and Professor and Chairman, Department of Statistics, Columbia University, New York.

Belgin Tekçe is a consultant with The Population Council, Cairo, Egypt.

James Trussell is Professor of Economics and Public Affairs and Faculty Associate, Office of Population Research, Princeton University.

Helen Ware is currently on secondment with the Federal Office of the Status of Women, Canberra, Australia.

Index

Acute diarrhea, death from, 157
Acute lower respiratory tract infections
        (ALRTI), 133–136
    etiology of, 134
    frequency of, 134
    mortality due to, 133–134
    nomenclature of, 134
    prevention of, 135–136
    risk factors in, 134–135
    socioeconomic status and, 135
    treatment of, 134–136
Acute respiratory infection (ARI), 133–136
Age of mother at birth of child, 343
Age-specific fertility, 152
Age-specific mortality rates, 326, 376
Amenorrhea
    and breastfeeding, 104
    equation converting mean duration of
        breastfeeding into mean duration
        of amenorrhea, 106
    suckling patterns and, 104–106
Amman (Jordan) study, 259–260
    conceptual framework of, 260
    diet in, 273–274
    feeding practices in, 273–274
    household income in, 263
    housing in, 262
    immunizations in, 272
    intermediate mechanisms in, 269–276
    maternal education in, 262, 277
    maternal reproductive behavior in, 271
    measure of child mortality in, 263–
        264
    nutritional status in, 274–277
    occupation of head of household in,
        263, 277–278
    personal hygiene in, 271–272
    sickness care in, 272–273
    socioeconomic determinants in, 260–
        267

statistical questions in, 267–269
    upgrading project described, 258–259
Amoebiasis, 142
Analytical framework, for study of child
        survival, 25–40; *see also*
        Proximate determinants model
    purpose of, 40
Anovulation, suckling and, 104
Anthropometry
    disadvantage of, 51
    as indicator of nutritional status, 51
    and mild and moderate undernutrition,
        130
    mortality and, 58–63
Arm circumference
    as measure, 65
    mortality and, 59, 61
Ascaris, 170, 174, 180
    lactase activity and, 176
    malnourishment and, 175
    measurement of, 179
    protein deficiency and, 177

Beliefs about disease causation, 36
Biological factors, in dietary intake, 85
Biological reproduction function, for child
        survival, 231
Biomedical research, 5–10
    on infectious diseases, 5–8
    on malnutrition, 9–10
    on parasitic diseases, 8–10
Birth intervals, 271
    breastfeeding and, 108–109, 271
    child's growth and, 297
    child's survival risks and, 262
    maternal education and, 262
    mortality and, 335
Birth order
    effects of, 336